# THE DISCOURSE OF DOMINATION

Northwestern University
Studies in Phenomenology
and
Existential Philosophy

# THE DISCOURSE OF DOMINATION

## From the Frankfurt School to Postmodernism

Ben Agger

Northwestern University Press
Evanston, Illinois

1992

Northwestern University Press
Evanston, Illinois 60201-2807

ISBN: cloth 0-8101-1004-0
       paper 0-8101-1029-6

**Library of Congress Cataloging-in-Publication Data**

Agger, Ben.
    The discourse of domination : from the Frankfurt School to
postmodernism / Ben Agger.
        p.      cm. —(Northwestern University studies in phenomenology
and existential philosophy)
    Includes bibliographical references and index.
    ISBN 0-8101-1004-0 (alk. paper); 0-8101-1029-6 (pbk.)
    1. Critical theory.    2. Postmodernism—Social aspects.
3. Ideology.    4. Marcuse, Herbert, 1898–     .  5. Frankfurt school of
sociology.    I. Title.    II. Series: Northwestern University studies
in phenomenology & existential philosophy.
HM24.A378    1992
301′.01—dc20                                                    91-38858
                                                                      CIP

For Sarah Rose and Beth Anne

# Contents

# Acknowledgments

I would like to thank Susan Harris at Northwestern University Press for facilitating this project from beginning to end. Her support and guidance have been wonderful. I would like to thank both of the manuscript reviewers for offering very useful suggestions for revision. The essays contained in this book owe their lives to more editors, reviewers, and friends than I can remember! Thanks to one and all.

Beth Anne Shelton, my partner, gave me the idea to do this book. Hugs and kisses to our new daughter, Sarah Rose Agger-Shelton, who was born just before this book was done!

Some of the essays collected in this volume were previously published and are reprinted here by permission of the following.

"Marxism 'or' the Frankfurt School?" in *Philosophy of the Social Sciences* 13 (1983): 347–365.

"The Crisis of the 'Crisis of Marxism' " in *Berkeley Journal of Sociology* 33 (1990): 187–207.

"The Micro-Macro Nonproblem" in *Human Studies* 14 (1991): 81–98. Copyright © 1989 by Kluwer Academic Publishers. Reprinted by permission.

"Marcuse's Growing Relevance" in *Dialectical Anthropology* 4 (1979): 135–45. Copyright © 1972 by Kluwer Academic Publishers. Reprinted by permission.

ACKNOWLEDGMENTS

"Marcuse's Freudian Marxism" in *Dialectical Anthropology* 6 (1982): 319–36. Copyright © 1982 by Kluwer Academic Publishers. Reprinted by permission.

"Marcuse's 'One-Dimensionality' " in *Dialectical Anthropology* 14 (1989): 315–29. Copyright © 1989 by Kluwer Academic Publishers. Reprinted by permission.

"Marcuse's Aesthetic Politics" in *Dialectical Anthropology* 12 (1988): 329–41. Copyright © 1988 by Kluwer Academic Publishers. Reprinted by permission.

"Work and Authority in Marcuse and Habermas" in *Human Studies* 2 (1979): 191–208. Copyright © 1979 by Kluwer Academic Publishers. Reprinted by permission.

"Marcuse and Habermas on New Science" in *Polity* 9 (1976): 151–81.

"On Happiness and the Damaged Life" in *On Critical Theory*, ed. John O'Neill (New York: Seabury/Continuum, 1976), 13–33.

"Critical Theory, Scientism, and Empiricism" in *Canadian Journal of Political and Social Theory* 1 (1977): 3–34.

"Toward a New Intellectuality" in *Canadian Journal of Political and Social Theory* 1 (1977): 47–57.

PART                    1

THE
LEFT'S
RIGHT

# Introduction:
# Beyond the End
# of Ideology

## Who's Left?

It is commonly said that civilization has entered an era (sometimes called postmodernity) in which political contention can be put behind. With the Germanys reunited and the USSR undergoing serious structural changes both internally and throughout the "evil empire," it is said that a new world order looms. Indeed, this was the justification for the United States' war against Iraq, which has greatly rekindled American patriotism and underscored an emerging faith that political contest is behind us. Political ideologies are viewed as anachronistic, further depoliticizing public discourse as well as legitimating our political guardians.

In this context, the crisis of Marxism requires a serious reappraisal of traditional left "certainties" such as the inevitability of capitalism's demise. Both *perestroika* and postmodernism seem to call into question venerable Marxist speculation about the direction of history. Everywhere old-guard leftists fall by the wayside, overtaken by all manner of political factions who have little use for the Marxist catechism. Some of these factions claim to be neoconservative, others post-Marxist. In any case, to be a Marxist today is to be unfashionable, especially when leftish social and cultural theorists disdain Marxism in favor of newer versions of European theory. Admittedly, some of this is welcome: Marxist orthodoxy was always too confining. Nevertheless, it poses profound problems for people who want to retain, albeit in modified form, Marx's epochal analysis of the self-contradictory nature of capitalist society. The crisis of Marxism makes it difficult to be a Marxist in old-fashioned terms—without apologies. My book is a response to the so-called crisis of Marxism as well as a proposal for a new Marxism that integrates a wide variety of theoretical insights from outside the Marxist canon, including postmodernism, feminism, communication theory, and phenomenology.

I am convinced that a good deal of the "crisis" of Marxism involves particular Marxists' failure of nerve; their faith has been shaken, and they either recant (e.g., neoconservatism) or move "beyond" Marxism (e.g., postmodernism). These erstwhile Marxists could not find enough to sustain them in the original Marxian edifice. In the North American university there are precious few Marxists, conservative caricatures notwithstanding. Marxism is hopelessly old-wave for the postmodern crowd, most of whom do not combine postmodernism with Marxism in a useful synthesis. Although Marxist insights have found their way into all sorts of disciplinary canons, they have lost a good deal of their political bite, having been methodologized as "tools" with which to do research. Meanwhile, fatally, Marxists have not exposed themselves to edification from outside Marxism proper; they have ignored the challenges of critical theory, feminism, and postmodernism.

I situate myself and my version of critical theory midway between orthodox Marxism and post-Marxism. Neither is dialectical enough to enable one to rethink Marx's approach to capitalism in relevant ways. But to claim Marxism somehow avoids the deconstructive necessity of grounding one's reading of Marx in the undecidable intertextuality that makes readings writings—Derrida's central insight. To put it in different terms, it is impossible to separate one's own knowledge-constitutive interests, as Habermas (1971) would say, from the readings of theory that condition one's own empirical and political diagnoses. Althusser and Balibar (1970) read *Capital* in a way that is continuous with their own political interests. Unfortunately, they do not recognize that their investment in a certain reading of Marx fundamentally vitiates the project of Marxist scientism (or what Althusser has called theoretical practice). One must argue for a certain version of Marx as a way of reading him; it is insufficient to stare at *Capital*, memorizing its technical economic formulations. One must also theorize the relationship between readings and texts—again, the central project of Derridean poststructuralism.

This is the very same reflexivity argued for and practiced by members of the Frankfurt school, both first and second generations. In Horkheimer's (1972) programmatic 1937 essay on the method of critical theory, he makes it clear that no Marxist reading Marx can escape positively from the hermeneutic circle of reading and writing intertextually. Our accounts of Marx reflect our present need to apply Marxist insights in ways that may have been unimaginable to Marx himself—for example, in explaining many dominations of gender and color ignored by Marx. The Frankfurt version of critical theory argues for the possibility of theoretical revisions formulated within the general frame of reference of Marx's emancipatory critical theory. Horkheimer, Adorno, and Marcuse did the important work of distilling the essence of Marx's analysis of the logic of domination so that we make use of this analytical framework in our own, later work. This led them to write the crucial *Dialectic of Enlightenment* (Horkheimer and Adorno 1972), *Negative Dialectics* (Adorno 1973b), *Eros and Civilization* (Marcuse 1955), and *One-Dimensional Man* (Marcuse 1964) that regrounded Marxism in a reflexive critique of domination. As I explain in chapter 2, they argue convincingly that Marxism is best seen as a particular instance of a generic critical theory, an argument that makes possible theoretical revisions absolutely essential for contemporary social analysis.

The Frankfurt theorists anticipated a number of Derridean positions when they argued that there are no singular or privileged readings of Marx. Instead, one must ground one's reading reflexively in the theoretical uses to which one wants to apply these readings. This is not to say that one can find anything in Marx; but one cannot simply take 1867 Marx into today's world without a great deal of selectivity and interpretation—the reflexively constitutive activities of theorizing. Simply to claim Marx as one's own is problematic, especially when people have been fighting about the verisimilitude of their versions of Marx from the beginning (necessarily so, Derrideans would say). Critical theory is the activity of establishing the lucid connection between one's reading of Marx and the uses to which one wants to put one's reading politically.

My essays in this volume attempt to meet the challenge posed by the delegitimation of Marxism. To do so, I retrieve important themes from the Frankfurt school while also appreciating the contribution of postmodern theory to a valuable rethinking and updating of Marxian categories. I have elsewhere (1989a) developed feminist theory's important additions to male Marxism. Here I argue that the original generation of the Frankfurt school, first assembled around the Institute for Social Research in Germany, produced a very important version of Marxian critical theory that continues to have significance today.

I frame my argument for the relevance of critical theory in counterpoint to orthodox Marxist dismissals of Frankfurt theory as politically apostate (e.g., Slater 1977) and to postmodern claims about the end of ideology (e.g., Lyotard 1984). I discuss what I call the Left's Right—conservative tendencies within Marxian social theory as well as postmodernism. I develop and defend the striking relevance of Marcuse's version of critical theory. I also contrast and compare Marcuse's and Habermas's versions of critical theory. Finally, I attempt to formulate a postnegative dialectic, a more positive version of critical theory that draws upon a variety of influences from Frankfurt aesthetic and cultural theory as well as from the most radical insights of postmodernism, which I reinterpret as an authentic version of critical theory.

Although some of these essays were composed a decade ago (and have been revised since), they have a contemporary significance in the context of global attacks on the Marxian project. Although many Marxists would disdain my own version of Marxism, rejecting its Hegelianism, Freudianism, and culturalism, I embrace the Frankfurt school's reinterpretation of Marxism as a version of an interdisciplinary critical theory. In these essays, I draw directly from the heritage of the original Frankfurt school, particularly from Marcuse and Adorno. I also begin to make use of insights from various European theories of interpretation and cultural criticism like postmodernism. The direction of my own work over the last decade reflects the general broadening of critical theory, moving from its foundation within Marxist discourse and analysis to wider perspectives in cultural, political, and ideological theory. Unlike some theorists (e.g., Poster 1989) who essentially replace critical theory with postmodernism and poststructuralism, I hold onto critical theory's Marxist underpinning while revising critical theory in light of empirical changes in world capitalism simply unforeseen by Marx.

I argue for an enduring, flexible critical theory. As such, my essays are arguments for Marxism, albeit formulated in a different way from Althusser's (1969). I interrogate what it means to be *for Marx*. I contend that Marxism has not become obsolete with *perestroika* and postmodernism. Indeed, I believe that it is impossible to analyze contemporary social problems without recourse to Marx's analysis of the self-contradictory logic of capital. These essays represent my own engagement with the complex heritage of critical theory: as such, they are personal statements. I resist the tendency to entomb the Frankfurt school in the museum of leftist intellectual history. Indeed, critical theory in its best sense is the generic activity of revising Marxism in response to intellectual and political transformations since Marx's death. Critical theory makes itself available for revision in light of its own methodological and substantive commitment to revisionism.

My interest in this book is not in establishing a definitive version of either Marxism or critical theory. Inasmuch as we are all strong readers capable of reading Marx deconstructively, scientistically, psychoanalytically, and/or as feminists, an argument "for" Marx is really an argument for oneself and one's sense of the world—for the reading that one's theory produces. But we do not read blindly, without being educated. Just as reading produces a new text, so texts inflect readings. One must learn to read both learnedly and naively—learnedly, in the sense that one recognizes the constitutive force of one's own selection, omission, and emphasis; naively, in the sense that one tries to read for the first time, to hear arguments anew, learning from them as well as imposing one's own erudition on them. This book can be read as readings that helped educate my own sense of theoretical priorities, opening the way for new readings of the people I discuss and of me—my discussions and revisions of them.

## The Structure of the Argument

The three parts of the book treat three interrelated themes: (1) the *integration and cooptation of Marxism and postmodernism*; (2) *Marcuse's critical theory* as it bridges between psychic and social-structural levels of social analysis (and especially as the distinctiveness of his problematic emerges in debate with Habermas); and (3) my development of a mode of *critical theory that functions as dialectical empiricism*—a mode of critical social science.

The first part confronts the ossification of Marxism as an intellectual and a political problem for the Left. I argue that the Left has developed its own right-wing rump composed of both orthodox Marxist and postmodern theorists. The second part pursues the importance of Marcuse's brand of critical theory; although Marcuse is well known for his writings in the 1960s, he is insufficiently appreciated as an important Freudian-Marxist critical theorist who develops many of the same themes as Merleau-Ponty, Sartre, and the feminists. It is in this second part that I clarify the Marcusean foundations of my own formulation of critical theory. The third part in a sense "applies" the Marcusean foundation discussed in part 2 to a broadly critical social science and social theory. In this section I address the ways in which critical theory can

function politically, concluding with a chapter that attempts to reinte-
grate the most radical insights from postmodernism into my own approach to critical theory, producing what I call a radical cultural studies
(see Agger 1990, 1991a).

That is the obvious structure of the book, reflecting the development of my argument from start to finish. But certain themes cut across
the chapters and sections, suggesting a different way of reading the book
to find integrating and cohesive meanings. These common themes include: (1) the Frankfurt school's critique of positivism as ideology; (2)
Marcuse's stress on the embodiment of the subject; (3) a critique of orthodox Marxism's positivism; (4) a dialectical notion of the relationship
between the economy and culture; (5) a critique of the disciplinary integration of leftist thought, particularly in mainstream American sociology; (6) a deconstructive concept of the undecidability of all texts, hence
empowering reading strongly to rewrite as well as merely receive meaning; (7) retention of the concepts of subjectivity and totality, against
postmodern skepticism about these notions; (8) a defense of the relative
autonomy of critical theory against attempts to reduce it mechanically to
science; and (9) openness to efforts by postmodernists, poststructuralists, and feminists to expand the Marxist agenda, fundamentally transforming the ways in which Marxists think about their own scientificity,
textuality, and sexuality.

These themes, and others, surface repeatedly throughout the
book. They have been central to my thought since the 1970s, and they
continue to be refined as I rethink the issues of critical social theory,
stimulated by both empirical and intellectual changes since the nineteenth century, when Marx first formulated the categories of his analysis
of capital's contradictions. I am a Marxist inasmuch as I accept Marx's
notion that capitalism is an internally and externally contradictory social
order, both robbing labor and despoiling the environment. I have tried
to expand the Marxist theory of the domination of labor to include a
focus on the domination of reproduction, as my discussion in *Fast Capitalism* (1989a) suggests. Along with the Frankfurt theorists, I broaden
Marx's critique of the alienation of labor to include all aspects of domination—class, race, gender, nature. In *Fast Capitalism* I introduced my
notion of the domination of production over reproduction to suggest a
critical theory of all hierarchies.

My argument is that the central logic of domination in Western
civilization hierarchizes the productive and valuable over the re- or un-
productive and valueless. This is the particular way in which I contextu-

alize the original Frankfurt school's broadening of Marx's concept of the alienation of labor into their larger category of domination. For me, fast capitalism is the second stage of late or monopoly capitalism, in which it is virtually impossible to disentangle the productive and reproductive, labor and text, science and fiction, men and women, white and non-white, base and superstructure. This sets an agenda for third-generation critical theory to locate the logic of domination in surprising, often quotidian forms, notably in the language games of a positivist or, as Marcuse (1964) called it, "one-dimensional" everyday life.

In my recent work I have tried to deepen this framework of postmodernist-influenced Frankfurt critical theory in order to address aspects of empirical social reality unforeseen even by the Frankfurt critics. Where Adorno, Horkheimer, and Marcuse argued that one could criticize domination from the distant vantage of critical theory, I argue that it is increasingly impossible to privilege theoretical activity that somehow escapes its own banalization and integration. Critical theory has itself been integrated into the academy, legitimated as a series of courses, books, journals, and conferences. The academization of critical theory, in part owing to Habermas's success in mainstreaming critical theory into and across the academic disciplines, has been a mixed blessing. On the one hand, people read and study the Frankfurt school. On the other, it neutralizes the explosive insights of Adorno and his colleagues, who defied disciplinary integration and legitimation. This is very much the theme of Russell Jacoby's *The Last Intellectuals: American Culture in the Age of Academe* (1987), where he laments the absence of broadgauged critical intellectuals under the age of forty-five in the United States. The angry rebels of the New Left have donned tweed blazers, earned tenure, and become timid in the North American university.

Although Jacoby does not exempt himself from his own autocritique—nor any of us who "do" critical theory for an academic living—he has not got off lightly for his trenchant iconoclasm. Many of his theoretical colleagues, including some of the *Telos* group, have defensively savaged Jacoby, arguing that he either misses genuine examples of public intellectuality or exaggerates the self-defeating obscurantism of the radical tenured class. I am fully in sympathy with his argument, which I think is both theoretically and empirically accurate: we on the erstwhile New Left have paid an enormous price for our academic sinecures. Our engagements with critical theory have become comfortable cultivation, little different from the minute and self-reproducing "scholarship" that we so decried in our professors during the 1960s.

## Critical Theory as Intellectual Production

By now critical theory has become a minor cottage industry, spinning off doctoral degrees, academic publications, international conferences, publishers' profits. Interestingly, the institutionalization of the Frankfurt school's critical theory has quickly led to the eclipse of that theory itself. Today, many who claim to specialize in critical theory are merely exegetes, close readers of Habermas, Adorno, and, lately, New French Theory (Derrida, Foucault, Baudrillard, Lyotard, et al.). Forgotten is the methodical injunction of the original Frankfurt thinkers *to historicize*— to apply the overall method of negative dialectics to the particular historical formations of capital and culture that bear ideology criticism. As a result, few write new versions of critical theory; instead, they read theorists and produce expositions of them.

As I remarked earlier, this is a false dichotomy. Every reading rewrites, given the undecidability of every text. Thus, even the most descriptive monograph on Foucault retheorizes him. But this is usually a meager payoff compared to what could be said and learned. Even a casual glance at the immense oeuvres of Marcuse, Adorno, and Horkheimer demonstrates their incredible creativity and virtuosity. They ranged effortlessly across substantive social theory, cultural criticism, intellectual history, and political economy, covering a huge range of topics. In the traditions of Marx and Weber, the Frankfurt theorists did not partition their work into theoretical and empirical parts, nor did they content themselves with textual exegesis (even though their more interpretive essays are gems of close reading and speculative reconstruction). Today, few write with the encyclopedic sweep and power of the original Frankfurt theorists, who were among the last generation of European intellectuals to attempt to reflect the totality in every particular piece of work. Instead, critical theorists have become students of critical theory, little more.

So my defense of critical theory, conducted over more than a dozen chapters, is not without its own ambivalence about the degeneration of theory today. In a sense, these chapters represent my engagements with other thinkers en route to developing my own theoretical identity. That identity is already prefigured in some of my earlier essays on Marcuse and on other theoretical topics. I have rewritten each to integrate them and to point beyond them toward larger issues of substantive social theory, thus somehow protecting these more exegetical studies against their own self-academization. I work very much in the spirit of the original Frankfurt school, albeit with some new inflections largely introduced from New French Theory and cultural studies. In this volume, I hope to engage with some of the best that critical theory has had to offer in politically motivated social theory and to demonstrate a style of theorizing that in part 3 I call "dialectical sensibility."

These chapters do not represent the last word on various issues of substance. They are engagements, interrogations. They have forced me to take seriously an enormous corpus of critical social theory, always challenging me to make my own contribution to that corpus. Although I, too, am a Marxist reader, I am also a Marxist writer. These halves of one's identity cannot be cleanly separated: we are what we have read, and we write beyond the marginal notes that we have jotted in the dog-eared texts that we have made our own. My own copy of Marcuse's *Eros and Civilization* (1955) is a case in point. The pages, heavily underlined and annotated, are literally falling from the book. I have to struggle to keep my copy together, using paper clips and tape. By having read the life out of the book, I have gone on to write my own books, necessarily trading on what I have read and where I have been. Each time I pick up and pore over my bedraggled copy of Marcuse's classic, I learn something—I see something in a new way, or I understand something better. This forces me to rethink what I have written about Marcuse, making me question my own writerly certainties about my subject.

This is good; it is the way of reading and writing. There are no singular or final readings, or definitive writings. I imagine that Marcuse worked the same way himself, having mastered a number of civilizational thinkers like Freud, Hegel, and Marx. Here is the challenge as I see it: we who profess critical theory must not get so far from the library that we forget our connection to these civilizational narratives that have brought us to where we are today; but neither must we lose our way out of the library into the street, squeezing the life out of texts and ideas without putting our own imprimatur on them, ensuring them a new life. Critical theory is ever a digging at foundations, a perpetual questioning. It is a way of being political at a time when politics is found nearly everywhere but in the official political arena, notably in the ways that texts are nucleic societies of readers and writers through which power is transacted. The effort of readers to become writers, hence citizens, is perhaps the most fundamental way in which we can challenge power today. These essays were written in that spirit, recording my own education in my attempt to master critical theory without being mastered by it.

## Toward a Lifeworld-Grounded
## Critical Theory

Ultimately, these essays move toward what I call *a lifeworld-grounded critical theory*, outlined most concretely in the last four chapters. I draw a great deal from Adorno's negativizing formulation of critical theory (which makes it impossible to ignore deception disguised in the banalities of the quotidian as well as in the outright falsehoods of philosophy and social theory). At the same time, as I begin to argue in chapters 12 and 13, Horkheimer and Adorno's (1972) theses of the decline of the individual and eclipse of reason leave a good deal to be desired in the way of practical interventions. Although friendly fascism, disguised as liberalism, abounds today, the metaphor of society as a concentration camp is overly undifferentiated. Just as the announcement of the end of ideology is premature, so must we rethink Adorno's negative totalization of the damaged life. There are still pockets and possibilities of resistance—what Marcuse (1964) calls "the chance of the alternatives." There are new social movements (Habermas 1981b) that pose threats to domination largely because they embody heterodox theoretical assumptions about the nature of the administered society (and thus they attack the system heterogeneously). I side with Marcuse in this book, first against early Habermas's truncated theoretical agenda (chaps. 10–11) (but borrowing from his theory of new social movements) and then against Adorno's gloom (chaps. 12–14). I supplement Marcuse with insights from postmodernism, feminism, and phenomenology.

A lifeworld-grounded critical theory theorizes nontraditional modes of personal and interpersonal resistance, identifying their prepolitical potential. The model of this engagement with political heterodoxy is found in Marcuse's writings about the counterculture and New Left (1969). A lifeworld-grounded critical theory also theorizes *itself*, attempting to adopt a more public discourse in order to prefigure democratic relations between writers and readers. Marx wondered who would educate the educators—the political vanguard. I wonder who will write the texts that educate the educators. I also wonder how educators (writers, critics, theorists, political leaders) will live—how their own lives can mesh with those whom they theorize, building socialist and feminist consensus out of privatization. These are largely questions of discourse and desire, requiring us to think hard about the relationship between the ways we write and work, on the one hand, and the ways we love, on the other.

For the most part, attention to questions of discourse has come from postmodernists and poststructuralists (see Agger 1991b). Attention to questions of desire has come from feminists. Interestingly, Marcuse, alone among the Frankfurt school theorists, raised many of the same questions, although his last book (*The Aesthetic Dimension* [1978]) was composed before he could fully appreciate the theoretical implications of feminism or come to grips with theories of interpretation that emerged from French theorists involved in the May Movement. Marcuse's *Essay on Liberation* (1969) anticipates the feminist stress on the politics of the personal as well as postmodern and poststructural themes of discourse and culture. In that book, which is pivotal in my own lifeworld-grounded critical theory, Marcuse argues that "new sensibilities" prefigure a good society by our treating ourselves, each other, and nature well in the here and now.

I combine these diverse and overlapping theoretical traditions in my own version of critical theory. For me, this is the best way to come to grips with the depoliticization of public life and the stagnation of Marxism. I am not ready to throw in the political towel. Capitalism, sexism, and racism continue to ravage nature as well as people's minds and bodies. The thesis of the end of ideology is ideological—now more than ever, when so much appears to be going wrong. But we need new theory with which to comprehend what is happening and to begin to live different lives. These essays represent my own attempt to confront this theoretical challenge. They stand or fall on their ability to repoliticize critical theory.

# 2

# Marxism
# "or"
# the Frankfurt School?

## Marxism as Method

This book begins with four essays that address different critiques of Marxism—even from within Marxism itself. I begin with readings of other authors as a way of establishing my own argument as counterpoint. Each of these four chapters deals in one way or another with my overall thesis: Marxism can be invigorated only by rebuffing both orthodox Marxism and orthodox anti-Marxism, a task best accomplished by adapting Marxist critical theory creatively to present circumstances. Orthodox Marxists ensure Marxist obsolescence by insisting on Marx's imperviousness to revisions (e.g., Slater in the present chapter). Other Marxists translate Marxism into a positivist science, reducing it to scientism (e.g., Wright in chap. 3). Orthodox anti-Marxists who dominate American sociological theory sociologize Marx, spuriously assimilating him to the canon of bourgeois sociological theory (e.g., the main project of Alexander, discussed in chap. 4). Finally, certain postmodernists (chap. 5) abandon Marxism altogether, regarding it as the spent passion of nineteenth-century ideologues.

These essays are directed at the Left's Right, which is gathering momentum today as people celebrate the supposed end of ideology, contestation, conflict. I argue that to be a Marxist requires more than simple self-identification. Indeed, one must insist on the plausibility of a Marxism that refuses to take for granted its own unproblematic relationship to Marx's texts—in fact, to textuality in general. As I shall argue in this chapter, to be Marxist is continually to interrogate Marxist belief and disbelief. My discussion of Slater and Connerton suggests some of the problems involved in appraising the Frankfurt school's Marxism. I submit that Marxism is a particular version of critical theory and argue for its essential flexibility and adaptability. Slater dismisses the Frankfurt theorists as leftist traitors, where Connerton rejects them as theoretical failures. Both arguments are exemplary attacks on critical theory and need to be addressed.

Since the major works of members of the so-called Frankfurt school began to be published in English in the early 1970s, critical debates have flourished in England and North America about the brand of the Frankfurt Marxism. Some sympathetic critics have taken the position that the members of the Frankfurt school advanced one step beyond traditional Marxism, a view often associated with appraisals of Habermas's work (Wellmer 1971; Schroyer 1973). Others (Jacoby 1975b) argue that the Frankfurt critical theory was an ingenious deepening of categories implicit in Marx, an interpretive line associated generally with the political scholarship of the *Telos* group. Unsympathetic critics have been equally quick off the mark in assessing Frankfurt Marxism. Here there have also been two prevailing schools of thought: one views Frankfurt theory skeptically through the lenses of analytic philosophy and Vienna Circle empiricism. This view is seemingly shared by most practicing social science empiricists in North America, who regard theories as valuable only when they can produce testable hypotheses. The other school rejects the Frankfurt theory as an unjustified recanting of what are taken to be fundamental Marxist positions.

It is the latter reading that will concern me here inasmuch as it informs two books that exemplify two typical misreadings of the Frankfurt school and necessitate clarifications that help me extend critical theory beyond its origins in Frankfurt—the project of this book. Although their authors differ on many points of substance, what they share is more interesting and instructive. Connerton's (1980), particularly, is a sophisticated attempt to probe weaknesses in the Frankfurt theory from the point of view of a sympathetic materialism. Although Slater (1977) also apparently accepts the original Frankfurt bifurcation of traditional and critical theory (e.g., Horkheimer 1972), his impatience with the ideology-critical focus of Frankfurt work is ill concealed, emerging in what amounts to a rejection of the entire Hegelian-Marxist enterprise. They share a belief, increasingly prevalent among Marxists of a more orthodox persuasion who resist philosophical and psychoanalytic revisions of Marxism, that the Frankfurt thinkers failed to produce a viable response to fascism and to emerging monopoly capitalism. This is allegedly because they rejected basic aspects of Marx's legacy. Of all the readings of Frankfurt critical theory, this is the most interesting. I reject it but find in it the occasion to raise what I regard as pertinent questions about the future of Marxism that occupy this whole book.

What sort of standards of evidence ought to be applied in the evaluation of this orthodox Marxist appraisal of Frankfurt theory? I believe it makes no sense to talk of a single "Marx" but only of a variety of possible readings that are suited to time and place. This is not to deny certain continuities between Marx's legacy and subsequent uses of Marx, as I have argued elsewhere (Agger 1979, esp. 5–74). I maintain that Marx developed a *method*, part and parcel of all critical theories, that later theorists can employ in adapting his analytic categories to their own historical and political needs. There is wide disagreement about what this method is, as even cursory readings of Slater and Connerton indicate.

In general, one can speak of an orthodox Marxist reading of the Frankfurt theory. It argues that the Frankfurt thinkers abandon the working class and its economic struggles as the prime movers of social history, substituting in their place the power of critical ideas in social change. It is argued in this vein that the Frankfurt theory borrows more from the German idealist tradition than from Marxian materialism. Related to this is the argument that Frankfurt neo-idealism leads to the enthronement of a purely contemplative subjectivism that replaces the active materialism of Marx and Engels. Social change is elevated to the realm of spirit, with dissident intellectuals replacing the proletariat as agents of social change. This, in turn, is seen to lead to the fetishism of cultural and psychological themes, in alleged ignorance of the economic. Below I will show how and to what extent Slater and Connerton share in these criticisms.

The "abandonment" of the working class in favor of a critical negativity that has no grounding in collective political movements is thought by many orthodox Marxists (Mandel 1975, 500–507; Mattick 1972; Anderson 1976) to weaken fatally the Frankfurt perspective on late capitalism. It is argued that to be a Marxist one must view the metamorphosis of a contradiction-laden capitalism in terms of inexorably sharpening tensions between the classes. I would agree that all who embrace Marx's dialectical method must view social history as a history of class struggle and capitalism as a social system defined by deep structural antagonisms between capital and labor. But orthodox Marxists, in accusing the Frankfurt theory of ideological apostasy and dismissing it, fail, I contend, to read deeply enough into the Frankfurt works themselves. In the important programmatic essay of 1937, Horkheimer (1972) makes it clear that the political-economic concerns of original Marxism are not abandoned by critical theory but rather strengthened by a reevaluation of relations between so-called base and superstructure. Here Horkheimer suggests that the apparently cultural and psychological orientation of the Frankfurt school responds to the growing linkage between base and superstructure in the "authoritarian state" of monopoly capitalism (just beginning to emerge in the 1930s). He suggests that culture in late capitalism is more than ever tied to the imperatives of capital and social control, indeed, that in the illusions of the autonomy of culture and the spiritual realm lies a powerful source of "total administration," a theme repeated often in early Frankfurt work (e.g., Marcuse 1968a) and in its adaptations by second-generation associates (Piccone 1976, 1978).

Horkheimer here is saying that critical theory pursues economic determination further than orthodox Marxism—which erects, according to him, too rigid a distinction between the economic and the noneconomic. He suggests that Marx as a dialectical theorist recognized that ideology retains its powerful, placating hold on individuals by virtue of its stress on the opportunities available to those who obey the iron laws of the economic marketplace in fulfilling their ascribed duties in the division of labor. This is among the most distinctive contributions of the Frankfurt theorists; they elaborate the theory of ideology beyond sketchy comments in *The German Ideology* by Marx and Engels (1947) in attempting to understand how socioeconomic crises were contained in the 1920s and 1930s through deepened obedience to liberal ideology and the virtual eradication of distinctions between the "first" dimension of an apparent surface reality and the "second" dimension of dialectical critique and utopian vision. It is precisely in the illusion of the autonomy of the individual that people are led to accept what is presented to them as immutable (laws of the marketplace) and to follow through on their imputed social duty, which is to exchange a certain degree of the alienation of their labor in return for consumer blandishments. The illusion of the autonomy of culture, according to Horkheimer, must be unmasked by a critical theory that recognizes, as Marx did, the ties between the economic and the ideological.

I do not believe the Frankfurt scholars thought that they were abandoning Marx's central understanding of the internal contradictions of capitalism or the role of the working class when they shifted the terms of their analysis from economic crisis pure and simple to cultural and psychological critique. Horkheimer and his associates felt that the failure of the European proletariat in the early twentieth century had to be explained in a Marxian way through a fresh understanding of the increasingly binding force of an affirmative culture. As I shall discuss in chapter 8, one-dimensionality, as Marcuse (1964; Breines 1970) termed it, was a central motif in subsequent Frankfurt work, extending Horkheimer's insights in a more sociological direction. Does this change Marx? Only if one reads Marx in literal terms as requiring a necessary falling rate of profit and the subsequent "expropriation of the expropriators," as he called it in *Capital*.

As I have suggested, there are two distinctive approaches to Marx here. Orthodox Marxists regard Marx's prophecies of a necessary apocalypse of capitalism brought about by a single type of Jacobin-like class warfare, based on his sketch of certain economic crisis tendencies exhaustively documented in *Capital,* as binding on all future social thinkers. Nonorthodox or "Western" Marxists, like the Frankfurt theorists, do not take Marx literally in this sense. Instead, they read *Capital* as presenting a method for the subsequent contextual analysis of socioeconomic crises as these spring from the deeply embedded internal contradictions of the capitalist system. At the center of disagreements over the currency of Marxism is the relationship between Marx's depiction of the abstract structural properties of a social system divided between capital and labor and contingent empirical analyses of the context-bound irruption of these contradictions.

The orthodox Marxist reads *Capital* as presenting both a formal analysis of deep structure and an empirical analysis of the precise stages of the breakdown, such as, in Marx's terms, the rising organic composition of capital, the falling rate of profit, the growing industrial reserve army, and deepening class consciousness. Orthodox Marxists fail, however, to disentangle these two analytic levels sufficiently; thus they fall into the trap of retaining a contingent empirical analysis of crisis from Marx that may be quite outdated today. But another way of reading *Capital* is to understand the relationship between structural and empirical levels of Marx's analysis as dialectical. This interpretation draws a distinction between things that "must" happen in a capitalist system and things that could happen. In capitalism there must, by definition, be a structural contradiction between the interests of capital and labor. At the same time, there may be numerous contingent manifestations of this contradiction in the real world, depending on such things as culture, degree of economic advancement, state of technology, and, of course, character of class consciousness. For Horkheimer in 1937, when he stated the basic premises of a philosophically grounded critique of political economy, all capitalist systems contain this structural contradiction between capital and labor. However, the actual emergence of this contradiction in, for example, central Europe of the 1930s was a matter for empirical sociological analysis.

Curiously enough, this is to reverse the charge, from both non-Marxists and orthodox Marxists, that Frankfurt theory is philosophical to the point where it neglects all engagement with the empirical here and now. I am suggesting, by distinguishing between Marx's analysis of deep structural aspects of the clash between capital and labor and the more mutable manifestations of these in economic and social crisis, that the Frankfurt thinkers opened the door to fresh analyses of these shifting forces. An orthodox Marxist faithfully assumes that there is an evolutionary direction of sharpening contradictions, according to the given motif of the *Manifesto* and *Capital;* Horkheimer argued that there is no such guarantee but only contingent advances and retreats in the struggle for human liberation.

Thus, in working through Slater's and Connerton's books, I want to remember this basic disagreement over what it means to be a Marxist. They take the Frankfurt thinkers to task for abandoning what they regard as an essential theme in Marx, namely, a belief in the inevitability of a class revolution to be carried out according to Marx's sketch of precipitating crises such as falling profit, increasing organic composition of capital, and rising unemployment. The Frankfurt thinkers reject this optimism but accept most of the insights into the mechanisms of the alienation of labor that remained central in Marx's work from 1844 through volume 1 of *Capital*. Indeed, the Frankfurt theory is in a certain way more economistic than orthodox critics would concede precisely because it follows the alienation of labor to its roots in belief and desire. The Freudian revision of Marx's economic analysis of alienation does not so much change Marx as give Marxism a firmer grounding on a libidinal substratum, thus explaining how capitalism can continue long past Marx's expectations of the date for its demise. Without this subjective turn, the Frankfurt thinkers believed, it would be impossible to explain early twentieth-century revolutionary failures in Europe and the rise of fascism and its metamorphosis into one-dimensional society. They extend the original economic categories into apparently noneconomic areas, implicitly calling on a reading of Marx that distinguishes, as noted above, between the structural logic of contradictions and their empirical emergence in history. This distinction between deep core and surface, they remind us often, is dialectical and not rigid.

It is easy to become disenchanted with Frankfurt theory—not simply as lacking class optimism but as lacking all optimism about the eventual dialectical emergence of negative critique into positive social change. Here it may be necessary to distinguish between the various tones of a critical theory that has suffered many vicissitudes since Marx. There are definite shifts between Horkheimer and Adorno (1972) in *Dialectic of Enlightenment*, where they suggest that the dialectical alternation of myth and a false enlightenment is to be eternal, or where Adorno (1973b) in the sober *Negative Dialectics* elevates the death camp to a nearly philosophical universal in idealistic identity theory, and the Marcuse of *Eros and Civilization* (1955) and *An Essay on Liberation* (1969), and, certainly, the more rationalistic Habermas (1984, 1987b) of communication theory. Disputes within the school have generally not been about lack of economic rigor but about whether there has been so much rigor that the phrasings of critical theory are restricted either to atonal music or to dismal aphorisms (Adorno 1973c, 1974), a theme I pursue further in chapter 12. Connerton, as we shall see below, has much to say about this subject.

The orthodox Marxist would probably respond to this by saying that, without an explicit class optimism, critical theory degenerates into the swan song of an aging, disaffected intelligentsia who no longer recognize "class struggle." Yet there may be other emancipatory theories that draw on Marx's own critical method but do not regard it as having a single unique application. I think it is an exaggeration to read Horkheimer and Adorno as cosmological reductionists like the later Hegel. As I discuss in chapter 13, they were too much the acute sociologists for that, as demonstrated in the quantity of important sociocultural and psychological research that they conducted while in the United States during and immediately after World War II (Jay 1973; Hughes 1975). It is evident in works like *The Authoritarian Personality* (Adorno et al. 1950) as well as in Adorno's later philosophical and aesthetic treatises (1973c, 1984) that they could find few symptoms of a resurgent transformative movement in the mass culture of postwar North America.

Orthodox Marxists tracing this inability to the Frankfurt "rejection" of Marxism, on a profound philosophical or social theoretical level, misunderstand the pessimism of Horkheimer and Adorno. They were pessimistic on the evidence and not because childish faith had soured in adulthood. Indeed, none of the Frankfurt thinkers went through this cycle of conversion and disenchantment—unlike, for example, numerous American intellectuals who lost political faith during the Stalin period and subsequently took up the banner of a bitter neoconservatism. This is not to say that in the 1960s Horkheimer and Adorno embraced the New Left and its incipient authoritarianism. The Frankfurt thinkers were careful political sociologists who required more than faith in texts to sustain an emancipatory philosophy of history.

One must ask whether political disenchantment is warranted today. For the Frankfurt theorists, a living Marxism was relegated to theoretical texts and the cultural counterexpressions of Schoenberg, for Adorno, and of Beethoven and Bob Dylan, for Marcuse. One also wonders whether empirical evidence of an imminent class revolution underlies the orthodox Marxist critique of the alleged Frankfurt apostasy. Certainly, failing Western economies today do not automatically produce the revival of working-class solidarity or a renewed consciousness of socialist possibility; the elections of Reagan in the United States and Thatcher in Britain bespoke the powerful hold of an ideology of bitter individualism as a response to the confusions and crises of a technocratically managed capitalism. It is difficult to see how the revival of theoretical Marxism in the West can have any significant catalytic influence on thought and practice that have become far more ideologized than Marx ever imagined. Critical theory, as I will argue more fully in the balance of this chapter and throughout this book, must register interruptions in the emancipatory struggle as well as—and as a way of—contributing to its advances.

## On the Abandonment
## of Agitational Theory

In turning to the books themselves, we find that my characterization of the typical orthodox Marxist reading of Frankfurt theory holds for Slater and Connerton. Yet their interpretive styles are quite different. Slater presents his work as something of a definitive "Marxist" account of the origins, both political and philosophical, of critical theory. Connerton is more concerned with explicating and evaluating the internal philosophical problematics of the Frankfurt school's leading expositors. Both books are useful for a number of reasons. Slater presents a wealth of historical and political material in a condensed form, reviewing in his early chapters the travails of early twentieth-century German socialism and of the socialist theory of the time. He situates the early work published in the Frankfurt journal *Zeitschrift für Sozialforschung* in this lively political context and adeptly draws out differences between, for example, Kautsky, Bernstein, and Luxemburg and the more Hegelian Marxists like Lukács, Korsch, and the Frankfurt thinkers. It has been remarked that Slater's book reads like a dissertation assembled largely through the careful culling of numerous 3 × 5 cards, a stylistic aspect that informs the theoretical content, perhaps too much. There is an absence of sustained argument, as if he were writing for an audience (I have readers and authors of the *New Left Review* in mind, particularly) whose members generally agree on the theoretical substance of Marxism. In later chapters, he goes too briefly into the psychological and aesthetic concerns of people like Fromm and Marcuse, approving more of Marcuse than of the other Frankfurt thinkers for his temporary ties to the 1960s student movement.

Stylistically and hermeneutically, his book has better competitors, an important consideration for a book advertised with words like "origin" and "significance." I found Martin Jay's (1973) by now well-thumbed *The Dialectical Imagination*, tracing developments in the thought of members of the school from 1923 to 1950, both more readable and more philosophically sophisticated. Jay is not as dismissive as Slater—largely because he sympathizes with the philosophical and political orientations of the school, and also because he is much more austere in his judgments of his subject matter. Jay's book, a version of his Harvard doctoral dissertation in history, reads much less like a patchwork of names and dates than Slater's. Jay manages, within the limitations of intellectual history, to advance a more coherent thesis about the relation between early European Marxisms and Frankfurt theory. Although his book has itself been hotly debated on political grounds (Kellner 1975)—certain nonorthodox Marxists claim that he was not Marxist enough in his interpretations—it is more generally useful than Slater's to the reader looking for a clear exposition of basic Frankfurt themes, especially for those who have not yet read the original sources. Slater's book, in contrast, is addressed to those who have already read and dismissed the Frankfurt works but require a systematic rationale for rejecting them in the name of authentic "Marxism."

The best thing about Slater is that he does provide just such a rationale for orthodox Marxists seeking the last word on Frankfurt theory. In the process, he helps to clarify differences between orthodox and Hegelian readings of Marx. Unfortunately, Slater had done much of his research before the works of Habermas had begun to evolve into a distinctive whole. The Habermas industry has quickly become a major one in European and North American social science, on both sides of the ideological line. Habermas's writing is more stylistically tortured even than Adorno's, combining German declarativeness with a cumbersome vocabulary. But he is also more empirically and philosophically eclectic than any of the original Frankfurt scholars and is himself critical of what he regards as their romanticism about utopian possibilities, especially the Frankfurt vision of "a new science and new technology" (Habermas 1970b; 1971, 32–33; also see chaps. 10 and 11 below). This eclecticism, mixed with a good deal of deference to Anglo-Saxon rationalism and empirical method, has made Habermas of concern to both non-Marxists and Marxists. The internal politics of critical theory, and especially of second-generation Frankfurt school commentators, has been pivotal both in determining the content of the original theory and in establishing interpretive and ideological continuity between the past and present.

Further, his gradually emerging communication theory of society (Habermas 1970a, 1970d, 1976, 1979, 1984, 1987b; McCarthy 1978) is in other important ways a distinct challenge to some of the psychoanalytic foundations of Horkheimer, Adorno, and Marcuse. That Slater does not deal with Habermas, whether Habermas is best located in or somewhat outside of the Frankfurt school per se, is a serious problem for the coherence of Slater's scholarship and his politics. For what it is worth, I align myself here with Jacoby's view that the original Frankfurt thinkers did not abandon Marxian aims or method; I depart from many other commentators who, I believe, make a cult of Frankfurt and shy away from fresh critical analysis of empirical tendencies. Thus, in terms of this chapter, there is as much uncreative idolatry among die-hard Frankfurt expositors as there is among those who, like Slater and Connerton, regard critical theory as a betrayal of Marx.

Like many dissertations in social theory, Slater's book begins with an unambiguous thesis:

> The following study propounds the following thesis: the Frankfurt School of the 1930s and early 1940s made a serious contribution to the elucidation and articulation of historical materialism but, at the same time, failed to achieve the relation to praxis which is central to the Marxian project. [Slater 1977, xiii–xiv]

Slater rejects Frankfurt theory because as a "Marxist" he regards it as a "tendential idealization of the values the critical theory of society drew from liberal ideology" (Slater 1977, 87). He is concerned above all to debunk critical theory as untrue to Marx because it severs what he calls the theory-praxis linkage in the name of purely cultural analysis. Throughout his book Slater returns to this theme, creating the unfortunate stylistic impression of an argument that could have stood greater tightening and repeating the orthodox Marxist rejection of critical theory as elitist, allegedly unconcerned with issues of working-class praxis.

In his own terms, of course, Slater is accurate in his depiction of Adorno and Horkheimer's growing despair, evident as early as the 1930s, about the possibilities of a socialist revolution of the kind Marx had called for. One of the better descriptive sections of the book is the last chapter, on "Historical Materialist Aesthetics," where he delves into the aesthetic theories of Adorno and Marcuse. And certainly Adorno, in his posthumously published *Aesthetic Theory* (1984), was unequivocally resigned to artistic praxis conceived as "total negation." Even in 1932 Adorno was convinced that art was to communicate the uncommunicable:

> Here and now, music can do no more than to present, in its own structure, the social antinomies which, amongst other things, carry the responsibility for music's isolation. It will succeed all the better, the more deeply it manages to form, within itself, the force of those contradictions and the need to resolve them in society, and the more precisely it expresses, in the antinomies of its own language and forms, the miseries of the status quo, emphatically calling, through the ciphered language of suffering, for change. [Adorno, quoted in Slater 1977, 142–43]

Adorno had in effect given up on the possibility that an organized transformative praxis, of the kind Marx had wishfully prophesied in *Capital*, would break through the economic contradictions of a capitalist society. Throughout his book, Slater finds the Frankfurt theorists easily characterized as having "abandoned" the working class and neglected to further its organization through what he peculiarly calls the analysis of economic "manipulation." He disparages their theory for rejecting "an active agitational role in directing this change" (Slater 1977, 89), continually comparing them to others either more directly involved in the political fray (Luxemburg, Trotsky, Lenin, the "anti-authoritarian student movement" of the 1960s) or advocates of cultural opposition—like Brecht—who conceived of their art as a "call to the oppressed to rise up against the oppressors" rather than as "total negation" (Slater 1977, 144).

"The Frankfurt School . . . held no hopes for changing the world; so they set about explaining it. That explanation, though dialectical, did not throw up any concepts for an anti-authoritarian strategy, and even failed to emphasize the need for such a strategy" (Slater 1977, 114). Here he does bring out certain important differences between Adorno and Horkheimer, on the one hand, and Marcuse (and to a lesser extent Walter Benjamin). He suggests that Marcuse was more receptive to 1960s student activism and the struggles of racial and ethnic minorities and women, and thus, apparently, the search for a new collective political agent, than were Horkheimer and Adorno, who remained where they began in the late 1930s, convinced that fascism signaled the total, eternal darkness of a degenerate liberal society. Unfortunately, Slater does not seem to realize that in Marcuse's own 1930s *Zeitschrift* essays, his view of the continuity between liberalism and fascism, as well as his emerging perspective on the USSR, was nearly identical with those of Horkheimer and Adorno and actually remained so through *One-Dimensional Man* (1964) and his last book, *The Aesthetic Dimension* (1978). When Slater dismisses the Frankfurt school for having rejected theories of class praxis while giving backhanded praise to the later Marcuse of *An Essay on Liberation* (1969) for having sought out—or, perhaps better, stumbled on—new "agitational" agents, he is merely reflecting the fact that Marcuse was able to adapt his theory more closely to the postwar American circumstance than did Adorno and Horkheimer and thus gave temporary credence to the "new sensibility" of the 1960s. But even then Marcuse rejected this ephemeral cultural irruption as apolitical (1972), returning to the original pessimism of the 1930s and of his own *One-Dimensional Man* (1964).

Marcuse differed from Adorno and Horkheimer not in his large parametric assumptions about the evolutionary course of capitalism but in the stresses he gave to the dialectical balance of hope and despair. His 1955 book on Freud enabled Marcuse to ground subjective rebellion (to flourish briefly and incompletely in the 1960s) in a libidinal substratum that, with the aid of Freud's distinction between the socialized motives of the ego and the primitive impulses of the id, he perceived as a source of indomitable emancipatory thrusts to be transformed, through basic but not "surplus" repression, into political acts. Where Adorno used Freud to explain the "total administration" of subjectivity, Marcuse, while obviously sharing Adorno's view of the psychological tentacles of a deepened alienation, also read Freud as pointing to a way beyond the internalized alienation, "surplus repression," of late capitalism, an issue I pursue further in chapters 6–7. I think this does not indicate a rupture of Marcuse with Frankfurt but reveals in Marcuse's thought a more intense yearning, in postwar America, for even the most inchoate manifestation of a critical, struggling sensibility. It was obvious to Marcuse, however, that the student movement was too unsophisticated and atheoretical to be a likely collective subject of a serious socialist kind.

But even on its own terms, Slater's argument for rejecting Frankfurt theory on grounds of unfaithfulness to the Marxian theme of praxis is not convincing. There are fundamental disagreements about the function of critical theory. Slater believes that theorists should directly abet the working-class struggle to overcome capitalism, while he characterizes Horkheimer's programmatic (1972) view in the following terms: "Horkheimer's differentiation of class and theory goes beyond Lenin's conception: whereas the latter saw the revolutionary theoreticians and the political avant-garde as one, Horkheimer envisages a separate category of critical intellectuals over and above the theoreticians of the avant garde" (Slater 1977, 57).

This remark is to aid Slater in building a case against Frankfurt theorists on grounds that they ignored certain political developments of the 1920s and 1930s, like the crisis of the European working class and the Russian Revolution, and instead sought to elevate themselves as a new world-historical elite. Alternatively, Slater proposes a theory in dialogue with such currents as Trotskyism, Luxemburgism, and the council-communist movement. (He makes an unconvincing attempt to paint the Frankfurt "team," as he calls them, as elitist by maintaining that they ignored the work of Pannekoek and "steered clear of any debate which had direct political implications" [Slater 1977, 74].) He concludes the pivotal chapter in which his historical indictment of Frankfurt theory receives its fullest exposure with the following profundity: "Class-war is thus a need, a duty, and an irresistible fact of life for the labor movement" (Slater 1977, 79). In allegedly isolating itself from "organized oppositional groupings" (Slater 1977, 81), the Frankfurt theorists descended to a "spontaneity-theory" (Slater 1977, 82) that makes intellectual criticism, and eventually art itself, a substitute for organized political praxis—a kind of negativizing praxis that surpasses ordinary discourse in order to achieve a transcendental truth unmuddied by practical contingencies or commitments. This "spontaneity-theory," writes Slater, "takes the place of an embarrassed silence" (Slater 1977, 87).

However, this is to conceive of the social role of critical theories in exceedingly crude terms. I suggest that both original and later affiliates to the Frankfurt tradition would not disagree with Slater that the role of theory ought to be in some way political, oriented to nurturing "organized occupational groupings." Habermas does so (1984, 1987b) through a "universal pragmatics" that emphasizes the everyday prospect for "consensus formation" around issues of class praxis (a "Marxist social psychology," as he terms it), Marcuse (see chap. 10) through efforts to destroy the technical division of labor and to create a realm of freedom within the production process itself (an aim that Slater peculiarly acknowledges and applauds—peculiarly, because it is not a Marcusean idiosyncrasy to think in terms of images of the merger of productive work and creative play, but part and parcel of the Frankfurt Marxism from the very beginning, as Habermas has acknowledged).

Where the Frankfurt thinkers part company from Slater is on the precise semantic content of critical theory. I believe they would say, with Marx, that a suitably "agitational" theory—agitational in the sense of opening people's eyes to their own exploitation and projecting for them the vision of a dialectical alternative—cannot always be cast in neat discursive terms, especially ones taken from a historical period a hundred years earlier. Where exactly is Slater's own critical vocabulary more directly engaged with the concerns of "praxis"? He approvingly cites Brecht's "despising" of "Horkheimer's team" on grounds that theirs was a "passive dialectical critique of culture, which he saw as evidence of their academic perspective" (Slater 1977, 145). But can Slater's own text, freed from its dust covers, stand in public? And can his plodding, highly technical hermeneutic language make itself available to citizens? Surely not. Then this makes his own critique of Frankfurt more than slightly disingenuous. It is a cliché of orthodox Marxism to blame Frankfurt theory for the absence of a concerted working-class politics when, in fact, as Horkheimer (1972) noted in 1937, theory is but a reaction, albeit a dialectical one, to a social constellation that has its own developmental momentum. Must Adorno (1973b) be condemned for the absence of a "positive" dialectics anchored in real historical possibilities? And if so, does Slater have a grip on a more directly constructive theoretical language?

Slater addresses this problem as follows: "Merely showing the necessity of contradictions and making them conscious is not enough; a real revolutionary theory involves a theory of organization and political action. What is needed is a practical-critical theory. And precisely this is lacking in the Frankfurt School's conception" (Slater 1977, 28). Slater documents the political episodes in the early twentieth century, such as Stalinism, that he believes the Frankfurt school failed to address, largely, we are told, because they were not interested in a class politics and instead endorsed what can be construed as a Mannheimian independence from ideological imperatives. But was Marx, notably in *Capital*, doing anything more than, to use Slater's own words, "showing the necessity of contradictions and making them conscious"? One can read Marx in his later work as having retreated from the revolutionary exuberance of the *Manifesto*, having become more circumspect about the possibility of successful class struggle. Volume 1 of *Capital* contains suggestions about the internal coping mechanisms that the capitalist economic system can employ in deflecting the threatening crisis tendencies that render it, on the nether level of its deep structure, an internally contradictory system. But, as I suggested above, Marx at once presented an elegant formal scheme for understanding these internal contradictions and possible scenarios of their undoing (notably in vol. 3). One cannot escape the impression that the imagery of the expropriation of the expropriators was tacked on at the end to satisfy Marx's own utopian optimism. In fact, he realized that countercyclical mechanisms in the economic system (such as international imperialism, variable rates of profit, and a fluctuating industrial reserve army) could preserve the system for many years to come (see Agger 1979, 65–72).

Slater would be disappointed, I contend, if he applied the same rigorous criteria of orientation-to-praxis to Marx that he applies to the Frankfurt school. For that matter, where in the Third International were theory and action more successfully bridged? It was precisely Leninism's failure and the slide of liberalism into fascism that spawned the Hegelian reading of Marxism, first in Lukács and Korsch and later among the Frankfurt theorists. Slater surveys this development but fails to understand that critical theory took life as a response to the growing distance between theory and praxis after 1914, the year the Second International collapsed. Instead, he reads critical theory as turning away from the political successes of Luxemburg, Lenin, Pannekoek. At best, this indicates a seriously flawed romanticism about the failed class struggles of the German and Russian proletariats. His conclusion (really his premise) that critical theory was not sufficiently agitational misses its very reason for being: there was no conceivable revolutionary subject after the collapse of the Second International, nothing to agitate *for*.

Finally, Slater, like many Marxist critics, dismisses Frankfurt theorists because their "analyses were largely superstructural, and basically lacking in terms of economic concreteness" (Slater 1977, 47). This comes right after Slater's acknowledgment that Horkheimer in 1937 and 1938 stated plainly that critical theory was to concentrate on culture and the analysis of ideology because in monopoly capitalism these were more tightly linked to the imperatives of the reproduction of capital than in the earlier entrepreneurial stage when Marx wrote. Slater does not make sufficient use of his own quotations. What Horkheimer is saying is that critical theory, in the face of numerous socialist political failures, must address the ideological occlusion of liberatory possibilities that has dampened working-class ardor and served to prolong the economic system. Here Slater's book ultimately fails. He does not come to grips with the dialectical implications of this critique of ideology. The Frankfurt theorists are not saying that the "base" no longer matters in late capitalism or that alienation is now strictly a cultural and psychological phenomenon. They are claiming that economic imperatives penetrate deeper into what Marx, almost a century earlier in a more rudimentary stage of capitalism, had regarded as a relatively autonomous realm of false consciousness.

Slater does not understand the thoroughly Marxian implications of the Frankfurt concepts of "total administration" and "one-dimensionality." He thinks that the Frankfurt theorists willingly abandon their own agitational roles. In fact, they merely register theoretically what has happened in the global evolution of capitalism, namely, that organized opposition against the system is increasingly defused by being robbed of both a viable utopian vision and a coherent language through which to organize itself and others. This sort of cultural-ideological analysis is dismissed out of hand by Slater because he reads a Marx who rigidly divided social forces into economic and noneconomic. As early as 1937, Horkheimer insisted that the importance of ideology grows in direct proportion to the deepening of capitalist internal contradictions. As Marcuse (1955) indicates, the more the objective necessity of social control is loosened by enormous technological advances, the more tightly people must be libidinally and cognitively bound into dominant modes of thought and behavior. It is thus no accident that his concept of "surplus repression" both parallels and extends Marx's original concept of surplus value, as I shall discuss in chapters 6–7.

Slater dismisses the Frankfurt school by relegating it to a stage in chronological history obviously superseded. But his own Marxism begs for an elucidation that would convincingly demonstrate its modern relevance. Horkheimer and Adorno always believed that the renewal of critical theory must address changing socioeconomic circumstances. Thus Slater's preoccupation with early Frankfurt works and his avoidance of Marcuse and Habermas doom his project. What is enduring about critical theory is its attempt to restore, as Lukács and Korsch had done in

1923, the Hegelian roots of the Marxian critique of political economy as a means of rescuing Marxism from an eventually fatal mechanism and determinism. Their special contribution to the restoration of Marxism has been the analysis and critique of an increasingly immobilizing ideology that, as Marcuse (1964) suggests, has been so thoroughly "introjected" by people that it virtually takes on a life of its own. In this way, base becomes superstructure, superstructure base. Slater suggests that critical theory has eschewed the analysis of "economic manipulation" and thereby opted out of the class struggle. I suggest that, over time, economic manipulation has become so effective that it has spun off a superstructure that no longer stands "out there," offering clearly falsifiable claims about the alleged rationality of the universe, but is experienced inwardly as reality itself, without the mediation of discursive arguments (see Agger 1989a). Thus the impulse to imagine and work toward a better world is denied at its roots, producing a one-dimensional world of experience without action. If this is not an analysis of evolving forms of economic manipulation, what is it? Slater, unfortunately, provides no clear answer except that, by turning away from economics, the Frankfurt theorists turned away from socialist commitment. In my view there has been no turning away from economics, only a different sort of analysis of the imperatives of capital.

## On the Death of Enlightenment and the Birth of Tragedy

Connerton's book has a much denser philosophical texture than Slater's and appears to show a greater sympathy toward the Frankfurt works. Unlike Slater, Connerton does not baldly charge intellectual elitism, although his criticism of critical theory is no less trenchant and deserves equally close examination. While Connerton's writing is less obviously hostile than Slater's, avoiding the dismissive language of a self-proclaimed orthodox Marxism, his message and conclusion are no less decisive. He believes that the Frankfurt thinkers failed to produce an adequate critical theory that resembles, as Horkheimer hoped in 1937, Marx's own critique of political economy. Connerton's book, too, reads like a doctoral dissertation, with chapters devoted to each of the school's original members. It is only in his final two chapters that we receive his conclusion and what he calls a "critique of critical theory." I will concentrate on those chapters. The balance of his book offers more or less direct textual accounts of the individual theorists, although these, too, bear the mark of his overall critique of the school, which revolves around the charge of "depoliticization" (Connerton 1980, 108).

Connerton agrees with Slater that critical theory failed because it did not retain contact with possible agents of social change.

> When critical theory is measured against the claims it makes for itself as a general procedure of social investigation, serious doubts arise. By explicitly taking Marx's *Critique of Political Economy* as the paradigm for their analysis of the contemporary situation, critical theorists open themselves to the question as to whether, in fact, they have succeeded in constructing a theory for their own society comparable in coherence and explanatory force with that produced by Marx for his society. Marx, as I have suggested, may be said to have produced an analysis of liberal capitalism that was critical in the sense that he analyzed that system of production from the standpoint of the possible change inherent in its basic structure; he sought to locate the objective possibilities of change as they were already present, though latent, in pre-revolutionary conditions. But the analyses of the technically most advanced areas of the contemporary world produced by the main exponents of critical theory do not suffice to justify the claim that they have constructed a modern critical theory in this strong sense of the term critical. It is true of course that in shifting attention from the infrastructure to the superstructure they successfully highlighted the emergence of new dimensions of domination. But once they replaced the critique of political economy with that of instrumental rationality, they began to develop variants of an analysis which, although containing within them insights many of which were correct, or at the very least suggestive, did not amount, when they were viewed as a general frame of reference, to a fully coherent model that could be called critical in the sense in which that term can, quite justifiably, be applied to Marx's analysis. [Connerton 1980, 109]

We hear the familiar repetition of the orthodox critique of Frankfurt theory: neglecting to adopt the standpoint of the proletariat; alleged shift from concerns of political economy to those of culture and ideology; lack of coherence when measured against Marx. Connerton's particular contribution is to explain the Frankfurt failure in terms of two interrelated themes: first, its insufficient break with the Enlightenment tradition that culminated in Hegel's philosophy of history, suggesting that historical progress will produce a unique subject who has attained autonomy; and second, its affiliation with the German tradition of

> tragic pessimism . . . [that] found expression in the belief that the new network of institutions [of industrial society] . . . had acquired an autonomy independent of human needs, that they had assumed a dynamism which was hardly any longer suscepti- ble to human control, and that this dynamism worked in direct opposition to the intentions which originally lay behind the creation of these new social structures. This is the characteris- tic topos of German sociology: the thesis of heteronomy. Means have become ends in themselves. The attitude of tragic pessimism gave rise to a general theory of alienation. [Conner- ton 1980, 119–20]

Here Connerton suggests that Frankfurt theory is but the latest expression of this tragic tradition, which has its sociological roots in Sim- mel, Weber, and Toennies and is a response to the fading Enlightenment ideals of subjective autonomy and reason in an emerging industrial age. Connerton suggests that Frankfurt theory merely continued in this vein, especially where the Frankfurt thinkers allegedly replaced the critique of political economy with a critique of instrumental rationality in general, shifting the focus from capitalist exploitation to the "domination" built into the machine system of all industrial societies. He finds this idea of the decline of enlightened reason into tragic pessimism most central in such works as Horkheimer and Adorno's (1972) *Dialectic of Enlighten- ment,* Marcuse's (1964) *One-Dimensional Man,* and, finally, most coher- ently, in Habermas's (1971) distinction between instrumental and communicative types of action. This assimilation of critical theory to the disappointed pessimism of Simmel and Weber—two distinctively Ger- man social thinkers, we are told—leads to Connerton's rejection of criti- cal theory as un-Marxist.

According to Connerton, these two themes of a world-historical trend toward autonomy coupled with tragic pessimism when enlighten- ment turns into its opposite, fascism, doom the Frankfurt enterprise. Throughout his book he returns to the Frankfurt theorists' alleged re- placement of the indictment of capitalist economic arrangements with the critique of "instrumental rationality" in general. "For whereas Marx had connected the principle of commodity exchange with a specific sys- tem of property ownership, Adorno detaches commodity exchange from a particular historical type of economic organization, and views it instead as the most complete expression of instrumental rationality" (Connerton 1980, 128). Earlier, Connerton suggests that Marcuse produced a technological determinism that causes his "swing from hope to despair" in the decade between *Eros and Civilization* and *One-Dimensional Man*. This is said to result in a lack of specificity about both the concept of domination and possible emancipatory routes left open to us. Connerton believes that the Frankfurt thinkers were too much creatures of the Enlightenment and of its tragic evolution into despair in the 1930s and 1940s; they could not be Marxists, he implies, because they "assimilated [too much] metaphysical and sociological ballast," thus producing an "enveloping orgy of abstractions" (Connerton 1980, 134) that end up on Connerton's last page ignoring the "possibilities of organizing the working class."

Slater suggests plainly that critical theory eschewed the analysis of what he calls "economic manipulation." Connerton, in what seems to be a more sophisticated way, says that Frankfurt theory replaced the critique of political economy with the critique of instrumental rationality under the twin influences of the eighteenth-century Enlightenment, taking the final form in Hegel of a world-historical Reason, and the late nineteenth- and early twentieth-century sociological articulation of the "tragedy of enlightenment" in what Weber called the "iron cage" of the bureaucratic machine age. He develops this argument in the course of his exposition of the various Frankfurt works. He suggests that Horkheimer and Adorno's *Dialectic of Enlightenment* was pivotal in the way it attempted to confront the failures of the Enlightenment. But Connerton thinks it was an inadequate confrontation for it led the Frankfurt authors to substitute the vague concept of "domination," referring to all person-nature as well as person-person relations, for Marx's sharper economic concept of the exploitation of labor. This led, through the influence of Marcuse's own well-known address and paper on Weber (Marcuse 1968b) and his *One-Dimensional Man*, to Habermas's ultimate reformulation of the critique of political economy. Here Connerton, referring to Habermas's distinction between instrumental and communicative action (Habermas 1971, 1973) that took its most nearly complete form in his (1984, 1987b) "communication theory of society," suggests that Habermas summarizes and completes the defective Frankfurt tradition:

> Habermas believes that the anticipation of a form of social life in which autonomy and responsibility are possible is prefigured in the structure of speech itself. Hence he views the theoretical and the practical consequences of his distinction

between instrumental and communicative action as inextricably connected. His claim therefore is that the normative basis of critical theory is not an arbitrary one, but that it is inherent in the structure of social action which it analyses. In this way his theory of communicative competence may be seen to take the place of the analysis of the work process, once Marx's philosophical anthropology has been abandoned. [Connerton 1980, 104]

Habermas is rejected for raising the ideals of the Enlightenment—emancipation, autonomy, reason—to the level of a teleology of the structure of communication itself. The "ideal speech situation," as Habermas calls it, is rejected as an orienting concept for a latter-day critical theory because, presumably, it substitutes talk for action, confirming Connerton's final verdict that "Habermas' essays are exercises in a mode of thought that can no longer be our own; so that, despite his strenuous efforts to reestablish their topicality, they are politically defective in the current social context" (Connerton 1980, 107).

It is interesting to compare Slater and Connerton here. The former rejects Frankfurt theory for being too "cultural" in its analysis of advanced capitalism, while the latter rejects the Frankfurt tradition for replacing the critique of capitalism per se with the critique of instrumental rationality, in very much the style of German sociologists, like Simmel and Weber, who were heirs to a failed Enlightenment tradition. The Enlightenment failed most conspicuously in late nineteenth-century Germany, where industrialization was taking place without the aid of a supporting liberal political tradition, ultimately leading to statism and fascism. I think these arguments are essentially identical inasmuch as they take their departure from Marx's materialism and his alleged linkage of theory and praxis. But I suspect that Connerton's own case (much like that of Slater) is insensitive to what was really going on politically and theoretically in the Frankfurt work. This leads him first to combine critical theory with the Enlightenment worldviews of the philosophes, Kant, and finally Hegel, and then to suggest that, as this worldview was proved practically hopeless by the fascists, the Frankfurt thinkers abandoned Marxism in favor of a fin de siècle cultural pessimism, the "tragedy of enlightenment," according to which all modernity is seen to be degenerate, based as it is on the "instrumental rationality" of the machine system. In my opinion, he has not made his case convincingly because he has failed to understand (although in places he comes close) that the Frankfurt critique of domination was not a substitute for the earlier cri-

tique of political economy, with all of its supposed directly political implications, but an extrapolation from it in an era of ideological and
cultural darkness.

Connerton, with Slater, blames critical theorists for giving up
what he calls "the western concept of publicity" (Connerton 1980,
139)—presumably the class struggle—and for registering their disenchantment in virtually ontological excurses on the eternal failures of instrumentality, technology, and science (very much the theme I take up in
chap. 13). He does not seem to credit the possibility that, as I remarked
when discussing Slater, the Frankfurt thinkers were responding empirically, albeit in works as apparently abstract as *Dialectic of Enlightenment*,
to the growing linkage among economics, politics, culture, and psychology in an overdetermined stage of capitalism.

This is a serious failure because it leads to nostalgia for Marx's
own literal version of the critique of political economy. It is never clear
whether we are to retrieve Marx literally or in some revised form. Connerton is even less clear than Slater about what a properly politicized
theory would say to us today, in transcendence of the Frankfurt gloom.
If one rejects the imagery of autonomous subjectivity taken from the
Enlightenment, as well as the thoroughly sociological analyses of culture
and ideology found throughout the Frankfurt corpus, how exactly is a
contemporary Marxism to be phrased? Connerton is no more helpful
than Slater here, although he is certainly more deft in building a philosophical and historical case against Frankfurt. His argument that
Horkheimer, Adorno, Marcuse, and Habermas failed because they were
too close to the Enlightenment (reason, autonomy, subjecthood) and
(therefore?) too bitterly disappointed by the failure of the early twentieth-century workers' movements is a very compelling one. It is to say,
with Slater, that when all is said and done the Frankfurt thinkers were
never really "Marxists"—merely wistful descendants of an earlier and
more optimistic rationalism that, under German fascism, led them to
"fear that socialist action from the left might set loose precisely that
which they oppose—the potential of fascist terror from the right." The
Frankfurt theorists, we are finally told, were true German intellectuals in
that they so feared the expansion of the state, unchallenged in the absence of a liberal tradition during Germany's industrialization, that they
rejected politics altogether—Connerton says that they shared the beliefs
of Simmel and Weber "that collective political practice is necessarily destructive of critical awareness" (Connerton 1980, 130).

I think the key word here is "necessarily." I suggest that the
Frankfurt theorists had no problem whatsoever in accepting Marx's rev-

olutionary materialism as an adequate rupture with Enlightenment idealism and rationalism. They merely contended, from the 1930s through Habermas's latest writings on communication theory, that "collective political practice" is often completely without aim, either easily co-optable, as the analysis of one-dimensionality has demonstrated, or else too susceptible to misdirection by an authoritarian elite. Neither Slater nor Connerton has made a case that there have been actual "collective political practices" worth supporting by someone who reads a dialectical Marx. Indeed, the Frankfurt theorists, in their analysis of "introjected" or "surplus" exploitation, attempt to explain exactly *how* capitalism has managed to bleed off potentially revolutionary dissent, thus temporarily (but not necessarily permanently) blunting the internal contradictions of capital.

Connerton's argument fails because he says that critical theory was "necessarily" allergic to a class politics; there is no "necessity" of this kind in their works. Rather than allowing an original idealism and rationalism to crash down in a tragic cynicism, the Frankfurt theorists, I contend, were nothing more or less than skeptics, trying their best to describe empirically how the imperatives of political economy now penetrate nearly all of our "private" interiors and turn us unwittingly into agents of our own bondage. Their skepticism has roots not in a subterranean affiliation of Frankfurt theory to the bourgeois Enlightenment (although all of us, notably Marx himself, who value autonomy, rationality, undistorted communication have some investment in Enlightenment notions of liberal freedom [see Ackerman 1980; Agger 1981]) but in Marx's original materialism. The argument that critical theory is Hegelian and not Marxist—and that is what Connerton is really trying to argue—is in my opinion unsupportable.

Why, then, does it continue to be such a popular way of reading critical theory? I think the answer is that there are all sorts of "Marxists" uncomfortable with the way in which theorists from Lukács to Habermas have developed new conceptual languages to describe unprecedented developments in capitalist society, thus appearing to deviate from the theoretical logic of literal Marx. Such Marxists believe that these linguistic and conceptual transformations—alienation into reification and domination, for example—betray a rejection of Marx's method and vision. They cling to an archaic discourse because they cannot bear to learn a new one. A psychoanalytic analysis of left-wing mimesis might be apposite here. Instead of reading critical theory as building on ideas in Marx and extending them in new directions in order to describe an evolving object—historical capitalism—these critics of Frankfurt theory

cannot go beyond denouncing the tone of political pessimism and terminological deviation as evidence of embourgeoisement. Both Slater's and
Connerton's books are examples of this tendency to denounce all revisions as ideologically unfaithful. They fail to deal with the much more
interesting challenge of thinking through whether critical theory does
accurately describe the evolution of capitalism—which, if met, could
then lead to discussions of strategic issues of praxis. In neither book are
we told whether one-dimensionality is a real, meaningful phenomenon,
requiring modifications of Marx. The authors are content to note the
obvious. A scan of the indexes of Marx's various books does not reveal
the term "one-dimensional."

## Critical Theory as Empirical Theory

Slater and Connerton regard critical theory as having failed because of
assumptions that weakened or altogether doomed its relationship to
working-class praxis. This neglects the practical role, however minuscule
in these times, of theory itself as a type of ideology critique that awakens
a dormant critical subjectivity in face of an increasingly preponderant
social totality—my argument in chapters 12–15. Orthodox Marxists
rightly, I believe, fear intellectual elitism but at the same time misunderstand the Frankfurt attitude toward the impotence of traditional working-class politics. The critical theorists "abandon" praxis only because
they feel that the prospects of collective subjecthood, in Marx's and
Lukács's sense, have so diminished as to make a working-class politics
today either thoroughly reformist or downright reactionary for its
avowed individualism in face of economic crises (e.g., neoconservatism).
Critics of Frankfurt theory misread the retreat from a discursive theoretical language that is, in Slater's terms, "agitational" as elitism instead of
understanding it as a response to all contemporary oppositional projects
that tend to be reduced to terms of conventional thought and action and
are thus defused.

As I argue in chapter 9, the Frankfurt turn toward aesthetics was
less in positive hope than from despair. It makes Adorno and Marcuse
not less Marxist but perhaps more so. By refusing to repeat tired recipes
of class agitation, they allowed themselves to take a fresh look at the shifting constellation of institutional and ideological forces in advanced capitalism. Frankfurt theory does not exaggerate its own role in these
developments but recognizes the impotence of nearly all political pro-

jects, whether of entrepreneurs in a world of corporate giants striking out after their first million or of Marxists trying to organize the working class, thoroughly embittered and apolitical, around themes of their own alienation. The orthodox Marxist does not see that the most effective political theory and action today may be those that try to provoke a halting first step toward what Habermas calls the formation of a new socialist consensus, requiring a critical negativity liberated from subservience to dominant ideologies that offer the comfort of faith in exchange for duty. Marx: "I am not a Marxist."

Both Slater and Connerton have dismissed critical theory prematurely on the grounds that its theoretical vocabulary is quite unlike that of Marx. This has raised their suspicion of a revisionism slanted in the direction of the fin de siècle intellectual elitism that characterized much bourgeois social theory then. But it is not enough, I believe, merely to acknowledge these terminological differences. Instead, Slater and Connerton should have probed whether, in fact, the Frankfurt analyses of introjected domination and one-dimensionality make any empirical sense as ways of describing the evolution of capitalism since Marx. Simply to reject Frankfurt because their language is abstruse—seemingly "cultural" and not "economic"—and because they offer no strategic advice to radical agents is to miss their point that their own revisions have been a response to a general retreat from praxis. In this they do not reject Marx's vital understanding of the deep contradiction in capitalist societies between capital and labor but rather try to understand why that very contradiction has not caused eruptions in system-wrenching crises with the advent of more contemporary forms of a private enterprise economy. Critics of Frankfurt theory who suggest that the Frankfurt critique broadens the concept of alienation too much, and thus occludes the possibility of political action, fail to see that the Frankfurt thinkers believe on the evidence that alienation has been broadened and deepened over time. Whether this is actually the case would make for interesting discussion. As it is, however, critics like Slater and Connerton waste their energies denouncing critical theory on grounds of what is an obvious terminological deviation.

My view is that it does not matter very much whether we are to call the Frankfurt thinkers "Marxist" in the weak sense of adhering to literal formulations in *Capital* (20 percent of the formulations, 80 percent—how many must one accept to be a "Marxist"?). I think that in the strong sense of accepting Marx's basic understanding of capitalism as internally contradictory, containing the hidden germ of a possible society beyond alienation, the Frankfurt theorists are Marxists. And, more than that, their very allegiance to the dialectical tradition has caused them to seek out reasons for capitalism's longevity. It does not take a great deal of interpretive know-how to realize that books like *Dialectic of Enlightenment* and *Eros and Civilization* are less about Homer and Freud than about modernity. Orthodox Marxists do not read works of critical theory in a sufficiently metaphoric way, as having a dialectical relationship to their topics (Homer, e.g.) that goes beyond the topic to the world itself. Slater and Connerton cannot see that critical theory is empirical theory that tries, albeit in allusive ways, to suggest how capitalism has changed (and remained the same) since Marx. Critics of this sort do not work hard enough to uncover empirical content but instead regard a "Freudian turn" or writing about Schoenberg as prima facie evidence of what they thought they suspected all along: The Frankfurt thinkers are merely bourgeois culture critics dressed up in leftish garb.

The work we should be doing, I propose, is assessing whether capitalism has changed in important ways since Marx and trying to see what sorts of implications this may have for a non-authoritarian political practice. Obviously, this is a huge task, and under way in many different areas today (e.g., Habermas's [1984, 1987b] communication theory, Offe's [1984, 1985] work on the state, Leiss's [1976] work on needs, commodities, and advertising). It should not be stifled by a fetishism of holy words and true belief. By the same token, devotees of critical theory ought not to treat the original works as icons—a real temptation when the works are presented as not only straightforward theoretical works but also as aesthetic objects whose allusive obscurity may be seen as precious. We may ultimately find that Marxism is but another critical theory that probes an internally contradictory society for signs of a new world that it would create through its very "progress." Better to say that Marxism is critical theory than the other way around. Such a theory joins sober appraisal of a damaged present with an imagination that tries to foster a creative negativity on the basis of its own apparent pessimism. What Slater and Connerton forget is that optimism about class struggle today may be a betrayal of the very critical science Marx thought he was writing.

In the next chapter, I turn to the Marxism of Erik Olin Wright, a leading expositor of quantitative Marxism. Like Slater, he rejects critical theory as a betrayal of Marx's revolutionary political project. I need to respond to Wright's positivism inasmuch as it reflects many of the pathologies of positivism attacked by Marcuse (chaps. 6–9). In the context of that argument, I shall suggest the possibilities of critical theory's renewal, to be pursued conclusively in chapters 12–15.

## 3

# The Crisis
# of the
# "Crisis of Marxism"

L et me set the stage for this chapter (see the Burawoy-Wright "debate" [1987]). The Wisconsin quantitative Marxist, Erik Olin Wright, has been invited to join the Department of Sociology at Berkeley. Graduate students, who run the estimable *Berkeley Journal of Sociology,* pose a number of questions to him and publish the results in their journal. Meanwhile, Michael Burawoy, his Marxist colleague and friend from Berkeley, answers Wright, who responds briefly in turn. I, representing critical theory, am invited to comment on their debate. The issue in this chapter, as in the preceding one, is what it means to be a Marxist. My answer, framed here, informs my later arguments in this book for a repoliticized version of critical theory that is influenced by a variety of European theories of interpretation, including feminism, poststructuralism, and postmodernism.

In itself, there is nothing particularly strange in debating the meaning of Marxism. People have been doing this for over a hundred years. It is a good way to run a journal, opening it to lively discussion of central matters. Intellectual and political controversy stirs the blood and focuses attention, especially when it is carried out with a minimum of Scholasticism. I am pleased to participate. However, on another level, there is something decidedly strange about all this. Although they are learned and articulate, Wright and Burawoy seem peculiarly untutored by the long history of controversy within Marxism, beginning with the First International and extending through Lukács, Korsch, the Frankfurt school, and Althusser. At issue, now as before, is the question of Marxism's scientificity.

For the few of us who work within critical theory in the United States (see Jay [1984], who lists fifty critical theorists in the United States) the controversy over Marxism's scientificity has long been settled. Wright and Burawoy add next to nothing; they repeat timeworn versions of Marxist scientism and Marxist pragmatism, respectively. What is going on, then? Wright has garnered some recent notoriety in mainstream United States sociology for his labored attempt to define and then quantify the middle class (Wright and Perrone 1977; Wright et al. 1982); indeed, much of his side of the *BJS* debate is a reflection on his book, *Classes* (Wright 1985; see Kamolnick 1988). Wright's contribution to the Wright-Burawoy debate could simply be read as an attempt at self-clarification; Burawoy, for his part, offers an intelligent response to the viability of Wright-wing Marxism.

Fine. But, as I said, the debate has been held scores of times before, and people have failed to learn from it. Where Wright defends the scientificity of Marxism in terms of Roemer's notion of "analytical Marxism" (Roemer 1986), Burawoy argues for a more closely welded theory and practice springing directly from the shop floor, the point of production. These are old positions; calling Wright's version "analytical Marxism" does little except more openly affiliate that version of Marxism to Anglo-American analytic philosophy. And Burawoy's engagement has been seen before; his autocriticism of his earlier Althusserianism serves his exuberant contention that revolutionary science and revolutionary politics are conjoined.

Thus, without stating all of my arguments at the outset, I suggest that the Wright-Burawoy debate should be read closely at the level of its subtext—the silences, echoes, and lapses inhabiting the words themselves. After all, as I acknowledge throughout this book, the "text" has been written before, notably in Lukács's (1971) *History and Class Consciousness,* Korsch's (1970) *Marxism and Philosophy,* and Horkheimer's (1972) "Traditional and Critical Theory." If I am right, and the debate over Marxist scientificity has been settled, what is going on here? Eventually, I shall argue that Wright's Marxism is positivist—at least, I shall clarify the senses in which we can understand the word "positivism," setting the stage for my later discussion of Marcuse's critique of positivism. Unfortunately, positivism has become a slogan of blind approval or disapproval, obscuring real issues involved in the politics of the philosophy of science.

## "Propositionalizing" Marxism

Wright wants to sociologize Marxism, making it into a social science with explanatory power (see Kamolnick 1988, esp. chap. 1). His response to the "crisis of Marxism" is epistemological; evidence plus methodological and conceptual acuity will refurbish the Marxist edifice. Wright inveighs against Marxist Scholasticism, rethinking sacred categories in light of their subsequent empirical evolution. Analytical Marxism is the name Wright and Roemer give to their refurbishing of old Marxism; they strip down Marxism into some differentiated propositions that are then put to the empirical test. "Analytical Marxism insists on the necessity of laying bare the assumptions that underlie these concepts and spelling out as clearly and systematically as possible the steps involved in linking them together within a theory" (Wright 1987, 25).

Burawoy responds by saying that Wright betrays Marxism for sociology; instead, Marxists must do science from the shop floor, whether in South Chicago, Zambia or Hungary (Burawoy's research sites). Burawoy: "Of all Wright's claims I find the one that science and revolution are antithetical the most disturbing" (1987, 52). He argues that Wright "unrigorously" cleaves science from politics, distancing Marxism further from the concerns of those involved in political struggle. Counterposing "positivist" and "practical" knowledge, Burawoy argues that "political struggles do not contaminate the pursuit of truth, they are the pursuit of truth" (1987, 65). Finally, "if social scientists want to shape the world they must work very closely with those whose interests they seek to defend" (1987, 62).

Burawoy rejects Wright's version of "analytical Marxism" (see Roemer 1981, 1982; Kamolnick 1988, chap. 2; also see Sober et al. 1987). Correctly, in my opinion, Wright wants to " 'save sociology' from the sins of bourgeois thought as well as to 'save Marxism' from the sins of dogmatism" (1987, 27). But this salvation is to come from "the joining of statistical methods with conceptual rigor . . . stress[ing] the importance of formulating explicit causal models of *variations* in the theoretical objects of the research" (1987, 27–28). This is the strong version of Wright's quantitative Marxism, establishing his affiliation to an earlier tradition of left scientism (see Lenin 1952; also see chap. 11 below).

Wright's version of Marxism claims a great deal for itself, notably that a "propositionalized" Marxism validated by impartial observers earns epistemological legitimacy.

But is this affiliation between a propositional Marxism concerned with explaining the "variance" of variables (like class) and the garden-variety positivism reducing knowledge to a mirrorlike reflection of the object world really necessary? Can one "propositionalize" and then test Marxism *without* endorsing the so-called reflection theory of knowledge that turns human subjects into disempowered vessels of direct experience? For that matter, what is *wrong* with positivism? By calling Wright a "positivist" here I am trying to use shorthand; further on in this chapter, I will separate his work into its various nuances. Some who use the term "positivism" differently from me may absolve Wright of positivism but agree with my negative characterization of his version of Marxism. Concepts—words—cannot do all of our analytical work for us. We must think *through* the tendency of thought to congeal into slogans, clichés, used only to dismiss or approve.

Let me briefly outline the three senses in which people use the term positivism. Positivism I refers to the view, originating with Locke, that knowledge mutely mirrors the world "out there," unmediated by ontological, theoretical, political assumptions. Positivism II requires knowledge to be formulated in terms of causality, arrived at by testing, rejecting, improving hypotheses—if/then statements. Positivism III simply advocates empirical research as a basis of objective knowledge. Later, I will argue that Wright is a positivist II and III, although all "real" Marxists and feminists ought to be positivist IIIs—indeed, *positivism III*, as I call it here, *is not really positivism at all* but merely empiricism, a good thing, defended vigorously in chapter 13 below. Finally, I do not know whether Wright is a positivist I; he would probably deny that he is, even if his work seems to imply it.

Fending off attacks that strong claims about his positivism embody, especially the conflation of positivism II and III in my sense, Wright suggests that "*if* positivism is simply the view that theory and empirical research need to be 'balanced' in some kind of systematic interaction, then indeed I would describe my work as 'positivism' " (Wright 1987, 33). Now this is the weaker version of Wright's "positivism"—my positivism III. On the one hand, above, Wright wants propositions to be tested, albeit Marxist propositions (my positivism II). On the other hand, here, Wright simply wants to avoid what he calls "empiricism" and "theoreticism" (atheoretical research and hagiography) by finding a middle way between them, a project with which few people working and acting on the Left would disagree. By seeming to back away from positivism I (which Wright never explicitly endorses or rejects) and instead confessing his positivism III (*all* empiricism), Wright deftly conceals the sense in which one can legitimately characterize his work as positivist—his insistence on hypothesis testing, *the* central feature of Viennese logical positivism (now animating "scientific" Marxism as well).

What *is* Wright's project? He is ambivalent about his own position on Marxist scientificity. On the one hand, he recommends Marxist hypothesis testing, or positivism II; on the other, he simply calls for empirical revisions of original Marxism, balancing empirical research and theory building (or, better, informing theory with the empirical)—positivism III. And there is little evidence to indicate that for Wright knowledge reflects the world presuppositionlessly, without ontological and political assumptions—positivism I. Wright's last sentence (1987, 45) offers a hint about the nature of his project: "Marxism is to be a contending theory within social science." He had already reflected on his more youthful fantasies about "glorious paradigm battles, with lances drawn and the valiant Marxist knight unseating the bourgeois rival in a dramatic quantitative joust" (1987, 44). Recognizing that bourgeois sociology will not play on his epistemological field, Wright attempts to secure greater institutional respectability for Marxism. Thus, he justifies his overall attempt to "propositionalize" Marxism, reducing it to the testable hypotheses so dearly valued by bourgeois social science, the epitome of positivism II.

Anyone on the Left who wants to survive in academe, and even do the modest political/pedagogical work available to Marxist academics, will support academization, at least as a survival strategy. Although Jacoby's *Last Intellectuals* (1987, esp. chaps. 5 and 6) laments the academization of the New Left, decrying university Marxism for its studied obscurantism and self-importance, Jacoby would undoubtedly agree that it is better to have some sort of institutional support, if only to put bread on the table. But certain disciplinary defensive maneuvers designed to protect (the few) leftists against the mainstream do not require one to "propositionalize" knowledge, thus endorsing precisely the postulate of social laws debunked by Marx himself as ideological. "Socialist" laws are still laws, diminishing free agency and hence only compounding domination. Although Wright recants his earlier optimism about beating back bourgeois sociology on its own quantitative turf, settling for more modest spoils (academic jobs, tenure, grants, journal space—just what?), Burawoy is reacting to the version of Wright's positivism that not only balances concept formation and empirical research but also attempts to test causal models exactly in the fashion of bourgeois natural science—a project that Burawoy, with all Western Marxists, rejects as politically inappropriate.

Even allowing for his initial vacillation about a strong or weak version of Marxist positivism, Wright is remarkably candid about his disciplinary intentions. His effort to elaborate a concept of the middle class is more than an effort to mainstream Marxism; he translates Marxism into testable propositions *to see whether Marxism is right or wrong.* Adopting mainstream discourse for publication in mainstream journals is one thing (after all, Marx engaged bourgeois political economy in its own terms); it is quite another to suppose that Marxism can be evaluated hypothetically with reference to data—that Marxism is simply a perspective on certain obdurate facts and not a total framework within which social reality is both interpreted and constituted. Although only intellectual dinosaurs believe that Marxism need not be extrapolated far beyond the rudimentary capitalism of the mid-nineteenth century, a nonpositivist empirical Marxism (positivism III) is entirely different from a multivariate Marxism standing or falling on the evidence (positivism II). Indeed, people who conflate positivism and all objective knowledge are anti-*science*, not just opposed to the reflection theory of knowledge (positivism I) or "propositionalization" (positivism II). Such people include certain Heideggerians and poststructuralists.

Burawoy is right that Wright is wrong to counterpose science and politics. Marxism is not a correspondence theory whose concepts simply dissolve in an obdurate, one-dimensional world of appearances; nor can allegedly impartial observers in the "marketplace of ideas" evaluate Marxist truth claims on the evidence. *The adjudication of claims about truth is itself theoretical practice,* constituting as much as reflecting the world it addresses. Ultimately, ontological disputes cannot be resolved epistemologically; no amount of evidence (or methodology) will settle what are essentially ontological and political disputes. For Wright, Burawoy, myself, and most other Marxists, it is second nature that contemporary capitalism, because of its built-in contradictions, tends to lurch from one crisis to another, always threatening to come apart. But for bourgeois social scientists, not to mention Republicans, Marxism is increasingly debunked by empirical falsification. Not even Dukakis could convince otherwise sane Americans of the obvious: The American economy has been stranded in the shoals of its structural contradictions.

Wright wants to enhance Marxism's institutional respectability by reducing it to causal modeling. In the process, he vitiates Marxism politically; scientific Marxism is all science, no Marxism. Regression Marxism only causes Marxism to regress. These debates have been held before, and resolved. Critics of the scientific Marxism of the Second and Third Internationals laid to rest the notion of a dialectic of nature; Western Marxism rethinks the empirical world, and thus Marxian theory, precisely to reinvigorate the conformist Marxisms of Engels, Kautsky, Lenin, and Althusser (see Jay 1973; Held 1980; Agger 1979). In Burawoy's terms, science and politics are inseparable. Yet Burawoy's spontaneous alternative is no alternative, after all. The notion that science stems from struggle on the shop floor is no more compelling as an argument against positivisms I and II than is the idea that power comes out of the barrels of guns. Unwittingly, perhaps, Burawoy's engaged version of Marxism converges with so-called feminist methodology, arguing that researchers must be intimate with their research subjects in the interests of both truth and politics (an especially problematic notion, given the poststructuralist critique of the idea of a stable, truth-telling "self").

But this is an empirical issue. At a time when there is precious little struggle of any kind in advanced capitalist countries, except in the most banal forms (environmentalism, liberal feminism, parliamentary politics), it is hopeless to expect Marxism to take wing from the political lifeworlds of rebels. Most such rebels are too busy at the shopping mall or on the Yuppie fast track. Without endorsing the empirically overdrawn Frankfurt thesis of one-dimensionality or total administration, I contend that the Frankfurt theorists are correct to notice the virtual absence of transformative politics, or even intelligent thought, in modern capitalism (see Marcuse 1964; Habermas 1984, 1987b). Everything and everyone seem to have been integrated, made safe—notably including academic Marxism (see Jacoby 1987).

Burawoy self-critically admits that he and Wright were former devotees of Althusser. Burawoy accepts Wright's theoretical practice or science as the only alternative to his own collapsing of theory and practice into radical politics. He laments that "theoretical practice now justifies a rigorous science at odds with radical politics" (Burawoy 1987, 69), and continues:

> Political quiescence has cut Marxists adrift within the university to find a new equilibrium, one that is shaped by interests within the liberal university. Professionalization threatens to reduce Marxism to an ideology of intellectuals whose interests are systematically concealed by the veil of neutrality surrounding the pursuit of science. [P. 69]

Professionalized Marxism is more professional than Marxist; Marxism is not another occupation like dentistry, corporate law, social work. When Burawoy refers to left intellectuals' interests, he may well be describing the ample salaries of the left glitterati, their adoration by student syco-phants, their academic networks.

But his alternative is no more credible:

> Venturing beyond the narrow community of Marxist aca-demics and engaging people with other interests has two bene-fits, apart from the possibility of directly affecting change. It makes us aware of our interests as academics and it fosters the solution and generation of anomalies that define the Marxist research program. [P. 69]

Marxist professors who have undergone embourgeoisement are, of course, professors first. But what does "engaging people with other in-terests" mean? Is the revolution to be found in the factories, streets, classrooms? Must it be? Just because it is not to be found at Berkeley or Wisconsin does not mean it is elsewhere, especially at the points of pro-duction by now so incredibly Taylorized that the only resistance to be found in workplaces is absenteeism, drug use, petty theft. Of course, we all want things to change, to nurture rebellion into full-blown transfor-mations; Marx's model of passionate intellectuality continues to fan the embers of hope. But the antidote to Wright's causal modeling, his misbe-gotten effort to "test" Marxism and thus give it academic reputability, is not a Rambo Marxism; left intellectuals learn little from those who strug-gle outside the university that they did not already know, notably how ineffectual 99 percent of "resistance" really is (see Cleaver 1979).

The crisis of Marxism is not to be resolved by more Marxism. Our exhausting interpretive labor has been exhaustive: We have read Marx, Lukács, Gramsci, Frankfurt, left feminism, world systems theory, etc., etc. The contours of the global totality have been charted. We basically understand the blockages to radical transformation, outlined further in the course of this book. The state continues to forestall economic crisis just as culture ameliorates psychic crisis. Why things do not change for the better is summarized simply enough in words like "power" and "domination"—external coercion and false consciousness. We do not have to model Marxism causally, mainstream it, give it respectability, or send it back to the factory. These things do not revivify Marxism; they only contribute to its falling rate of intelligence. The problem is not the absence of correct theory but of practice (including theoretical practice) that makes a difference (see chap. 2).


## Avoiding Wrightophobia

It is tempting to use more ink on Wright; at least Burawoy seems to have his political heart in the right place. We should resist the temptation to demonize Wright's version of Marxism, reducing it to political apostasy. Things are never that simple. Marxism has been called science from the beginning, and even by Marx. What is new about Wright is his attempt to add "class" to the standard regression equations, a project easily integrated by bourgeois sociology. I am not against science, as some post-structuralists are, but I am against both its positivist formulation as presuppositionless representation, the mirrorlike reflection of the world "out there" (my positivism I), and its "propositionalization" (positivism II). The best work on the Left empirically reformulates Marxist and feminist categories; the enduring character of capitalism, sexism, racism, and the domination of nature challenges the Left to understand them as dialectical processes, thus reversing them.

Much of the debate generated by Wright's version of Marxist sociology has to do with the brand of his positivism—that much-belabored animus of the Left. Of course, there are as many positivisms as there are critics of positivism; indeed, I have tried to distinguish between Wright's own strong insistence that Marxists test Marxism propositionally and his much weaker insistence that Marxism engage itself with the empirical world—my positivisms II and III. Only the first insistence is objectionable to those of us who accept the notion in the eleventh thesis on Feuerbach that science and practice merge dialectically. Virtually no materialist disagrees with Wright that Marxism must address the empirical world. As I have said, positivism III is not positivism at all. Wherever Wright stands on positivism I—reflection theory—the Wright who "propositionalizes" and then operationalizes Marxism betrays the eleventh thesis on Feuerbach: theory is proved in practice, as well as enlightened by it.

I suspect that Wright would disclaim positivism as a theory of knowledge rooted in sheer reflection—positivism I; he probably agrees that all knowledge is filtered through theoretical, ontological, political categories. Thus, I want to reverse the tendency of my own critique of Wright to substitute slogans for analysis: when I call Wright a positivist, I am using shorthand to characterize his attempt to reduce Marxism to causal propositions. This is positivism II. One could "propositionalize" Marxism without accepting positivist epistemological strictures: one can be positivist II without being positivist I. In that case, one could characterize Wright as a nonpositivist causal Marxist. So be it. In fact, most social scientists who reduce knowledge to sheer mirrorlike reflection of the world out there also believe that social science must test hypotheses to arrive at laws that then enable prediction. There is a correlation between positivisms I and II—judging by the people who publish in *American Sociological Review,* the correlation is probably as high as 0.98! Most bourgeois empiricists have never thought about whether knowledge immediately or mediately represents the object world. Epistemology is a waste of their time, something left behind after the first few weeks of graduate-level research methodology seminars. It is precisely these unreflexive empiricists who produce the impression of positivism as a monolith.

Indeed, this number-crunching empiricism begets a number-crunching Marxism. The difference between Wright and the usual *American Sociological Review* authors is that Wright drinks deeply of epistemology: his guard is up against Western Marxists who recognize logical positivism (i.e., "propositionalization") when they see it. We Western Marxists reject positivism in the strict sense of mirrorlike reflection; we also reject "propositionalization" (whether or not we characterize it as a logically necessary feature of mirrorlike positivism); most of us favor empiricism as an alternative to theoreticism. *Like* Wright, we are unashamedly positivists III—we are empiricists.

Wright, his students, and his disciplinary opponents take him more seriously than his work deserves. For that matter, "analytical Marxism" as a whole is moribund; it is just another name for Marxist scientism, determinism, economism. People are attracted to Wright because his multivariate Marxism endlessly proliferates itself; Wright's *Classes* is a typical example of the self-referential logic chopping promoted by those who force Marxism through the "propositionalizing" meat grinder of positivism. People oppose Wright because they do not recognize that his attempt to render Marxism scientific has been tried, and failed, before, beginning with Engels. For their part, most mainstream sociologists virtually ignore Wright, either treating him as merely another citation in the vast literature of the discipline or plundering his work for the variable, class, that they add to their regression models.

The Wright-Burawoy debate aside, do books like Wright's *Classes* add anything to our empirical and theoretical knowledge? Wright has constituted the distinctiveness of his own intellectual problematic through academic journal writing, endless self-reflection, and conference papers. For most Marxists, critical theorists, and feminists, Wright is a nonentity; his empirical work is trivial, his grandiose philosophizing wrong, his importance self-manufactured. Only in American sociology could Wright arrogate to himself the left center stage. Publishing "Marxism" in the *American Sociological Review* is oxymoronic. Anyone who follows mainstream American sociology in its leading journals, books, and conferences knows that the discipline exists to *discipline* rebellion, resistance, reason.

Burawoy raises real questions about the relationship between theory and practice. I think his answers are wrong, or at least naive. Yes, I too would rather save Marxism than sociology, but I do not see that returning to the point of production and interviewing workers is going to improve matters for Marxists. Buroway and I clearly share a critique of the pretentious analytical Marxism suggested by Wright and Roemer. I do not know Burawoy's views of mainstream sociology, except that I have read some of his work and know that he coedited the infamous special issue of *American Journal of Sociology* on Marxist research a few years back (Burawoy 1982, 1985). (That special issue, coedited with Theda Skocpol, excluded just about every intellectually and politically vibrant brand of Marxism in the United States at the time.) I suspect that Burawoy defends intellectual democracy as a nucleic form of the real thing; his dialogue with Wright is conducted in that spirit. He would probably make a good comrade.

## Critical Theory's Modest Agenda

Where do we go from here?—this book's theme, taken up more systematically in the book's last section. Let me offer some initial indications here. If Marxist causal modeling is hopeless, if the disciplinary mainstreams across academe successfully resist their own transformation by subversives burrowing from within, if class struggle is virtually nonexistent, what ought left intellectuals to do? As Adorno and his other first-generation Frankfurt colleagues convincingly demonstrate, the absence of an answer is the most truthful answer of all. For his part, Habermas eviscerates the political project of critical theory by professionalizing it via sociological theory—Durkheim, Weber, Mead, especially Parsons (see Habermas [1984, xlii], where he writes, "To be sure, these remarks touch upon only the motivational background to this work and not its actual theme. I have written this book for those who have a professional interest in the foundations of social theory"). His two-volume *Theory of Communicative Action* (1984, 1987b) is no more revealingly political than Wright's analytical Marxism; the Parsonianization of Marxism has the same depoliticizing effect as its Wisconsinization.

Yet to suggest reading Adorno as adequate "practice," even in the self-infinitizing practice of negative dialectics, is bogus, too. Although one has to master all of German idealism, Marxism, and feminism to grasp the totality today, revolutionary nostalgia is no answer, either. Jacoby (1987) struggles with this issue in his *Last Intellectuals*. His critique of left academics is inevitably read to heroize earlier generations of "publicists," including C. Wright Mills, Mary McCarthy, Irving Howe, Edmund Wilson—people who could write the "big" book for intelligent nonacademic readers. I agree with Jacoby that academization has taken its toll. In my own work I have tried to understand the decline of discourse somewhat more structurally than he does, perhaps only reflecting our different roots—intellectual history versus social science (see Agger 1990).

Ultimately, the theory-practice question can be rephrased this way: What ought the practice of theory to be in these times? In spite of Burawoy's cavils against "theoretical practice" (I completely agree with his swipes at Althusser's version of it), this is just another way to formulate the problem of left intellectuality. I do not think the answer is easy, although we must recognize that we are hardly the first to ask the question; that is why we should read the Wright-Burawoy debate in the larger context of historic discussions of the politics of Marxist epistemology, discussions repeated systematically in chapter 13 below.

Without being exhaustive, let me offer a few suggestions, amplified further in chapters 12–15.

1. Cease exegesis; do only empirical theory.
2. Engage in political education; attack positivism.
3. Avoid heroic interventions.

1. We do not need more exegesis. The crisis of Marxism reflects crisis itself: Professional left academics have run out of things to read and dissect; that is largely why left theorists have begun to read the postmodern and poststructural convolutions of Barthes, Lacan, Foucault, Derrida, Irigaray, Kristeva (see Culler 1982; Eagleton 1983; Ryan 1982; Agger 1991b). Given their opacity and density, the texts written by these people will keep us in business for generations to come, even though they solve next to nothing of our political problems. Although

deconstruction can be politicized, as in chapter 15, it typically resides in English departments as yet another interpretive methodology. Literary theory does not translate into social theory automatically; the connection must be made. Wright, Burawoy, and I all agree with Marx that, at some level, theory (science) must have empirical referents; it must explain the world, even if explanation cannot exhaust empirical phenomena but exists in discursive and dialectical counterpoint to them.

Saying that facts exist does not mean that they can be presuppositionlessly reflected; that is positivism—positivism I. But facts are not constituted only in the rhetorics used to discuss them; that is the trendy idealism of poststructuralism. Deconstructive methodologies appeal largely because they avoid social and political analysis, instead reducing theory to textuality. Derrida (see Agger 1989a) is wrong to say that "the text has no outside." At the risk of a reductive sociology of knowledge, it is fair to say that poststructuralist literary theory is currently so "hot" because it affords yet another excuse to avoid grappling with the thorniest of all empirical problems: How does capitalism survive Marx's quite reasonable expectation of its demise? To recognize that language helps constitute reality does not mean that all reality is language. The world is not a text, although all texts, all language games, are social relationships. Precisely in this way can we politicize deconstruction as critical theory.

So if we are going to theorize, it had better be empirical theory—theory that addresses the world. This must, of course, include cultural and ideological critique for culture and ideology are forces complexly entwining us in mythology. I believe that we have nearly enough empirical theory of this kind, given the immense labors of left researchers and thinkers over the past half-century. We have learned significant things about the capitalist city (Harvey; Castells), the class-gender connection (Dalla Costa; James; Eisenstein; Hartmann; Delphy; etc.), the class-race connection (Reich; Wilson), world systems and imperialism (Wallerstein), the labor process (Braverman; Edwards), the politics of communication (Habermas), social control (Foucault), and the state (Offe; O'Connor; Poulantzas). This list could be elaborated extensively by those of us doing one kind of left research or another.

At most, perhaps, we can use the insights afforded by this Promethean empirical and theoretical work in (2) political education—cracking the codes of bourgeois mystification (see, e.g., Freire 1970; Mueller 1973; O'Neill 1976; Misgeld 1985) in order to create nucleic forms of alternative community in the here and now. Political education is more than ever necessary at a time when people thoughtlessly continue their bondage as second nature. Positivism itself is a feature of this thoughtlessness, as the Frankfurt theorists systematically argued (e.g., Horkheimer and Adorno's *Dialectic of Enlightenment*, Marcuse's *One-Dimensional Man*). Positivism today is more than epistemology; it is a form of life (Wittgenstein) inducing people to extend their own servitude. This is a thoroughly Marxist notion. The first form of capitalist positivism, reflecting the existent as the essential, is the *fictio juris* of the labor contract, as Marx called it; workers continue their own alienation by participating in ostensibly just relationships with their employers.

Given the integration of Marxist academics, it would seem that Marxist positivism is not a central source of mystification today. But the example of erstwhile state socialism, based on Lenin–Stalin-era dialectical materialism, suggests otherwise. Although Wright is not a Soviet Marxist, and although his *American Sociological Review* articles are read by perhaps thousands, not millions, he adds value to positivism in his quantitative version of Marxism. His voice is important only inasmuch as it is drowned out in the general cacophony of affirmation; for its part, negative dialectics (Adorno 1973b) can be heard to evoke the dissonant rage of protest. Ignoring positivism only entrenches it.

Political education sounds like agitprop; for those sensitive to these echoes, perhaps it is better to call it ideology critique. In any case, the Left must change minds not about epiphenomenal issues like political party choice but about deeper ontological matters. People must be shown that history is fluid and that their own seemingly implacable fates as eternal subordinates are merely constructions and self-constructions—imposed and then self-imposed. Political education of this kind solves the crisis of Marxism not with equations and evidence but with a palpable sense of utopian otherness, a better life.

The crisis of Marxism: While Bush sweeps the country and our students major in engineering and business, Marxists and feminists talk exegesis and split hairs ad infinitum. At this depressing juncture in disciplinary, national and world history, it is tempting to pose the problem of Marxism's alleged crisis in terms of going back to the drawing board, the library, the secondary literature. Unfortunately, (3) heroic interventions, whether extraparliamentary or exegetical, are insufficient. Sociologizing Marxism, Marxizing sociology, decolonizing the lifeworld, squaring the hermeneutic circle—these do nothing more than keep academics in business. I am in sympathy with Burawoy's attempt to find political things-in-themselves, to break away from Marxology and Marxization—from Marxist bookishness—to more concrete tasks. But as Merleau-Ponty once wrote, nothing guarantees a good end:

[Hegelian Marxism] continues to see the revolutionary event as contingent and finds the date of the revolution written on no wall nor in any metaphysical heaven. . . . Marxism is unique in that it invites us to make the logic of history triumph over its contingency without offering any metaphysical guarantees.
[1964, 81–82]

Too frequently, Marxism and feminism degenerate into slogans; they become life-styles and shelves full of books, merely symbols of affiliation. Radical temperament, emotional commitment, intellectual rigor all fail in themselves to shift power. That is the real issue. Today, virtually everything is arrayed against political and theoretical heroics.

This acknowledgment usually leads to structuralism, that peculiarly French version of the standard economic determinism (Eagleton 1985). But saying that structures, whether overdetermined or otherwise, frustrate radical intervention is not to endorse them; on the contrary, the sober reckoning of real political possibilities can spark resistance, struggle, even, over the long term, transformation. I may sound as if I am betraying left intellectuality in a fit of pique about the sort of Marxological obscurantism only compounded by theoretical "debates." I am for debates and against theoretical simplemindedness. But the fact remains that Wisconsin and Berkeley sociologists (like those from SUNY-Buffalo or the CUNY Graduate Center) count for precious little against the enormity of the totality. If this sounds Hegelian, it is; at least, it is the Hegel read and transvalued by Marx (see Adorno 1974).

A minimalist agenda: Ask not, What to do? but, How to avoid political and intellectual mistakes that only make the bad more dismal? If exegetes trace this version of Marxism to Nietzsche in dismissing it, so much the worse for exegesis. Truth prospers at the expense of heroism; only thus can real heroes be born.

In this chapter, as in the preceding one, I discussed the liabilities involved in the heroization of Marx, which leads to an inflexible orthodoxy. I argued that Marx should be read as a critical theorist who, as such, needs a great deal of extrapolation from the perspectives of hindsight and of other theoretical and critical traditions simply unimagined by Marx (e.g., feminism, which focuses Marxist attention on the whole sphere of reproductive labor). In the next chapter, I discuss the deheroization of Marx—which is equally fatal. In particular, I examine the extirpation of Marxism from the canon of orthodox American sociological theory. In many ways, these are two equally problematic sorts of orthodoxy: one freezes Marx into a never-changing economistic catechism, as in Slater and Wright; the other mummifies Marx in the museum of failed sociological theories. Although both arguments are wrong, they need to be addressed not least because they are efficacious forms of ideology today.

# 4

# The
# Micro-Macro
# Nonproblem

The preceding two chapters addressed Marxist critiques of critical theory. In this chapter, I engage the critique of Marxism mounted from within mainstream sociological theory. Although Jeffrey Alexander praises Marx's "brilliance," his project is to eviscerate Marxism of all political content. In this reading, I attempt to delineate crucial points of difference between Marxist critical theory and neo-Parsonian social theory (which disingenuously borrows certain rhetorical gestures from Marxism). Here and in the next chapter, I engage arguments against critical theory that pretend little sympathy for critical theory's emancipatory project. Even though both Alexander in this chapter and world-weary postmodernists in the next claim a cosmopolitan familiarity with Marxism, they drain Marxism of politics.

The publication of the multieditored *The Micro-Macro Link* (Alexander et al. 1987) further entrenches the alliance of American and European sociological theorists bent on displacing Marxism once and for all from mainstream sociology (Agger 1989b). Admittedly, my fulminations against sociologized anti-Marxism are fighting words; typically, this sort of ideological polemic indicates thoughtlessness, another expression of left-wing infantilism (Jacoby 1987, 112–90). Yet there is something decidedly strange going on in this collection written by such "names" as

Jeffrey Alexander, Peter Blau, Niklas Luhmann, James Coleman, Neil Smelser. As a way of introducing my discussion of the particular issues in question, let me glance at the underlying intellectual and political changes transpiring in Western sociology that largely occasion the neo-functionalist effort to unify the field under the banner of the so-called micro-macro problem and condition the attack on Marxism.

## Situating Neofunctionalism Politically

The Parsonianization of American sociological theory is best understood in terms of a sociology of knowledge-cum-critique of cultural hegemony that situates neo-Parsonianism politically. Let me not pretend that Parsonianism has more influence than in fact it does. What goes on in mainstream American sociology is only tenuously related to the larger political world. Yet this is no reason to ignore the politics of theory. As I say repeatedly in this book, politics in late capitalism is found everywhere and nowhere (Agger 1989a); that is precisely why it is so difficult to criticize ideology in the traditional Marxist way. People like Alexander (1982, 1985) reinvent functionalism as neofunctionalism in order to restore the dominance of Parsonian theory in American sociology (Sica 1983; Turner 1985). Although Marxists do not proliferate in the American university, least of all in the midwestern-empiricist discipline of sociology, they are sufficiently abundant to offer "neofunctionalists" a target at which to aim their own self-serving critiques. Parsons, as ever, is most useful where he offers an alternative to the Hegelian Marxism that has prevailed in Europe since the 1920s, discussed systematically in chapter 13 (Lukács 1971; Marcuse 1960). He does not provide much empirical sustenance for the number crunchers who analyze regression. Parsons functions mainly as a political signifier in contemporary American sociology, differentiating non-Marxists from Marxists.

Thus, I want to understand the neo-Parsonian project as a political one. Of course, Parsons was attacked from the beginning as an advocate of "stasis," hence of stable Eisenhower-era American society; now he is even accused of fascist sympathies. His *Structure of Social Action* (1937) prepares the ground for his *Social System* (1951), in which he systematizes his structural functionalism. Parsons in effect Americanizes Weber, obliterating Weber's own Nietzschean pessimism about the fate of bureaucratic capitalist civilization—an angst he shared with numerous fin de siècle thinkers like Freud, Wittgenstein, and Simmel. As I discuss in chapter 10, there are two Webers: there is the Parsonian Weber who cheerfully plotted the course of puritan capitalism, and there is the conflict-theoretic Weber who underlies all sorts of non-Marxist perspectives on class and class conflict (Lenski [1966]; Dahrendorf [1959]; Giddens [1973]; Gouldner [1970, 1976, 1980]; even—perhaps—the Habermas of *The Theory of Communicative Action* [1984, 1987b]).

Although critical theorists, who derive their intellectual perspective from the original Frankfurt school (Adorno, Horkheimer, Marcuse), believe that there is not much difference between these two Webers (as Marcuse [1968b] indicates in his paper on Weber), it is telling that the Weber restored by Alexander et al. is not the pessimist fundamentally ambivalent about whether capitalism is good or not. The sunny Parsonian Weber gives rise later to the pattern variables, those seamless ontological constructs meshing individual self-interest and societal interests in order and stability. Today, these two analytic levels are called micro and macro; hence the topic of the volume under discussion. Indeed, the claim on the back cover of the paperback edition of the book is indicative:

> [A] new cadre of scholars, both established and young, has
> come to appreciate the need for a new, integrative approach
> [to linking micro and macro analysis]. The authors and editors
> of *The Micro-Macro Link* share the general conviction that the
> two levels of analysis are complementary and synthetic, not op-
> posed. Their work, informed by that conviction, stands at the
> forefront of contemporary sociological theory and will no
> doubt influence both theoretical dialogue and empirical re-
> search for years to come.

Yet a careful reading of the various chapters shows that there may not be complete consensus among the contributors about how the so-called micro-macro problem, viewed through neofunctionalist lenses, can successfully reorient the theoretical labors of the discipline. Schegloff, for example ("Between Macro and Micro: Contexts and Other Connections"), seems not to place a great deal of stock in the micro-macro question as an axis around which sociology can pivot; of course, this is unsurprising, given his own investment in ethnomethodology. Other authors (e.g., Raymond Boudon, "The Individualistic Tradition in Sociology"; Peter Blau, "Contrasting Theoretical Perspectives"; and Niklas Luhmann, "The Evolutionary Differentiation between Society and Interaction") offer interesting contributions to sociological theorizing but do not distinctly advance Alexander's argument about how the micro-macro fusion in itself can solve a whole host of sociological problems.

A version of Parsons that canonizes him as the legitimate heir of Weber serves his essentially ideological project well. Parsons's happy, hopeful version of Weber's theory of rationalization effectively deflates the Marxist attempt to pose an alternative perspective on rationalization for which the end of history is not IBM and Donald Trump but socialism. At issue, now as before in Parsons scholarship, is the deep matter of social ontology: What is the good society? Of course, to read Parsons this way is contentious precisely because, parroting Weber's (1968) strictures on objectivity in the social sciences, Parsons argued vigorously that sociology is supposed to be value-free. In any case, it is not difficult to exhume the metaphysical/political constructions embedded in Parsons's pattern variables in terms of the ideological work they are supposed to do. Parsons, like Weber and Marx, contains a political theory, a sense of what is, what is possible, and what should be—in spite of his professed value freedom. I want to see the rehabilitation of Parsons in this light because I am interested in contesting the continuing—no, the mounting—hegemony of anti-Marxists in American sociological theory, the very people who since Bell (1973) have pronounced ideology dead.

This is not to deny that there may be as many Marxes as there are Webers, indeed, probably more. I have already acknowledged the undecidability of the Marx question in chapter 2. My Marx, for what he is worth, is a socialist, feminist, and democrat as well as an empiricist and dialectician. The two-Marx problem posed by Althusser, among others, has been settled satisfactorily: Marx combined humanist passion with a rigorous empiricism (O'Neill 1972a, 1984). In any event, it is necessary to situate Parsonianism, whether first-generation structural functionalism (Parsons's Americanization of Weber) or second-generation neofunctionalism (Alexander's brand), in political counterpoint to Marxism. Now as before, functionalists deflect the socialist challenge on metaphysical grounds. Parsons and Parsonians suggest that radical social change is impossible and, in any event, undesirable. To read the functionalist and neofunctionalist literatures this way requires a good deal of interpretive dexterity, notably sustained attention to political subtexts, for Parsons's latter-day expositors seem to resist ideology-critical readings precisely by integrating what Alexander calls Marx's "brilliance" into their supposedly synthetic version.

Indeed, virtually all of the essays in *The Micro-Macro Link* seem "above," or beyond, politics. In the cover's own language, neofunctionalists are searching for "a new, integrative approach" to micro-macro integration. Politics is disdained implicitly. On the very first page of their introductory article, Alexander and Giesen say:

> We will argue that the micro-macro dichotomy should be viewed as an analytic distinction and that all attempts to link it to concrete dichotomies—such as "individual versus society" or "action versus order"—are fundamentally misplaced. [P. 1]

They continue: "Only if it is viewed analytically, moreover, can the linkage between micro and macro be achieved." What is meant by "analytically"? Later in their chapter, Alexander and Giesen suggest that:

> Parsons insisted on distinguishing between what he called the "analytical" and the "concrete" individual. When he wrote about the "actor" in his concept of the "unit act" . . . he meant to refer only to the analytical individual, not to a real individual in his or her concrete empirical form. What defines the analytical individual is the utter contingency of his or her acts, a quality Parsons identifies as effort. What defines the concrete individual, however, is not only effort but all manner of social constraints. [P. 22]

The so-called analytic individual is free, whereas the concrete individual is a combination of agency and determination. This is precisely what critics of Parsons have averred since the early 1950s. The smoothly equilibrating systems of patterned action that Parsons depicts bear little resemblance to the real world (Mills 1959). Similarly, here, to distinguish between unreal-but-free individuals and real-but-constrained individuals is equally hopeless. It resolves the micro-macro problem only metaphysically, not in terms of real empirical referents. This raises the obvious question: What *is* the micro-macro problem addressed by neofunctionalists?

## The Problem

Unfortunately, for some at work on the micro-macro question or micro-macro link, the problem is self-evident. As Alexander puts it, the search is for "linkage"; this, of course, assumes an initial disjunction. But the rhetoric of micro-macro is a deliberate choice; the "problem," such as it is, does not fall from the sky. Here are some of the ways the editors and contributors to *The Micro-Macro Link* (Alexander et al. 1987) articulate the problem:

> Microsociology analyzes the underlying social processes that engender relations between persons. . . . Macrosociology analyzes the structure of different positions in a population and their constraints on social relations. [P. 71]

> Behind the many controversies that rage in sociology, general agreement on a minimal program seems to exist: The central task of sociology consists of showing how social behavior and collective phenomena . . . are socially determined . . . How . . . can collective phenomena be explained? This question is often phrased in terms relevant to the conference on which this book is based: How can macrosocial phenomena be explained? This is the master question behind many interpretations of the so-called micro-macro problem. [P. 135]

> How can macrostructure be composed out of micro events? Clearly it is so composed: What is "empirical" meets us only in the form of micro encounters, and any macrostructure, no matter how large, consists only of the repeated experiences of large numbers of persons in time and space. [P. 195]

> Most sociologists will agree that macroanalyses deal with collectivities, and microanalyses with social processes between two or more individuals—that is, with small groups. Few of them, however, can agree on a satisfactory way to move from micro to macro levels of analysis. [P. 237]

> Both microscopic processes that constitute the web of interactions in society and the macroscopic frameworks that result from and condition those processes are essential levels for understanding and explaining social life. Moreover, those who have argued polemically that one level is more fundamental than the other . . . or who have argued for the complete independence of the two levels, must be regarded as in error. [P. 385]

There is some agreement that the micro-macro link solves the problem of disjointed analytic levels, even if a number of contributors do not agree that the micro-macro problem is sociology's central issue.

There is some consensus that social analysis should connect the micro-analysis of small groups with the macroanalysis of collective behavior and structure. Most of the book's contributors suggest "emergent" properties of group life bridging these two analytic levels. But which social scientists, other than certain ethnomethodologists, reject the notion of social structure?

Phenomenologically, at least, we can readily understand that studying how we relate to our mates or colleagues differs from the way we study aggregate voting behavior, economic inequality, cultural transmission. Randall Collins ("Interaction Ritual Chains, Power and Property: The Micro-Macro Connection as an Empirically Based Theoretical Problem") derives macrophenomena from micro-level interaction chains in the fashion of both Homans's exchange theory and other versions of network analysis. James Coleman ("Microfoundations and Macrosocial Behavior") proposes essentially neoclassical economic models of social behavior as a way of bridging micro- and macro-analytical levels. Still others (Edith Kurzweil, Karl Otto Hondrich, and Neil J. Smelser) attempt to establish psychoanalytic links between these two levels.

Much of this work, in its way of conceptualizing the micro-macro problem, derives directly from earlier discussions surrounding methodological individualism and holism, a tradition usefully reviewed by Alexander and Giesen in their opening essay. Must we choose between explanations of group life reducing all social reality to interaction chains, and thus individual choice, and explanations that, with Durkheim and Marx, suggest that macrostructure is an "emergent" reality quite apart from the interaction chains constituting it? Alexander and Giesen lionize Weber precisely because he appears to offer a third way between individualism and what one may loosely call structuralism or collectivism.

> The path toward linkage and the implied possibilities for theoretical synthesis were prepared by the earlier theorizing of Max Weber and Talcott Parsons. Their theories resist classification as either micro or macro. The current movement from reduction to linkage is inspired by the example set by these first great attempts at micro-macro synthesis, even when they do not follow the theories themselves. [Alexander et al. 1987, 3]

The methodological individualism/holism debate (O'Neill 1973) between Hayek (1944, 1964) and Popper (1961, 1963), on the one hand, and Marxists, on the other (Adorno et al. 1976), is repeated here. Although Alexander claims to distance himself from strict individualism, his account of how Parsons's Weber solves the micro-macro problem via what he calls "emergentism" (as opposed to reductionism) differs little from the earlier views of soi-disant methodological individualists. After all, if Parsons is not talking about "concrete" (i.e., real) individuals but only about "analytic" (i.e., transcendental) ones, he differs little from the methodological individualists who rebut Marxism on metaphysical grounds, notably rejecting Marx's alleged determinism.

Parsons divides reality into two levels only to connect them by the pattern variables. In this, he derives his inspiration from a version of Weber that basically concentrates on Weber's methodological writings (*Verstehende Sociologie*, etc.). The neofunctionalist construction of a "problem" virtually decides its solution in its own terms: once neofunctionalists announce that micro- and macro-level analyses cleave along certain ontological and epistemological dimensions, they move to secure what Alexander calls linkage. I do not oppose generic methodological postures that allow us to read the structural in the everyday and vice versa; but I read the neofunctionalist version of the micro-macro problem as an *implied critique of putative Marxian determinism*.

Earlier critics of holism like Popper and Hayek alleged that Marxism is determinism and that determinism, in canceling the prospect of free will, leads to political tyranny. This has become a standard variant of anti-Marxism within the bourgeois philosophy of science. Hegelian and other Western Marxists (Agger 1979; Antonio 1983) reject this version of Marxism, claiming instead that Marx dialectically addressed the alternation between agency and determination (or what a Durkheimian might call external constraint). As such, their non-Soviet Marxism both maximizes political freedom (self-determination, etc.) and offers a penetrating critique of capitalist political economy. Although certain critical theorists like Habermas (1971) contend that Marx insufficiently separated agency (what he calls self-reflection and communicative reason) from determination (what he, with Weber, calls technical or instrumental rationality), most non-Soviet Marxists have little trouble locating this dialectical version of Marxism in a unified oeuvre spanning both the 1844 manuscripts and *Capital* (Agger 1979).

This returns me to my claim that the neofunctionalists invent the micro-macro problem as yet another attack on Marxism, essentially using Parsons's Weber to rebut the holism originally rejected by Popper as the source of political tyranny. Alexander and Giesen do not make these alleged political deficits of Marxism thematic in the way Popper did. After all, they are talking about "analytic," not "concrete," reality. Alexan-

der proclaims Marxism dead on other grounds, even as he passingly calls
Marx "brilliant" (Alexander et al. 1987, 7). Of course, what he calls brilliant about Marx is, strangely, his supposed "empirical elaboration of
instrumental action and of the way it is restricted by macrostructures"
(p. 7). Immediately, though, to ensure that the evaluative adjective "brilliant" does not have too much influence, he recants his enthusiasm for
Marx and Marxism by indicating that "this structural emphasis has created fundamental problems for Western neo-Marxism, which has tried
to reinstate the centrality of consciousness to critical theory" (p. 7).

It is not clear that Marx empirically elaborated instrumental action and the way it is restricted by macrostructures; that is a Weberian/
Parsonian reconstruction of Marx's project unfortunately shared by the
Habermas of *Knowledge and Human Interests* (1971) and pursued further
in chapters 10 and 11 below. Nor is it evident that Western Marxism has
failed to reinstate the centrality of consciousness to critical theory. The
work of Lukács, Korsch, Adorno, Horkheimer, Marcuse, Sartre, and
Merleau-Ponty attests to their ingenious version of a dialectical Marxism
intellectually and politically continuous with original Marx (Jay 1984).
Alexander and Giesen merely mouth a conventional dismissal of Marxism: Marxism amounts to structuralism, obliterating what Parsons called
the analytic individual. I think this critique is as wrong as ever; indeed, all
manner of so-called Western Marxists since the Russian Revolution have
written eloquently about the possibilities of a nondeterminist Marxism
that has enormous methodological relevance for many intellectual
problems as well as political relevance for building a democratic
socialism.

Now, Alexander and Giesen do not rest with Marx. They also con-
demn Durkheim (1950) for his exaggeration of the ontological power of
the social, a critique that makes more sense (Agger 1989b). Yet they conflate Durkheim and Marx: "Durkheim and Marx, then, for all the com-
plexities and possibilities of their work, produced strongly polemical
arguments for a one-sidedly macro emphasis" (Alexander 1984a, cited
in Alexander et al. 1987, 8). Durkheim and Marx are not identical; Durkheim was a structuralist in Alexander's sense, whereas Marx was a dialectician, a nonreductionist. But Alexander makes his strange case through
innuendo ("strongly polemical arguments")—as if Weber and Parsons
were not polemicists in their way—and by citing *himself*. It is hard to
imagine that this attack on Marxism could have much credibility in a
postmodern academic world saturated with "Marxist scholarship," the
mainstreaming of Marxism into a whole range of disciplinary rhetorics.
But academic McCarthyism is still with us (Lewis 1988; Schrecker 1986),

especially in mainstream American sociology dominated by positivism. Today, though, political censure does not require HUAC; the resistance of mainstream publication outlets to nonpositivist work, especially Marxism and feminism, constrains intellectual and political heterodoxy: without publications, people on the Left inevitably perish (assuming they have found academic jobs in the first place). In fact, the appearance of a thriving Marxism is conjured by conservative demonologists in order to disqualify Marxism (and feminism) yet again. That Marx was polemical does not make him a macro thinker, a reductionist. In fact, *Marx had already anticipated and resolved the micro-macro problem,* an irony to which I return later in this chapter.

As always, the mainstream's version of Marxism is a caricature. On pages 26–29, Alexander and Giesen (1987) run through a variety of possible and actual positions on the micro-macro problem. On page 29, they list a number of "structuralist" versions of it, including those of Althusser, Skocpol, Wright, Treiman, and Lieberson. This is questionable in two ways. First, there are nonstructuralist, nonorthodox Marxists who ignore neither the macro nor voluntarism. To assign historical structures enormous causal weight is not the same as structural*ism*, an ahistorical version (e.g., Lévi-Strauss 1963, 1966) essentially making this structural overdetermination unavoidable (DiTomaso 1982). The Western Marxists offer nonreductionist versions of structural social science, as do their latter-day expositors. Second, Alexander and Giesen reduce Marxism to a peculiarly narrow list of leftish American sociologists. Treiman? It is arguable whether Skocpol is a Marxist at all; and to call Wright structuralist misses his effort to improve individualistic status-attainment research by adding "class" variables to the standard regression equations (see preceding chapter). Alexander and Giesen seriously misrepresent Marxism by reducing it to a structuralist determinism, thus ignoring both the logic of Marx's open-ended historical materialism and the numerous latter-day Marxists who do empirical and theoretical work highly sensitive to agency.

One page later, Alexander and Giesen add nuance to their blanket dismissal of Marxism:

> The major effort to counter this disregard for the micro level also emerged from within the Marxian camp. Exegetically based on the philosophy of the young Marx . . . "praxis philosophy" . . . and "critical theory" . . . stressed the revolutionary role of subjectivity, reflection, and dialectical fantasy in opposition to the "repressive structures of society." [P. 30]

But

> Because of the scarcity of theoretical resources within Marx-
> ism, and because of ideological constraints as well, this
> micromovement within Marxism was eventually charged with
> being scarcely more than a critical methodology. Some of the
> key participants in the earlier subjectivist movement returned
> to orthodox structuralist assumptions and political economy
> (Offe . . . Hirsch). They focused on the function of the state in
> capitalist accumulation and tried to derive social problems and
> crises from "inevitable" state intervention. [P. 30]

On the one hand, the authors now admit that there was a "micromove-
ment within Marxism" itself that parallels their own effort to preserve
dynamic tension between micro and macro levels of analysis. Even here,
though, a mocking innuendo prevails: Alexander and Giesen pose
micro-Marxism's critical object or topic as "repressive structures of society." Quotation marks are added by the authors to lampoon the seemingly polemical tone of these words. Of course, they are not quoting
Marx or anyone else in this. By implication, their own value freedom
improves on the zealotry of (nameless) people who view capitalism as a
"repressive structure."

On the other hand, returning to their earlier blanket dismissal of
Marxism, the authors add that Marxism suffers from a "scarcity of theoretical resources." What is this to mean? Have Marxists not been theorizing voluminously since Marx, the Russian Revolution, Stalin? Is such
theory inadequate? In addition, the cliché—"ideological constraints as
well"—is a convenient subtext on which the political disqualification of
Marxism is inscribed. Again, one asks, what ideological constraints? Are
Alexander and Giesen trying to pin the Gulag on Marxist methodology,
as many have done since the Third International?

Finally, the notion that "some of the key participants in the earlier subjectivist movement returned to orthodox structuralist assumptions and political economy" is either irrelevant or wrong. How many is
"some"? For the authors to cite Claus Offe as an example of this is pat-
ently ridiculous; his analysis of the state derives from the theoretical apparatus of Habermas, whom many of the contributors to this volume cite
approvingly in their validation of his occasionally weird Parsonian version of critical theory (Keane 1984; Offe 1984, 1985). And the study of
"political economy" in no way requires that one adopt structuralist, determinist, or antisubjectivist tenets. Indeed, as I argued in chapter 2,

much of the original Frankfurt work on the "authoritarian state" (Horkheimer 1973) creatively blended political economy with cultural and ideological analyses, one of the enduring hallmarks of Frankfurt Marxism (Horkheimer 1972). Alexander and Giesen give no evidence that they know such work; if they did, they would have a much more difficult time dismissing Marxism as structuralism and determinism.

## Rethinking the Problem

Alexander and Giesen justify their attention to the micro-macro problem in terms of a critique of Marxian determinism:

> There are social and institutional as well as intellectual reasons for this new phase in contemporary sociological theory. Certainly one important factor is the changing political climate in the United States and Europe. Most radical social movements have faded away, and in the eyes of many intellectuals Marxism has been morally delegitimated. The ideological thrust that fueled anti-Parsonianism in both its micro and macro form in the United States, and that stimulated Marxist structuralism on the Continent, has now been spent. [1987, 32]

So Marxism is vitiated by "the changing political climate," the fact that "most radical social movements have faded away," and that among "intellectuals Marxism has been morally delegitimated." At long last, opponents of Parsonianism have finally been disarmed; their "fuel" is "spent." All of the conceptual gymnastics and revisionist intellectual histories are shown to be superfluous in light of this approach to theoretical legitimacy that derives concept formation from an ideological sociology of knowledge. Parsonianism, in particular Parsons's signature approach to the micro-macro problem, is given new life now that the Marxist opposition has been diverted or altogether eliminated. This last passage shows the neofunctionalist project—the rehabilitation of Parsons as sociology's prime theoretical mover—to be the political project it is. Parsons justifies state-managed capitalism in his seamless ontology that knits together self-interest and societal functional requisites, the micro and macro.

Parsons and Parsonians are interested in these seemingly separate analytical levels because, in fact, micro and macro are central ideological categories in bourgeois social theory (Institute for Social Research 1973,

37–53). Micro refers to what neoclassical economists have always understood as self-interest; macro refers to the postulated functional requisites of capitalist bureaucratic order—what the "social system" (Parsons
1951) requires to function effectively. The pattern variables magically,
metaphysically identify self- and societal interests (or micro and macro,
in the current parlance of neofunctionalism) to elicit exactly the pattern-
maintaining individual behaviors that both prolong the system and
effectively constrain unit actors from bursting out of their largely self-
imposed bondage to supposed social laws.

Parsonianism is intended to function ideologically, not merely
"justifying" the status quo, as early critics suggested (Gouldner 1970;
also see O'Neill 1972a) but elaborating a whole social metaphysic—the
mythic pattern variables—encoding the unit actor's subordination to
postulated system requisites like capitalism, Judeo-Christianity, bureau-
cracy, patriarchy. Although perhaps Parsons did not really believe that
his version of this metaphysic would replace the Bible, *Wealth of Nations*,
or apple pie and motherhood as central rubrics of this American ideology, his structural functionalism was to frame the everyday empirical research of those committed to this benign view of capitalist
modernization. Alexander and his ilk dust off the classical tomes of Parsons's functionalism under the guise of micro-macro theory, yet another
assault on godless Marxism.

In the last analysis, the micro-macro problem is just words; one
could as well call it the problem of order (Hobbes), self and society
(Mead), or lifeworld and system (Habermas). All of these writers have
tried to resolve how people accept social constraint in face of the evident
loss of individual freedom it entails.

Marx was the only Western intellectual in the classical tradition of
European high theory to reject this formulation of the problem. He believed that social individuals could maximize freedom as long as the relations of material production (and, feminists would correctly add,
reproduction) are organized nonhierarchically. Parsons derives from a
long list of people, including St. Paul, Luther, Kant, and Hegel, who
located freedom in the alleged realm of necessity. Marx, although indebted to early Hegel's formulation of the process of coming to consciousness through labor, broke with this tradition of bourgeois
metaphysics by arguing that people make history even when they appear
to be made by it. Marx thus posited a realm of freedom *within* necessity—socialism—characterized by the simultaneity of creative and productive activity. This very insight enables Marcuse to project the
possibility of eroticized labor, as I discuss in chapters 6, 7, and 10. Marx

rejected ontologies of bourgeois renunciation such as classical political economy and religion; he called these idealism, mystifying the subordination of the person to social and economic structure in the name of supposed developmental imperatives encoded in the "laws" of social science.

Parsonians gild Weber's iron cage in the traditional terms of idealism (Collins 1975; Gerth and Mills 1946, 50; Mitzman 1971). As such, neofunctionalism functions ideologically. It is unsurprising that these conservative times would provoke the restoration of the Parsonian metaphysic. After all, Reagan's optimistic claim that the glass half empty is also half full merely extends the traditional theme: although victims of the forward march of an inexorable history (whether laws of supply and demand or pattern variables), people ought to be viewed—and thus to view themselves—as "analytic individuals," capable of gratifying themselves even as they submit to what Parsons and Henderson (translating Weber in 1947) first called "imperative coordination," a telling translation of Weber's *Herrschaft* or domination. The political project of Parsonians is as clear as ever: Marxism is to be disqualified as a utopian, authoritarian chimera. Even if Alexander appears to heroize Marx by calling him "brilliant," he fails to learn from his critique of bourgeois social science vainly pursuing laws.

However implausible it sounds to people who recognize the enormous ideologizing power of megainstitutions like mass media and education, Parsonians want sociology to be a social text provoking our social fate, inducing us even to love fate—Nietzsche's *amor fati*. By recognizing, hence enacting, postulated social laws, people help bring them about. In Parsons's own (Parsons and Bales 1955) terms, the thesis of eternally stratified gender relations in the bourgeois family is to produce familied practices, thus ironically proving his notion of instrumental male and expressive female roles (Agger 1989c). But if Parsonianism is read as an ideologizing text, not as ontology, then Parsons's attempt to reproduce social nature by freezing it conceptually—ever the mission of ideology—will be laid bare. Indeed, one of the most important contributions to this venerable project of ideology critique, in its original Marxist formulation, comes from left literary theorists who enrich the Marxian theory of ideology with discourse-analytic formulations from poststructuralism as well as feminism (Culler 1982; Eagleton 1983; Ryan 1982).

Let me conclude this chapter by reconsidering the micro-macro problem. I have argued that this construction of sociology's central problematic is a way of reintroducing the Parsonian metaphysic at a time when the Left seems to be on the run. Calling functionalism neofunctionalism advances theory only neologistically. As ever, Parsons's project is preserved: the individual unit actor is to subordinate himself/herself to presumed systemic imperatives. Meanwhile, sociology tries to integrate these analytic levels in order to improve the rhetoric with which it tries to enmesh people seamlessly in the patterned fabric of modernity. I risk homogenizing an apparently diverse discipline; but the appearance of intellectual, theoretical, and political heterogeneity is largely a construction of the very people who oppose it.

There is nothing inherent in the rhetoric of micro-macro that should prevent us from using these words in different, non-Parsonian ways. Indeed, the Alexander collection includes some evenhanded attempts to preserve the possibilities of Marxist approaches to the micro-macro interpenetration, whether through Habermas or in different terms. The concluding chapter by Munch and Smelser suggests (Alexander et al. 1987, 383) that Marxism is a legitimate perspective on the dialectic of "macrostructure" and "microprocesses." This chapter has little of the ideological vitriol of the introductory Alexander-Giesen article, perhaps only indicating that the neo-Parsonians are not homogeneous—or, indeed, that some of these people are not even neo-Parsonians at all. Munch and Smelser conclude their synthesizing closing essay with these reasonable thoughts:

> Both microscopic processes that constitute the web of inter-
> actions in society and the macroscopic frameworks that result
> from and condition these processes are essential levels for un-
> derstanding and explaining social life. Moreover, those who
> have argued polemically that one level is more fundamental
> than the other . . . must be regarded as in error. Virtually ev-
> ery contributor to this volume has correctly insisted on the mu-
> tual interrelations between micro and macro levels, and on the
> necessity of characterizing transitional and emergent processes
> moving in both directions. It seems to us that to strive for the
> better theoretical and empirical understanding of these pro-
> cesses constitutes a proper agenda for the coming years.
> [P. 385]

These are not particularly objectionable sentiments, although I would urge a very different research agenda (notably, the critique of ideology). They merely acknowledge that everyday life and social structure are encoded in each other. On the other hand, Alexander and Giesen offer a much stronger version of neo-Parsonianism, already discussed above. This version uses the micro-macro rhetoric further to disqualify

Marxism as untoward reductionism and determinism. Munch and Smelser acknowledge that Marx himself offered a version of micro-macro relations, although they insufficiently recognize the depth to which he traced the palimpsest of "macrostructure" in the "microprocesses" of both interpersonal and (via Marcuse's Freudian Marxism, later on) intrapsychic existence.

Since the 1920s, through Lukács's and Korsch's Hegelian Marxism, the original Frankfurt school and its Freudian Marxism (see chap. 7), and finally Habermas's theory of communicative action, Marx has been read by Western Marxists to account for both agency and structure, micro and macro. All this means—all it should mean, it seems to me—is that one must simultaneously recognize the imprint of social structure in people's daily lives (perhaps even in their unconscious lives, if one is inclined in a Freudian direction) and the intersubjectively constitutive nature of overarching structures. This is precisely the methodological agenda of the Frankfurt school, in both its Adorno-Horkheimer-Marcuse and Habermas gestations. In Adorno's terms, critical theory and the social research it spawns must recognize the "objectivity of subjectivity," especially the penetration of overwhelming structures into the core of individual sensibilities (Adorno 1967, 1968, 1978); for Habermas (1984, 1987b), social science must address the dynamic relationship between what he calls system and lifeworld.

On this basis, both the first- and second-generation Frankfurt thinkers have generated enormously rich research programs ranging over state intervention, social psychology, cultural analysis, and the study of ideology. The leitmotif of the Frankfurt school is the interpenetration of object and subject, structure and consciousness (Agger 1989a; Marcuse 1955); unlike Parsonians, who, after all, are positivists chasing invariant social laws, they historicize these relations because they recognize that what Habermas calls the "colonization" of the lifeworld by an imperial social system is a *variable*—and, through political action, can be changed. Marxists of all sorts want to restore constitutiveness—political and economic agency—to unit actors heretofore denied agency by the crushing forces of capitalism, state socialism, sexism, racism, and the domination of nature, among other things.

Thus, even in its weak formulation, the micro-macro problem is a nonproblem unless it is understood in terms of a theory of history that allows us to read, and thus potentially reverse, the deformations of subjectivity. The weaker version of the micro-macro problem fails to recognize that the story of microprocesses has been dismal; for most of history, unit actors have suffered one or another kind of heteronomy. As for the stronger, neofunctionalist version, it purposely tries to occlude the historicity of domination in exactly the fashion of those who, since Smith, Ricardo, Comte, Durkheim, Weber, and Parsons, have posited enduring social laws in order to inflate the social text of those accounts (e.g., economic theory, sociology, psychology) into fate. The Parsonian integration of micro and macro conceals their hierarchy; Parsonians would reproduce by ontologizing, a world in which the macro holds sway. Thus, their research program is little more than one of social pathology, tracing domination in the lives wasted in the name of allegedly higher developmental imperatives.

At best, the micro-macro problem misses the historicity of micro-macro relations. At worst, the strong version of the micro-macro problem deliberately suppresses the Marxist dialectic of personal life and social structure: the neofunctionalist opposition to Marxism converts into intellectual capital, where its proponents present themselves as saviors of a fractious, ideologized discipline. As such, the micro-macro problem is hardly news; people have been castigating Marxism for over a hundred years, especially since Marxism entered academic disciplines as a competing intellectual position. Parsons is Parsons is Parsons. Nothing will redeem his effort to freeze Eisenhower's America into eternal patterns of social life. At the very least, we can read Parsonianism as the political text it is. And we must dispute its claims to break new theoretical ground when it says, prosaically, that we cannot comprehend society without understanding both individuals and social structure. That is but an apology for subordinating the former to the latter, ever the posture of ideology.

In this chapter, I have responded to an increasingly fashionable neoconservative critique of Marxism, grounded in the long end-of-ideology tradition that begins with Weber and Mannheim and extends through Daniel Bell (1973) and Lyotard (1984). In the next chapter, I shall begin to confront Lyotard's postmodernism and banalizations of it, arguing that postmodernism in its affirmative version continues the end-of-ideology tradition discussed in this chapter. Like neofunctionalism, postmodernism is far from ideological. This will set the stage for my contention in chapter 15 that there are possible versions of postmodernism that are in fact critical and political. Just as there are orthodox and heterodox versions of Marx, so there are apologetic and dialectical varieties of postmodernism.

# 5

# The
# Problem
# of Postmodernism

T his chapter concludes the first section of this book. I caution here against embracing postmodernism, even though I have self-consciously affiliated myself to a critical theory that makes ample use of certain postmodern as well as feminist insights. Postmodernism in its Establishment versions ignores social problems of the public sphere altogether, resolving postmodern anxiety with doses of commodities and popular culture. The postmodernism hawked on every Yuppie streetcorner must be rejected by those seriously concerned with transforming large-scale social structures. In fast capitalism, cultural and intellectual trends, the postmodernism craze included, are ephemeral. Unfortunately, the Establishment postmodernism so prevalent today blocks attempts to reformulate a radical vocabulary of social change among both feminists and Marxists. In this chapter, I examine the modalities of the culture industry's own postmodernism—which, I conclude, is far removed from the radical Nietzschean transvaluation of all values that converges with what Marxists later called the critique of ideology. Instead of being a critique of ideology, which it could be in its best sense, an affirmative postmodernism lamely celebrates the end of ideology, thus hastening its demise.

## Is Postmodernism the Solution
## or the Problem?

Postmodernism is just about the hottest cultural and intellectual trend around. People across the humanities and social sciences publish articles and books and organize conferences and panels on postmodernism. "Pomo" has become a minor cottage industry, giving bored postleftist academics something new to do and read. Although, as I demonstrate in my concluding chapter, there is a great deal to be said about the more theoretical versions of postmodernism that seriously engage with world-historical issues of social theory and social change, I am more concerned here with postmodernism as ideology—or, more precisely, with postmodernism as the end of ideology, which it intends to be. Here I am not talking mainly about the literate postmodernisms of Baudrillard (1983), Lyotard (1984), and Foucault (1976, 1977, 1980), although I allude to these people in passing, but about the postmodernism of the American cultural establishment and culture industry—what I call a *New York Times* postmodernism (see Gitlin 1988). This chapter is designed as a political introduction to the fads and fashions of *New York Times* postmodernism. I am mostly dismissive of this version of postmodernism, although one can merge certain postmodern insights with the political and theoretical agenda of the Frankfurt school, neo-Marxism, and feminism. I am increasingly convinced that the mainstream discourse of postmodernism, like those of *perestroika* and post-Marxism, is merely the latest, trendiest attack on the Left. Here I suggest some ways in which postmodernism not only ignores social problems but becomes a problem in its own right.

My critique will possibly be heard as yet another attack on heterodox European theory that breaks the mold of Marxism-Leninism. But we must not be bound by the simplistic dichotomies that force us to choose between Marxism and postmodernism. One can (and must!) fashion a Marxist version of postmodernism as well as a postmodern Marxism that genuinely contributes critical insights to new social movements. Aronowitz (1990), Huyssen (1986), Kellner (Best and Kellner 1991), Jameson (1981), T. Luke (1989), Fraser (1989) and I (1990) have offered examples of this convergence. Here, I criticize an Establishment version of postmodernism in order to demonstrate the affinity between a peculiarly uncritical postmodernism, on the one hand, and perennial bourgeois social thought, on the other. Intellectual fads must be resisted and debunked, that around postmodernism especially. This does not preclude a serious engagement with the discourse of the postmodern, which remains one of the most exciting theoretical challenges. It simply ac-knowledges that such engagements do not typify the celebration of postmodernism currently taking place across the university and in main-stream culture. Like all celebrations, this one must be viewed skeptically, especially from the vantage point of critical social theory.

Here I consider the tendencies of a glitzy, Manhattanized postmodernism to monopolize the terrain of cultural production and reception, as well as of the capitalist-built environment. One finds postmodernism as an identifying slogan in nearly every avant-garde bookstore, magazine, television show, and movie as well as in the build-ings and malls housing cultural producers and consumers. Strolling through Soho and Tribeca in New York or along Queen Street West in Toronto, one discovers the cultural hegemony of postmodernism. Hip-sters dressed in black wander and shop and dine under the zeitgeist of the postmodern, whatever that is supposed to mean. Postmodernism does mean something in these formulations and manifestations: it repre-sents a thoroughgoing aversion to political discussion and contention, embodying the narcissism addressed by Lasch (1979) as early as the late 1970s.

It is not strictly accurate to conflate Lyotard's (1984) nuanced, if relentless, critique of Marxist grand narratives with the pedestrian postmodernism of the New York galleries, clubs, and critics. At least, Lyotard, like Bell (1976) before him, was aware of Marxism, recognizing it as a genuine subversion of capitalist pluralism. Thus, one could argue with Lyotard in his own terms, as Habermas (1981a) has done. The peo-ple who sell and live postmodernism in the United States do not inflate their participation in the zeitgeist with a serious ideological critique of the Left. In fact, they do not view themselves in terms of a philosophy of history at all. For them, postmodernism is largely a consumer movement.

In my concluding chapter, I distinguish between Lyotard's ver-sion of Bell's end of ideology and postindustrial society theses, on the one hand, and a radicalized postmodernism with a political intent, on the other; here, I want to discuss a third variant of postmodernism that in some respects is really a subcategory of Lyotard's neoconservative ver-sion, although without the philosophical patina from Nietzsche and Hei-degger. This *New York Times* version of postmodernism is simply not theoretical enough to warrant extended discussion as a full-fledged ver-sion of cultural and social theory, although it is prevalent. It is the sort of postmodernism found in *Rolling Stone*, mentioned in the *New York Times*, developed in *The New Yorker*, and cited in urbane Sunday supplement pieces on the cultural beat and in various critical and trade publications on the arts. This *New York Times* postmodernism epitomizes a range of cultural attitudes and gestures encoding deeper political content. Of course, the essence of postmodernism is to conceal politics underneath the veneer of the rejection of politics, now as before a posture of value freedom. Unlike the more self-consciously ideological approaches of Lyotard and Bell, this postmodernism is not defined by its opposition to left-wing radicalism. Rather, it is signified by Lasch's (1979) narcissism, Macpherson's (1962) possessive individualism, and Marcuse's (1955) repressive desublimation. Not that these are texts read by *New York Times* postmodernists! But these texts help explain some of the valences of this postmodernism especially as it issues in the distinctive cultural creation and criticism typical of this perspective. In the rest of this chapter, I will identify some of the features of this untheorized postmodernism in order to uncover its secret political affiliations.

## Four Modalities of Affirmative Postmodernism

1. *New York Times* postmodernism rejects political discourse as out of date, shabby, irrelevant. Politics is not a venue of meaning because all political movements and personalities are viewed as venal to the point of Nixonian absurdity. One might periodize *New York Times* postmodernism as post-Watergate, although there were stirrings of it in the counterculture, further demonstrating a certain distance between *New York Times* postmodernism and Bell's end-of-ideology perspective, especially as rendered in his *Cultural Contradictions of Capitalism* (1976). As Gitlin (1987) indicates, one must divide the 1960s into a genuinely political rump (e.g., the Port Huron statement of the early SDS) and a depoliticized counterculture devoted to many of the same cultural significations as *New York Times* postmodernism.

The aversion to politics is more temperamental than doctrinal. Since Marxism is not a specter haunting the United States, American postmodernism, unlike the French variety, does not take its bearings from a considered rejection of Marxism. It is tempting to date this postmodern denial of the political as a feature of the post-baby boom generation. But that would be incorrect: Yuppies, borne of the 1960s, are quintessentially postmodern in their consumerist individualism and political cynicism. They derive whatever semblance of theoreticity they possess from periodicals like the *The New York Times* and *Esquire* as well as from television shows like "thirtysomething." The post-baby boom co-hort is no more apolitical than their Yuppie predecessors. Perhaps the only difference is that Yuppies can call on the rhetoric of the 1960s as proof of their social commitments—disingenuous, because most baby boomers in the 1960s were pot-smoking conformists and not serious political rebels.

2. *New York Times* postmodernism endorses consumer capitalism and hence, by implication, rejects the possibility of radical social change—for example, socialism. If social change is addressed at all, it is addressed piecemeal. A more structural radicalism is regarded as hubris. Radicals themselves are branded as failed personalities somehow still mired in the adolescent passions of the 1960s. Although in other respects *New York Times* postmodernism places value on retro gestures that encompass the less political manifestations of the counterculture (like the Rolling Stones appearing in Budweiser ads and McCartney shilling for VISA cards), the angry radicalism of the 1960s is dismissed as both antediluvian and excessive. At best, mainstream postmodernism is liberal on social issues like abortion, the First Amendment, and the environment but conservative on fiscal matters.

3. *New York Times* postmodernism celebrates popular culture unashamedly, failing to make distinctions (rejected as modernist and mandarin). This robs postmodernism of the ability to expose and debunk the political codes of culture. Postmodern cultural criticism adds value to the popular, which is thoroughly commodified. This validation of popular culture reinforces a common generational experience of the world, albeit mass mediated, which substitutes for real community. Every baby boomer understands that we are defined by common televisual events like the broadcasts of the Kennedy assassinations or of the first moonwalk. But what we want to remember about these collective experiences is not simply the events themselves but the text and texture of the cultural experience of identity formation watching Dan Rather break the first news from Dallas and living the event from Friday through the funeral cortege. These experiences are focused retrospectively not on what they were and what they meant but on the ways they formed us, affording us both identity and values. My own adolescence, which is typical in this respect, can be reproduced diachronically in terms of how the mass mediated unfolding of these events and experiences paralleled and signified my own passage through successive stages of the life cycle, especially adolescence. A pedestrian, depoliticized postmodernism helps us reexperience these public events for their contributions to our own ego formation, which is imperiled by all of the colonizing forces threatening

to turn us into what Lasch (1984), borrowing from the Frankfurt school, called minimal selves.

Although I decry this banalization of postmodern cultural criticism, especially where I (Agger 1991a) contend that radical cultural studies is the single best manifestation of the erstwhile critique of ideology, there is no denying the influence of this sort of retrospectively self-referential analysis of culture. Like most baby boomers, I too reexperience myself in terms of my participation in these aspects of the popular, although for me most of these events take on political significance inasmuch as they help me chronicle my own formation as a social critic, not a contented Yuppie. One of the reasons that academic baby boomers are attracted to cultural studies is that we experience our own selfhoods in terms of their constitution by the popular, refracted through the analysis of these public spectacles in which we can relocate central aspects of our ego formation.

There is nothing wrong with wanting to understand one's own constitution by the popular, especially where the popular encodes deep political meanings. For example, the television to which we were exposed in the 1950s and 1960s tried to turn us into men, women, parents, citizens, and consumers. But *New York Times* postmodernism prevents us from critically examining our differential experiences of the popular and the hierarchies of access and accumulation embedded in it. It is far more important that the media presented a manufactured Vietnam War than that we came of age watching the coverage of the Tet offensive, which we then insert retrospectively into the reconstructed pastiche of our identity formation—just another relativized cultural experience that we examine self-referentially but not in terms of the million Vietnamese who died during the war, an issue given important contemporary significance in the mass mediated discourse about the Persian Gulf War (e.g., "collateral damage" referring to civilian casualties).

The reexperience of the formation of self through pop culture analysis is less important than the critical evaluation of ways in which the popular is itself a differential field that not only constitutes us but also deceives us in fundamental respects. After all, the mass mediation of social reality proceeds apace; the lessons we learn about the 1960s as spectacle (see Debord 1983) can be applied today in helping us resist the most insidious aspects of cultural and personality formation, as well as the deflection of political mobilization, caused by popular culture. As I develop in my book *Cultural Studies as Critical Theory* (1991a), a radical cultural studies can help us read and resist mass culture as what Adorno called "an objective context of delusion" (1973b, 406).

4. *New York Times* postmodernism purposely replaces substance with style, installing ironic detachment as the central social value. But neither cynicism nor irony is an appropriate political posture, especially where so much is going wrong. Both accelerate the venality of politics and the commodification of public discourse. Post-baby boomers are especially impervious to social problems, which they perceive as having little relationship to their own lives, devoted to the consumption and celebration of commodified popular culture. Teachers of social science confront a growing psychologism on the part of students that inures them to larger structural understandings of what is going wrong. We cannot simply attribute what is wrong to the Reagan and Thatcher regimes, as some critics do. Certainly the 1980s were not an aberration in the sense that they are now over and will not recur. Making social issues private is part and parcel of capitalism. We noticed this self-aggrandizing trend during the 1980s because it was especially pronounced in the images of the homeless huddled outside Trump Tower. Some leftist critics of this sociopolitical ennui blamed it on the supposedly new ideology of postmodernism, failing to recognize that narcissism and possessive individualism are ways in which capitalism defends itself against the threat of collective insurrection.

As I noted earlier, *New York Times* postmodernism has a soft spot for the environment. It is easy for Yuppie and post-Yuppie possessive individualists to relate to the degradation of the built and natural environments because they relate so obsessively to commodities. Ironically, postmodern environmentalism commodifies environmentalism while indicting the commodification of the environment. Witness the numerous corporate tie-ins to the environmental movement: companies sell environmental awareness as proof of their own social concern. This is not to deny the possibility of a radicalized environmentalism but only to note the self-contradictory postmodernization of environmentalism in the context of capitalist consumerism.

## Postmodernism, Post-Marxism, Postindustrialism

These four features of an affirmative postmodernism contribute to block a genuine radical cultural critique that can intervene in the cultural field as a counterhegemonic force of its own—the central purpose of my version of critical theory. The postmodernization of everyday life is a thin veneer for its further depoliticization, which has been gathering momentum since the collapse of the First International and the dream of an international socialist revolution. The postmodernism of shopping malls and "Miami Vice" defuses political disputation in the name of the so-called end of history—a warmed-over version of Bell's (1973) postindustrialism. Of course, neither ideology nor capitalism has ended, in spite of the spectacularization of the "end of communism" that, in fact, only signals the failure of Stalinist command economies that Western Marxists have denounced for the past seventy years. Postmodernism does not best Marxism any more than *perestroika* does; it simply transmogrifies anti-Marxism into another cultural commodity, readily gobbled up by the cultural and political establishment.

Indeed, the end-of-ideology thesis, captured figuratively and in gesture in the lived experience of postmodernity (see Harvey 1989), props up capitalism by diverting attention from substantive social, economic, and cultural alternatives. As Horkheimer and Adorno (1972) noted in the 1940s, the culture industry exists in large measure to represent capitalism as a rational social order, hence perpetuating the commodification of all experience.

Horkheimer and Adorno were first exposed to Hollywood culture and American mass media from which they developed the theory of the culture industry in the 1940s. Where half a century ago ideology could be more readily debunked as egregious falsification, today ideology has gone underground, encoded in Baudrillard's simulations (see Baudrillard 1983) of what I (Agger 1989a) have called fast capitalism, in which the boundary between the textual and material has virtually disappeared, disabling social criticism as a result. Today, texts commanding experience are not found between covers but in the imagery, infrastructure, and discourse of a postmodernized everyday life—what Baudrillard (1983) calls hyperreality—in which people believe that we live at the edge of the end of history, in the eternal present posited by Nietzsche as the fated destination of the Enlightenment gone wrong.

Nietzsche despised the linear liberalism and rationalism that were enthroned as a new religion of positive thinking. But *New York Times* postmodernists do not read Nietzsche. Thus, they cannot appreciate the ways Nietzsche grounds both the Frankfurt school's Marxism and the postmodernism of Lyotard and Foucault. The closest they get to Nietzsche is Ayn Rand, a central possessive-individualist culture hero. The *New York Times* postmodernism that dominates our urban environment and its urbane cultural discourse celebrates what Nietzsche viewed as the antithesis of reason. Meaninglessness is frozen into a monument to capitalism, now neologistically called postmodernity. But capitalism is thoroughly modernist in its essential logic; postmodern architecture and culture only embellish a modernist public space with borrowings from premodern epochs (see Gottdiener 1991), producing the trivially different buildings that dominate the skylines of Manhattan, London, Houston, and Atlanta. We have not yet entered a genuine postmodernity, which would have to be postcapitalist. We can make a halting step toward that genuine postmodernity by reversing the momentum of the postmodernizing culture industry that eschews ideology while perpetuating it at every turn.

The Establishment postmodernism that I decry threatens to engulf postmodern tendencies in social science and the humanities. Although I and others have tried to borrow the more critical insights of postmodernism and poststructuralism in our own theorizing (e.g., see Fraser 1989; Best and Kellner 1991), I hesitate to endorse the postmodernization of sociology when postmodernism typically is yet another version of post-Marxism. This is not to say that Marxism is a monolith; the critical feminist Marxism that I advocate gave up on state socialism long before it was fashionable on the American Left to do so. Pitting Marxism against postmodernism prevents their interpenetration and dialogue. Nevertheless, we who care about the structural roots of social problems should be on guard against an affirmative version of postmodernism at a time when the celebration of the so-called end of Marxism becomes what Hegel called a "bacchanalian whirl in which no member is not drunken" (1966, 70).

Later in this book, I attempt to blend postmodernism with other themes in critical theory. As this chapter demonstrates, certain versions of postmodernism function ideologically where they oppose the very radicalism giving rise to my proposed theoretical synthesis. This demonstrates again that subversive ideas can be deployed against themselves when they are reduced to clichés. Notwithstanding that, I am hopeful that postmodernism, like feminism, poses a fundamental challenge to Marxism that can be met only by rethinking some basic Marxist positions on the relation between discourse and social change. Like feminism, postmodernism helps Marxism strengthen itself at a time when the nineteenth-century prophecy of class struggle seems extremely remote. I have attempted to preserve Marx's vision of a better society by formulating it in discourse-theoretic terms, with the aid of postmodernism and feminist theory. Against the commodified postmodernism discussed in the present chapter, I believe that we can revivify the public sphere and transform our political agenda, but only if we rethink aspects of Marxism that have lost their vitality and relevance. A feminist postmodern critical theory contributes to this rethinking, affording us a perspective from which to address social problems of modernity and postmodernity—including theory's own obfuscation of these social problems. It remains to be seen whether feminist postmodern critical theorists can address the public in comprehensible, compelling terms, deacademizing their own discourse. I hope that this work at least raises the possibility of such deacademization and of the repoliticization of critical theory.

In the next section, I turn directly to the theoretical contributions of the Frankfurt school, particularly Marcuse and Habermas. I explore Marcuse's contributions to the reconstruction of Marx's historical materialism (chaps. 6–9); then I address his dispute with Habermas about the emancipatory scope of critical theory (chaps. 10–11). This section will prepare the way for a more positive formulation of critical theory in my concluding chapters, resting in part on a politicized version of the very postmodernism decried in this chapter.

PART                    2


# BACK
# TO
# FRANKFURT

# 6

# Marcuse's
# Growing
# Relevance

I n this section, I return to debates within the Frankfurt school and
their implications for the future of critical theory. I concentrate on
Marcuse's version of critical theory, focusing on his Freudianization
of Marxism (chap. 7), his theory of false needs (chap. 8), and his aesthetic-political theory (chap. 9). In this chapter, I introduce the general
relevance of Marcuse's thought for my own version of critical theory,
which I continue to elaborate in this and the last section. I also focus on
Marcuse's debates with Habermas about the nature of organizational
rationality (chap. 10) and science and technology (chap. 11).

Here I examine aspects of Herbert Marcuse's more recent work
in the context of a general examination and critique of contemporary
Western Marxism. In this sense, I propose to treat Marcuse as the harbinger of a new perspective in the Marxist tradition as well as one of the
most articulate expositors of the "old" Western Marxism, entombed
once and for all in the 1960s. My argument is that Marcuse, in spite of
his 1978 descent into aesthetic resignation before an apparently inflexible capitalist totality of domination (paralleling Adorno's [1984] own
critique in this regard), illuminates certain current dilemmas of Western
Marxism and points the way toward their resolution. Most notably, I believe, Marcuse understands the dialectic between individual and group

levels of socialist and feminist struggle, offering a Marxist perspective on the micro-macro problem addressed in chapter 4. He thus guides us beyond a monadic, inner-directed socialist asceticism (in spite of his own inability to creatively transform his own late 1960s insights in this respect).

## The Problem of Radical Subjectivity

As I discuss throughout this part of the book, Marcuse (1969) recognizes the requirements of a nonauthoritarian socialist movement that arise from the struggling individual—the "new sensibility." I intend to read Marcuse in this sense as a theorist who does not treat the liberation of the singular individual as the end point of socialist praxis but only as the beginning. This interpretation of Marcuse violates certain received canons. However, I argue that reading a theoretical text is as much an act of creation as of "objective" comprehension. I shall read Marcuse deconstructively against himself in searching his work for clues to the transcendence of what can be termed aesthetic Marxism. Marcuse, I contend, outlines an important theory of the objectification of subjectivity that has been almost universally ignored by both sympathetic and unsympathetic commentators in their rush to style him merely an exemplar of the Freudian-inspired new sensibility. Indeed, left-wing misreadings of Marcuse largely stem from an inability to appreciate the significance of his work on the psychoanalytic grounds of critical theory (*Eros and Civilization*, 1955), and notably the distinction he draws between basic repression and sublimation (required for all mature culture creation), on the one hand, and surplus repression, on the other.

Elsewhere (see chaps. 10–12 and Agger 1979) I argue that Marcuse has left himself open to being read as endorsing "total liberation" from the civilizing, binding restraints of what Freud viewed as basic repression. This misinterpretation has allowed many of his readers to concentrate on the aesthetic and sexual dimensions of Marcuse's theory, ignoring its political import. In *An Essay of Liberation* (1969), his most programmatic political tract, he called for "new and durable work relations" springing from the life activity and self-externalization of the new sensibility. I want to protect the nature of Marcuse's Marxism against caricatures from the Left and the Right that paint him, critically or enthusiastically, as a theorist who has moved "beyond" Marxism.

To move beyond Marxism implies that one abandons class struggle as the motive force of historical transformation. It also implies that one abandons Marx's aim of the dealienation of labor and its transformation into creative praxis. Marcuse does none of these things, although he is hazy enough about Marx to have opened the way for such readings. Marcuse can be more fruitfully read as a Marxist who argues that class struggle—and this *is* genuinely beyond Marx—must spring today from individuated foundations. His argument in *An Essay on Liberation* is that liberation must not be postponed until "after" the revolution; indeed, there is no clear-cut "before" and "after" but only an extended process through which transforming/transformed human beings transform society. Marcuse, in this sense, agrees with Korsch and Lukács when they argued, in the early 1930s, that the socialist revolution would not be a leap so much as a process, a gradual metamorphosis of capitalism into socialism that, in its very gradualness, would retain the possibility of a qualitative transformation. Marcuse also rejects the notion of a leap into socialism because he argues that such metaphors connote a "dictatorship of the proletariat" phase that merely licenses the socialist domination of labor as an ostensible precondition of the full and democratic maturation of the new society. Marcuse in this sense understands that Leninism went wrong at the very moment that Lenin excused "idiotic" peasants and backward workers from the necessary travail of self-transformation in the context of their needs and value assumptions.

In *An Essay on Liberation,* Marcuse states that the revolution will not be sudden in a collective and structural sense, punctuating history definitively. Yet it will have to be sudden in a personal sense, as human beings choose decisively to reject capitalist everyday life, that is, values and needs inculcated by the dominant ideology. However, his position is not incrementalist because he argues that there can be massive and sudden changes on the level of sensibility that can, in turn, create new types of group struggle. Thus Marcuse breaks with most orthodox Marxists, who ignore the dialectic of individual and class, supposing that class struggle demands no subjective self-transformation. Marcuse operates on a different level because he is convinced that capitalist alienation has penetrated deep into the substratum of the individual, transforming the subject into an agent of capitalist social control and ideological conformity, an argument he develops through his reading of Freud (chap. 7) and in his theory of false needs (chap. 8). Thus, to Marcuse, transformative praxis involves the struggle to transform the need and value patterns of the individual as a prelude to new class and group formations.

## The Continuum of Domination

Marcuse's contribution to Western Marxism is, above all, this notion that human beings must come to terms with their false needs and thus rupture the continuum of domination. The *Essay on Liberation* is an eloquent if somewhat epigrammatic brief on behalf of human beings who can and must begin to live in different ways, becoming agents of what he terms instinctual and environmental "pacification." The concept of false needs was first introduced systematically in *One-Dimensional Man* (1964, 4–5), which, unfortunately, remains the best known of Marcuse's works and thus provides all sorts of ammunition for a caricature of his position on the impossibility of class struggle today. But even there Marcuse clearly stated that the situation of the working class and its revolutionary possibilities were "ambiguous" (xiv–xv), "one-dimensionality" being neither eternal nor total. He suggested that false needs are human needs imposed on pliant and ideologically obedient consumers. Marcuse did not mean that certain needs are false because he, a cultural mandarin, did not "like" them; they are false simply because they are not freely arrived at through rational reflection. Human beings become habituated to a range of commodities the consumption of which they perceive as compensation for enduring alienated labor (see Kontos 1975; Leiss 1976).

According to Marcuse, needs are false because they are designed to compensate for injustices suffered in the workplace. A true need, by implication, would bridge the activities of consumption and production so that the person could no longer separate "free" leisure time (given over primarily to consumption) from the "unfree" working day controlled and managed by administrators. Marcuse here is not only attacking the capitalist split between labor and leisure but the very notion of "labor" that is generated in the breach between productivity and creativity. Human needs are often false because they do not unite productivity and creativity—or, put differently, because human beings under capitalism do not find their work to be creative and nonalienated (see chap. 10 below). Marcuse is often criticized for postulating a definitive set of true needs, based, presumably, on his own idiosyncratic preferences. This is a serious misreading inasmuch as he simply suggests societal conditions under which human beings could spontaneously determine their own needs, whatever they might be. He argues that one-dimensionality is a function of the collapse of the universe of reflection and discourse within which people can make informed choices about commodity consumption and can seek the pursuit of existential satisfaction in work as well as beyond it.

In this sense, then, Marcuse is merely reiterating Marx's 1844 strictures on the nature of alienated labor under capitalism. Foremost for Marx was the notion that capitalism fractures human existence into work and nonwork components, with the result that alienated labor is seen as the cost of material attainment. Marcuse is here repeating early Marx's theory of alienated labor, which, as I noted earlier, cannot be identified only with the young Marx but informs the entire corpus of Marx's work, including *Capital* (see Hyppolite 1970). Early Marx contended that alienated labor destroys creativity and individuality because human beings approach labor, as constituted under capitalism, as an odious obligation to be escaped in a consumption-oriented realm of leisure. Correspondingly, Marcuse argues, following up on Horkheimer and Adorno's (1972) culture industry thesis, that in a society of unprecedented material abundance the realm of consumption and culture is no more emancipated than the realm of labor. Human beings endlessly consume commodities that have little intrinsic value or meaning apart from their ephemeral appearances mediated through advertising and popular culture. One-dimensionality, in short, is the penetration of alienation into the realm of leisure existence and consumption.

In *One-Dimensional Man* Marcuse only hints at the possibility of overcoming the condition he describes. It is, on balance, a very bleak book. But in *An Essay on Liberation,* published only five years later during the politically volatile 1960s, he is much more hopeful about the possibilities of emancipatory praxis. While he does not retract his earlier analysis of the co-optation of dissent and the homogenization of critical thought, he appears to be hopeful about new types of socialist transformation, which he characterizes as the potential of the new sensibility. By *new sensibility* he refers to the human being who begins to transform his or her existence and everyday life in a nonalienating way, refusing to postpone liberation to a distant future. This new sensibility refuses to oppress others in the name of future liberation and takes responsibility for his or her own liberation. Marcuse's new sensibility implicitly opposes Lenin's concept of the vanguardist, who postpones fundamental personal and interpersonal liberation until that magic moment of revolutionary victory, after the so-called dictatorship of the proletariat has fulfilled its mission and eradicated the vestiges of capitalist economics and culture. As noble as the Leninist aim may have been, Marcuse (following Lukács, Korsch, Adorno, and Horkheimer) believes that it is wrong on two counts (see Marcuse 1958).

In the first place, Lenin's vanguard model requires enormous sacrifices of liberty and perhaps life itself. Lenin's image of the revolutionary dictatorship of the proletariat—so-called democratic centralism—becomes a euphemistic reflection of total control by the Communist Party of the Soviet Union, directed by a few bold revolutionary tacticians. The longer it survives, the more deeply it seeks to entrench itself, producing Djilas's (1964) new class. Indeed, Marcuse concludes that this is in the nature of Leninism, with its central statist power and the deferral of democracy.

In the second place, Leninism assumes the persisting, inevitable existence of false needs among peasants and workers. As a result, it does not even attempt to involve them in their own liberation. Lenin's famous analysis of working-class stupidity was used by him to justify theoretical and ideological hegemony by the vanguard party. Not only is this ultimately fatal in that it undercuts socialist democracy; in the short term it renders workers and peasants incapable of becoming what Marx called self-managing new people. These workers and peasants remain captives of the old system that the Soviets were presumably trying to replace—hence reproducing it.

Marcuse argues that, by ignoring the short-term requirements of personal self-transformation and societal prefiguration, Lenin and his allies doomed the socialist experiment before it could be effectively begun. By refusing seriously to contribute to the reeducation of workers and peasants, promoting the conditions for self-development and critical independence required in any system of democratic socialist workers' control, the Bolsheviks guaranteed that the gap between revolutionary vanguard and recalcitrant masses would only widen. Marcuse is alarmed by this because he contends that short-term organizational democracy in the socialist movement is indispensable if the workers' state is not to become a bureaucratized duplicate of the capitalist system it is trying to replace.

Thus Marcuse argues for a short-term rupture in the continuum of domination so that human beings can begin to think through for themselves the meaning of socialist praxis. The socialist process is as important as the socialist product; indeed, artificially to separate process and product, as Lenin did, is to invite political disaster. Marcuse nowhere implies, however, that process and product are identical. The difference between them, it may be said, is dialectical and not absolute. Marcuse does not suggest (in classic socialist-utopian or anarchist fashion) that personal liberation is equivalent to collective liberation. He merely points out the dialectic between these two moments, a dialectic effaced by most orthodox Marxists and Leninists, who ignore the subjective moment of consciousness formation and self-transformation of needs.

Marcuse contends, then, that subjective self-transformation is necessary in order to achieve structural transformation; it is the beginning of collective liberation. In this way, he calls for the realization and organization of radical subjectivity as a means for broadening the new sensibility in its initial attempts to break through the continuum of domination. The new sensibility brings to this transforming praxis a non-authoritarian temperament and interpersonal demeanor that ultimately emerge in a non-Leninist type of socialism.

## Marcuse on Work and Desire

The new sensibility emerges and is organized largely in terms of the productive work (including unwaged reproductive labor) that must be done. Marcuse, in *Essay on Liberation,* offers several suggestive hints about the character of the objectification and organization of radical subjectivity; these will serve me here as the basis for a fuller discussion in the next five chapters. I read Marcuse as implying that the subject is never without a latent objectivity in the ways it relates to other subjects, in its instinctual erotic core, and in its interaction with nature. Marcuse sets us the challenge of creating a newly energized working and houseworking class capable of structurally realizing the aims and ideals of the new sensibility— a theme to which I return in chapter 10. I have already noted that one of Marcuse's important contributions to Western Marxism is his idea of the rupture in the continuum of domination and the self-transcendence of false needs. Another is the notion that human beings could begin to merge work and play, or productive and nonproductive/creative work, in their own daily lives, a theme I pursue further in chapter 10. In his 1969 book, he posits, but does not explicate, the possibility of blurring the distinction between work and play to the point of virtual indistinguishability.

This blurring, in Marcuse's sense, flows from what he terms the "erotization of labor" (1955, 196–202). By erotization of labor, he means that a type of work can become the creative and productive self-externalization of polymorphous erotic individuals who have been freed from surplus repression imposed by capitalism. Marcuse recognizes that Freud had deep insights into the psycholibidinal character of mature adulthood. But Freud paid insufficient attention to historical variations in the quantity and intensity of the basic repression required to let individuals grow away from their infantile pasts and thus assume a nonneurotic role in adult civilization. In other words, Freud understood the character of culture creation and of work insofar as they depend on a successful mastery and channeling of desire. Marcuse, following Freud, argues that all human beings have an erotic core that they must master if they are to function effectively as bearers of culture and as workers.

Marcuse valorizes psychoanalysis, suggesting that the basic mastery of desire will be enhanced by the liberation of human beings from surplus repression. Freud did not perceive surplus repression as historical because he believed that domination was an ineluctable part of every successful civilization. Hence, Freud was deeply pessimistic; he argued that the burdens of repression and sublimation would eventually become too heavy for the individual as society would require increasingly diligent work and stricter obedience. Marcuse suggests that Freud, captive of his times, did not and could not conceive of the possibility of a nonalienated civilization resting firmly on the individuated ground of successful basic repression and sublimation of instinctual energies. Marcuse historicizes Freud without jettisoning his theory of desire and all it implies. He thus stresses the variability of the quantity of repression foisted on (and self-generated by) the individual. Marcuse argues that surplus repression is a product of a peculiarly advanced technological order that has no other way of exacting strict work discipline and ideological obedience. Alienation is internalized and deepened by the individual in such a way that the potentially vast technological creation of abundance is ignored. Thus the opportunity to liberate creative praxis from the regime of alienated labor is lost.

Marcuse argues for the end of alienated labor, based on the rational mastery of existing technology, a topic I take up in chapters 10–11; he suggests that surplus repression is historically specific to societies rooted in such labor. Once surplus repression is removed, the objective consequence of alienated labor will disappear, and human beings will be able to regain contact with their own constructive desires. With Freud, Marcuse believes that there is an umbilical relation between work and desire (Eros). Work is a sublimated, repressed form of desire, culturebuilding activity in which free human beings freely engage. Marcuse does not suggest (whatever certain conservative misinterpretations and caricatures are made of his position) that human beings in a nonalienated social order would engage in unbridled expressions of individualism. Rather, they would engage in praxis, the externalization of what Marx termed social freedom, uniting productive and creative work and eventually obliterating the distinction between necessity and freedom peculiar to class society.

This blurring of the distinctions between productivity and creativity and between work and play is what Marcuse is aiming at in his notion of new and durable work relations grounded in the polymorphous eroticism of the new sensibility. He suggests that, by breaking through the continuum of surplus repressive (false) needs, the human being is freed not for endless narcissistic self-indulgence but for creative/productive praxis, in the early Marx's sense. Marcuse, then, is inspired by the Marx of 1844 in projecting, first in *Eros and Civilization* and later in *An Essay on Liberation,* the possibility of nonalienated labor. But he grounds Marx's notion of creative praxis in psychoanalytic terms. He shows that the abolition of surplus repression will not necessarily spell that of basic repression. To this extent, human beings, when freed from alienation, could then, via basic repression and sublimation of Eros (the life-instincts, id-energies, desire), throw themselves into productive/creative praxis of precisely the kind Marx envisaged.

Marcuse requires this psychoanalytic grounding of critical theory. In the first place, he needs to show how alienation has sunk ever deeper into the libidinal and emotional substrata of the human individual in late capitalism. He must explain false needs (although, parenthetically, the concept of false needs was not to take explicit form until nearly a decade later; it existed in embryonic form in the book on Freud); he needed to explain how human beings did not come to consciousness about the potential world-historical mission of the proletariat in the straightforward way Marx and Engels had prophesied. Why does the working class not revolt against a system in which the contradictions are sharpening inexorably? Marcuse does not explain this lack of class consciousness crudely by suggesting that capitalism has somehow "overcome" its internal contradictions; he tries to show how domination/alienation has been internalized by human beings who have begun to depend libidinally on a surplus repressive reality principle that, in turn, has kept them in productive and ideological check.

Thus, Marcuse's psychoanalytic grounding of critical theory explains why surplus repression exists and how it reinforces prevailing structures of domination. He goes on: The analytic reconstruction of Marxism demonstrates that alienation is never total but that there always exists a libidinal political substratum that orients the human being toward potential freedom. Ten years before he wrote the book on one-dimensionality, Marcuse was already convinced that one-dimensionality is never total. The work on Freud anticipates his later argument in *An*

*Essay on Liberation* to the effect that the one-dimensionality thesis, in its pure form, is undialectical because it ignores the subjective potential for revolt (via the new sensibility). In Marcuse's view, desire drives the human being to desire liberation. In this sense, erotic desire is a directly political moment in the constellation of false needs, capitalist alienation, and emancipatory praxis. Desire, in the Freudian sense of the gratification of past (repressed) wishes, could conceivably push the human being to rupture the continuum of domination, which is now viewed as historical and not eternal.

Marcuse thus makes double use of psychoanalytic theory, to show the libidinal depths to which capitalist alienation has penetrated, and to demonstrate the potential for revolt arising from that same libidinal core. His critical theory in general is consistently double-edged in this way. He moves between the almost complete manipulation of the human subject by the ideological imperatives of late capitalism and the growing objective and subjective potential for liberation. What concerns me here is the possibility that this libidinal-erotic core may erupt, in transcendence of false needs, toward new work relations, new forms of creative praxis. These forms, as noted, are rooted in Marx's 1844 vision of creative praxis; they also go beyond Marx, as I will argue shortly.

The psychoanalytic grounding of critical theory allows Marcuse to make the case for a bonding of desire and work. He takes Freud's concept of the pleasure principle and suggests that it can also become a new reality principle. The conjunction and blending of these two principles—thought by Freud, in his undialectical fashion, to be categorically opposed (as they indeed were in the capitalism of his time)—is the source of Marcuse's optimism about creating new forms of work that are both creative and re-creative, both libidinally satisfying and socially responsible (see chaps. 13–14). For Marcuse, the manifestation of desire in everyday life is threatening only when desire is improperly repressed and sublimated. Such impulses, when channeled constructively via successful basic repression and sublimation, can result in the fruitful joining of libidinal and intellectual rationality. Marcuse's innovations in critical theory rest on this notion of the possible merging of creativity and productivity, leisure and work. All of this is still drawn from the inspiration of Marx.

But Marcuse goes beyond Marx. Whereas Marx suggested that creativity and productivity could begin to merge in a nonalienated social order, he did not believe that human beings, here and now, could actually effect that prefigurative merger. Marx maintained that a fully mature socialism, taking generations to create once capitalism has been overthrown, would slowly evolve in such a way that the gap between work and creativity could be narrowed. But Marx did not believe that men and women, in the revolutionary short run, could begin to create the institutional infrastructure of present and future socialism. In *An Essay on Liberation*, Marcuse suggests that Marx was too much a captive of the mainstream Western philosophical tradition separating freedom and necessity, leisure and work; Marcuse argues for synthetic fusions and thus transformations of these antitheses. He suggests that human beings, in the present, can create alternative forms and organizations of work through the self-management of the productive and reproductive apparatus and through direct democracy in other nonproductive spheres of life.

New types of non-authoritarian cooperation can be forged as a way of mediating between present capitalism and future mature socialism. These short-run alternative institutions are counterhegemonic in Gramsci's (1971) sense. They serve both to undermine capitalism and to create a future society. The problem with Marcuse's deepening of Marx's theory of creative praxis is simply that he does not become explicit enough in his modeling of the new and durable work relations of his new sensibility. Of course, his project is not merely revolutionary blueprinting. It is, more significantly, a critique of Marxian ideology rooted in the overall Frankfurt assumption that Marxism is not radical enough in its anticipation of the prefigurative transition to a better society. Marcuse states clearly that human beings must not oppress each other in the short run in order to enjoy distant future liberation. Similarly, they must not let "old" patterns of false needs persist into the socialist future but must, instead, attempt to overcome and replace those patterns in the present. As a critique of conventional Marxism, Marcuse's psychoanalytically informed Marxism points toward important new insights into the dialectic between subjective and objective liberation. His new sensibility is a bridge between individual and collective modes of struggle.

## Dialectical of Individual and Class: The Objectification of Subjectivity

Marcuse avers that human beings can begin to live different, democratic, and socialist lives in the present—that they can develop nonalienated needs and begin to merge work and play. His new sensibility is the libidinal and intellectual repository of this emancipation. Specifically, the new sensibility for Marcuse (1969) was expressed in the archetype of bohemian revolt against both dominant bourgeois culture and the political foibles of the advanced capitalist state. The hippie notion of a new dimension of transcendent experience is harnessed by Marcuse to his own, more explicitly socialist and rationalist, notion of a rupture in the continuum of domination. Marcuse mines the hippie episode for further phenomenological evidence of the possibility of a socialist new sensibility (a matter I develop in chap. 12).

This is not to say that Marcuse fully vindicates the American New Left and counterculture. Indeed, his *Counterrevolution and Revolt* (1972) suggests that the New Left and counterculture unnecessarily jettisoned aspects of traditional Marxian rationality in their rush to create an anticulture and antisystem. Marcuse retreats from the extravagances of the 1960s such as the drug culture at precisely the point where he believed that these impulses lost their critical and dialectical thrusts, their counterhegemonic potential. He treated the new sensibility as a regulative idea, in the Kantian sense, and not as a finished socialist product. Marcuse never hypostatized aspects of the 1960s sensibility, for he knew that the essence of nonalienated needs is their adaptability to the ever-changing material, cultural, and symbolic universe. As this universe changes, so will true needs change. Thus Marcuse does not suggest that marijuana will be a universal form of relaxing transcendence, nor does he eternalize the communal forms of the 1960s. He merely treats the new sensibility as an archetype that points the way toward new dialectical syntheses.

The new sensibility interposes itself between the struggling, rebellious individual and larger issues of class and group struggle. Marcuse revitalizes Marxism by adding a radical subjectivism to an otherwise overly structural theory of dialectical change; but he does not go far enough in outlining the actual mediations that will allow the new sensibility to grow into a full-blown social movement located in ideologically self-conscious classes and groups. Anticipating Habermas's new social movements theory, Marcuse suggests in *An Essay on Liberation* that new types of struggle might spring from the heterogeneous lifeworlds of new sensibilities. These forms of struggle will be unorthodox in that they will spontaneously arise from the particular "generative themes" (in Paulo Freire's [1970] sense) that make life meaningful for human beings. Marcuse thus suggests that one-dimensionality is never total, that there is always "space" in which emancipatory projects can be undertaken and group praxis initiated.

This linkage between microscopic and macroscopic praxis, between rebellion and strategic action, informs Marcuse's revision of orthodox Marxism. He believes that he can protect the non-authoritarian character of the socialist movement if that movement preserves the spontaneity of the new sensibility's attempts to forge a new world in the immediate present, no matter how difficult that world making may be. By preserving the new sensibility's attempt to overcome the continuum of domination and to forge the tentative merger of work and play, the socialist movement, Marcuse believes, will be both non-authoritarian and deeply utopian, refusing to accept short-term vanguard dictatorship as the price of future collective liberation. He is one of the few Marxists unwilling to accept the Leninist sacrifice of short-term liberty and spontaneity to longer-term goals such as capital accumulation. In this advanced industrial society, implies Marcuse, we need not postpone liberation on grounds of material insufficiency. Instead, we can master the technological apparatus in such a way that human beings today and tomorrow can be freed from the regime of alienated labor and surplus repression (the theme of chap. 11 below). His dialectic between individual spontaneity and strategic group action is rooted in this appreciation of the emancipating effects of technological abundance.

In this sense, Marcuse takes Marx seriously when the latter suggests that new social forms emerge only when old forms have been fully developed. It is not a matter of returning to a Luddite past or to primitive society for Marcuse. Rather, it is one of reintegrating the primitive and the romantic into a future order that does not negate primitive communism but makes it objectively possible. Marcuse's romantic utopianism is objectively grounded. He is mistakenly interpreted by critics as endorsing regression to a "primal" (psychic and civilizational) past. But he argues rather that the nonantagonistic rapprochement between humanity and nature can be re-created in a supertechnological order in which technology is mastered by human beings rather than vice versa.

The present social order is intrinsically post-one-dimensional, as I explore in chapter 8. Subjectivity has not disappeared. Indeed, the system now cultivates this otherness, this artificial dissidence, because monopoly capitalism will grind to a halt without a certain disharmony between subjectivity and objectivity. In the words of Paul Piccone (1976, 1978), "artificial negativity" is generated by the system in order to provide that system with sources of the individual, idiosyncratic creativity without which it would simply stagnate, both economically and culturally—somewhat along the lines of Habermas's (1975) argument about legitimation crises.

This artificial negativity is one step beyond one-dimensionality for it reopens the universe of spontaneous (or pseudospontaneous) subjectivity. This reopening, it seems to me, can be either co-opted by dominant ideologies or authentically radicalized, with the result that the new sensibility may reappear at any time. There is a tendency to see the *Essay on Liberation* and its vindication of subjective radicalism as a period piece of the late 1960s. But I argue that the double-edged character of artificial negativity today resurrects the possibility of new types of sensibility as the point of departure for socialist and feminist struggle. Artificial negativity may take the form of politically harmless attempts at "self-help," expressive of the vaunted narcissism of the decade (see Lasch 1979). Or it may assume the form of a deepened socialist radicalism sharpened by the blatant economic, ecological, and political crises of the moment. If, as Piccone suggests, one-dimensionality has outlasted its functional utility, then the space for radical subjectivity (as well as for cloying, politically irrelevant narcissism) again becomes enlarged.

At issue here are the objectification and organization of radical subjectivity. In his 1969 manifesto on subjective liberation, Marcuse was never very explicit about the emancipatory forms that struggling subjectivity would take. It is useless to read that book for hints about present mediations between the individual and group. We have instead to preserve insights into the dialectic between individual and group, in support of a non-authoritarian socialism, and to build on these insights by suggesting alternative counterhegemonic forms of work and leisure that break through the disciplinary society (see O'Neill 1986; Agger 1989c).

The organization and objectification of radical subjectivity require actual mediations between individual and class praxes. In a Gramscian sense, these counterhegemonic mediations bridge the capitalist present and the socialist future. They create both continuity and rupture between these two poles. Marcuse believes that the rupture will be gradual, emerging from the choices and actions people make and do in their daily lives. It is useless to attempt to specify what comes first, change of consciousness and sensibility or the adoption of certain potentially counterhegemonic cultural and institutional forms. There may be all sorts of potentially counterhegemonic forms that superficially, seen in terms of the dominant ideology of advanced capitalism, appear to be merely reformist and not revolutionary. It is precisely the project of radical theory to create non-authoritarian socialist frameworks and discourses that allow these counterhegemonic forms to be broadened, both materially and in consciousness, into a real alternative. This is the kind of work that Gramsci (e.g., 1971) was engaged in during his political struggles in Italy during the early part of the century and that Marcuse implicitly licenses.

Marcuse does not ignore subjectivity but argues that subjectivity is the wellspring of a future objectivity—a class in and for itself, working to create a humane socialism. Marcuse sketches the mediations between the spontaneous new sensibility, responding in its struggle to the generative themes of capitalist everyday life, and larger forms of collective praxis. He is none too clear about these mediations simply because they change with the times. The counterculture New Left sensibility of the 1960s was a Dionysian response to the 1950s one-dimensionality. The new sensibility of the present may be quite different, less oriented to overcoming the repressive one-dimensionality of the 1950s and middle 1960s and more oriented to the international economic and ecological crises of the present. In this sense, one can hope that the sensibility of the late twentieth century will be embodied in a rigorous theoretical radicalism more receptive to the imperatives of socialist and feminist struggle than was that of the spaced-out (but not for that reason culturally or ideologically irrelevant) children of the 1960s.

In chapter 7, I specifically discuss Marcuse's Freudianization of Marxism, concentrating on his *Eros and Civilization* (1955). That close reading develops out of the more general outline of his thought presented in this chapter, and it prepares the way for a discussion of his theory of one-dimensionality in the subsequent chapter. Where chapter 7 focuses on Marcuse's Freud book, chapter 8 concentrates on *One-Dimensional Man* (1964), and chapter 9 on *The Aesthetic Dimension* (1978), three of Marcuse's classic texts.

# 7

# Marcuse's Freudian Marxism

## The Objective Character of Subjectivity

Marcuse's early essays (1930s) on the emancipatory content of German idealism and bourgeois culture prepared for a materialist concept of reason that could anchor emancipatory struggle, largely individuated at first, during advanced capitalism's "total mobilization." Indeed, this was the raison d'être of critical theory as a whole, although Marcuse is distanced from Horkheimer and Adorno (and especially from Habermas, as I explore in chaps. 10 and 11) by his reading of Freud. Adorno viewed Freud entirely as a profound analyst of the social manipulation of our inner desires; Marcuse treated Freud both as a perceptive critic of bourgeois repression and as a prophet of liberation (see, e.g., Adorno 1967, 1968). This more than anything else has made enemies for Marcuse on the Right and Left. He is read either as an undisciplined Epicurean who endorses "total" liberation from bourgeois morality or as a misdirected instinct theorist who substitutes biologism for economism. The latter reading is to some extent conditioned by the affiliation between Wilhelm Reich's writings on psychoanalysis and dialectical materialism and Marcuse's *Eros and Civilization* (1955) (see Horowitz 1977).

In the preceding chapter I outlined the general contours of Marcuse's psychoanalytically grounded critical theory. In this chapter, I develop his reading of Freud in greater detail. Marcuse's Freudian Marxism is the mature outcome of his earlier *Zeitschrift* speculations about a materialist synthesis of cognition and sensuality. Marcuse wanted to overcome philosophical dualism and introduce a synthesis that would become the telos of an emancipatory political theory. The dualism of the realms of freedom and necessity is merely a reflection of "antagonistic" societies in which work and leisure are sundered. Marcuse suggests that, unless emancipatory impulses are grounded in an autonomous interiority motivated by both reason and desire, left social theory will simply repeat tired nineteenth-century recipes and fail to reinvigorate the proletariat. This is especially troublesome in the present period of capitalism's total mobilization because, according to Marcuse, alienation is now internalized on such a deep level that the early bourgeois distinction between the first dimension of material production and the second dimension of cultural critique disappears. As a result, revolutionary ideology loses all reference to the present historical moment. Socialist possibility is banished as metaphysical nonsense by a culture in which positivism is both a metatheory of science and a mode of everyday knowledge (Verstand).

The utility of Freudian psychoanalysis is to explain how domination has penetrated so deeply and so effectively into our inner beings; on the other hand, Marcuse reads Freud as a utopian who points beyond this. The psychoanalytic model of personality explains why false consciousness and false needs persist and at the same time why their hold on interiority can never be total, holding out the prospect of eventual liberation. Marcuse's critical theory is inherently dialectical, moving between the polarities of domination and liberation. And this is why Marcuse never gave up hope.

For Marcuse, psychological categories have become political categories (1955, xvii). Freud is not purely a "biological" thinker, as neo-Freudians have argued in justifying their addition to psychoanalytic theory of "sociological" correctives; he is also a social thinker who embeds sociological content in his very categories of desire. Freud is most interesting where biological and sociological content merge; indeed it is the Frankfurt school's contention that capitalist subjectivity is laden with objective content, determined by both the political-economic and cultural requirements of total mobilization. Here Marcuse pursues themes broached in the early essays where he attempts to protect bourgeois interiority against all-encompassing socialization. The objectification of subjectivity is extended in Freud's psychoanalysis exactly where psycho-analytic categories have political and ideological content and where the process of "private" ego formation, repression, and sublimation is over-laid by the objective requirements of the dominant social system (Jacoby 1975b; also see chap. 12).

The objective character of subjectivity, its biological ground, is treated by Marcuse as a resource for social freedom, not as a hindrance to ideal(ist) freedom. It is in and through the joining of desire and reason that we can fashion a new rationality that shatters the fettering, dominat-ing dualisms of the present. Our biological constitutions are the vehicles of liberation; they open from the realm of necessity (desire) onto the plateau of freedom (reason). So, for Marcuse, the Freudian foundation provides a better source of individuation than the Hegelian concept of reason. The emancipatory impulse must, he contends, be grounded in individual need, in instinct, understood dialectically to be inherently and irrepressibly social. And this instinct must be channeled by a rationality that partakes of the realms of both necessity and freedom. Marcuse wants to expand the category of sexuality, in accord with the later Freud's preferences, into the larger category of Eros or desire, the life instincts. It is only in and through the life instincts, he suggests, that we can re-create labor as a gratifying as well as socially useful activity. In-deed, in the remembrance of infantile desires Marcuse finds one of the greatest resources for adult liberation, as we shall see.

Marcuse finds Freud's hidden objectivism, his critical theory of desire, both suggestive and false. It is suggestive in that Freud recog-nized how subjectivity contains a dynamic instinctual core; it is false where Freud accepts at face value the equation of progress and repres-sion, the loss of happiness as the cost of civilizational advance. Marcuse does not want to give the categories that Freud passed down superfluous sociological content from the outside but to historicize and render dia-lectical the content they already have. Freud, he contends, offers a vital analytical tool for understanding the generic character of domination, rejoining themes that Marcuse had begun to air in the early *Zeitschrift* essays.

Most important among these early themes of Freud's psychoana-lytic theory that Marcuse pursues is the concept of domination, the oblit-eration of bourgeois interiority by the forces of total mobilization. Marcuse in the 1930s offered no adequate explanation of why the work-ing class in the early twentieth century failed to accept and realize the historical mission explicated in Marxian theory. The early essays on bourgeois culture and hedonism grasped that this bourgeois interiority, once preserved only as an ideal on the transcendental plane of high culture, had succumbed to the further linkage of economy and culture as well as the total mobilization of human experience required in the era of advanced capitalism. Marcuse's work, through his book on Hegel in 1941 (Marcuse 1960), dealt with the collapse of the idealist concept of reason. But as yet he had found no adequate basis for developing a materialist concept and practice of reason other than the Hegelian concept of negative thinking; he could describe the fall of interiority but provide no suggestions about its possible restoration.

Deepened alienation, the Frankfurt thinkers discovered, could not be adequately opposed by appealing to idealist ontology; the counterfeit identity of the real and the rational was simply impenetrable by negative reason. And Marcuse could not join rationality and sensuousness solely with the categories of Hegelian phenomenology. After all, Hegel's human being had itself become pure spirit, rising above the exigencies of the externalized world. So, for Marcuse, the analytic problem was how to understand this deepened alienation or domination in categories that went beyond the purely rationalistic and that could thus both penetrate to domination's modus operandi and point toward its self-abolition. He found Freud's theory of desire made to order. But before he could credibly use the Freudian apparatus he had to separate Freud's writings from all sorts of right and left misreadings. Psychoanalysis was perceived by the Left in the mid-twentieth century as a repressive tool of class society: at best, Freud was a biological determinist; at worst, he was a dangerous metaphysician who, in later books like *Civilization and Its Discontents,* "justified" heightened repression in defense of capitalism. Indeed, Freud is commonly read on the Left as an instinctual determinist with an apocalyptic, hence ideological, view of the telos of Western civilization. Marcuse thus had to show first that "his" Freud was a dialectical theorist of desire and not a simplistic and ultimately regressive reductionist.

*Eros and Civilization* announces itself as a philosophical reading of Freudian categories; indeed, Marcuse wants to display the hidden sociological and philosophical content of what are usually taken to be purely biological categories. But Marcuse's Freud extrapolates from ontogenetic experience to the social structural concerns of the species as a whole. And whereas there is no coherent theory of society in Freud, there are important hints about what he took to be the fated relation of the life and death instincts and the reality and pleasure principles. Freud is so important for Marcuse *because* he treats the individual's instincts as at once subjective and objective forces; their subjectivity is rooted in our unique developmental experiences, and their objectivity involves the deep imprinting of phylogenetic forces on the developing and developed individual. Thus we must all work through the conflict of life and death instincts in ways mediated by society.

It is Freud's postulate of the objective character of subjectivity that interests Marcuse most. There is a dialectical relationship between self and society—not strict barriers, as Durkheimian (Durkheim 1950) sociologists suggest. Freud indicates that the objectivity of desire is always shaped by its subjective expression, that is, by personality. Indeed, he describes the structure of personality in terms of an objective id or erotic inner core and a more subjective ego formed in the clash of id and social order. This structure of personality guarantees that there is never complete co-optation of the person by the social system because residues of libido always remain. For Marcuse, this is the emancipatory resource for which he had been searching in the 1930s. Freud's structural theory of personality related sensuousness and reason, the objective and subjective, as a universal requirement of human nature. At last, Marcuse found in the objective character of human subjectivity, our instinctual core, a barricade against total mobilization. But he also found a new wellspring of domination. The plasticity of our biological structures allows us to be more deeply manipulated.

Desire thus constitutes an inner barrier against the eradication of bourgeois interiority, a type of inner second dimension that replaces bourgeois culture with the dynamic potential of resistance and transcendence. But where the second dimension of nineteenth-century bourgeois culture was intrinsically lacking in objectivity, its very essence being its spirituality, the libidinal center, Marcuse recognized, is the nexus of culture and civilization, the ideal and material. In this sense, what I call the inner second dimension is much more important for Marcuse's critical theory than was affirmative culture because it underlies both culture and material reproduction. There is nothing in the objectified world not touched by desire; thus, the forces of resistance and liberation must necessarily pass through the instinctual core that Freud postulated in his profound structural theory of personality. Bourgeois culture was doomed from the start merely to placate those who suffered alienation in the historical present. Its conciliatory power was precisely its aloofness. The instincts, in contrast, are anything but aloof.

> The concept of man that emerges from Freudian theory is the most irrefutable indictment of Western civilization—and at the same time the most unshakable defense of this civilization.

> According to Freud, the history of man is the history of his re-
> pression. Culture constrains not only parts of the human being
> but his instinctual structure itself. However, such constraint is
> the very precondition of progress. [Marcuse 1955, 11]

Freud is indeed critical of the present order, which represses desire in
order to facilitate material progress.

How does desire function as a source of emancipatory impulses?
Marcuse suggests that the function of the unconscious is to drive toward
the unity of freedom and necessity in sensuous gratification; thus the
unconscious joins what had been philosophically sundered since Aris-
totle, if only on the level of memory and dream. Freud, as a citizen of the
bourgeois world, felt that the progress of civilization required increasing
libidinal repression, thus vitiating the possibility of happiness. But, according to Marcuse, the "truth" of the unconscious "continues to haunt
the mind; it preserves the memory of past stages of individual development at which integral gratification is obtained" (1955, 17). Thus memory has a truth value that begins the struggle, first against deeply
internalized domination (false needs), and then against class society as a
whole. Memory comes to perform the function of a transcendent culture.

> The psychoanalytic liberation of memory explodes the ratio-
> nality of the repressed individual. As cognition gives way to re-
> cognition, the forbidden images and impulses of childhood be-
> gin to tell the truth that reason denies.
> Regression assumes a progressive function. The rediscov-
> ered past yields critical standards which are tabooed by the
> present. Moreover, the restoration of memory is accompanied
> by the restoration of the cognitive content of phantasy. Psycho-
> analytic theory removes these mental faculties from the non-
> committal sphere of day dreaming and fiction and recaptures
> their strict truths. The weight of these discoveries must eventu-
> ally shatter the framework in which they were made and con-
> fined. The liberation of the past does not end in its
> reconciliation with the present. Against the self-imposed re-
> straint of the discoverer, the orientation of the past tends to-
> ward an orientation on the future. The *recherche du temps perdu*
> becomes the vehicle of future liberation. [Marcuse 1955, 18]

Marcuse here links memory to the liberating function of fantasy, returning us directly to the concerns of the early *Zeitschrift* essays. Fantasy

grounded in the memory of infantile gratifications can show us the way beyond the present reality principle that subordinates gratification to a strict regimen of surplus labor and surplus consumption. Fantasy does not, however, dwell within the infantile but is a resource for planning a different civilizational order. Marcuse here prefigures his views on the emancipatory function of art (discussed in chap. 9).

> Freud's metapsychology here restores imagination to its rights. As a fundamental, independent mental process, fantasy has a truth value of its own, which corresponds to an experience of its own—namely, the surmounting of the antagonistic human reality. Imagination envisions the reconciliation of the individual with the whole, of desire with realization, of happiness with reason. While this harmony has been removed into utopia by the established reality principle, fantasy insists that it must and can become real, that behind the illusion lies knowledge. The truths of imagination are first realized when fantasy itself takes form, when it creates a universe of perception and comprehension—a subjective and at the same time objective universe. This occurs in art. The analysis of the cognitive function of fantasy is thus led to aesthetics as the "science of beauty": behind the aesthetic form lies the repressed harmony of sensuousness and reason—the eternal protest against the organization of life by the logic of domination, the critique of the performance principle. [1955, 130]

Interestingly, Marcuse resurrects art as a liberating medium where in the 1930s he lamented its demise, its integration into the one-dimensional. By grounding art in the fantastic functions of the unconscious, Marcuse strengthens its resolve and further insulates it against the co-opting forces of society. Of course, art is insufficient by itself to transform the given order; it merely gives fantasy a form and begins the long struggle to abolish alienation. The form is usually of such a kind that art serves to reawaken sensuous pleasure in us. Art, while unpractical, sides with sensuousness against a repressive reality principle—not to elevate the sensuous above the realm of material reproduction, as in hedonism, but to point toward a synthesis of the two realms.

> The philosophical effort to mediate, in the aesthetic dimension, between sensuousness and reason thus appears as an attempt to reconcile the two spheres of the human existence which were torn asunder by a repressive reality principle. The

mediating function is performed by the aesthetic faculty, which is akin to sensuousness, pertaining to the senses. Consequently, the aesthetic reconciliation implies strengthening sensuousness as against the tyranny of reason and, ultimately, even calls for the liberation of sensuousness from the repressive domination of reason. [1955, 164]

Marcuse thus does not celebrate art or fantasy per se; he utilizes them to harness the power of the unconscious and its memory of past gratifications—the *recherche du temps perdu*. According to Marcuse, recollection can be much more than a therapeutic tool in the psychoanalytic encounter; it can also be a mode of rebellion and resistance inasmuch as it plumbs the past (the analogue of the unconscious on a phylogenetic level) for the forgotten possibility of beauty and happiness. While the civilizational past has been barren of workable utopias, the ontogenetic past, according to Freud, is a veritable Garden of Eden. The necessity to grow out of the oceanic phase in which the infant tries to engulf the world in satisfying raw libidinal needs does not detract from the liberating "polymorphous eroticism" of the small child. The recollection of this eroticism, harshly overcome in class society as adults face up to their "duties" as workers and citizens, can be a powerful spur to critique and praxis. Marcuse does not substitute recollection, captured in fantasy and art, for transformative action but suggests that one may prepare the way for the other.

This is readily caricatured by more sober Marxists, like Slater (see chap. 2 above), who do not concern themselves with the dynamics of ontogeny. Class struggle, according to orthodox Marxism, will emerge full grown from the womb of capitalist internal contradictions. But Marcuse is writing when, he contends, bourgeois subjectivity has been eclipsed by the all-embracing forces of administration. This notion of the decline of the individual is addressed in a number of Frankfurt studies, notably in Horkheimer's 1947 lectures in New York which appeared as *Eclipse of Reason* (1974; also see chap. 13 below). The individual's defenses against mobilization are drastically weakened, and ennui replaces the critical anxiety that would otherwise arise from knowledge of the social totality's falsehood. This prefigures the more systematic statement, in *One-Dimensional Man* (1964), discussed in chapter 8.

We have suggested that the individual's awareness of the prevailing repression is blunted by the manipulated restriction of his consciousness. This process alters the contents of happiness. The concept denotes a more-than-private, more-than-subjective condition; happiness is not in the mere feeling of satisfaction but in the reality of freedom and satisfaction. Happiness involves knowledge; it is the prerogative of the *animale rationale*. With the decline in consciousness, with the control of information, with the absorption of the individual into mass communication, knowledge is administered and confined. The individual does not really know what is going on; the overpowering machine of education and entertainment unites him with all the others in a state of anaesthesia from which all detrimental ideas tend to be excluded. And since knowledge of the whole truth is hardly conducive to happiness, such general anaesthesia makes individuals happy. If anxiety is more than a general malaise, if it is an existential condition, then this so-called "age of anxiety" is distinguished by the extent to which anxiety has disappeared from expression. [1955, 94]

The key to Marcuse's analysis of the decline of an autonomous individual is his thesis of the decline of a bourgeois mode of socialization rooted in patriarchal authority. The decline of the socialization functions of the family hastens what he, Horkheimer, and Adorno call the decline of the individual (treated further in chap. 13). Somehow the stage of successful ego formation is skipped.

Now, however, under the rule of economic, political, and cultural monopolies, the formation of the mature superego seems to skip the stage of individuation: the generic atom becomes directly a social atom. The repressive organization of the instincts seems to be collective, and the ego seems to be prematurely socialized by a whole system of extra-familial agents and agencies. [1955, 88]

This development becomes even more marked in the 1970s, addressed by Christopher Lasch's *Haven in a Heartless World: The Family Besieged* (1977) and his subsequent *The Culture of Narcissism* (1979), where he essentially popularizes themes laid out by the Frankfurt school thirty years before. According to Marcuse, domination is streamlined as the "social atom" replaces the earlier rugged individual, insulated to some extent from the surrounding social system. In this analysis Marcuse does not glorify bourgeois individualism or the patriarchal family but suggests that they, like idealist culture, at least preserved the ideal of ego autonomy that, he recognizes, is required in an emancipatory system. So the notion of declining ego autonomy emerges from Marcuse's attempt to preserve what is valuable in psychoanalytic concepts. The ideal of mature adulthood, rediscovered more recently by Habermas as the goal of critical theory, is contained in the psychoanalytic structure of ego development and preserved by Marcuse as a resource of subjective autonomy (see Habermas 1973; also see McCarthy 1978, 77-91). This autonomy is not sufficient in itself but is the necessary point of departure for a full-blown social activism, even class struggle.

## Basic and Surplus Repression

The objective character of subjectivity requires that we confront the crucial interaction of culture and biology; Freud, according to Marcuse, offered a profound if ahistorical analysis of the alternation between cultural progress and biological repression. Freud did not foresee the possibility of dialectical and not simply unilinear historical development; thus, his metapsychology tended to pit life instinct against death instinct. He concluded that progress in civilization would be instinctually unrewarding. Marcuse adds Marxism to Freud where he suggests that the amount of libidinal repression is variable and can be altered by changing the social structure. This is a possibility that Freud's sociology of instinct could not admit—not, it must be noted, because he was a partisan of late nineteenth-century Viennese capitalism but because he, like Max Weber, was fatalistic about what he took to be the inevitable trade-off between progress and happiness. This fin de siècle fatalism characterizes a wide range of important bourgeois intellectual developments, including Freud's psychoanalysis, Weber's sociology, and Wittgenstein's philosophy. All of these thinkers in different ways provided immanent critiques of late bourgeois civilization, indicating its contradictions but providing no solution.

In preserving an objective theory of subjectivity, Marcuse could grapple with the historical relationship between biology and culture and show simultaneously the new depths of domination in administered society and the biological ground of rebellion in the unconscious, through fantasy, memory, and art (Kontos 1974). He felt that the truth of Freud's science of the unconscious lay in his profound recognition of the trajectory of ego development, its passage through the infantile stages. But Freud, in moving from ontogeny to phylogeny, suggested that culture must necessarily triumph over biology. Marcuse as a Marxist reads the relationship between culture and biology as dialectical, and thus he suggests that the amount of repression exacted by civilization can be lessened and the human being freed from what he calls a repressive reality principle (see Diamond 1974). Here Marcuse introduces one of the central concepts of his critical reading of Freudian psychoanalysis—the notion of surplus repression.

Marcuse suggests that Freud erred when he characterized the historical reality of scarcity as necessitating the repression of desire on both a biological and a sociohistorical level. Marcuse wants to distinguish between what is "basic" in our phylogenetic inheritance and what as "surplus" can be eliminated. As I discussed in the preceding chapter, repression in the biological sense properly refers to the process by which the human individual comes to grips with his or her infantile past and unfulfilled desires and channels them through sublimation into socially useful activity. Yet repression in the sociohistorical sense arises not from the fact of scarcity per se but from its social organization in class society.

> [Freud's argument] is fallacious in so far as it applies to the brute fact of scarcity what actually is the consequence of a specific organization of scarcity, and of a specific existential attitude enforced by this organization. The prevalent scarcity has, throughout civilization (although in very different modes), been organized in such a way that it has not been distributed collectively in accordance with individuals' needs, nor has the procurement of goods for the satisfaction of needs been organized with the objective of best satisfying the developing needs of the individuals. [Marcuse 1955, 33)

Thus it is not the reality principle per se that dominates individuals but "the specific interests of domination [that] introduce additional control over and above those indispensable for civilized human association" (1955, 34). Marcuse envisages a type of reality principle that organizes scarcity so that society does not dominate individuals but allows them to satisfy their needs within the realm of necessity through self-creative work. He makes it clear, however, that the basic organization of mature personality required in every civilization via repression and sublimation is not to be undone; he does not endorse liberation from the reality principle but only from its present-day form, the "performance principle." This principle subordinates all human experience and instinct to mobilization by a social order premised on the pursuit of private

profit and discipline. Surplus repression exceeds the biological requirements of an organized adult ego; it describes the way in which human
beings in advanced capitalism eschew the promise of liberation, func-
tioning both as dutiful workers and busy consumers. Surplus repression
is internalized alienation that protects the system by diverting human
beings from the promise of an end to toil.

A great deal of criticism has been directed at Marcuse's subsequent utopian concept of "non-repressive sublimation." Some critics
take this to mean that beyond the performance principle people will no
longer engage in even basic repression of libidinal energies. But this is
not what Marcuse suggests. He sketches a dialectical relation between
biology and culture such that the elimination of surplus repression will
not require the elimination of basic repression; by nonrepressive sublimation he simply means that basic repression can itself be transformed
under the rule of a "rationality of gratification" (1955, 205). While the
process of ego formation will, according to Freudian theory, never be
entirely painless, its pain can be lessened and indeed transformed into
what one may call mastered necessity. Freud's dualism of biology and
culture reproduces the epochal Western dualism of necessity and freedom. But Marcuse suggests that in a nonantagonistic social order the
biological necessities may be made virtually painless.

We do not have categories of discourse that adequately express
the synthesis of freedom and necessity. The term "repression" itself implies unfreedom. But when the biological necessities are situated in a
nonantagonistic social order, they may lose their character as necessities,
just as Marcuse suggests at the end of *Eros and Civilization* that death
itself may become painless. So Marcuse here repeats the early Marx's
suggestion that productive and creative work can meet on the common
ground between necessity and freedom, thus blurring them to the point
of virtual identity. We can know how painful biological necessity will be
only when we liberate it from the surplus repression of a social order
premised on unequal reward. In the meantime, it is imperative to point
out that desire and culture have a historical relation and need not be
seen as perpetual antagonists.

Indeed, Eros is a force that joins biology and culture through
nonrepressive sublimation, hence liberating sexuality from narrow restriction to the genital zones. In a free society, all sorts of nongenital
activities could be eroticized without losing their inherence in the realm
of necessity (e.g., productive work), as I shall discuss in the last section of
this chapter.

> [B]etween pleasure principle and reality principle, between
> sexuality and civilization, militates the idea of the unifying and
> gratifying power of Eros, chained and worn out in a sick civili-
> zation. This idea would imply that the free Eros does not pre-
> clude lasting civilized societal relationships—that it repels only
> the suprarepressive organization of societal relationships under
> a principle which is the negation of the pleasure principle.
> [Marcuse 1955, 39].

Marcuse suggests that the character of the realm of necessity is itself
historical; he characterizes scarcity as an "excuse" (1955, 84) that keeps
people in chains, where actually scarcity can be organized in such a way
that labor is freed from the performance principle. Technological progress, coupled with our increasing mastery of nature, "enhances the
means for fulfilling human needs with a minimum of toil" (1955, 84).
This is not to suggest, as Marcuse cautioned in the early *Zeitschrift* essays,
that "necessity" will disappear; it will be mastered in such a way that it
can become optimally a realm of freedom as well. In this sense, Marcuse
implodes the Western dualist conception of necessity as an obstacle to
freedom, indeed as something to be conquered.

For Marcuse, necessities, whether those of material reproduction
or of biology, are not hindrances to freedom but vehicles for maximizing
social freedom. With the early Hegel, Marcuse believes that we humanize
ourselves in and through work; with Freud, he believes that we achieve
mature adulthood in and through the mastery of desire. The objective
character of subjectivity, in the case of the instincts, means that we cannot escape our biology. Marcuse in *Eros and Civilization* suggests that
Eros partakes equally of the realms of freedom and necessity, at once
biological and rational.

Thus desire and culture can be liberated only together, the one
through the other. By coming to grips with the exigencies of material
reproduction and erotic desire, we liberate ourselves for creative work
and polymorphous eroticism. But today these possibilities are closed off
the more we master the realm of necessity.

> But the closer the real possibility of liberating the individual
> from the constraints once justified by scarcity and immaturity,
> the greater the need for maintaining and streamlining these
> constraints lest the established order of domination dissolve.
> Civilization has to defend itself against the specter of a world
> which could be free. If society cannot use its growing produc-
> tivity for reducing repression . . . productivity must be turned

against the individuals; it becomes itself an instrument of universal control. Totalitarianism spreads over late industrial civilization wherever the interests of domination prevail upon productivity, arresting and diverting its potentialities. The people have to be kept in a state of permanent mobilization, internal and external. [Marcuse 1955, 85]

Marcuse suggests that surplus repression is necessary in a system where technological abundance threatens to liberate human beings from an ascetic regime of self-denial. The virtual conquest of scarcity must be shielded from individuals who, in the interests of both social control and profit, must keep their noses to the grindstone. The regimentation of sexuality is increasingly necessary in such an order; along with the ever-sharper distinction between a sexuality confined to the genital area and generalized Eros grows the distinction between the realms of necessity and freedom. But the realm of freedom is increasingly mobilized in a narcotized leisure time. A generalized desire would spill over into the realm of necessity and would threaten to eroticize and liberate work. This is why surplus repression must keep desire increasingly in check through the institutions of the disciplinary society, notably the culture industry (see Foucault 1977; O'Neill 1986). The memory of infantile gratification must be stifled lest the remembrance of a *temps perdu* become a liberating mode of revolutionary fantasy (see Lenhardt 1975).

The emancipatory vision of nonrepressive sublimation, the eroticization and liberation of the body and of work, is countered in totally administered society by what Marcuse calls repressive desublimation, superficial release of sexual and genital perversions that, like hedonism, do not challenge the prevailing order. Thus sexual promiscuity, based on the anonymous market principles of fair exchange (body for body), does not challenge bourgeois monogamy. This monogamy, based on strict genital organization and sexual exclusivity, is best challenged not by a series of insensitive one-night stands but by deep and intimate sharing between mature egos who temporarily banish (and thus rise above) total administration. Marcuse can defend true diadic intimacy because like bourgeois culture in an earlier period, it nurtures community. An erotic solidarity that challenges the atomization of late bourgeois society is captured in the practice of enduring love.

It is in this sense that Marcuse argues for an end to surplus repression and the return to polymorphous eroticism rooted not in indiscriminate infantile gratifications but in a mature adulthood that has overcome strict genital organization in the service of the performance principle. Marcuse's call for polymorphous eroticism is caricatured as 1960s free love by those who do not appreciate his distinction between basic and surplus repression (see Marcuse 1972, 129). The eroticized body-subject will engage in successful repression and sublimation; indeed, as I remarked earlier, the strict notion of repression will itself change under a social order based on true eroticization. Marcuse here aims for a blurring of the distinction between the sexual and sensual such that all sorts of productive and interpersonal activities, once eroticized, will afford sensual as well as intellectual gratification. People will touch and be touched without the inevitable arrival at genital encounters; indeed, polymorphous eroticism will very possibly involve some measure of bisexuality, where people of the same sex can share intimacy without shame. As the strict demarcation between sexuality and sensuality is blurred, the very character of repression and sublimation will change; they will lose their odious quality.

> [C]ivilization has subjugated sensuousness to reason in such a manner that the former, if it reasserts itself, does so in destructive and "savage" forms, while the tyranny of reason impoverishes and barbarizes sensuousness. The conflict must be resolved if human potentialities are to realize themselves freely. [Marcuse 1955, 170]

Marcuse takes great pains to argue that the liberation of Eros—nonrepressive sublimation—is not monadic but eminently social. Freud's generalization of the opposition between biology and culture is paralleled by his notion that personal and social freedom are antithetical. As Marcuse notes, Freud was never sanguine about the possibility of happiness in advanced civilization. But this historically correct interpretation can itself be superseded in a social order where individuals are not pitted against each other either as economic combatants in the marketplace or sexual combatants in the genital erogenous zone. And implicit in this notion of sexual freedom as social freedom is a powerful feminist impulse, where human beings ultimately incline toward greater androgyny and where men, particularly, undergo "feminization" (eroticization) (see Mitchell 1974).

Marcuse suggests that nonrepressive sublimation will break the shackles of surplus repression, historically peculiar to late capitalism, and liberate human beings both for polymorphous erotic encounters and, in a Marxian vein, for what Marcuse terms "libidinal work relations." In his penultimate chapter of the Freud book, he calls for "the transformation of sexuality into Eros" as the basis of a new rationality of both work and play. When freed from its strictly procreative function, sexuality will imprint itself in successfully sublimated form on all sorts of human activities, notably on work. It is here that Marcuse finds his solution to the dualism of freedom and necessity. He discovers, with the help of Freud's categories, that the erotic life instinct can be harnessed to push work from the realm of strictly species-reproductive toil into a more nearly artistic and sensual realm without losing its productive content. This, according to Marcuse, is the goal of socialism: to produce a "rationality of gratification," wherein work and play are reunited.

## "Libidinal Work Relations": Toward a "Rationality of Gratification"

Desire, according to Marcuse, contains both work and play elements, lying in the common ground between freedom and necessity. In this sense, the universality and inviolability of Eros are equivalent to the universality and inviolability of reason in the idealist tradition; however, it is broader than reason and includes it. Thus ends Marcuse's search for a biological and cultural principle of synthesis that overcomes the ancient Greek separation of the realms of material reproduction and freedom and beauty. These forces of work and freedom spring from a common source in the life instincts, Eros. In this way, Freud's psychoanalysis, liberated from its historical fetters, augurs a new rationality that does not choose between necessity and freedom but joins them in common cause.

A "rationality of gratification" replaces the repressive reality principle, the performance principle, and joins happiness and freedom.

> To the degree to which the struggle for existence becomes cooperation for the free development and fulfillment of individual needs, repressive reason gives way to a new rationality of gratification in which reason and happiness converge. It creates its own division of labor, its own priorities, its own hierarchy. [Marcuse 1955, 205]

Marcuse takes pains to show that the elimination of surplus repression does not spell the end of repression and the abolition of work per se, a theme to which I return in chapter 10. A rationality of gratification is still oriented to human self-externalization in nature. The "necessity" of reproducing the material conditions of existence affords the fortuitous "freedoms" of self-expression, as Hegel and the early Marx both recognized. Freud, too, recognizes the deep mystery that our biological destiny—having to grow up, properly repressing infantile desires, and so forth—is also a token of our freedom, although he is less optimistic than Marcuse that freedom could result in happiness.

Those critics who suggest that Marcuse disdains the economic in favor of the aesthetic accuse him of what he takes to be a false choice:

> We have suggested that the prevalent instinctual repression
> resulted not so much from the necessity of labor, but from the
> specific social organization of labor imposed by the interest in
> domination—that repression was largely surplus repression.
> Content to eliminate, not labor, but the organization of the hu-
> man existence into an instrument of labor. If this is true, the
> emergence of a non-repressive reality principle would alter
> rather than destroy the social organization of labor; the libera-
> tion of Eros could create new and durable work relations.
> [Marcuse 1955, 140]

Marcuse here opposes both orthodox Marxists, who misinterpret Marx to suggest that freedom and necessity must be further sundered and labor organized from above by a party elite, and those neo-Weberians who believe that freedom can be attained only in a post-industrial society wherein all work has been automated and leisure time greatly expanded (e.g., Bell 1973). This neo-Weberian view functions as ideology by sanctioning the division of work time and leisure time in the here and now, compensating workers for ungratifying work by giving them ever-increasing doses of commodities in leisure time. As capitalism undergoes total mobilization, leisure is increasingly linked to the needs of political economy, making the escape from work a false solution to the problem of alienation:

> Progress beyond the performance principle is not promoted
> through improving or supplementing the present existence by
> more contemplation, "higher values," through elevating one-
> self and one's life. Such ideas belong to the cultural household
> of the performance principle itself. [1955, 142]

Alienation in work can be overcome only by reconstructing work according to a rationality of gratification; this will not make work and freedom identical, but it will blur the distinction. In this way, Marcuse avoids both left-wing and right-wing economisms that enshrine an ethic of productivity and promise freedom either in a distant future age (as Lenin did) or in the "private" hours of leisure time, spent in endless consumption and other inauthentic cultural pursuits. Leisure is governed in this society by the irrationality of repressive desublimation.

In a very important passage in *Eros and Civilization,* Marcuse confronts the notion of instinctual liberation and suggests that, instead of tearing apart vital social institutions, it would inhibit its own aims. The liberation of desire manifests itself in mature eroticization and not perverse sexualization under the tyranny of strict genital organization. As I have noted, the transition from narrow sexuality to broader Eros has the effect of transforming libidinal impulses that are now self-sublimating.

> These prospects seem to confirm the expectation that instinctual liberation can lead only to a society of sex maniacs—that is, to no society. However, the process just outlined involves not simply a release but a transformation of the libido: from sexuality constrained under the genital supremacy to eroticization of the entire personality. It is a spread rather than an explosion of libido. [Marcuse 1955, 184]

While inhibiting its own aims, this nonsurplus repressive libido would also achieve erotic gratification in a great many activities, including work, heretofore thought to be devoid of sensual elements. The instinct is not deflected from its aim. It is gratified in activities and relations that are not sexual in the sense of genital sexuality and yet are erotic (Marcuse 1955, 190).

Marcuse suggests that work can be eroticized while remaining productive:

> If work were accompanied by a reactivation of pregenital polymorphous eroticism, it would tend to become gratifying in itself without losing its work content. Now it is precisely such a reactivation of polymorphous eroticism which appeared as the consequence of the conquest of scarcity and alienation. The altered societal conditions would therefore create an instinctual basis for the transformation of work into play. [1955, 196–97]

This idea of preserving work's content (material reproduction) while retaining its eroticization is a rephrasing through Freudian vocabulary of the early Marx's vision of work that is at once productive and creative (see chap. 10). Marcuse goes further and suggests that creative work is necessarily instinctually gratifying, self-sublimating. Again, this ruptures the dualist philosophical tradition that in its latter-day sociological translation glorifies productivity as a virtue, the triumph of duty over individual happiness. Marcuse suggests that socially useful work can also fulfill individual needs so long as it is performed under a rationality of gratification and is not subject to surplus repression.

A great deal of controversy surrounds Marcuse's image of "libidinal work relations" largely because he did not spell out its actual sociohistorical parameters. In chapter 10, I attempt to expand on Marcuse's imagery by suggesting that nonsurplus repressed eroticized work would be self-managed, subject to what Marcuse terms rational administration. Because his book on Freud was addressed to a largely non-Marxist audience, and because of the inherent limitation of his subject matter, Marcuse did not develop his theory of eroticized labor. I join the early Marx on the nature of nonalienated labor with Marcuse on the rationality of gratification in order to show more concretely what libidinal work relations may mean. I suggest that, for work to be experienced as a fusion of work and play components, it must be both owned and directly controlled by workers, including houseworkers. This is to address the question that many critics of Marcuse have raised about what they contend is the hidden authoritarianism and utopianism of his approach. Just how, they ask, is eroticized labor to be organized? What will its institutional forms be? In the final chapter of the book on Freud, he sketches the outlines of an answer, although he leaves unresolved the problem of how eroticized labor is actually to be administered in a non-authoritarian way. Marcuse addresses more directly the concrete implications of the rationality of gratification for he realizes that it is not enough to leave the image of Eros unspecified as to its institutional underpinning. He plots the ultimate synthesis of desire and reason.

## Eros and Thanatos

Explication of Marcuse's investigation of the instinctual grounds of liberation is incomplete without considering the institutional and moral implications of nonrepressive sublimation. Throughout this discussion, I have noted the tendency of his critics to fasten on notions such as polymorphous eroticism that seem to unhinge civilized rationality as well as surplus repression. Marcuse's earlier distinction between basic and surplus repression is deepened in his discussion of the life and death instincts, Eros and Thanatos:

> The striving for lasting gratification makes not only for an
> enlarged order of libidinal relations ("community") but also
> for the perpetuation of this order on a higher scale. The pleas-
> ure principle extends to consciousness. Eros redefines reason
> in its own terms. Reasonable is what sustains the order of grati-
> fication. [1955, 204–5]

Here Marcuse wants to suggest that desire must be mediated by reason in order to secure a lasting place in human community; after all, the theory of instincts per se is not a theory of political institutions. Here, in the brief final chapter of his book, Marcuse moves beyond his reading of psychoanalytic theory and confronts the more explicitly Marxian question of what sort of institutional shape these impulses should take in the social world. His remarks are only suggestive because he presupposes and does not explicate his debt to a non-authoritarian reading of the Marxist tradition; indeed, apart from a vague reference in the original preface to Horkheimer and the Institute for Social Research in Frankfurt, Marcuse leaves the uninformed reader in the dark about his own theoretical investment. Only Marxists trained in recondite European philosophy and social theory will recognize that *Eros and Civilization* moves in a thoroughly Marxian orbit and is a direct contribution to critical theory. Only the initiated will connect Marcuse's early *Zeitschrift* essays and those of his Frankfurt colleagues to his discussion of Freud. In fact, the book is less about Freud than it is about advanced capitalist social structure.

In a few concluding pages, Marcuse confronts the great problem of political theory from Plato to Rousseau, the nature of authority (see my chap. 10). The convergence of reason and happiness implies distinctive relations of authority and a division of labor; the "liberated" individual is not left floating in air, unconnected to the body politic.

> Hierarchical relationships are not unfree per se; civilization
> relies to a great extent on rational authority, based on knowl-
> edge and necessity, and aiming at the protection and preserva-
> tion of life. Such is the authority of the engineer, of the traffic
> policeman, of the airplane pilot in flight. Once again, the dis-
> tinction between repression and surplus-repression must be re-
> called. If a child feels the "need" to cross the street any time at

its will, repression of this "need" is not repressive of human potentialities. It may be the opposite. The need to "relax" in the entertainments furnished by the culture industry is itself repressive, and its repression is a step toward freedom. Where repression has become so effective that, for the repressed, it assumes the (illusory) form of freedom, the abolition of such freedom readily appears as a totalitarian act. Here, the old conflict arises again: human freedom is not only a private affair—but it is nothing at all unless it is also a private affair. Once privacy must no longer be maintained apart from and against the public existence, the liberty of the individual and that of the whole may perhaps be reconciled by a "general will" taking shape in institutions which are directed toward the individual needs. The renunciations and delays demanded by the general will must not be opaque and inhuman; nor must their reason be authoritarian. However, the question remains: how can civilization freely generate freedom, when unfreedom has become part and parcel of the mental apparatus? And if not who is entitled to establish and enforce the objective standards? [1955, 205–6]

The problem of educating the educators has been paramount in Marxian theory since Marx wrote the theses on Feuerbach. But the traditional authoritarian answer, to impose truth on the masses, is no longer satisfactory in liberal society. Marcuse here explicitly comes out on the side of anti-authoritarianism in spite of what some of his "democratic" critics suggest about his elitism. Marcuse makes it clear that critical theory is not another vanguardist project and states clearly that its truths are available to everyone on the basis of reason. "Utopias are susceptible to unrealistic blueprints; the conditions for a free society are not. They are a matter of reason" (Marcuse 1955, 206). Marcuse maintains this posture throughout his oeuvre. He suggests in *One-Dimensional Man* that false needs are simply those not arrived at rationally, in a self-determining fashion. Similarly, he postulates a socialist general will, borrowing Rousseau's image, made up of human beings who recognize the truths of social freedom, praxis, community, and Eros. True needs are left to chance, admittedly, and Marcuse never itemizes what he predicts they will be once the veil of domination has been lifted. But he thinks there is a good chance that individuals through reason will agree on what they should be. And if they do not, he has already provided for the function of recognized authority such as that of the pilot or police officer.

Reason and desire must be joined for "instinct itself is beyond good and evil" (Marcuse 1955, 206). Marcuse here suggests that there is a tension between personal and general freedom. And this tension is at the center of human existence. My erotic desires for another person may not be reciprocated; and in a free society they would not have to be. We might not find each other compatible. The identity between personal and general freedom is not guaranteed but is a product of the institutionalization of a kind of rationality that grounds social freedom and sets up limits to the gratification of private desire. These are, of course, the normal bounds of civilization, although in a socialist society they will be freely erected and obeyed, not imposed by force.

While Marcuse has suggested the possibility of nonrepressive sublimation, where the person inhibits the aim of libidinal desire and bends it in a constructive direction, it is not guaranteed. Authority must deal with those cases where aim inhibition is imperfect. In this way, Marcuse never abrogates the dialectic of particular and general or, in another context, of individual and class. The group is always to some extent opaque to the individual; it exists before and will outlast the individual. The clash between desire and reason can be resolved only in provisional ways and not eternally. And this clash is mirrored in Freudian terms by the clash between Eros and Thanatos, life and death instincts. Here, in the recognition of a longing for eternal bliss in death, Freud profoundly confronted our mortality and the problem of its relation to the immortality of the species and society. Marcuse has noted that human freedom "is nothing at all unless it is also a private affair" (1955, 205). As a Marxist he will not tolerate a history that sacrifices individuals. This is why he upholds individual biological need as the dynamic core of his critical theory; but at the same time history is disappointing anyway since we all must die. Does the fact of ineluctable mortality, captured by Freud in his notion of Thanatos, cancel transformative possibility? Is the urge to transform society in radical ways not a form of neurosis, given our mortal limitations?

If death is inevitable, why should we struggle? Marcuse responds that "the necessity of death does not refute the possibility of final liberation" (1955, 216). He seeks to redefine Thanatos not as the death instinct but as an instinct that wants to avoid pain. Otherwise, death's inevitability makes it impossible for us to relish the present since we cannot triumph in the end.

> The mere anticipation of the inevitable end, present in every instant, introduces a repressive element into all libidinal relations and renders pleasure itself painful. This primary frustra-

tion in the instinctual structure of man becomes the inexhaustible source of all other frustrations–and of their social effectiveness. Man learns that "it cannot last anyway," that every pleasure is short, that for all finite things the hour of their birth is the hour of their death—that it couldn't be otherwise. He is resigned before society forces him to practice resignation methodically. The flux of time is society's most natural ally in maintaining law and order, conformity, and the institutions that relegate freedom to a perpetual utopia; the flux of time helps men to forget what was and what can be; it makes them oblivious to the better past and the better future. [1955, 211–12]

But Marcuse suggests that the harsh contradiction between Eros and Thanatos can be ameliorated if Thanatos is reinterpreted as Nirvana, the longing for the absence not of life but of pain. "The conflict between life and death is the more reduced, the closer life approximates the state of gratification" (1955, 214–15).

He suggests that reason and desire can unite in the struggle, not against death per se but against unreasonable death, premature and painful at the hands of class society. He decries the therapeutic cult of death that prepares us for dying; a "death with dignity" is impossible when life itself has no dignity.

Theology and philosophy today compete with each other in celebrating death as an existential category. Perverting a biological fact into an ontological essence, they bestow transcendental blessing on the guilt of mankind which they help to perpetuate—they betray the promise of utopia. [Marcuse 1955, 216]

He is referring here to Heidegger's existential philosophy; and today he would refer to works like Kübler-Ross's on dignified death. Marcuse is not denying death as a biological fact but suggesting that the death wish and its cult in the present society are deeply conservative. By transforming Thanatos into Nirvana, Marcuse suggests that desire can be harnessed not to aggressive and self-destructive projects but to the perpetuation of gratification. And this will also require reason for, as he noted earlier, instincts are beyond good and evil; a completely privatized Nirvana principle would necessarily fail unless it were channeled into socially acceptable modes of gratification. Pure Nirvana would result in the endless drug high and not the gratification of real needs; and yet, by replacing Thanatos with Nirvana, Marcuse suggests that there is an instinctual basis for liberation rooted in our perpetual quest for the absence of pain.

A complete reconciliation of reason and desire would involve a combination of pleasure and pain; Nirvana would not be unproblematically given but would have to be achieved. After all, the biological fact of death is omnipresent. And desire is inherently contradictory to the aims of civilization. Only by binding reason and desire can Marcuse utilize the Nirvana principle in the struggle for liberation from an order that glorifies death by equating stoic acceptance of it with bourgeois duty.

> In contrast, a philosophy that does not work as the hand-maiden of repression responds to the fact of death with the Great Refusal—the refusal of Orpheus the liberator. Death can become a token of freedom . . . Like the other necessities it can be made rational—painless. Men can die without anxiety if they know what they love is protected from misery and oblivion. After a fulfilled life, they may take it upon themselves to die—at a moment of their own choosing. [1955, 216]

Indeed, the recognition of our mortality is at once a sign of disappointment and a token of our liberating possibilities. By grounding rebellion in desire as well as reason, Marcuse reveals the deep ambiguity in his thought and in all of Marxism. The individual is driven to desire liberation, according to Marcuse, and to join a revolutionary group even when his or her own mortality cancels the possibility of final liberation. The tension between particular and general can never be undone; while the person is mortal, the species, "humanity," may be eternal. But humanity cannot be free unless individuals are free.

Eros thus is the wellspring of liberating possibilities, never totally manipulable by dominant interests and, at the same time, the token of our mortality. Marcuse's thought dwells within this dialectic and never tries to cancel it. This dialectic of desire and reason is mirrored by the dialectic of individual and class. Whereas in general terms the class can express individuals' interests, it can never embody every particular interest. Similarly, reason must always temper desire in the interest of preserving social institutions. So although institutions have to be created to provide for individual needs, they also tend to entrap the individual. Marcuse suggests that this is an inevitable fact of human existence. But because reason and desire (or individual and class) are not identical, they need not be seen as eternal enemies. Freud is important because he points out the biological grounds of social rationality and, once properly historicized, serves as an optimistic prophet of enhanced rationality—one of gratification and not repression.

Marcuse is one of the few Marxists to confront the inexorable tension between the biological and cultural. While social transformation is obviously important, it must not ignore the grounds of individual desire and needs. These needs are important because it is in their name and through them that social change is sought. Marcuse opposes epistemological and normative relativism by suggesting that reason and desire are inviolable. The truth of a nonrepressive order is obvious, he implies; this truth can be uncovered only through sustained self-reflection and introspection (see Habermas 1971). Against those who view Freud as an alchemist of mind, always avoiding empirical evidence against the existence of desire, Marcuse suggests that Freud's findings can be duplicated through self-examination. These truths about the inviolability of reason and desire are available to everyone. Once domination has been lifted, the identity of reason and desire, merged through a new rationality of gratification, will be transparent. Marcuse is not elitist, illuminating a biological or intellectual darkness that only he can see, but dialectical. Once we are free to reason we will recognize the identity of our self-interests and social interests. And the essence of social freedom is precisely the opportunity to determine our needs free of social control. He is profoundly optimistic that reason and desire, once liberated together, will emerge in an order premised on nonrepressive sublimation.

In this sense, as well as in his reinterpretation of the death instinct, Marcuse attempts to supply a missing materialist theory of human nature; where Marx only hinted at the biological core of human nature, Marcuse confronts our biological heritage directly and makes of the objectivity of subjectivity a resource for liberating struggle. In our mortality, Marcuse implies, lies the promise of a truthful existence where we are not pitted against ourselves. The individuation of rationality is imperative lest we sacrifice individuals to a history over their heads, embodying "reason" in the party and its apparatus of terror. And the biological foundation Freud provides is just that source of individuation that Marcuse was seeking in his early essays. Reason as negative thinking is powerless without a body; by itself reason is impotent because it can never penetrate externalized domination. After all, as Marcuse notes in his final chapter on life and death instincts, it is reasonable to succumb to the facticity of the present: we are dead anyway. But reason in harness to the life instincts rises above the damaged present in seeking a new order that fulfills the primal desires of our infantile pasts. In the repressed

material of the unconscious Marcuse finds the most powerful weapon
against present domination; its false promises are reinterpreted not as
infantile desires, inherently unfulfillable, but as rational goals of social
change. In this sense instinctual repression opens the door to mature
eroticization and eventually emancipatory praxis.

> Freud has established a substantive link between human
> freedom and happiness on the one hand and sexuality on the
> other: the latter provided the primary source for the former
> and at the same time the ground for their necessary restriction
> in civilization. [Marcuse 1955, 245]

The pitfall of philosophical dualism, which contained a hidden political theory separating work and freedom, was the gulf it perceived between mind and matter. Marcuse draws on Freud to show that reason is
not a "pure" function but affected by instinctual content, biology. And
this instinctual core is what joins human and nonhuman nature, in a way
that Marx first noted in the 1844 manuscripts where he urged the simultaneous liberation of human and material nature. We are our bodies: this
insight is paralleled later in the existential phenomenologies of Sartre and
Merleau-Ponty. Marcuse suggests that desire is a natural force that inter-
acts with reason as the infant matures; biology is always historical. He suggests that Freud falsely equated the fact of scarcity with its hierarchical
organization and thus derived a theory of invariant repression. But the
amount of repression required is variable precisely because "scarcity" can
be ameliorated by a rational social organization of labor. Thus Marcuse
postulated the prospect of nonrepressive sublimation rooted in our technological capacity to master nature rationally and thus to liberate ourselves for creative, eroticized labor. Whereas others have also postulated
the conquest of scarcity, they have not adequately speculated about the
liberating effects this could have on desire. And they have tended to define the abolition of scarcity in terms of thoroughgoing automation and
not in light of a more rational, non-authoritarian organization of labor
(see chap. 10 below).

Marcuse eases the distinction between culture and biology because he understands what the early Marx called our embeddedness in
nature. And he reflects that it is only through our interactions with nature that we can become truly human. What he adds to the early Marx's
vision is that our true humanity resides not only in the liberation of labor, but also in the liberation of our desire. Eros is both a rational and a
natural force; it binds us to nature and at once lifts us above it. The

unique character of human existence is our ability to engage in transcendental activity that allows us to imprint our own wills on a world to which we belong. Thus Marcuse grounds emancipatory activity not in pure mind but in a reason that confronts its own objectivity and attempts to master it without being mastered by it. The gratifications we experience from "eroticized" labor are both intellectual and sensual; indeed, as Marcuse's critical theory so eloquently suggests, we can no longer adequately distinguish between the two. The problem of philosophical dualism is resolved as freedom and necessity are subsumed under the overarching category of Eros.

## From Rationality to Praxis

The signal contribution of Marcuse's *Eros and Civilization* is to generate a theory of subjectivity that grounds emancipatory struggle in desire as well as in reason, the body as well as the body politic. He resolves the philosophical problem of dualism by suggesting that necessity and freedom inhere in our life instincts; thus it is possible, he postulates, to create a mature rationality of gratification that harnesses libidinal energy to socially useful activity. He reinterprets Freud's categories and historicizes them through his distinction between basic and surplus repression, the one universal and the other a particular product of class domination. Thus the elimination of surplus repression, along with that of surplus value, becomes a desideratum of socialist theory.

But this return to subjectivity as a way of explaining the depth and persistence of false consciousness while preserving the possibility of libidinal revolt is more a philosophical corrective than a direct contribution to a theory of praxis. Indeed, in 1955 Marcuse did not have a theory of praxis. Western capitalism was in the midst of postwar reconstruction and the consequent obliteration of critical consciousness. Marcuse could not count on an informed philosophical audience for his book on Freud, let alone a political one. The Eisenhower years were the apex of what Marcuse was later to call one-dimensionality (see Agger 1979, 145-88). So in the 1950s his political theory remained dormant, hidden in the nuances of his reading of Freud. As in earlier decades, critical theory lacked a volatile political situation in which to apply philosophy directly to action.

The relevance of the rationality of gratification was not to come for another decade, until the late 1960s and the rise of the New Left.

And even that was an equivocal phenomenon, located somewhere between populism and Marxism. But the rise of the New Left and counterculture at least challenged neo-Marxists to speculate about necessary revisions to the theory of class struggle, most notably in terms of a critical theory of subjectivity. In this sense, Marcuse's Freudianism acquired political significance, if only an ephemeral one, in the late 1960s. When he wrote *Eros and Civilization* he was more concerned with working out a coherent materialist concept of reason on the level of philosophy and psychology. But before he addressed the turmoil of the late 1960s, Marcuse needed to take the theory of subjectivity one step further and to explain on a sociological level how the phenomenon of domination operated. The book on Freud was a necessary prologue, because it solved the problem of philosophical dualism first stated in the early *Zeitschrift* essays. But it was thin in its treatment of the new socio-historical configuration of late capitalism. Marcuse asserted in *Eros,* with the aid of Freud, that subjectivity was objective. Yet he did not sufficiently apply that understanding to actual social analysis. That was not to happen until he wrote *One-Dimensional Man.* There the categories that he drew from Freud and refashioned dialectically were applied to his important analysis of "false needs" and "one-dimensional" consciousness.

In chapter 8, I move ahead nearly a decade in Marcuse's oeuvre to his 1964 work, *One-Dimensional Man.* There Marcuse extends the discussion of surplus repression and repressive desublimation found in *Eros and Civilization* to a coherent social theory of ideological hegemony. Of particular interest is his theory of false needs, which remains a focus for critics of the Frankfurt school's putative mandarinism and elitism.

# 8

# Marcuse's "One-Dimensionality"

## Total Mobilization in Advanced Capitalism

In his book on Freud (1955), Herbert Marcuse set the stage for much of his later work. Whereas his essays in *Zeitschrift für Sozialforschung* and *Eros and Civilization* were largely philosophical excurses, his work from 1964, the year of publication of *One-Dimensional Man,* was more directly political. The publication of *One-Dimensional Man* indicated that Marcuse had settled accounts with the tradition of philosophical dualism and was now prepared, with the notion of the "rationality of gratification," to apply these insights in sociohistorical analysis. This was a product both of his own self-development and of his new reading of the structural forces within capitalism. In the 1930s, the authoritarian state was only beginning to take shape; by the late 1950s, it was clear to all of the Frankfurt thinkers just where Marx's earlier theories of the crisis needed to be amended (see Habermas 1975). In spite of the conventional wisdom among more doctrinaire Marxists that critical theory veers away from Marxism, it is my contention that Marx's method is flexible and as such requires unceasing historical adaptations. What is enduring about Marxian theory is Marx's critique of alienation, his vision of nonalienated work, and his theory of internal contradictions. But these contradictions have a wide range of vicissitudes; in fact, where Freud charted the historical vicissitudes of desire, Marx mapped the vicissitudes of domination. Marx would have agreed that capitalist social structures are not invariant but are transformed by historical change. Thus the Frankfurt thinkers distinguished early from advanced or "late" capitalism (see Mandel 1975, 502–3). They believed that the manifestations of Marx's "internal contradictions" had changed by the end of World War Il, necessitating vital theoretical revisions.

The Frankfurt theorists used the concept of domination to describe the deep internalization of alienation, via what Marcuse in *Eros and Civilization* called surplus repression. It was argued that during the transformation of early entrepreneurial capitalism into later state-regulated international forms, crucial new needs arose for heightened social control and for the total mobilization of human experience. In the first place, human beings can taste the promise of substantive freedom once the technological infrastructure is sufficiently advanced that it can emancipate people for lives of creative work and leisure. In the second place, as Marx recognized in *Capital,* capitalism requires a continual cycle between production and consumption; without programmed consumption, the production process, the lifeblood of the profit system, stagnates. The need for heightened social control and the manipulation of consumer preferences is realized by the internalization of alienation, "introjection," as Marcuse describes it in his 1955 book.

According to Marcuse, the new reality of domination, rooted in the instinctual structure of individuals, is more difficult to dispel than was previous economic exploitation; domination covers exploitation with illusions of false harmony and material abundance but does not eliminate it (see Schroyer 1973; Jay 1973). It is important to recognize that the Frankfurt thinkers were not suggesting that capitalism had solved its internal contradictions and overcome alienation but only that in its more "mature" stage it protected itself internally by sending alienation ever deeper into personality and desire. Instinct and experience must be mobilized in order to ensure social control and endless consumption in an increasingly advanced technological order, rooted in the sundering of work time and leisure time. Where bourgeois ideology has before fostered what Marx called false consciousness, in late capitalism this ideology pervades the very interior of human personality and cannot be easily expunged through rational critique. Lukács (1971) thought he could penetrate the haze of a reifying false consciousness simply by explaining the proletariat's world-historical mission to it; today individuals are tightly bound in the seamless web of domination. Their obedience is no longer problematic, and the promises of a socialist future are viewed skeptically.

This emergence of domination, or more deeply internalized alienation, was a function of ever-tightening links between political economy and culture, termed by Marcuse, in *One-Dimensional Man,* the "first" and "second" dimensions. The vicissitudes of capitalist social structure tightened the connection between base and superstructure in the interest of both discipline and profit. Marx did not foresee the extent to which the second dimension of culture and personality could be integrated into the requirements of political economy; for him, the false consciousness of the working class could be dispelled through rational critique and consciousness raising. After all, rampant unemployment, then the prevalent manifestation of crisis in an earlier capitalism unprotected by a Keynesian state, would directly trigger deep working-class resentment. But Marx did not foresee the checks and balances, including the culture industry, that a Keynesian state could employ to protect the system from within. And thus he did not recognize the depth to which false consciousness would penetrate in becoming what the Frankfurt thinkers called domination.

It has often been contended by critics of the Frankfurt school that they have merely substituted cultural for economic radicalism and thus deemphasized the scientific foundation of Marx's critique of political economy. For example, as I discussed in chapter 2, Phil Slater (1977, 147–48) suggests that the Frankfurt school lost touch with the theory-praxis nexus largely because its adherents overemphasized cultural manipulation and ignored political economy. But from the beginning, the Frankfurt position was that culture and political economy have become inextricably intertwined as the individual is increasingly manipulated by affirmative forces. In this sense, the Frankfurt thinkers are more economics oriented than many orthodox Marxists, who view the relationship between base and superstructure as static and who repeat arguments in *The German Ideology* about the mechanical determination of superstructure by base, thus implying that they are separate to some extent. But the Frankfurt position is that the superstructural sphere— art, politics, quotidian experience—is increasingly "economized" in face of the imperatives of social control and profit in capitalism. Surplus repression involves the penetration of political-economic imperatives into culture and personality, producing what Marcuse in *One-Dimensional Man* called the identity of the real and the rational (Marcuse 1964, 11). Culture and political economy are more entangled in late capitalism than in the mid-nineteenth century, which is why Marx appears to have accorded more ideology-critical efficacy to socialist ideas than do the Frankfurt thinkers. It is important to explain why citizens (who are still objectively alienated from ownership and control of the production process, according to Marxist criteria) have not taken up the revolutionary banner in the straightforward way that Marx predicted in *Capital,* where he suggested, in exuberant optimism, that "the expropriators would be expropriated."

So Marcuse's critical theory in the late 1950s and 1960s began to apply some of his earlier philosophical concerns to sociohistorical analysis. His central topic, to explain why the working class had not revolted and to indicate future liberating possibilities, required Marcuse to develop more fully the theory of domination on the basis of an elaboration of his own concept of false needs. Above all, Marcuse, in *One-Dimensional Man,* tries to explain how positivism, a philosophical theory of scientific investigation, has itself become a dominant form of ideology and intensified domination by collapsing the first and second dimensions of consciousness. In this analysis, he utilizes categories he had drawn from his investigations of German idealism and of psychoanalysis that serve to explain how these two dimensions can actually fuse. The outcome of this analysis is a theory of the one-dimensional.

One-dimensionality, according to Marcuse, describes the fusion of the levels of cultural critique and political economy, a phenomenon that I pursue more systematically in the next section of this chapter. Here it is vital to note that one-dimensionality was conceived by Marcuse as a direct outcome of the new requirements of total mobilization in late capitalism and not simply as a result of philosophical "mistakes" made by dualists from the Greeks through the positivists of the Vienna Circle. Marcuse here goes beyond philosophical categories pure and simple and, on the basis of his work on German idealism and desire, suggests that one-dimensionality is a pervasive feature of capitalism, used to keep human needs as well as human consciousness in perpetual check. One-dimensionality is the translation of philosophical identity theory, where reality is thought to correspond to reason, into a principle of social organization. This, for Marcuse, is not a development simply of ideology but also of social practice. To the extent to which we accept the given as rational, we function as dutiful workers and consumers. Thus the power of the one-dimensional is not simply to implant false ideas in us but also to relate those ideas about the alleged rationality of the real to our quotidian social practices.

Marcuse goes further to ground an argument about the new ide-

ology of late capitalism in a discussion of human needs, the central problematic of *One-Dimensional Man* (see Leiss 1976; Heller 1976). The
collapse of bourgeois interiority charted philosophically and psychologi-
cally in his earlier work results in what Marcuse takes to be "false" patterns of human needs in advanced capitalism; indeed, domination is
"corporealized" in this translation of deeply internalized false consciousness (via what in the Freud book he called surplus repression) into
false needs. And this shift from the level of false consciousness to that of
false needs is consonant with Marcuse's attempt to explain new sociohistorical developments; he breaks out of the orbit of philosophy where he
believes that philosophical and psychoanalytic categories have become
political ones.

"Thus emerges a pattern of *one-dimensional thought and behavior* in
which ideas, aspirations, and objectives that, by their content, transcend
the established universe of discourses and action are either repelled or
reduced to terms of the given system and of its quantitative extension"
(Marcuse 1964, 12). One-dimensionality is thus intended to explain what
happens when capitalist political economy uses culture and personality
to reproduce alienation both in work and leisure. This tightening of the
bond between economy and culture, according to Marcuse, occurs as a
result of the expansion of the Keynesian management of domestic capitalist economies and of capitalism's global expansion. Marcuse was here
heavily influenced by his arrival in the United States in the 1940s. In this
sense, *One-Dimensional Man* could only have been written in response to
the American political and cultural moment, inasmuch as the United
States, during the postwar reconstruction period, was the most "advanced" capitalist society in the West.

It is not surprising that Hegelian Marxists in the 1930s took the
absence of collective subjectivity as their point of departure, seeking to
preserve whatever free space had been created for bourgeois individuality. In carrying out this theoretical retreat, the Hegelian Marxists in the
1930s called themselves critical theorists and concentrated their analyses
on culture and desire. They were not only developing new conceptual
forms for new historical contents; they also found themselves doing so
on a new continent. The rise of nazism and an accompanying anti-
Marxism and anti-Semitism made it impossible for the Frankfurt school
to work in Germany. So they were confronted, in their American exile,
with a full-blown product of a process of social transformation that was
still unfolding in Germany. In spite of its references to European culture, critical theory came into its own during the late 1930s and early
1940s specifically as a theory of American society. Although it still spoke

German and had no initial influence in the United States, either intellectually or politically, critical theory had irrevocably moved beyond its European origins.

This suggests an important periodization of critical theory. In early monopoly capitalism (the rise of the authoritarian state and beginning of capitalism's total mobilization, starting in the 1930s and extending through the 1950s and early 1960s), critical theory sought to preserve any viable remnant of bourgeois interiority, first through cultural and philosophical analysis and then through the use of psychoanalysis. But this temporary abandonment of Lukács's (1971) 1923 collective subject for a more individuated concept of opposition is itself historically specific; indeed, in later monopoly capitalism starting with the turmoil of the 1960s, the system loosens total administration in order to provide itself with the idiosyncratic sources of creativity without which it would simply stagnate. The overrationalization and overbureaucratization of social life, as Max Weber himself saw, result in the stagnation of the entrepreneurial system that erected bureaucracies in the first place as sources of efficiency and innovation. Thus, according to Piccone (1976, 1978), the challenge for Marxists in late monopoly capitalism is to exploit this "artificial negativity" as a genuine possibility of non-authoritarian thought and action. The bright young people recruited by the corporations and culture may equally well become the critical thinkers of the future.

## The Dialectic of Enlightenment

In 1944, Horkheimer and Adorno published what has come to be considered the landmark work of the Frankfurt school (1972). *Dialectic of Enlightenment* can reasonably be read as a more esoteric version of Marcuse's later *One-Dimensional Man* (1964). In *Eros and Civilization,* Marcuse (1955) drew heavily on Horkheimer and Adorno's book for his own arguments.

Horkheimer and Adorno contended that positivism, when generalized from a metatheoretical principle of scientific investigation into a lived principle of culture and ideology, becomes a powerful force of domination. The dialectic of enlightenment refers to the recurring alternation between preindustrial mythology and "rational" science. In this regard, the Frankfurt critics were concerned to confront the problem of enlightenment and rationalization in a more dialectical way than Weber had done (Horkheimer and Adorno 1972, 9). They suggest that, under the rule of positivism, we fetishize immediacy and factuality and thus reinforce a false consciousness that prevents us from recognizing dialectical possibilities of liberation concealed in the present.

> The dutiful child of modern civilization is possessed by a fear of departing from the facts which, in the very act of perception, the dominant conventions of science, commerce, and politics—cliché-like—have already molded; his anxiety is none other than the fear of social deviation. [Horkheimer and Adorno 1972, xiv].

Marcuse draws on this analysis of the dialectic of enlightenment and adds to it a critique of a technological rationality that he perceives to be linked to positivism as ideology. This technological rationality serves to achieve "economic-technical coordination" of human needs, weaving a seamless web of domination in which human beings, once stuck, can no longer think rationally and critically about their needs. Speaking of the inauthentic, dominated character of needs in a totally mobilized society, Marcuse says "false are those which are superimposed upon the individual by particular social interests in his repression: the needs which perpetuate toil, aggressiveness, misery and injustice" (1964, 10–11).

Bourgeois interiority, which earlier could protest against the imposition of social on individual need, whether directly through ideology critique or indirectly through "transcendent" works of high culture, has been "invaded and whittled down by technological reality." This results in what Marcuse calls mimetic behavior, repetition of the immediately given. Here Marcuse evokes a theme of Horkheimer's 1947 *Eclipse of Reason* (1974); positivism sanctions imitation of the given because it cannot admit metaphysical concepts. False needs are imposed on the individual by a surrounding social order, in Habermas's later (1984, 1987b) terms reflecting the colonization of the lifeworld by the system; the individual repeats his or her programming in fulfillment of Kantian duty. Here it is important to distinguish between duty and mimesis as agents of domination. Marcuse implies an important distinction between modes of social control in early and late capitalism. Where before workers' obedience was exacted by imposing on them an ideological conception of dutiful behavior, today they are kept in harness in a culture that purges all memories and visions of transcendental possibility. The modern person works, not out of an obligation to contribute to the common weal (duty), but because he or she equates the necessity of work with the "freedom" of abundant leisure. False needs thus are false not simply because their content is damaging (fast-food restaurants, television, violent sports) but also because they cannot be examined rationally and critically. The person no longer feels a sense of duty but works and plays mimetically, in accord with what he or she believes to be the "only possible" reality. Life can be no other way, according to positivists; it is what it appears to be. Thus needs are formed by a cultural apparatus that imposes the imperative of infinite consumption on people who view it as natural to divide existence into obligated work and programmed leisure.

> In the last analysis, the question of what are true and false needs must be answered by the individuals themselves, but only in the last analysis; that is, if and when they are free to give their own answer. As long as they are kept incapable of being autonomous, as long as they are indoctrinated and manipulated (down to their very instincts), their answer to this question cannot be taken as their own. By the same token, however, no tribunal can justly arrogate to itself the right to decide which needs should be developed and satisfied. Any such tribunal is reprehensible, although our revulsion does not do away with the question: How can the people who have been the object of effective and productive domination by themselves create the conditions of freedom? [Marcuse 1964, 6]

The harmony of early bourgeois society had to be achieved by persuading the worker to act against his or her immediate self-interest; today, immediate gratification can be tasted in the panoply of cultural and consumer pursuits that surround us. Where early capitalism was penurious and uncertain, late capitalism requires massive Keynesian planning of markets and fiscal policy as well as programmed consumption. The manipulation of taste is a vital component of the contemporary technocrat's agenda. The internalization of false consciousness becomes an automatic response, mimesis, for we lose all reference to a past or future order qualitatively different from the present one.

In an important neo-Frankfurt study, Jacoby (1975b) terms this loss of memory "social amnesia," by which he means our loss of memory, which serves to erase the distinction between the rational and the possible. He draws on a sentence from Horkheimer and Adorno's (1972) *Dialectic of Enlightenment*, "all reification is a forgetting." Jacoby adds that "the syndrome is a general one. In brief, society has lost its memory, and with it, its mind. The inability or refusal to think back takes its toll in the inability to think." Thus he decries the New Left's rejection of theorizing and historical analysis in favor of a spontaneity that he contends was doomed to failure. A naive progressivism fails to recognize the historical nature of the present and leads either to utopian thinking or to mere reformism. One-dimensional thinking is a direct example of social amnesia for it suggests that the present is grounded neither in past nor future but is an "eternal present." A dialectical analysis of the present must show where it came from historically and where it may move in the future. This dialectical motion, according to which the present is both a concretion of the past and the promise of something new, cannot be captured by a unilinear concept of causality or by a positivist fixation on immediate appearances. Social amnesia leads to a superficial understanding of phenomena, a presuppositionless empiricism, that fails to examine deep structure underneath the surface of the present. One-dimensionality, in effect, obliterates the past in order to keep the future hidden.

In late capitalism, enlightenment is celebrated as the faculty of competent adjustment to the given. To be rational is to be realistic, not to aim for the stars. In *One-Dimensional Man,* Marcuse suggests that the power of positivism is its ability to deny implausible hypotheses about future social betterment and thus to justify whatever currently exists as the apex of social development. He suggests further, in a theme I will take up in the next section of this chapter, that technological rationality excludes other possible rationalities such as the rationality of gratification; in defining reason as a way of relating given means at hand to desired ends, technocrats collapse the categories of what Weber called formal and substantive reason. The hidden substance of modern rationality is contained in its superficial pragmatism that is defined by whatever is imposed from on high. Thus technical rationality—the logic of the instrument—comes to prevail as thought is reduced to operational definitions, formal logic, and mathematics.

> The new mode of thought is today the predominant tendency in philosophy, psychology, sociology, and other fields. Many of the most seriously troublesome concepts are being "eliminated" by showing that no adequate account of them in terms of operations or behavior can be given. The radical empiricist onslaught thus provides the methodological justification for the debunking of the mind by the intellectuals—a positivism which, in its denial of the transcending elements of reason, forms the academic counterpart of the socially required behavior. [Marcuse 1964, 13]

Interestingly, Marcuse treated Weber as one of the most perceptive of positivist sociologists, an early apologist of capitalist rationality but also an immanent critic of it. Weber lamented the "iron cage" of technical reason but saw it as inevitable; he was never sanguine about the human consequences of this technical reason that ingests all substantive meaning and values in its path. Marcuse here rejects technical reason—the logic of efficiency—on grounds that its apparent formalism contains hidden content, namely, profit maximization in capitalism. Weber erred not in his morbid description of runaway rationality that ignores human values but in his exoneration of a purely technical rationality. Marcuse suggests that such a rationality does not and cannot exist. Indeed, one of the hallmarks of one-dimensional society is its reduction of value and moral questions to operational problems (e.g., poverty defined simply in terms of "social indicators" such as per capita income).

Marcuse's critique of the one-dimensional is thus a critique of Weber, a theme I develop in chapters 10 and 11. They lament the absorption of the second dimension of transcendent culture into the quotidian. They differ in their views on the function of this second dimension. For Weber, cultural values were to leaven the pure purposiveness of instrumental rationality; they were to be overlaid on the mundanities of material reproduction such that captains of industry were to dabble in philosophy and attend the opera. But Marcuse suggests that this is doomed to fail because the second dimension, and the valuable bourgeois interiority it protects, is bound to succumb to the pull of political economy and the culture industry. By separating material reproduction and a "higher" sphere of cultural values, Weber fails to protect culture as a world apart. Only by refusing to deal in a "pure" technique allegedly devoid of values can this gravitational pull be resisted. So Marcuse suggests that what is an apparently value-free rationality of purposiveness, pragmatism, technique, and efficiency actually contains the substantive ethos of profit maximization and domination; indeed, it is the very objectivity of enlightenment in this sense that allows it surreptitiously to become ideology. There is no such thing as pure reason.

## The Critique of Technological Rationality

The dialectic of enlightenment serves to banish the metaphysical as nonsense and to perpetuate a one-dimensional existence. The dominant rationality is not pure after all but is always in service to particular ideologies carefully concealed in the name of social control. Workers must think that they are participating in the noiseless evolution of benign social laws under the guidance of omniscient technocrats who kowtow to no party line. Rationality is implicit in "reality," which unfolds dialectically. This leads Marcuse to speculate not simply about the dialectic of enlightenment in this sense but also about the ethos of science and technology that is the new idol, a theme pursued further in chapter 11 below.

> The most advanced areas of industrial society exhibit throughout these two features: a trend towards consummation of technological rationality, and intensive efforts to contain this trend within the established institutions. Here is the internal contradiction of this civilization: the irrational element in its rationality. It is the token of its achievements. The industrial society which makes technology and science its own is organized for the ever-more-effective domination of man and nature, for the ever-more-effective utilization of its resources. It becomes irrational when the success of these efforts opens new dimensions of human realization. Organization for peace is different from organization for war; the institutions which served the struggle for existence cannot serve pacification of existence. Life as an end is qualitatively different from life as a means. [Marcuse 1964, 17]

His critique of science and technology as embodying oppressive rationalities is also indebted to Horkheimer and Adorno's argument in *Dialectic of Enlightenment*. Marcuse adds the distinctively Freudian rationality of gratification to their earlier critique of civilization, arguing that science and technology, as modes of human self-externalization, can themselves be erotized. This gives rise to the striking concept of a new science and technology that will liberate nature and serve as nonalienated forms of human praxis. On the orthodox Left, this concept of a new science and technology has often been treated as a central symptom of Marcuse's underground utopianism. Habermas (1970b, 88) himself has rejected the postulate of a new science on transcendental grounds, as I explore further in chapter 11, where I explicitly contrast Marcuse's and Habermas's views on science as a way of amplifying larger differences in their approaches to critical theory. Habermas rejects Marcuse's vision of a reconstructed science and technology largely because he rejects the instinctual and biological foundation of Marcuse's critical theory. At issue here is whether science and technology as human projects can be self-expressive and self-creative at all or whether they are oriented purely to the mastery of nature. Marcuse's position, first sketched in *One-Dimensional Man* (1964) and later expanded in *Essay on Liberation* (1969), is that science can become a playful mode of activity carried out under the "aesthetic ethos," a mode of joyful, nonexploitive interaction with nature, explored further in the next chapter.

Marcuse is talking about science in two senses: It is an institutional practice guided by certain political and economic purposes. For the most part this type of science is carried out in universities. It is also an everyday practice, an attitude toward the quotidian, characterized by the lack of critical insight. Positivism is a theory of knowledge governing both types of science, according to Marcuse. It suggests that knowledge simply reflects an inert reality. As such, the knower is passive, acquiescing to the pregiven nature of what exists "out there," whether in esoteric or everyday terms.

The problem with positivism in the first place is that it does not accurately represent the actual process of knowing, of doing science, whether on the part of academics or ordinary citizens. Instead, Marcuse suggests, science is a deeply value-laden practice that brings pregiven perspectives to bear on the process of knowing. For this reason alone, positivism weirdly exempts itself from its own critique of mythology.

Marcuse argues that scientism—belief in positivist science as a panacea for all social problems—is the characteristic epistemology of one-dimensional thought. I have already suggested how crude positivism, according to Marcuse, banishes all metaphysical and normative ideas as nonsense. But he goes further and argues that to suggest that science and technique have value-free rationalities is ideological; indeed, his concept of a new science is a rebuttal of this thesis of the disinterested character of science. The belief that social problems can be solved technically, without reference to values, is a vital component of technocratic capitalist ideology that hands over the keys of power to experts responsible for charting the unfolding of putative evolutionary laws of progress (charted by socio[onto]logists like Durkheim, Weber, and Parsons; see Agger 1989c). The ethos of scientism is so powerful because in its name we willingly relinquish our control of society.

The critique of science and technology developed in *An Essay on Liberation* was given its first coherent airing in the 1964 book, although Marcuse, in *Eros and Civilization*, had mentioned that nature ought not to be ruthlessly plundered but should be conceived as a garden in which science and technique are benign forms of free self-expression, exuding Schiller's "play-impulse." By suggesting the concept of a happy, joyous science, Marcuse does violence to the Weberian notion that science is the preserve of dispassionate technicians, unconcerned with matters of transcendence. The dualism of science and philosophy is yet another instance of Western philosophical dualism separating matter and mind. Positivism is the culmination of this dualism, because it suggests that nature unproblematically presents itself to the eye of the scientist and requires no interpretation. In the 1964 work, Marcuse does not pursue this image of a playful science but indicates, in a negative sense, just where technological domination has become a force of one-dimensionality. Technological rationality, by pretending to be concerned with efficiency and the pragmatic accomplishment of tasks and not human values, appears inviolable; it flattens out the distinction between the real and the possible and banishes "idle" speculation about utopia. In this sense, the technological ethos is indicted by Marcuse not, as it is by dystopian Luddites, because machines impose their unique evil on us, but because Marcuse contends that the technical ethos pervades existent capitalist technology, including its social organization. In this sense, as I argue in chapter 11, Marcuse disagrees with Habermas' contention that there is a science and technology "as such."

> In the social reality, despite all change, the domination of
> man by man is still the historical continuum that links pre-
> technological and technological Reason. However, the society
> which projects and undertakes the technological transforma-
> tion of nature alters the base of domination by gradually re-
> placing personal dependence (of the slave on the master, the
> serf on the lord of the manor, the lord on the donor of the
> fief, etc.) with dependence on the "objective order of things"
> (on economic laws, the market, etc.). To be sure, the "objective
> order of things" is itself the result of domination, but it is nev-
> ertheless true that domination now generates a higher rational-
> ity—that of a society which sustains its hierarchic structure
> while exploiting ever more efficiently the natural and mental
> resources, and distributing the benefits of this exploitation on
> an ever-larger scale. The limits of this rationality, and its sinis-
> ter force, appear in the progressive enslavement of man by a
> productive apparatus which perpetuates the struggle for exis-
> tence and extends it to a total international struggle which ru-
> ins the lives of those who build and use this apparatus.
> [Marcuse 1964, 144]

An alternative science and technology would contain within it a mode of gratification derived from molding and mastering nature. Marcuse in this sense relies on his earlier resolution of philosophical dualism and its split between the realms of freedom and necessity. Science transformed into a mode of self-gratification would not lose its cognitive content, its objectivity; rather, its objectivity would be merged with a playful subjectivity that delights in investigating and manipulating the external world. Similarly, technique would not give up its instrumental rationality but would also embody a play impulse through which we derive pleasure from touching and molding nature. Marcuse's vision thus presupposes an advanced industrial order in which basic needs can be satisfied. He merely suggests that science is always imbued with deep subjectivity; hence, he wants a different science, not antiscience. The ideological strictures of positivism are so destructive, he contends, because they suggest that the external world is static and contains a sufficient rationality, thus canceling the possibility of future dialectical motion—social change.

While Marcuse does not agree with scientific Marxists like Engels that there is a dialectic of nature similar to the dialectic of history, he maintains that science and technique are modes of self-externalization that contain important ontological and political recommendations about the relationship of person to world. Positivism contemplates a world supposedly beyond human control. One-dimensionality collapses the distinction between political economy and transcendental culture and binds us even more closely to the reified present. Marcuse's argument about the constraining effect of one-dimensional thought, purveyed by positivism, science, or technology, is incomplete without a further discussion of false needs.

## True and False Needs

As discussed earlier, one-dimensional thought becomes a form of social action "introjected" in the form of needs.

> No wonder then that, in the most advanced areas of this civilization, the social controls have been introjected to the point where even individual protest is affected at its roots. The intellectual and emotional refusal "to go along" appears neurotic and impotent. This is the socio-psychological aspect of the political event that marks the contemporary period: the passing of the historical forces which, at the preceding stage of indus-

trial society, seemed to represent the possibility of new forms
of existence.

But the term "introjection" perhaps no longer describes the
way in which the individual by himself reproduces and perpetuates the external controls exercised by his society. Introjection
suggests a variety of relatively spontaneous processes by which
a Self (Ego) transposes the "outer" into the "inner." Thus introjection implies the existence of an inner dimension distinguished from, and even antagonistic to, the external
exigencies—an individual consciousness and an individual unconscious *apart from* public opinion and behavior. The idea of
"inner freedom" here has its reality: it designates the private
space in which man may become and remain "himself."

Today this private space has been invaded and whittled
down by technological reality. Mass production and mass distribution claim the entire individual, and industrial psychology
has long since ceased to be confined to the factory. The mani-
fold processes of introjection seem to be ossified in almost mechanical reactions. The result is, not adjustment but *mimesis:*
immediate identification of the individual with his society and,
through it, with the society as a whole. [Marcuse 1964, 9–10]

The object of *One-Dimensional Man* is to document sociohistori-
cally the collapse of bourgeois interiority on the level of human needs.
Advanced capitalism creates what Marcuse calls "euphoria in unhappiness," willing bondage on the part of citizens who come to relish their
own total mobilization. False needs are the outcome of this introjection
of the ethos of one-dimensionality, according to which this is not only
the best of all possible worlds but also the only possible one. Marcuse
suggests that Marxists require a theory of human needs in order to better understand the institutionalized forms of false consciousness today,
especially where the everyday has become (falsely) a plenitude of existence.

This follows from the discussion of surplus repression and repressive desublimation in his Freud book: The individual against his or her
own objective interests internalizes excessive discipline and eschews the
abundant promises of liberation. In advanced capitalism, according to
the Frankfurt argument, this total mobilization of experience is necessary to deflect human beings from recognizing that liberation can be
achieved here and now. Marcuse's theory of false needs adds to his earlier argument about the introjection and internalization of domination.
And this argument is advanced in the context of the Frankfurt school's

immigration to postwar America in which total mobilization was a vital requirement. *One-Dimensional Man* both popularizes and Americanizes themes that emerged in the 1930s more as tendential arguments than as sociohistorical analysis. It was almost as if the Frankfurt critical theory found direct application only in the 1950s United States, where ideological conformity and the introjection of domination in the form of false needs had advanced over anything Marcuse and his colleagues had seen in Europe.

A number of features distinguished the New World setting of critical theory. First, the extent of Keynesian state management of the economy was greater in the United States during the postwar reconstruction than in Europe (which was itself being rebuilt under the Marshall Plan). Second, the postwar boom following wartime abstinence created a cornucopia of consumer commodities and raised consumer expectations. Third, since there had never been a socialist movement of note in the United States, class conflict was considerably blunted, allowing state intervention and the endless manipulation of human needs to proceed unhindered. With no coherent left opposition, the postwar reconstruction was increasingly phrased in Cold War terms, thus creating the "artificial negativity" of an external enemy that was useful in enhancing patriotism and fostering civic obedience. The political and psychological harmony of advanced capitalism in the 1950s United States required the actualization of the theoretical categories used originally in the *Zeitschrift* essays to describe the eclipse of bourgeois interiority.

Marcuse's discussion of human needs builds on Marx's image of private needs as social needs. But because Marcuse recaptures the biological core, he adds to Marx's theory of the social determination of need a vision of true needs springing from the nonrepressive sublimation of desire. Marx did not spend much time speculating about either false or true needs because, in the early stage of entrepreneurial capitalism, needs in general were unproblematic; the problem of introjection had not yet appeared. Workers' poverty compelled them to act; this, according to Marx, was to be the mainspring of revolutionary transformation. Marx simply did not foresee the structural requirements of the mobilization of bourgeois interiority in a more advanced stage of capitalism.

Marcuse adds to Marx a biological dimension that allows one to explain both true and false needs: false needs are those that are not freely arrived at in a state of self-determination; those needs are true that emerge through nonrepressive desublimation from the externalizations of desire. In early Marx's terms, true needs involve self-externalization through creative praxis. The particular content of these needs does not preoccupy Marcuse; in *An Essay on Liberation* he suggests that it is uto-pian to itemize what their contents could be. Only in the exuberant pro-cess of self-liberation will the needs be determined; and Marcuse retains what he calls Marx's (Marx and Engels 1947) "joking-ironical" image of the fisher-hunter-critic, able to move easily across roles and distin-guished by the catholicity of his or her self-expressions. Marcuse agrees with Marx that in a state of freedom there will be incredible diversity in patterns of need and creative work.

In the theory of false needs, Marcuse applies the analysis of the oppressive functions of scientific and technological rationality in a posi-tivist culture to human biology. One-dimensionality is not a transper-sonal ether that envelops us without our knowing it; it is reproduced on the phenomenologically real level of individual desire, defining the quo-tidian. Thus we come to relish the numerous gadgets and objects that fill our stores as balms for the anxiety of exploited and unfilling work. The split between labor and leisure sanctioned by the ancient dualism of Aris-totle creates a situation in which needs are relegated to the domain of consumption and culture. But Marcuse, following the early Marx, sug-gests that the truest needs are those bridging production and consump-tion, where we realize our humanity in work that is at once productive and creative. Where Marx in the *Grundrisse* sketches the close relation-ship between production and consumption, Marcuse takes the argument many steps further in analyzing the systemic function of the work-leisure dualism in the service of false needs. Through one-dimensional con-sciousness we forget that satisfaction and pleasure, even erotic gratifica-tion, are attainable in work as well as leisure.

Later examinations of needs and consumption by authors such as Heller (1976) and Leiss (1976) suggest that false needs in Marcuse's sense are unsatisfiable; Leiss suggests that there comes a point where the busy consumer cannot keep up with the ceaselessly shifting appearances and allure of commodities. Ecological radicals argue further that the provision of a never-ending cornucopia of products to placate alienated worker-consumers is rapidly becoming impossible in the face of immi-nent energy and resource shortages. What will happen when advanced capitalism simply cannot afford to churn out commodities? Can capital-ism survive in a steady state? Indeed, frustrated consumer expectation is one of *the* crisis points in late capitalism. False needs may be inherently ephemeral, at least insofar as their satisfaction is becoming ecologically irrational.

Leiss, a former student of Marcuse's, suggests that one solution lies in providing modes of satisfaction that are alternatives to what he calls the high-intensity market setting [1976, 104–13]. Small-scale production and consumption have constituted a desideratum of much socialist literature from Godwin through Marx. In this sense, the Hegelian interpretation of Marxism has always avoided hypostatizing centralized forms of political economy (as in the state socialist model), recognizing that technological decentralization goes hand in hand with the decentralization and deconcentration of wealth and power. Indeed, incipient limits to growth and ecological constraints could provide fortuitous opportunities to transform society in radical ways; in the American context, populist resentment of big government and big business could be transformed into a yearning for small-scale socialism rooted in closer harmonies between production and consumption and work and leisure.

Piccone, in his analysis of "artificial negativity," suggests that Marcuse's depiction of one-dimensionality is historically peculiar to the most repressive and integrative period of early monopoly capitalism. He argues that the system methodically loosens the bonds on subjectivity in its later stage of development, that Marcuse, like Horkheimer and Adorno, falsely eternalizes the reality of total mobilization in suggesting that false needs are virtually inescapable. The system, in its more mature phase, finds that it cannot survive without inputs of creative subjectivity that guarantee future profit through knowledgeable long-term planning. A bureaucratized capitalism, where all experience is administered, necessarily stagnates. Piccone, I believe, is correct in periodizing the phase of one-dimensionality. Today the system cultivates needs that superficially break out of the consumption-conformity syndrome of the 1950s. Artificial negativity is bred as life-style, involving sustained attention to "personal growth" and the cultivation of meaning. Piccone is undecided whether this negativity, produced by the system itself, can be radicalized as the counterculture critique of the 1960s is broadened into a sober theoretical radicalism in the 1990s.

The periodization of one-dimensionality is important lest critical theory lose its own dialectical character. To suggest that one-dimensionality has become total denies what Marcuse himself, in the 1964 book, calls "the chance of the alternatives." And in the introduction to *One-Dimensional Man,* he characterizes the revolutionary situation as ambiguous and not totally hopeless. The very recognition of one-dimensionality constitutes what Marcuse at the end of his book calls the Great Refusal, the negation of false needs through individual reason and choice. The crucial question in his post-World War II theoretical work was whether this initially individualized refusal could be more than simple negation— might actually connect individual resistance to large-scale types of rebellion. In 1964, Marcuse could barely perceive the historicity of one-dimensionality, and he thus tended to eternalize false needs, providing little hope of their abolition. The criticism that *One-Dimensional Man* is "only" a book about ideology and consciousness misses the point; in the late 1950s and early 1960s, there were no credible political vehicles for converting the Great Refusal into political action. And Marcuse, in the spirit of his 1930s essays, suggests that the fall of bourgeois interiority must be resisted at all costs, even if only in initially privatized terms.

> Does this mean that the critical theory of society abdicates and leaves the field to an empirical sociology which, freed from all theoretical guidance except a methodological one, succumbs to the fallacies of misplaced concreteness, thus performing an ideological service while proclaiming the limitation of value judgments? Or do the dialectical concepts once again testify to their truth—by comprehending their own situation as that of the society which they analyze? A response might suggest itself if one considers the critical theory precisely at the point of its greatest weakness—its inability to demonstrate the liberating tendencies within the established society.
>
> The critical theory of society, was, at the time of its origin, confronted with the presence of real forces (objective and subjective) in the established society which moved (or could be guided to move) toward more rational and freer institutions by abolishing the existing ones which has become obstacles to progress. These were the empirical grounds on which the theory was erected, and from these empirical grounds derived the idea of the liberation of inherent possibilities—the development, otherwise blocked and distorted, of material and intellectual productivity, faculties and needs. Without the demonstration of such forces, the critique of society would still be valid and rational, but it would be incapable of translating its rationality into terms of historical practice. The conclusion? "Liberation of inherent possibilities" no longer adequately expresses the historical alternatives. [Marcuse 1964, 254-55]

This raises the crucial problem of the possible self-transcendence of false needs. Marcuse here rejoins, if implicitly, the great themes of Western Marxism since Lukács. The overcoming of these self-damaging needs is not guaranteed purely in the cosmic clash of self-contradictory economic structures. Since Marxism is not determinism, Marcuse stresses that the bourgeois individual must, through critical reflection, undo his or her own distorted needs, not simply on the level of consciousness but also on the level of desire. As I suggested in chapter 6, sensibility is the first battleground of transformative practice. Marcuse thus does not choose between individual self-transformation and class activism but suggests that the latter begins with the former. The individual is a battleground precisely because one-dimensionalization has threatened to destroy bourgeois individuality; without that individuality, affecting individuals who at least in thought and feeling hold out against total administration, class struggle is impossible. Lukács's collective subject can come to life only in and through struggling individuals.

## The Chance of the Alternatives

Marcuse ends *One-Dimensional Man* with considerable pessimism, suggesting that "nothing indicates that it will be a good end"; the individual can only engage in the Great Refusal, rejecting the seductive blandishments of consumer culture and its forced merger of reason and rationality.

> At its most advanced state, domination functions as administration, and in the overdeveloped areas of mass consumption, the administered life becomes the good life of the whole, in the defense of which the opposites are united. This is the pure form of domination. Conversely, its negation appears to be the pure demand for the end of domination—the only truly revolutionary exigency, and the event that would validate the achievements of industrial civilizations. In the face of its efficient denial by the established system, this negation appears in the politically impotent form of the "absolute refusal"—a refusal which seems the more unreasonable the more the established system develops its productivity and alleviates the burden of life. [1964, 255]

But it could also be the beginning of class-based transformative action. Indeed, it is with the Great Refusal that Marcuse initiates what I have called his dialectic of individual and class. This dialectic works to raise individual rebellion to the level of full-blown collective activism through suitable mediations that join the individual to social groups. These mediations were never spelled out by Marcuse until *An Essay on Liberation*, where he offers a number of hints but, even then, no hard and fast guidelines, given the historicity of liberation movements. While Marcuse's thought as a whole remains insufficiently programmatic in this sense, it is important to note that he envisages a dialectic of individual and class that does not reduce transformative activity to "change of consciousness" or strictly personal choice. Marcuse recognizes that social change will go nowhere unless people actively desire it and live it.

This dialectic of individual and class, from its foundation in the Great Refusal, is at once the strength and the weakness of Marcuse's critical theory. It is a strength because it seeks an individuated concept of reason with which to restore subjective autonomy in the face of total administration; Marcuse, through his merging of German idealism and psychoanalysis, discovers a key to solve philosophical dualism and thus hasten the restoration of the struggling individual as the basic resource of a nonauthoritarian Marxism. It is a weakness, however, where Marcuse restricts his analysis to the dominated individual and does not pursue relevant mediations that can relate the Great Refusal to a transindividual social praxis. In his opposition to the orthodox Marxist model of automatic class struggle, transpiring above the heads of men and women, Marcuse errs by avoiding discussion of what Habermas calls new social movements. Faced with revolutionary determinism, he shies away from serious programmatic thinking of a kind that could relate individual protest and self-liberation to the creation of institutional forms like workers' councils and the women's movement. This is largely because Marcuse inhabited a thoroughly unrevolutionary political culture, especially after World War II. But it may also be because Marcuse drank too deeply of bourgeois high culture, especially art, and often seemed to intimate that the revolution could be carried on only through aesthetic radicalism—necessarily a politics of abstraction.

His arguments about the transcendent function of art in his last work, *The Aesthetic Dimension* (1978), tend to perpetuate the abstract negation of the Great Refusal. Indeed, as I explore in chapter 9, Marcuse was torn between the nitty-gritty activism of the student movement in the late 1960s and a high-flown aesthetics as proper transformational vehicles. His 1972 critique of the New Left, *Counterrevolution and Revolt*, reveals his growing ambivalence. He suggests that the New Left was not attuned enough to the dialectic of individual and group.

> The new individualism raises the problem of the relation between personal and political rebellion, private liberation and social revolution. The inevitable antagonism, the tension between those, too easily collapse into an immediate identification, destroying the potential in both of them. True, no

qualitative social change, no socialism, is possible without the emergence of a new rationality and sensibility in the individuals themselves: no radical social change without a radical change of the individual agents of change. However, this individual liberation means transcendence beyond the bourgeois individuals: It means overcoming the bourgeois individual (who is constituted in the tension between personal, private realization and social performance) while at the same time restoring the dimension of self, of the privacy which the bourgeois culture had once created. [1972, 48]

On the one hand, he is saying the New Left was too individualistic; on the other, bourgeois culture is self-negating because it does not overcome its own interiority. Marcuse could not find an adequate concept of mediation in order to navigate between the Scylla of uninformed New Left subjectivism and the Charybdis of radical aesthetics, inherently distant from politics. While he had much more sympathy for the student movement than most Marxists at the time, he decried its insufficient rationality, its revolt against reason per se. But this is not to say that Marcuse found a better, more effective, mode of bridging the individual and collective.

I read Marcuse as wavering between the immediacy of New Left politics and the mediacy of bourgeois art as a form of immanent critique. Those who decry the apolitical character of critical theory miss the point; Marcuse could not find a collective subject capable of embodying the nonauthoritarian aims of the New Left, rising above spontaneity. His venture into aesthetic theory was occasioned by a political situation in the 1970s when radical politics had been integrated and the American working class and other collective subjects self-contradictingly embraced neoconservative solutions to the deepening economic and social crisis, as they still do. The charge that critical theory is apolitical says more about the prevalent political culture than about the theorists who were associated with the Frankfurt school. Indeed, more than any other Frankfurt thinker, Marcuse actively engaged the New Left and plumbed it for transformative significance. Marcuse ultimately found it to be wanting by the standards of German critical theory—too individualistic, too immediate. And his important critique of the New Left, *Counterrevolution and Revolt,* stands as a monument of sympathetic dialectical criticism. Instead of rendering ex cathedra judgments over the grave of the New Left, Marcuse tried to salvage its important oppositional content, just as he had tried to do more systematically in *An Essay on Liberation,* which remains the more important theoretical statement.

This ends my discussion of Marcuse's more hopeful political theory. By 1978, when he published *The Aesthetic Dimension* in English, Marcuse had come around to Adorno's (1984) pessimism about large-scale radical social movements. As I discuss in chapter 9, Marcuse's aesthetic politics continues the evolution of the logic of his critical theory, albeit in a direction that leads away from organized politics and social movements. As I shall argue, that makes his aesthetic critical theory no less political, especially where, in fast capitalism (Agger 1989a), politics is deceptively dispersed into the dense cultural fabric of the everyday in many of the ways indicated by Marcuse in *One-Dimensional Man.*

# 9

# Marcuse's Aesthetic Politics

## Toward an Aesthetic Socialism

Hegel suggested that art contains the sensuous appearance of the Idea, the symbol of a rationality of reason that is beyond words (Hegel 1920). Art is not language for Hegel because it is nondiscursive; it gives form to hidden, ineffable content. Marcuse in his later work came to regard art as the last refuge of critical insights in a totally mobilized society. In his last book, *The Aesthetic Dimension* (1978), he rejoins themes from his earliest *Zeitschrift* essays on the problems of truth and happiness (see Marcuse 1968d). Marcuse in the 1930s originally sought a materialist concept of reason with which to overcome philosophical dualisms, a theme he later pursued in his dialectical investigation of desire. What he called a "rationality of gratification" in 1955 joined intellect and instinct and overcame the mind-body dualism that he felt served to cement social bondage by relegating the ideal of freedom to the spiritual heavens, leaving Earth to the expropriated (Marcuse 1955, 205–6). In this chapter I trace Marcuse's mature aesthetic theory, focusing on his view of art's dual role as ideology critique and socialist ontology. Like Adorno (1984), Marcuse ended with art because he felt he could no longer talk about a rationality of gratification or give it comprehensible political form in the context of late capitalism. The cracks in one-dimensional society that showed faintly in the late 1960s were once again disappearing, leaving critical theory with no discourse other than art.

In one sense, then, Marcuse finishes with a discussion of art because he concludes, after the short-lived exuberance of the 1960s, that a traditional politics of class is hopeless. Yet in another sense he maintains his internal dialogue with the Marxist tradition and uses art, as he had used psychoanalysis earlier, to ensure that subject and object, individual and class, particular and general, could never gain complete identity, thus preserving the nonidentical relation between person and collectivity. Marcuse uses art both as a transcendent ideology-critical force that evokes the dream of freedom and as a vehicle for projecting the image of a humane socialism that refuses to separate process and product. He suggests that every social order, no matter how free of internal contradictions, will need media through which individuals can confront their own mortality. Art both rescues the dream and memory of freedom in a one-dimensional social order and allows us to confront our own mortality once we—and as we ourselves—are liberated. An almost aesthetic socialism preserves the ineradicable distance between the nonidentical subject and object and thus opposes an orthodox socialism—that of Leninists and economic determinists—that dispenses with ambiguity in favor of apodictic knowledge and hence political inflexibility.

## The Liberating Autonomy of Art

*The Aesthetic Dimension* is phrased as a challenge to orthodox Marxist aesthetics that reduces art to a vehicle of socialist counterpropaganda, "socialist realism."

> The political potential of art lies only in its own aesthetic dimension. Its relation to praxis is inexorably indirect, mediated, and frustrating. The more immediately political the work of art, the more it reduces the power of estrangement and the radical, transcendent goals of change. In this sense, there may be more subversive potential in the poetry of Baudelaire and Rimbaud than in the didactic plays of Brecht. [1978, xii-xiii]

Marcuse suggests that in its autonomy art remains a repository of radical hopes for social improvement. By refusing to succumb to the appearance of the given, art is "permanent subversion," giving form to hidden content amplifying the inherently dialectical character of the social world. The content is hidden, he contends, in *la prose du monde,* the attitude of one-dimensional common sense where things "are" as they appear to be, hence fatefully ensuring the identity of the real and rational. Marcuse suggests that art transforms our conventional perception because art is more evocative than what Hegel called Verstand, uncomprehending common sense. Instead, art grasps at the occluded possibility of a qualitatively different reality. And it is because total mobilization in advanced capitalism distorts and falsifies our immediate experience that we must resort to aesthetic transcendence in order to keep alive our dreams and memories of freedom and happiness.

> Inasmuch as art preserves, with the promise of happiness, the memory of the goals that failed, it can enter, as a "regulative idea," the desperate struggle for changing the world.
> Against all fetishism of the productive forces, against the continued enslavement of individuals by the objective conditions (which remain those of domination), art represents the ultimate goal of all revolutions: the freedom and happiness of the individual. [1978, 69]

Art is a proper revolutionary vehicle only in the distance it keeps from organized politics. Marcuse mistrusts socialist realism because it requires that art subordinate its own internal necessity to a crudely conceived model of class struggle, thus canceling the vital autonomy and hence flexibility of ideology-critical ideas. Art is valuable precisely because it prods consciousness, sensibility, and imagination in an era when they are virtually defunct, a recurring motif in Marcuse's work. He makes art thematic in his final book because he feels that the 1960s represented the last viable historical moment when the dialectic of individual and class might have been creatively activated and mediations developed between individual change of consciousness and new social movements. Art remains a political topic for Marcuse because he regards it as the last repository of imagination, a theme reminiscent of his writings in the mid-1930s on the affirmative character of culture (see Marcuse 1968a). Whereas the early essays on culture and philosophy from the 1930s were written in the lengthening shadow of Hitler's authoritarian state, his last book on art was conceived during the dawn of neoconservatism, with is glorification of pseudoinwardness and its celebration of the goods society. Marcuse acknowledges his growing despair early in the book:

In a situation where the miserable reality can be changed
only through radical political praxis, the concern with aesthetics demands justification. It would be senseless to deny the element of despair inherent in this concern: the retreat into a
world of fiction where existing conditions are changed and
overcome only in the realm of the imagination. [1978, 1]

However, he rejects the orthodox Marxist view that art must mechanically represent the interests of the "ascending class." Marcuse, with
other Western Marxists since early Lukács, rebels against the mechanical
schemata of base and superstructure imposed by "scientific" Marxists of
the Second International (including, ironically, Engels himself) on a few
passages lifted out of context from *The German Ideology* and other later
writings of Marx. Art, like religion and philosophy, is improperly relegated to the realm of the merely derivative and becomes a mirror, albeit of
the proletariat's "true" interests (see Fischer 1969). The contradiction in
orthodox Marxism, which Marcuse notes but does not explore in enough
depth, is that art is restricted by economic determinists to reproducing the
proletariat's class interest, and yet, according to determinism, art can have
no independent constitutive function. Thus socialist realism is an empty
category insofar as art merely reflects class conflicts and cannot energize
the revolutionary process. Indeed, socialist realism was conceived in the
context of postrevolutionary Russia, not as a prod to the class struggle,
but as a form of ideological self-justification. The portrayal of dutiful
thick-muscled Soviet workers—Heroes of Labor—reinforced the nearly
Kantian sense of duty that the Communist vanguard tried to instill in
workers. Thus socialist realism was actually socialist idealism, justifying the
real no matter how corrupt. So the orthodox Marxist discussion of art is a
rough equivalent of the Scholastic disputes about angels on pins; the denial of art's autonomy, indeed of the autonomy of consciousness, makes
art's content irrelevant except as an index of "substructural" conditions.

In more general terms, Marcuse suggests that this mechanical
base-superstructure model has the same effect in the state socialist world
as one-dimensionality does in the capitalist West. It devalues consciousness, subjectivity, and imagination in the name of transpersonal developmental imperatives. The person matters only inasmuch as he or she is a
cipher of surrounding social forces, notably as a representative of one or
the other of the warring classes. The denial of art's autonomy thus goes
hand in hand with the denial of subjectivity's autonomy.

Ideology becomes mere ideology, in spite of Engels' em-
phatic qualifications, and a devaluation of the entire realm of

subjectivity takes place, a devaluation not only of the subject as
ego cogito, the rational subject, but also of inwardness, emo-
tions, and imagination. The subjectivity of individuals, their
own consciousness and unconscious, tends to be dissolved into
class consciousness. Thereby, a major prerequisite of revolution is minimized, namely, the fact that the need for radical
change must he rooted in the subjectivity of individuals themselves, in their intelligence and their passions, their drives and
their goals. Marxist theory succumbed to that very reification
which it had exposed and combatted in society as a whole. Subjectivity became an atom of objectivity; even in its rebellious
form it was surrendered to a collective consciousness. The deterministic component of Marxist theory does not lie in its concept of the relationship between social existence and
consciousness, but in the reductionistic concept of consciousness which brackets the particular content of individual consciousness and, with it, the subjective potential for revolution.
[Marcuse 1978, 3–4]

Marcuse in 1978 defines the project of critical theory in exactly the way
he defined it in the early 1930s: it was to rescue bourgeois *Innerlichkeit*
(inwardness) from the forces of one-dimensionality (see Marcuse 1968d,
107–10; 1978, 38–39). What had changed in his perspective was the medium through which to restore critical inwardness. In the 1930s he and
his Frankfurt colleagues attempted to register the truth about the demise of interiority through a direct discourse of theory; in the late 1970s
Marcuse despairs of didactically intoning the name of domination as a
spur to counterhegemonic action but instead tries to evoke its sinister
reality through illusion (*Schein*), a theme I pursue in chapter 12. According to him, art is still autonomous and can reconstitute reality beyond
the media of everyday communication, which are necessarily banalizing
and affirmative. Like Adorno, Marcuse suggests that critical theory may
itself become a metalanguage that is more evocative than the straightforward analytic theory of Marx (although there are differences between
Marcuse and Adorno that I shall explore below).

Marcuse here rejoins his discussion of the "aesthetic ethos" in *An
Essay on Liberation* (1969, 31–32), addressed in the previous chapter. But
where in 1969 he suggested that the new sensibility of the New Left was
already an incipient positive force for social reconstruction, in the late
1970s he feels that this sensibility itself is under siege. Indeed, the spontaneity of the New Left may well have been its undoing, as he argued in
*Counterrevolution and Revolt* (Marcuse 1972, 29–36). By attempting to

erase the distinctions between art and reality and between theory and action, New Leftists did not protect their own irreducible interiority. The forces of one-dimensionality could thus integrate the counterrevolution—neoconservatism, the ruling ideology of Reagan's and Bush's America—and make it its own.

An autonomous art only superficially appears to abandon politics; actually art is most political where it provokes in us memory and dreams that liberate us from the flattened horizon of one-dimensional perception. In this sense art is vitally antipositivist for it suggests that things are not what they appear to be but possess hidden dialectical motion. Marcuse explicitly suggests that art as a form of dialectical imagination in this way has political content and is not merely spiritual or emotive. The second dimension can thus affect the first dimension as artistic autonomy issues in direct political sensibility. Here Marcuse, in the midst of political pessimism, rejoins the dialectic of individual and class (see chap. 6 above; also see Agger 1979, 230–37). His criticism of early affirmative culture was that it remained separate from political economy and the material base (1968d, 95–101). Marcuse indicts socialist realism because it subordinates art, ideology, and consciousness to the first dimension of material reproduction. Bourgeois culture, in the opposite way, keeps art on lofty heights and denies its contact with material reproduction. Marcuse suggests that both are false: artistic illusion can prepare the way for the fusion, through concerted revolutionary practice, of the first and second dimensions. Art begins on the level of mere consciousness in order, one day, to subvert the very distinction between consciousness and practice. Art will be mere art only when socialism has been brought into being, and "permanent aesthetic subversion" can be relaxed as art becomes a way of dealing with our individuated mortality, itself a vital humanizing aim of a non-authoritarian socialist ontology. While every social order requires art as perpetual witness to the inexorable tension between Eros and Thanatos, only corrupted social orders need art to remain autonomous as a way of preserving the memory and dream of political liberation.

## The Force of Transcendent Illusion

Marcuse alone among the Frankfurt theorists had patience for the stoned sensibility of the counterculture inasmuch as he felt it augured a rupture in the continuum of repressive experience that keeps dialectical imagination in check. But the new sensibility of the 1960s was not sufficiently dialectical and did not achieve those mediations between thought and sensibility that open onto the plateau of social reconstruction. Instead the drug high is an end in itself, the triumph of immediacy over mediacy—momentarily liberating but not able to sustain itself, via nonrepressive sublimation, in new institutions constructed with purpose and plan.

Art partakes of Brecht's estrangement effect by using materials at hand. It is of this world but also above it; it evokes the given in new and liberating ways.

> The encounter with the fictitious world restructures consciousness and gives sensual representation to a counter-societal experience. The aesthetic sublimation thus liberates and validates childhood and adult dreams of happiness and sorrow. [Marcuse 1978, 44]

Art is both celebration and mourning, comedy and tragedy; either way it can liberate the imagination so that it is able to distinguish between what is "surplus" and what is "basic" in the human condition. Surplus is needless suffering, tyranny, injustice, and domination. Basic is our mortality, existential aloneness, lovers' quarrels, and brokenheartedness, along with the *promesse de bonheur* of true socialism (see Schaff 1970). Great art does not make tragedy a timeless universal but sets up the profound counterpoint between happiness and tragedy, joy being the penumbra around the gray cloud of death and finitude. Marcuse clearly believes that socialism will not efface all human suffering but only that suffering produced by a repressive reality principle in the service of private interests (see Marcuse 1955, 211–16; Horowitz 1977).

Art for Marcuse works through illusion (*Schein*) that affords us greater realism than is offered in ordinary experience shackled by the constraints of positivism. Art is a mode of cognition alternative to positivism in that it deals with images, symbols, and shadows and not simply unmediated experience that refers directly to given objects in the world and the ideological claims made about them. Art aims at a subversion of experience that restores inwardness, sensibility, and imagination: "rebirth of the rebellious subjectivity" (Marcuse 1978, 6–7). Marcuse characterizes the process of aesthetic presentation as sublimation, where ordinary experiences and data are stylized in accord with the inner requirements of the form itself. Thus ordinary content is presented in an extraordinary way, shattering our preconceptions and clearing our perception of tired habits and the gravitational pull of the quotidian. We see behind the given appearances with the help of the artistic sublimation; we see death where it haunts life and joy where it holds out against unhappiness. All is not rosy in the work of art, of course; as I just noted, artistic consciousness helps us to distinguish between what is essential and superfluous in the human condition.

Artistic illusion calls up a deeper cosmos than we can experience in everyday life, especially under advanced capitalism. The rhythms of nature, as of life itself, are evoked in their majesty and sorrow; all things pass, and yet with that passage comes the renewal of hope. Marcuse is not a sloppy sentimentalist whose critical theorizing has grown senile. Rather he is more concerned than ever to rescue the experience of hope and sorrow from the banalities of popular culture. Writing in the late 1970s, Marcuse is aware that artificial negativity (see Piccone 1978, 53–54), carefully cultivated by the system in order to provide itself with pockets of creative subjectivity, takes the form of life-style, becoming a fetish of immediate experience, personal authenticity, and interpersonal sincerity. Of course, the "jargon of authenticity," as Adorno (1973a) scornfully referred to Heidegger's existenz philosophy (which easily became a justification of fascism), buttresses a totally administered society. The estranging experiences communicated in a great work of art are obliterated under the tyranny of popular thinking; life-style in modernity requires that people not subject themselves to the alarming truths of Schoenberg or Kafka lest their "personal growth" be disrupted. All of this cultural baggage is dismissed as an archaic remnant of early bourgeois society when the first and second dimensions were still to some extent distinct. Life-style has no patience for the estranging lessons of art because it is concerned with self and not with the world in which self is historically anchored. In a totally administered society, the preponderance of the object ultimately forces the subject to make a fetish of its own needs—really, its wants—and to dismiss the public sphere and indeed the entire objective world as irrelevant.

The culture of narcissism (Lasch 1979) perfects a bland positivism and has no use for illusion; the requirements of authenticity cancel the dialectical echoes of the double entendre, irony, and subtlety. Narcissistic personalities speak in the transparent chatter of gossip, which is the opposite of aesthetic illusion: the soul of the world is bared under the trivializing eye of the couch potato, fad follower, and voyeur of the lives of the powerful. The narcissist accepts at face value whatever is given and relates it to his or her own impoverished experience. The foreign, the unordinary, is dismissed with the lament, "I can't deal with it." The subject acquiesces to the object precisely in order to experience the certainty of "common sense" that is a comfort in a world gone mad. Perpetual uncertainty becomes itself a type of certainty; total administration administers everyone equally and, as Horkheimer and Adorno noted in *Dialectic of Enlightenment* (1972, 12–13), enlightenment is democratic for everything is demystified equally.

Marcuse's aesthetic theory is a challenge to this postmodern jargon of authenticity translated into life-style as well as socialist realism. He opposes the realism of Verstand with the idealism of transcendent knowledge and critique. He questions the possible grounds of human existence and the modalities of freedom. This is not an invalid questioning for, as Marcuse notes, art works with the given materials at hand—colors, words, sound. In the dialectic of form and content is contained the dialectic of the possible and the real.

> In its very elements (word, color, tone) art depends on the transmitted cultural material; art shares it with the existing society. And no matter how much art overturns the ordinary meanings of words and images, the transfiguration is still that of a given material. This is the case even when the words are broken, when new ones are invented—otherwise all communication would be severed. This limitation of aesthetic autonomy is the condition under which art can become a social factor. In this sense art is inevitably part of that which is and only as part of that which is does it speak against that which is. This contradiction is preserved and resolved (*aufgehoben*) in the aesthetic form which gives the familiar content and the familiar experience the power of estrangement—and which leads to the emergence of a new consciousness and a new perception. [Marcuse 1978, 41]

Only by being of this world can art indict it and at the same time reveal the promise of an undistorted order where beauty and tragedy, Eros and Thanatos, are in harmony. Art is not pure idealism but, in Merleau-Ponty's phrase, dialectical idealism; it uses given expressive material to point out its latent potential. And the vehicle of its critical capacity, in this Kantian sense, is its power of illusion.

> The indictment does not exhaust itself in the recognition of evil; art is also the promise of liberation. This promise, too, is a quality of aesthetic form, or more precisely, of the beautiful as a quality of aesthetic form. The promise is wrested from established reality. It invokes an image of the end of power, the ap-

pearance (*Schein*) of freedom. But only the appearance; clearly,
the fulfillment of this promise is not within the domain of art.
[Marcuse 1978, 41]

Marcuse opposes an anti-art that entirely erases the distinction
between form and content as well as between art and reality. Art cannot
become reality precisely because it is sublimated activity, channeling
available expressive material into an oeuvre. Art is vital precisely where it
preserves its autonomy and rises above the suctionlike forces of the one-
dimensional; anti-art would cancel this autonomy and would require art
to do battle with politics for its very survival. As Marcuse noted in *An
Essay on Liberation,* poetry never wins its contest with politics; thus, he
suggests that art can be most political precisely where it rises above the
fray (see Marcuse 1969, 40–41). This argument resembles his discussion
of psychoanalysis (1955), where he suggested that libido must always be
repressed and sublimated in order to enter the world as socially useful
activity (see 190–202). An unsublimated art would lose its aesthetic appeal as illusion and, like unmediated desire, would fail to inhibit its aims.
The lack of aim inhibition in art results in the dissolution of form and the
unmediated merging of artistic content with the "real" world. Art must
sublimate itself in order to achieve an epistemological status in reality
that prevents it from being swallowed up in the maelstrom of a positivist
culture that has no use for illusion or indirection. This sublimation, as
Marcuse recognizes, is very threatening to the dominant order precisely
because it maintains a high standard of maturity, autonomy, and rationality. An art that attempts to erase the boundaries between itself and
reality descends to infantilism, just like those who practice promiscuous
sexuality as a way out of bourgeois asceticism.

Marcuse here addresses the erotic character of art against those
orthodox Marxists who "sharply reject the idea of the Beautiful, the central category of 'bourgeois' aesthetics" (1978, 62). Marcuse argues:

> Appertaining to the domain of Eros, the Beautiful repre-
> sents the pleasure principle. Thus, it rebels against the prevail-
> ing reality principle of domination. The work of art speaks the
> liberating language, invokes the liberating images of the subor-
> dination of death and destruction to the will to live. This is the
> emancipatory element in aesthetic affirmation. [62–63]

Art objectifies the life instincts, which through their sensuous representation take the form of the beautiful. Marcuse is not suggesting that ugli-

ness as such will please us but that the internal necessity of a work like Picasso's *Guernica,* depicting Fascist forces' dive bombers killing peasants, allows the oeuvre as a whole to rise above the reductionist forces of one-dimensional consciousness. Brecht agonized over the proper political role of the artist; he wrote a poem about how only the horrors of politics and not the sensation of natural beauty moved him to his desk to write in protest. But Brecht's message is itself poetic, as is Picasso's in *Guernica.* Some of the most moving evocations of humanity struggling against fascism came from children in concentration camps; these were among the most powerful protests against the total horror of genocide because they challenged the grim imagery and reality of the camps with an alternative imagery of joy—the *promesse de bonheur* fascism could not entirely stifle. Art need not have a superficial beauty to partake of Eros and, in this sense, to remind the living that they are still alive and have much to live for.

Indeed beauty and tragedy merge in the artistic vision; is the inevitability of death any less beautiful than the inevitability of life and hope? In this sense, Marcuse presents not only an ideology critique of late capitalist domination, the explicit theme of his work since the early 1930s, but also a philosophy of socialist existence that is designed to be timeless. Art in this way fulfills a second important function: it reconciles us to our own mortality, defusing revolutionary arrogance, and prevents the inevitability of death from canceling liberating projects in the present. In this regard, art as ideology critique promises a politics of nonidentity, the basis of a socialist ontology.

## An Art and Politics of Nonidentity

In chapter 7 I addressed Marcuse's speculations about the interrelationship of life instinct and death instinct. His final book completes his view of the relationship of mortality to Marxism, this time in the explicit context of art.

> The institutions of a socialist society, even in their most democratic form, could never resolve all the conflicts between the universal and the particular, between human beings and nature, between individual and individual. Socialism does not and cannot liberate Eros from Thanatos. Here is the limit which drives the revolution beyond any accomplished stage of freedom: it is the struggle for the impossible, against the un-

conquerable whose domain can perhaps nevertheless be reduced. [1978, 71–72]

Death is the unconquerable. It is easy to see that this issue of the inevitability of death must have preoccupied Marcuse when, in the late 1970s,
he composed his final book. Here he takes his greatest risk in the composition of his critical theory: Whereas even the most obdurate of Marxists
can "forgive" his Freudianism, few have any patience for what seem to
be maudlin reflections in existentialism. What on earth does the dialectic
of particularity and universality, our mortality and the infinity of time
and the universe, have to do with revolutionary struggle? In the last sections of *The Aesthetic Dimension,* Marcuse confronts this problem directly,
sketching the outline of a socialist ontology based on nonidentity.

The need for such an ontology is in both the present and the future. Unless Marxism is made mortal it will retain a self-defeating arrogance, supposing that radical politics will resolve all dilemmas, solve all
problems. Such a prospect will not only prove to be impossible in an as-
yet-unseen socialist future; it dangerously distorts the struggle for that
order in the present.

> The universality of art cannot be grounded in the world and
> world outlook of a particular class, for art envisions a concrete
> universal, humanity, . . . which no particular class can incorpo-
> rate, not even the proletariat, Marx's "universal class." The in-
> exorable entanglement of joy and sorrow, celebration and
> despair, Eros and Thanatos cannot be dissolved into problems
> of class struggle. History is also grounded in nature. And
> Marxist theory has the least justification to ignore the metabo-
> lism between the human being and nature, and to denounce
> the insistence of this natural soil of society as an aggressive
> ideological conception. [Marcuse 1978, 16]

This interaction between humanity and nature takes place within each of
us, in the clash of mind and body, life and death instincts. Marcuse here
offers a deep meditation on the relation between human and nonhuman
nature. These reflections are remarkably similar to those of the late Mau-
rice Merleau-Ponty, who wedded existential phenomenological and
Marxian concerns in his unique synthesis, itself in perpetual dialogue
with the existential Marxism of Sartre. Merleau-Ponty (1964), like Marcuse, sought that interaction between reason and desire that is the riddle
of existence and cannot be surpassed by any understanding (see O'Neill

1974, 78–79). I read Marcuse together with Merleau-Ponty as authors of a mortal Marxism that takes as its resource the contingency of human existence. The dialectic of desire and despair will outlast every ideology. And Merleau-Ponty, like Marcuse, lived under the cloud of Stalinism, which muted forever his optimism about social transformation. But like Marcuse, Merleau-Ponty did not lose all hope. The fact of death does not refute the possibility of "final liberation"—at least from the constraints of domination, if not of mortality.

Art is thus a sign system through which we come to grips with our own stake in social movements. As mature adults we are not self-sacrificing without regard for our own happiness; and yet our happiness cannot be sought without reference to the terrible suffering of others. In the last pages of his 1978 book, Marcuse again evokes the memory of those who have already died and cannot be redeemed, except in memory.

> Art declares its *caveat* to the thesis according to which the time has come to change the world. While art bears witness to the necessity of liberation, it also testifies to its limits. What has been done cannot be undone; what has passed cannot be recaptured. History is guilt but not redemption. Eros and Thanatos are lovers as well as adversaries. Destructive energy may be brought into the service of life to an ever higher degree—Eros itself lives under the sign of finitude, of pain. The "eternity of joy" constitutes itself through the death of individuals. For them, this eternity is an abstract universal. And, perhaps, the eternity does not last very long. The world was not made for the sake of the human being and it has not become more human. [68–69]

In suggesting that the world is not our creation (although as passengers we can leave our mark, if not indelibly) Marcuse, like Derrideans later on, opposes all idealisms that put the subject at the center and thus commit the sin of pride. Instead, we can find ourselves only in the interaction between subjective constitution and what is objectively given (the world, desire, the body). It is through our body that we become truly human, mastering the world and making it our own. We cannot change everything, only particular things like the organization of production and reproduction and the distribution of wealth and power. We cannot change the subject matter of philosophy, poetry, and painting—the relation between our mortality and the universality of the world and cosmos. By suggesting falsely that we can transform all things—the Hegelian end of history—we invest struggle with a dangerous arrogance.

Here Marcuse's thought is carefully post-Hegelian. He individuates the concept of reason to divest it of its encompassing overtones; the whole is neither the false nor the true: neither Adorno nor Hegel was correct, the one in despair and the other in faith. Marcuse endorses the principle of nonidentity according to which we can never undo the connection between ourselves and the world, the particular and general, Eros and Thanatos. Philosophies of identity end either in utopianism or tyranny, where the subject vainly tries to rise above the distorted reality in pure contemplation—the *theoria* of the Greeks—or to impose one's own authoritarian solutions on it. In this sense Marcuse did not retain Lukács's Marxian version of Hegel's concept of totality—the identical subject-object of world history, the collective subjectivity of the proletariat—but created a Marxism of nonidentity that related individual and group dialectically, denying the possibility of a final synthesis. Marcuse's Marxism in this way is rooted in mortality and mediation.

Art is to capture this ontology of nonidentity through its creative sublimation of reality. Where political theory soars above the details of the particular in making a case for the possibility of a new universality—social freedom, in Marx's sense—art descends to the particular in setting up counterpoints between the given and the possible. Theory asserts, where art evokes, a distinction I challenge deconstructively from within a version of Marcusean critical theory in chapter 12. Both Adorno and Marcuse in their later work embrace this attitude of nonidentity that attempts to probe the nature of the universal through a deciphering and representation of the particular; they differ, however, in that Adorno attempts directly through theoretical language to achieve the evocative echo of art, while Marcuse feels that theory must remain discursive. This explains their differences of cultural sensibility (see chap. 12 below). Adorno thought the most radicalizing art immanently exploded the dialectic of form and content, as in Beckett and Schoenberg, while Marcuse could embrace the great bourgeois art of Beethoven as well as the carnal rock of the Rolling Stones. Adorno's (1973b) *Negative Dialectics* is incomprehensible without references to his (1984) attempt in *Aesthetic Theory* to make theory speak a discourse of nonidentity.

Adorno in his postwar pessimism had no theory of the political, no positive image of mediations between art and politics (see Buck-Morss 1977). Marcuse, in contrast, attempted to theorize positively about the "new sensibility," his central conceptual contribution to neo-Marxism. Whereas Marcuse remained disappointed about the ensuing lack of practical mediations between the new sensibility of the late 1960s and a possible new council communism in the post-1960s, he gives us crucial hints in his last book of how nonidentity could be developed into a veritable principle of political praxis. This counters his own aesthetic-political pessimism to some extent. The struggle to humanize our existence never ends; the very principle of nonidentity suggests that synthesis and solutions must be continually renewed. There are no guarantees of perpetual peace, although certainly, as a Marxist, Marcuse knows that things can be greatly improved. But he acknowledges that the liberation of imagination may not lead to Nirvana. Instead, the imagination, once freed from the fetters of the reality principle, may become melancholic, sad with wisdom. The moments of play and joy will be set against a darker background of life and death, of historical guilt and unrequited love. Socialism, after all, will only make us truly human—not superhuman. As a Freudian, Marcuse recognizes that our turbulent and volcanic desires must be mastered, painfully and haltingly, before we are fit to associate with our fellow human beings.

His argument about the function of art is sometimes read one-dimensionally to imply that art's only utility ought to be in the political here and now. But Marcuse also argues that art retrieves an essential aspect of the human condition, our particularity and mortality, and uses this as a revolutionary resource. Here he differs from those existentialists who infer that the awareness of our mortality means that to struggle in the short run is useless. It is rather because of our all-too-human mortality and individuality that we must effect radical social change, allowing our true humanity to emerge. Again, whether "repression" in a genuinely different society will still be repressive is an open question, answerable only in practice and through experiment (see chap. 14). Our humanness cannot be grasped in what Marx called "pre-history"; it will emerge only in the interaction of history and nature, subject and object.

Marcuse's Marxism is often dismissed for its apolitical overtones; the reduction of liberation to personal choice would seem to imply an optimism and idealism about social change unwarranted by historical circumstances. But Marcuse never forgets that liberation, which indeed must begin with a choice, can never compensate for past suffering, nor can it eliminate all future anxieties and social conflicts. He issues a necessary corrective to an unbalanced reading of his work as idealism:

> Art fights reification by making the petrified world speak,
> sing, perhaps dance. Forgetting past suffering and past joy alleviates life under a repressive reality principle. In contrast, remembrance spurs the drive for the conquest of suffering and the permanence of joy. But the force of remembrance is frus-

> trated: joy itself is overshadowed by pain. Inexorably so? The
> horizon of history is still open. If the remembrance of things
> past would become a motive power in the struggle for chang-
> ing the world, the struggle would be waged for a revolution
> hitherto suppressed in the previous historical revolutions.
> [1978, 73]

It is too easy to dismiss Marcuse's aesthetic theory as utopian; passages like this remind us that the liberating force of remembrance, culled from Freud's psychoanalysis, contains a retrospection on the tragedy that is by now millennial in its duration. That we can avoid this human tragedy in future social orders (if not the elemental tragedy of life and death) should not undo our memory of it. Revolutionary humility is bestowed on those who in their present struggle recognize that they have come only lately to the emancipatory task; the slave revolts are no different from the revolt of the moderns. Like Jacoby (1975b), Marcuse cautions against amnesia on the Left, suggesting that reconstruction can never fully redeem those who perished anonymously.

Art thus serves to particularize suffering by giving it a shape and a name. Not all art evokes joy or beauty. But even the remembrance of ugliness can be beautiful, joyful, transcending both the beautiful and the ugly (see Diamond 1987); it evokes the hopes of those who had hoped in vain. Remembrance restores the brutality of the past and shows how it made way for the society of the present; it no longer allows us to live in benign neglect of the anonymous martyrs of the past. It creates what one commentator has called "anamnestic solidarity," reminding us that we are by no means the first to invoke the names of liberation and justice (see Lenhardt 1975).

Indeed I suggest that much of Marcuse's effort to develop an aesthetic theory responds to the arrogance of orthodox Marxists who forget the past in the spirit of naive progressivism and who reduce conscious-ness to a mere reflex of the iron law of socialist development. This arro-gance leads to both vanguard tyranny and fatalism. Marcuse's writings on art can be read as a direct counterpoint to the growth of Marxian scientism, exemplified in the passionless structuralism of Althusser (1969; Althusser and Balibar 1970). The revolution is not guaranteed in the concepts we use to analyze capitalism, as the Frankfurt critique of science has reminded us often (see chap. 11). Scientism becomes an ide-ology in both capitalist and socialist spheres (see Habermas 1970b). Left scientism legitimizes the tyranny of an ideologically "correct" minority and cancels the need for subjective liberation.

Marcuse did not intend to say in the 1978 book that the newly sensible of the future must be artists by profession; they need only be alive to the nonidentity of individual and group, Eros and Thanatos, particular and general interest. Only if the new sensibility keeps nonidentity in mind can it avoid the false totality of authoritarian socialism and a utopianism that degenerates into tyranny. Art for Marcuse is merely one of the vehicles for keeping this guiding perception of nonidentity alive; it sublimates present reality in order to show the possibility of a future in which individual and group can be in harmony, although not identical. Art in this sense promotes a social setting in which the truly human— tragedy as well as beauty—can gain lucid outline. Marcuse's last speculations about the radical role of art help him create a Marxism based on nonidentity that is responsive to the contingencies of life and revolution as well as to their promises. The resource of mortal Marxism is at once its limitation: Eros promises liberation, but it also remains mortal, libidinal, and it cannot be eradicated. Marcuse in all his work has sketched a grounded rationality that is not Promethean precisely because it dwells within the interaction between history and nature. After all, history is situated in nature and must return to it. The ineluctability and ineradicability of desire ensure political humility and millennial hope. Thus Marcuse's Marxism is captured in the final phrases of his aesthetic theory and is not overcome, as so many commentators contend, in his evident political pessimism.

It is erroneous to read Marcuse as having moved from early optimism to mature pessimism; he has always been skeptical about the possibilities of liberation. By avoiding both cynicism and utopianism, however, Marcuse's skepticism has been suitably constrained in face of the massive task of social reconstruction. His Marxism is mortal precisely because it does not attempt heroically to end history. Marcuse knows that our mastery of inner and outer nature is always painful (although how painful is a question that can be answered only when "surplus" restraints have been removed); on the other hand, Marcuse knows that the deformations of domination penetrate deep into desire and are not merely manifestations of remediable economic exploitation. Both of these realizations distance him from orthodox Marxists who reduce domination to purely economic issues and fail to recognize its subjective manifestations and the subjective and intersubjective struggle required to overcome it. Just here, Marcuse's mortal Marxism takes on its finished form.

He reminds us that the class struggle cannot be conducted without coming to grips with, and attempting to reverse, the deformations of

subjectivity that occlude consciousness today. He contends that the mechanical repetition of Marx's objective categories does not do justice to
his dialectical method, which continually reassesses the modalities and
depths of domination. The objective character of subjectivity in late capitalism cannot be ignored simply because Marxists refuse to revise literal
Marx. Indeed a Marxist political economy today must necessarily grapple with the political economy of desire, the deep penetration of formerly objective institutional forces into the substratum of the
individual—into need, morality, psyche. His aesthetic theory confronts
the nearly total absorption of desire into political economy; although art
is not adequate politics, it is minimally political, prefiguring viable
counterinstitutions grounded in a rationality of gratification.

Art opens the way for change of consciousness and self-liberation.
While critics dismiss this prepolitical moment of liberation, Marcuse remained convinced that the class struggle would be fought on the battleground of inwardness. Without preserving bourgeois inwardness, social
movements stagnate, as early twentieth-century Marxists like Lukács and
Korsch quickly learned. A critic of Marcuse avers:

> The proposal of the principle of a "definite choice," the
> "great refusal," has a quasi-accidental and arbitrary quality. It
> is a decision. By limiting the focus to the here and now, this
> once again brackets out from his critical theory of society the
> problem of historical continuity; the standpoint of the existen-
> tialist "choice" is reproduced anew. Ironically, this position has
> a curious affinity to that which he sharply criticized in the same
> essay of 1934. His theory of a definite choice—which presup-
> poses the total negation of the prevailing order—stands in
> striking parallel to the repressive tendencies of "decisionism"
> which in 1934 he had not hesitated to describe as fascist. [Con-
> nerton 1980, 89–90]

But Marcuse contends that self-liberation is a choice that people can
make rationally only when they have been liberated from the tyranny of
the one-dimensional; yet liberation dialectically presupposes reason.
This liberation comes as a result of both education and self-education.
And one of the prods to self-education is the development of an aesthetic sensibility that peers behind and beyond the appearances of late
bourgeois society and searches for dialectical essence—the possibilities
of a free world.

Critics like Connerton, quoted directly above and discussed in chapter 2, indict Marcuse for reducing politics to existentialist choice; in the same vein, they dismiss Marcuse's preoccupation with art and its emancipatory desire. But Marcuse is interested in instinct and the aesthetic only as they have an objective dimension, opening from interiority to the external world. After all, his early criticism of the affirmative culture of German idealism was that it locked its truths inside contemplation and ignored the possible synthesis of materialism and idealism in "sensibility." Marcuse's critics do not understand what he means by the objectivity of subjectivity; they mistake it for subjective idealism when in fact it is dialectical, indeed more dialectical than the crude reductionism that reduces consciousness to a mere epiphenomenon of the material base.

What I call the art and politics of nonidentity is the guiding principle of Marcuse's search for a materialist concept of reason. Art evokes and hence preserves nonidentity, preserving the tension between itself and reality, between subject and object, and between particular and general. Marcuse's thought is profound, I contend, because he could accept what Merleau-Ponty (1964) called ambiguity. Our embeddedness in nature, our biological inheritances and constitutions, did not daunt Marcuse but instead challenged him to conceive new forms of subjective revolt and resistance adequate to the task of overthrowing the one-dimensional. Art evokes a liberating nonidentity in its sublimation of a reality with no apparent exit.

# 10

# Work and Authority in Marcuse and Habermas

## Overcoming the Work-Play Distinction

Having discussed Marcuse's view of art and aesthetic politics, I now turn to a further discussion of his views of work (in this chapter) and science (in the next chapter), the remaining components of his wide-ranging critical theory, which both retains and reformulates central Marxist assumptions about social change. His 1969 book, *An Essay on Liberation,* goes considerably beyond Marx's traditional bifurcation of work and play, necessity and freedom, toward a unified nondualist theory of productive human activity. This attempt has provoked recent critical theorists like Habermas to confront the issue of a Marxist theory of work and authority. My thesis is that Marcuse has frequently been misunderstood by both left and right critics who reject his work as a naive romantic glorification of a totally unrepressed social order, without civilizing decency or a collectivizing concept of authority and organization.

In chapters 6–9, I read Marcuse as a responsible Freudian who does not abandon repression and sublimation necessary for the successful individuation of every human being, but only surplus repression found in societies based on domination. Here, I explore Marcuse's views on work and authority, in counterpoint to Habermas's, to the end of

grasping certain fundamental issues of Marxian political and social theory—notably, the problem of rational authority and democracy. It is my
premise that a humane Marxism is contingent on optimally non-authoritarian forms of work organization and the transformation of work itself.
In this regard, my reading of Marcuse is rooted in the reappropriation of
early Marx's theory of self-humanizing praxis; my argument is that it is
imperative to preserve and broaden Marx's notion, embodied in the
1844 manuscripts, that work can conceivably become a form of social
freedom. In the next chapter, I extend this argument to science and
technology.

As I have indicated, Marcuse has built on Marx's early theory of
praxis and attempted to go beyond it by suggesting that Marx was insufficiently radical in his conception of the emancipation of labor. In *An Essay on Liberation*, Marcuse argues that Marx (especially the "later" one)
was not radical enough in his projections of the creative, even erotic,
character of humanized work under socialism:

> The early Marxian example of the free individuals alternat-
> ing between hunting, fishing, criticizing, and so on had a
> joking-ironical sound from the beginning, indicative of the im-
> possibility of anticipating the ways in which liberated human
> beings would use their freedom. However, the embarrassingly
> ridiculous sound may also indicate the degree to which this vi-
> sion has become obsolete and pertains to a stage of the devel-
> opment of the productive forces which has been surpassed.
> The later Marxian concept implies the continued separation
> between the realm of necessity and the realm of freedom, be-
> tween labor and leisure—not only in time but also in such a
> manner that the same subject lives a different life in the two
> realms. According to this Marxian conception, the realm of ne-
> cessity would continue under socialism to such an extent that
> real human freedom would prevail only outside the entire
> sphere of socially necessary labor. Marx rejects the idea that
> work can ever become play. [1969, 29]

Marcuse searches for a convergence of work and play, but one that does
not abandon the necessary productivity of the working process. Marcuse
is not unaware of the impinging reality of the necessity of human survival
before nature. Productive work must still take place until that magic moment of complete automation and servomechanistic control of the production process—a pipe dream at best, suggests Marcuse (1969), and a
reactionary ideology at worst, used to justify alienation "now" in return

for freedom from work "later," as in Daniel Bell (1973). Marcuse's aim is to salvage early Marx's vision of self-creative, socially useful praxis without appearing needlessly utopian.

Marcuse wants to argue that there can be simultaneously creative and productive work without severe elements of domination and alienation—that human beings, in a nonsurplus repressive social order, need not sacrifice themselves in their work, enjoying themselves (and even then "falsely") only in their time away from the job. At the root of Marcuse's reinterpretation of the Marxian concept of praxis is his vision that work and play could converge in such a way that human beings would be seen to engage in constructive useful work without abandoning their creative individuality.

As I have indicated, much of *An Essay on Liberation*, which is clearly a pivotal text of my version of critical theory, is given over to a discussion of a "new sensibility" in a person who has "developed an instinctual barrier against cruelty, brutality, ugliness" (Marcuse 1969, 30). This new sensibility "is conceivable as a factor of social change only if it enters the social division of labor, the production relations themselves" (1969, 3). Marcuse's point here is that socialists must remake the production process itself, and feminists the reproduction process, in a way that unifies work and play, fulfilling and surpassing Marx's 1844 vision of self-creative praxis.

As I discussed in chapter 7, Marcuse in *Eros and Civilization* argues that the production relations can be transformed under the rule of a "rationality of gratification," that is, through what Marcuse calls the "erotization of labor":

> The problem of work, of socially useful activity, without (repressive) sublimation can now be restated. It emerges as the problem of a change in the character of work by virtue of which the latter would be assimilated to play—the free play of human faculties. [1955, 195]

As indicated in chapter 7, Marcuse sought a psychoanalytic base on which he could argue for the transformation of work and authority. He suggested that the erotization of work would depend on a reactivation of polymorphous eroticism that would infuse work with new creative purposes.

When Marcuse talks about making work playful he is referring to the way in which people approach their work. He is also referring to the way in which work is structured. For him, these are inseparable parts of the same problem. Of course, for most of human history work was a degrading toil in which people would have to spend almost all of their waking hours. Even then work was rarely productive enough to afford most people respite. Not until the Industrial Revolution could anyone— elites—derive enough surplus from work that they could enjoy the realm of leisure. Marx indicated that the enjoyment of this surplus was achieved at the expense of others.

Marx was not entirely clear how the work/play duality could be eased, if not overcome completely. Marx's 1844 manuscripts speak eloquently about the humanization of toil, anchoring his subsequent political-economic critique of capitalism. Marcuse radicalizes Marx's vision in light of substantial technological changes that have occurred since the 1860s, when Marx composed his mature economic theory. For Marcuse, the prospect of an end to toil and the merger of work and play is much more credible. It would require the rational deployment of productive technologies, which would depend in large part on ending the arms race and redistributing wealth from developed to less developed nations.

Marcuse is not saying simply that people would come to "like" their work. Weber, too, wanted people to feel a minimum of workplace alienation. Rather, people would deeply identify themselves with their work and with the communities to which their work made an important contribution. Work would not be simply a life-style, as it is for workaholics on the fast track. It would be a personal poetry expressing one's deepest meanings and values.

The most provocative aspect of this argument is Marcuse's notion that the erotization of labor would require new relations of production and organizational forms within which work could be carried out. He maintains that this does not mean that human beings would act with total abandon, heedless of each other and of the collective imperatives of survival. Rather, a new division of labor and organizational rationality can emerge that fosters erotized nonalienated work. This would be the very basis of a new social structure to replace capitalism and state socialism.

Marcuse does not advocate the abolition of the division of labor or of rational authority; he does not endorse unbridled anarchy. Marx suggested in 1844 that human beings can enjoy social freedom (praxis) without abandoning personal freedoms and liberties and that this social freedom can be at once productive and recreative. Marcuse argues, against liberalism, that the individual is not an island. Marcuse, following early Marx in this regard, argues that the individual can fulfill himself or herself only in community, notably in a dialectic between his or her particular individuality (which must remain ultimately inviolable) and the general collectivity. Thus his solution to the problem of social freedom is to stress that we all inhabit a dialectic of particularity and generality, of self and community, that we cannot abrogate or wish away.

Marcuse is also saying that work and play can converge without abandoning the work character of work itself. He retains the rational organization of work without relinquishing the Marxian goal of creative praxis. As he notes, "hierarchical relationships are not unfree per se." That is, the possibility of liberation depends on the kind of hierarchy that informs the relationships. Marcuse's most vociferous critics have argued that he equates authority and hierarchy with alienation and thus advocates the abolition of all authority and hierarchy. But as we have just seen, Marcuse makes no such equation; he says rather that hierarchy and organization are a necessary feature of all social relationships, both capitalist and socialist. In the first place, Marcuse hints at a theory of work that rests on the merger of productive and creative components. His views in this regard are captured in his vision of the erotization of labor. In the second place, Marcuse suggests a form of organizational rationality that is nondominating. He suggests in *Eros and Civilization* and, fourteen years later, in *An Essay on Liberation,* that social institutions can be organized in such a way that they do not dominate creative individuality. Taken together, these two constitute his theory of work and authority.

Marcuse's theory of work and authority is directly opposed to the Weberian theory of organizational rationality, which dominates bourgeois social theory and mainstream sociology. Weber argued, against Marx, that it was impossible to create nondominated work relationships and furthermore that it was impossible to dispense with bureaucracies to organize and coordinate alienated work. Weber differed with Marx on the question of alienation. He said that a degree of alienation/estrangement from our work, ourselves, our communities, and nature is inevitable in advanced industrial societies and that we should accommodate ourselves to this alienation in pursuit of what he called rationality—the logic of modernity.

Throughout the Western philosophical tradition, the concept of rationality has been taken to mean that human beings, through mental activity, would comprehend the necessity of the external universe and then adjust themselves to the laws and imperatives of that universe. Marxism fundamentally rejected that. Marx said that it was not enough merely to contemplate the order of the universe passively; he argued that people must also change the laws that are seen to govern society at given moments in history. Marx suggested that there are no eternal, time-invariant "laws" of social life. Instead, there are particular structures of social and economic organization that extend through historical time and, as such, can be transformed. Marcuse agrees with Marx that people can change the world and its necessities. In effect, Marcuse, like Marx, challenges the notion that freedom and necessity are fundamentally opposed spheres of existence. Marcuse argues that freedom and necessity are dialectically intertwined; he opposes the view, applied by Weber to his sociological study of industrial capitalism, that human beings can hope to taste freedom only beyond the bureaucratic organization. Specifically, Marcuse argues for a "rationality of gratification" that reconstructs organizations so that work is experienced at once as productive and expressive.

The basis for Marcuse's reinterpretation and deepening of the Marxian critique of Western rationality is his Freudian-inspired theory of work and authority. The traditional view, most masterfully articulated by Weber in the late nineteenth century, maintains that work resides within the realm of necessity, responding to natural scarcity and the human will to win the struggle with external nature. Freedom is thus merely the time left over after work. As I discussed in chapter 7, the most that human beings can hope for is an enlargement of the realm of leisure, based on the further automation of the industrial production process. Marcuse responds to the Weberian theory of rationality in this sense by saying that there can be a rationality of gratification that refuses to fracture freedom and necessity. Marcuse suggests that the work-freedom distinction is peculiar to social orders based on domination. He argues that the creation of an authentically classless society will allow human beings to seek creativity and recreation on the job. (An articulate exposition of Weberian assumptions in this regard is to be found in Berger et al. [1973].)

An important reinterpretation of Marx's views on labor and leisure is in Leiss (1976). Following Marx and Marcuse, Leiss argues that people must be able to seek their satisfaction in creative work as well as in consumption, especially as natural resources gradually run out, forcing a slowing of industrial growth. Leiss contends that "the possibilities of human satisfaction must be rooted in the creation of a well-functioning sphere of shared activity and decision-making within which individuals would forge the means for satisfying their needs" (1976, 105). This sounds remarkably similar to the concepts of creative praxis and nonauthoritarian authority taken from Marcuse's theory of work and authority, which I further develop in this chapter.

Moreover, Leiss and Marcuse argue that this work need not be organized via severely authoritarian bureaucratic forms; it can be organized in such a way that the hierarchy of administration and authoritative decision making does not become a hierarchy of domination and alienation. For example, in a genuinely socialist society, workers together would determine the forms and quantities of their collective labor through the mechanism of workers' self-management. The non-authoritarian organization of labor, to Marcuse, is possible precisely because he believes that freedom and necessity (or leisure and work, in sociological terms) are not categorically divided but potentially dialectically intertwined. This allows him to challenge the Western tradition of rationality rooted in the dualism of mind and body, freedom and necessity, leisure and work, which, he argues, is the hallmark of a social order based on domination. Weber's sociology of work and authority is seen to be merely an ideological reflex of a capitalist order that wants to convince workers (and itself) that there will always be a degree of alienation in the working process and a degree of bureaucratic domination in the organization of that work. Marcuse's thought is fundamentally a critique of the Weberian articulation of Western dualist rationality—the ideology of domination.

Marcuse notes that Marx himself has failed to foresee clearly enough the possibility of a future socialist order in which work and play would become indistinguishable and in which authority could be cooperatively self-imposed without domination. In *An Essay on Liberation,* Marcuse begins by arguing:

> Marx and Engels refrained from developing concrete concepts of the possible forms of freedom in a socialist society; today, such restraint no longer seems justified. The growth of the productive forces suggests possibilities of human liberty very different from, and beyond those envisaged at the earlier stage. Moreover, these real possibilities suggest that the gap which separates a free society from the existing societies would be wider and deeper precisely to the degree to which the repressive power and productivity of the latter shape man and his environment in their image and interest. [1969, 15]

Marx was not utopian enough; he did not fully appreciate how freedom and necessity could merge under an order in which people could express their creativity in their work (social freedom) without being dominated by the organization of that work. Marx did not go as far as Marcuse because he was imbued with the tradition of Western rationality that disregarded the possibility of the erotization of labor and of nonauthoritarian socialist authority. While Marx transcended many of the assumptions of this traditional Western rationality (such as the implicit assumption that society must always be divided between property-owning rulers and propertyless ruled), he remained ensconced within its dualistic assumptions about necessity/freedom, work/play, labor/leisure, which Marcuse tries to transcend. With the help of psychoanalysis, Marcuse shows that we need not choose between body and mind, between desire and reason; we can instead create a rationality that joins reason and desire in a coherent and productive form of human sensibility.

## Habermas's Dualism

What I characterized above as the Weberian position on matters of rationality, work, and authority has curiously reemerged in the recent work (1971) of Habermas, a second-generation member of the Frankfurt school. It is curious that Habermas is read by many as a neo-Marxist; certainly he is a humane critic of technocratic capitalist society. However, Habermas's critique of the grounds of social science knowledge conflicts sharply with Marcuse's theory of work and authority. The contrast between their respective positions may shed further light on the nature of Marcuse's problem as well as on the disparity between full-fleshed Marxian and Weberian positions on work and authority.

Habermas attempts to correct the apparent "mysticism," as he has characterized it, of Marcuse's theory of work and authority. Habermas believes that Marx fundamentally blurs the necessary distinction between work and interaction (including speech), that Habermas (1984, 1987b) believes is at the core of all human action. Habermas submits that it is possible to distinguish between technique and praxis, between the logic of the instrument and that of human communication and interaction. Habermas's position is that there is a categorical difference between the way people work and the way they think and talk. In this sense, he says that there are three kinds of rationality: purposively rational or instrumental, self-reflective, and communicative. He draws a heavy line between the first and second types, arguing that instrumental rationality is incommensurable with self-reflection and speech.

Habermas's critique of Marcuse's mysticism is taken from his *Knowledge and Human Interests.*

> Marx, on the contrary, does not view nature under the category of another subject, but conversely the subject under the category of another nature. Hence, although their unity can

only be brought about by a subject, he does not comprehend it
as an absolute unity. The subject is originally a natural being
instead of nature being originally an aspect of the subject, as in
idealism. Therefore unity, which can only come about through
the activity of a subject, remains in some measure imposed on
nature by the subject. The resurrection of nature cannot be
logically conceived within materialism, no matter how much
the early Marx and the speculative minds in the Marxist tradition (Walter Benjamin, Ernst Bloch, Herbert Marcuse, Theodor W. Adorno) find themselves attracted by this heritage of
mysticism. Nature does not conform to the categories under
which the subject apprehends it in the unresisting way in which
a subject can conform to the understanding of another subject
on the basis of reciprocal recognition under categories that are
binding on both of them. [1971, 32–33]

In a mundane sense, of course, Habermas is not wrong. After all,
our tools and machines do not think or speak (except in the artificial
intelligence and voice of computers). But his is a direct challenge to Marcuse's creative reinterpretation of Marx's theory of praxis. In contrast to
Habermas's essentially Weberian dualism of instrumentality and reflec-
tion/communication, Marcuse would argue that the work we do is never
distinct from the ways we think about and speak about that work: our
work is a reflection of our unified embodied rationality, the unity of reason and desire.

Habermas disputes this equation of work and rationality because
he argues that work is categorically reducible to the logic of the instrument. His position refurbishes Weberian sociology, for Weber also argued that it is possible to separate purposive rationality from substantive
rationality. The former is a rationality of instrumentality, whereas the
latter is a rationality of decision making about the purposes of instruments. Weber did not favor a thoroughgoing preoccupation with instruments; indeed, he criticized capitalists for paying insufficient attention to
the substantive values that guide the choices we make about the uses of
instruments. Habermas swims within the Weberian stream for he argues
that purposive and substantive rationality are different in kind. He sees
the difference here as a dualism and not as a continuum or as a dialectical intertwining of separate but similar entities.

Marcuse, in contrast to Habermas and Weber and beyond Marx,
argues that work and play can converge, although he never abolishes
their dialectical distinction. Marcuse concedes that there is some difference between the way an artist paints a canvas and the way a child finger-

paints (or between building a house and building a dollhouse). The distinction is dialectical and not absolute. Habermas, in contrast, argues that it is possible to distinguish categorically between the ways we work and the ways we think and speak about the work we do. Habermas's position is enlightened and progressive inasmuch as he calls for greater communicative rationality—greater discussion in a democratic context of our collective goals and aims. Habermas's more recent work (1984, 1987b) on a communication theory of social organization urges the development of the "ideal speech situation" in which human beings democratically arrive at consensuses about the purposes of social life. The ideal speech situation is free of interpersonal domination as well as of ideological distortions of discourse.

Thus Habermas sees social change as the result of rational discussion about the purposes of social life, whereas Marcuse sees social change as emerging both from rational discussion and self-reflection and from the transformation of the ways we work on the world. It will be recalled from an earlier citation that Marcuse suggested that the new sensibility must enter the production relations themselves in qualitatively transforming the very character of work. Marcuse, unlike Habermas, believes that we can remake work in such a way that it becomes social freedom, performed in the context of a non-authoritarian organization of cooperative and self-managing workers. Habermas would respond that work cannot be transformed in its very essence, that the only realistic progressive desideratum is to create rational consensuses about the uses of social labor. In this sense Habermas would probably endorse the traditional argument for automation of the production process, contending that authentic freedom lies beyond the realm of "mere" necessity.

Habermas's dualism challenges Marcuse's attempt to synthesize work and play. Habermas dismisses Marcuse as a romantic optimist. In some sense, of course, Marcuse is a romantic: his vision of free work performed in a non-authoritarian social setting suggests that people can have their cake and eat it. But Marcuse does not believe that human beings must limit their freedom to the domain beyond labor; as a Marxist, he believes that the human purpose is to work on nature and to realize our humanity in the projects we undertake. In short, Habermas appears to abandon Marx's 1844 theory of praxis. He rejects Marx's early theory of praxis on the grounds that Marx unjustifiably combined "interaction and work under the label of social practice (Praxis)" (1971, 62). Marx, according to Habermas, confused the way we work *(Arbeit)* and the way we think and talk about the way we work. Marx thus gave rise to the illegitimate conflation of the logics of instrumentality and of self-reflection and speech, which had the ultimate consequence of creating an overly positivist mechanical Marxism in the Second International under the auspices of Engels and Kautsky. Had Marx been clearer about the difference between work and interaction, Habermas says, he would not have given the misleading impression that the socialist revolution would proceed automatically, instrumentally, without the assistance of class consciousness (arrived at, one presumes, through aggregated self-reflection).

Habermas is justified, I contend, in attacking the Marxism of the mainstream theorists of the Second International as mechanical and deterministic. But this is a far cry from saying that the source of determinism is in Marx himself. I argue, against Habermas, that Marx never abrogated the dialectic of consciousness and social being; Marx understood that socialist transformation would never be a matter purely of predetermined social-structural motion without the active intervention of an ideologically awakened working class. I read Marx's concept of praxis as unifying manual and mental activities, combining the logics of the instrument and of self-reflection (in Habermas's terms). Where Habermas sees Marx's concept of praxis as a sloppy confusion of two fundamentally distinctive kinds of rationality, I see (and I believe that Marcuse sees) the concept of praxis as the vital link between doing and being. Thus, social praxis is a unity of intellectual knowledge and conversation about reality and at the same time the movement toward a different reality via social change.

Habermas does not understand what Marx meant by praxis because he belongs to the Western tradition of dualism to which Weber contributed and in a sense summarized. Habermas, however, is closer to Marx than Weber because Habermas shares many of the radical democratic aspirations of the socialist and feminist movements. He opposes the monopoly of power and information under capitalism, and he argues convincingly that one of the best ways to shake that power is to give human beings the capacity to think and talk about their own alienation as a way of provoking critical action. Habermas and Marcuse differ most on the issue of the extent of social change.

## The Splitting of Critical Theory

The Habermas-Marcuse split can be understood as the difference between narrow and extensive radicalism (see Schroyer 1978). Habermas suggests that people can be freed by being encouraged to regain what Weber called substantive rationality, that is, the capacity to think critically about their lives and then to act on those insights via the creation of rational consensus. Marcuse believes that human beings must use intellectual and communicative rationality, to be sure, but he goes further than Habermas in arguing for the transformation of work. Habermas's ideal speech situation is the end point of social change, whereas Marcuse believes that the ideal speech situation is merely one agency of more fundamental kinds of transformation.

Habermas's radicalism is less extensive than that of Marcuse; it is narrower in its scope and its aims. Habermas wants to restore to people the capacity to reason that has been negated by capitalist ideology, which transforms them into passive consumers of dominant political and economic wisdom as well as commodities. Habermas's critique of the effects of an instrumentalist ideology coalesces with those offered by Paulo Freire and Ivan Illich in their critiques of capitalist education and the capitalist professions, respectively. Freire and Illich join Habermas in arguing that citizens have been fatally weakened by a social system that denies them the opportunity to determine their own fate, making them mere receptacles of ideology and commodities. Habermas argues that radical change optimally can return to people the capacity to direct their own lives as well as to create rational agreements about societal purposes. He joins Marcuse in arguing for a self-managing socialist authority rooted in the power of the strongest argument, as he has characterized it. Habermas in this sense has faith that human beings are rational creatures who can live peaceably in community as long as they allow the light of communicative rationality to shine, deferring to those who demonstrate superior competence.

Marcuse and Habermas agree that there can be non-authoritarian rationality and authority, but they disagree about the scope and character of the rationality. Although they share a model of communicative democracy, they differ in their views of work. Marcuse's position is more radical because he argues that the ideal speech situation is merely a tool for transforming the nature of work and for creating a society of praxis. Marcuse would see the ideal speech situation as a way of fostering new types of class and group consciousness, whereas Habermas, who rejects the possibility of qualitatively transforming the nature of work, sees it as an end in itself.

Habermas's growing appeal in North America can be attributed, I contend, to the way in which he salvages radical democracy without endorsing the full Marxian program (which, according to Marcuse, Marx himself never quite endorsed, unable to break with Western mind-body dualism). As I discuss further in chapter 11, Habermas urges the democratization of technology and of politics without advocating the abolition of capitalism. Habermas is a radical liberal who partakes of the Western tradition of dualism, refusing to believe, with Marcuse, that people can engage in unified work-play in the context of a cooperative community of coequal producers. Habermas's person is an initially isolated individual who temporarily enters the ideal speech situation not in order to humanize himself or herself through creative/productive praxis and discourse but merely in order to seek a consensually validated truth that can guide the uses of categorically immutable social labor.

Although Habermas's *Legitimation Crisis* (1975) appears to be a Marxist account of the crisis forms of advanced capitalism, I read it differently—as an account of how advanced capitalism, although beset with crises, can continue to function as long as it finds a new ideology to augment the ideology of just exchange and individual initiative that has evidently crumbled under the weight of state intervention in the capitalist mixed economy. Habermas conveniently says nothing about how new forms of class struggle (or for that matter personal struggle, in Marcuse's sense) can be generated in response to legitimation crisis. Although Habermas is not a strong Marxist, he shares with most Marxists a democratic orientation as well as a belief in non-authoritarian authority and rational consensus. In this sense, Habermas may best be seen not as a right-wing Marxist but as a left-wing Millian.

Marx saw praxis as a socially useful activity that would also humanize the individual by externalizing his or her values and aspirations. Marx's essential challenge to the Western dualist tradition was his claim, in the 1844 manuscripts, that we need not distinguish between the social utility of labor and its intrinsic creativity. This was a revolutionary sentiment for it freed social labor from the strictly circumscribed realm of necessity and paved the way for a theory of rationality rooted in the convergence of necessity and freedom. Marx thus postulated the possible identity of personal self-interest and collective interest. (The Marxian concept of praxis has been examined in all sorts of ways, by many authors, e.g., Sher [1978] on the Yugoslavian intellectual currents that resulted in the realization of their praxis philosophy in their experiments with workers' control and workers' councils. Also see Fromm [1965] and Schaff [1970] for more theoretical and philosophical discussions of the issue of praxis. At the root of all these works is the notion that socially useful work and creativity are not antithetical, as Habermas tends to assume.)

In this sense, Marx was a Rousseauean, positing the possible identity of individual self-interest and "general will." Rousseau could not have been a Marxist, however, because he did not recognize that the root of the individual's self-humanization lay in the socially necessary work that we must all perform in order to survive. Rousseau's theory of the identity of personal and general will was abstract and ungrounded because he ignored the centrality of labor. Habermas too is a Rousseauean. Yet his Rousseauean concept of the ideal speech situation lacks a Marxian twist: Habermas ignores the humanizing potential of socially necessary work. For Habermas, as for the Greeks, the highest good for people is the life of politics, given over to rational consensus formation through what he calls ideal speech. For Marcuse, the highest good is self-humanization through work and not simply rational consensus formation that, in Marxist terms, is merely a way station en route to the mobilization of class consciousness.

Habermas abandons the dynamism of class struggle as the motive force of historical transformation. His ideal speech situation involves two or more individuals but not two or more groups or classes. Marcuse stresses that his new sensibility, arising from the rationality of gratification, is but a mediation on the way toward full class consciousness and activism. At least in the 1960s, and notably in the *Essay on Liberation* (1969), Marcuse preserved Marxism's traditional focus on class struggle while adding a radical subjectivism that could help individuals move beyond their personal alienation toward a more structural appreciation of advanced capitalism. Marcuse's radical subjectivism was always in the service of the mobilization of new, appropriately contemporary types of class radicalism through which to transform the nature of social labor.

Habermas appeals to those who abandon class struggle; instead, he endorses a radical incrementalism based on communicative rationality. The Marxist would ask: How can communicative rationality dent the corporate capitalist power system with "mere words"? A Habermas adherent could respond by saying that communicative rationality, toward the end of consensus formation, is only a way of raising consciousness about evident structural domination. But Habermas explicitly rejects the Marxian-inspired aim of emancipating social labor in Marcuse's sense of fusing work and play or, in Habermas's own terms, of fusing instrumental rationality and self-reflection. It appears that his radical incrementalism could aim at certain piecemeal goals, such as the democratization and economic leveling of the capitalist welfare state, without trying for the full emancipation and transformation of social labor in the sense of dialectically unifying productivity and creativity.

Habermas's argument against the alleged mysticism of Marx's

theory of creative praxis appears to follow from his sober appraisal of the possibility of class radicalism in the 1970s. Habermas is often read as a "sensible" radical. Indeed, as I noted in the preceding chapters, Marcuse retreated from the possibility, announced by him during the late 1960s, of creating mediations between new sensibility and new types of class or group radicalism (e.g., Marcuse 1978). It is interesting to compare Marcuse's and Habermas's varieties of radical pessimism. Habermas's ideal speech situation is designed to be a directly practical alternative to class struggle, a way of achieving rational consensus. Marcuse's retreat to artistic allusion possesses no clear-cut practical directives but is self-consciously meant to be a retreat from collective praxis (without losing sight of its importance). Marcuse is saying that there are no existing mediations between new sensibility, on the individual level, and a collective type of opposition—no way of translating the individual consciousness of unbearable alienation into a class- or group-based political program. Art is not a substitute for class struggle but a reminder that class struggle is absent and a way of keeping alive socialist ideals in the midst of what Marcuse has termed one-dimensionality.

> The common denominator for the misplaced radicalism in the cultural revolution is the anti-intellectualism which it shares with the most reactionary representatives of the Establishment: revolt against Reason—not only against the Reason of capitalism, bourgeois society, and so on, but against Reason per se. [1972, 129]

But Marcuse adds that "with all its misplaced radicalism, the [student-radical] movement is still the most advanced counterforce" (1972, 129).

Habermas responds to the absence of class consciousness with a theory of communicative rationality. Marcuse responds to this absence with a theory of radical art designed to keep alive the promise of effectively mediated personal resistance, able to achieve its final form as socialist praxis. Marcuse's position is starkly realistic, refusing to substitute incrementalism for full radicalism. He does not endorse Habermas's communicative rationality because it is insufficient to the task of abolishing alienation. Better to keep alive the *promesse de bonheur* through artistic expression than to succumb to the clichés of liberal democracy that foster the illusion that calm discussion among coequal speakers will shake the foundations of domination.

## Realizing Marcuse's Theory of Work and Authority

My discussion of Habermas's Weberian-inspired critique of the Marxian theory of praxis, and its creative exposition by Marcuse, has been a necessary digression to situate Marcuse against the backdrop of traditional Western rationality. I now want to return to Marcuse's theory of work and authority and to relate it to historical and contemporary themes in a way that shows its practical significance. Marcuse has been interpreted above as suggesting that socially necessary work can also be seen as a form of social freedom, both creative and self-expressive. Is this to be taken to mean that Marcuse thinks that factory workers can somehow enjoy the monotony of the machine, seduced or narcotized by its rhythms and sounds? Traditional Marxists could take exactly that position, glorifying physical labor whatever its character or content. But Marcuse, as a theorist of praxis, certainly would not accept the stoned reverie of the daydreaming assembly-line attendant as a form of liberation (or, indeed, of class consciousness). Praxis must take other kinds of forms.

A Marcusean example of emancipated praxis that does not lose its "work" component is a group of self-managing carpenters building a house (much like the ones, perhaps, in Tracy Kidder's [1985] *House*). This exemplifies both the nature of unified work-play (social freedom) and the nature of non-authoritarian authority. In the first case, the carpenters engage in socially necessary activity that can also fulfill certain creative and artistic needs. These workers are not compelled to construct prefabricated homes resembling other such homes to be located in a monolithic space; they can inject their personality into their work, approaching that unity of work and creativity that is the essence of praxis. In the second case, the workers work together without having to institutionalize bureaucratic or imperatively coordinated lines of decision making. But the carpenters do not for that reason abandon all forms of hierarchy or authority. More experienced workers instruct inexperienced workers without aggrandizing power. Similarly, the workers can develop a division of labor without the individual's becoming identified with any one role that is then immutably imprinted on the individual's sensibility. Indeed, there can be rotation of functions, thus ensuring that the more odious and demanding chores can be performed by all.

The carpenters are Marcusean workers because they do not view their work as a chore, performed only in return for a wage; nor do they develop a strict authority structure that legitimizes the domination of the many by the few (e.g., of the workers by a foreperson). It seems that the relationship between the creative character of their work and the non-authoritarian character of their self-imposed supervision and division of labor suggests interesting models of socialist freedom. House building is not intrinsically "creative" work; in fact, it is work that many of us would not find existentially and aesthetically fulfilling, either because we do not view carpentry as artwork or because we are so unskilled in the intricacies of carpentry that we would view the work as mere toil (not possessing the skills, for lack of experience, necessary for enjoying the work). The work is self-expressive (social freedom) not so much because it is intrinsically artistic but rather because it is democratically self-managed and nondominating.

Marcuse's theory of work and authority hints at a model of radical workers' control. I contend that work could be experienced as creative praxis because it can be socially organized without domination. Thus, the possibility of nonauthoritarian authority is more crucial than the intrinsic character of the work itself. Marx in 1844 argued for the "free flowering of human individuality," implying that people would choose to do different kinds of things in a free socialist community. In *The German Ideology*, Marx and Engels (1947) proposed the famous archetype of the fisher-hunter-critic, the "all-round individual" who moves easily across roles. I contend that Marx felt that human beings, in their incredible diversity, would each choose different sorts of praxis in a socialist society. What was most important for Marx was the way in which workers relate to each other in the labor process, developing non-authoritarian relations of trust and interdependence. People can enjoy all sorts of praxis as long as that praxis is organized in an optimally democratic fashion, subject to the ultimate rationality of workers' control. (This model has been partially elaborated in many works by Yugoslav philosophers and industrial sociologists. An especially interesting treatment is found in Markovic [1974], where he argues against the bureaucratization of the Yugoslavian system of workers' control.)

The concept of workers' control is as old as the Paris Commune, yet its partial realization is relatively new. In contemporary Yugoslavia, since the early 1950s, workers' self-management, through the mechanism of the workers' council, has been the dominant ordering principle of the industrial production process. Workers' control is the living expression of the kind of authority that Marcuse desires. It is a form of direct democracy in which workers are able to develop relationships of authority and dependence as well as a division of labor without introducing the domination of the unskilled by the skilled. This is a type of organizational rationality that retains leadership and social differentiation without reifying the fluid relationships between leaders and led (for the led can be taught to become leaders).

But workers' control, as factory democracy, is insufficient to transform alienated work into creative and socially useful praxis of the kind that Marcuse desires. Along with workers' control of investment decisions and day-to-day logistics of production, the working process must be transformed so that machines do not dominate people but vice versa. It is conceivable that workers' control could obtain in a highly differentiated assembly-line system (such as a modern automobile factory). But this would not mean that the factory workers are necessarily engaged in creative praxis; alienation in Marx's sense can exist even in a system of workers' control.

What is needed here is an additional notion of the workers' control of the technological apparatus. This sort of control does not refer primarily to democratic decision making about investments, salaries, and daily logistics of production. It refers rather to the idea that workers are able to understand and manipulate the productive apparatus so that it does not dominate and discipline them. The Fordist assembly-line system is alienating primarily because the worker becomes a virtual cog in the machine, performing a narrow, piecemeal productive function, having little control over his or her relationship to technology, and, most important, remaining estranged from the fabrication of the total product. Thus there must also be direct workers' control of the technological apparatus to ensure that workers understand and master the productive means.

Workers' control has two integral components, then: workers' control of decision making regarding investment strategies and day-to-day operations of the plant or office; and workers' control of the technological apparatus such that workers do not become estranged from the productive means and dominated by those who have mastered them. In the West, the move toward workers' control, especially in Germany and Scandinavia, has often lacked the crucial second component. Instead, workers' control in those contexts means more effective participation of workers and unions in co-opting negotiations with government and corporations. The so-called tripartite system in Germany is a reflection of this tendency to truncate workers' control into a watered-down coping mechanism of the capitalist welfare state and big capital.

Real workers' control, in the Marcusean sense, requires workers' democracy in economic decision making. It also requires workers' control of the labor process itself. Marcuse's theory of creative praxis and of self-managing authority seems to suggest that, if workers' control in both senses obtains, then workers will tend to experience their work as creative praxis performed according to a "rationality of gratification," as he called it in the Freud book. Unless workers control the very production process and the technological apparatus that supports it, they will remain alienated from the possibilities of creative praxis.

In this chapter I have argued that Marcuse's notions of the merger of work and play and of the possibility of nondominating organizational rationality and authority fly in the face of the mainstream Weberian tradition that venerates the labor-leisure dualism and the bureaucratic coordination of labor. I have further argued that this Weberian current is reappropriated by Habermas in his work on the epistemological foundations of social science (1971). The contrast between Marcuse and Habermas reveals a split within modern critical theory between radicalism and incrementalism. Marcuse takes the more radical viewpoint, arguing that if work and leisure are dialectically merged and if work is organized democratically through workers' control, then social labor will be experienced, in Marx's early sense, as creative praxis—a type of self-externalizing activity that is both productive and creative. Habermas, in his reformulation of Weberian sociology, endorses an incrementalism that rejects the possibility of transforming labor into praxis, arguing instead for greater communicative democracy as a way of redirecting (what Habermas contends is categorically immutable) social labor toward more constructive ends such as the economic leveling of the capitalist welfare state.

In the next chapter, which concludes this section of my book, I turn to the debate between Marcuse and Habermas on the nature of science and technology. This debate follows from their disagreement about the nature of work and authority in advanced industrial society. As in this chapter, I favor Marcuse's more utopian version of critical theory, although I acknowledge that Habermas's (1984, 1987b) reconstruction of historical materialism is extremely provocative and challenging. Habermas, in his fully developed communication theory of society, raises a variety of very important questions that must be answered by critical theorists who want to take critical theory a stage beyond its original formulation in the 1930s. In this sense, an engagement with Habermas takes us beyond Frankfurt.

# 11

# Marcuse and Habermas on New Science

The meaning of Marx's materialism and the extent of Hegel's influence on his thought have been at the center of controversy among Marxists ever since the original publication in 1923 of Lukács's *History and Class Consciousness* (1971) and Korsch's *Marxism and Philosophy* (1970). The original Frankfurt school theorists, including Marcuse, embraced the Hegelian interpretation of Marxism. The controversy has resurfaced within the Frankfurt school in Habermas's (1971) critique of Marcuse's concept of a "new science and new technology." In this chapter, I contend that Marcuse's position reflects and deepens the thinking of Marx, whereas Habermas's rejection of Marcuse's critique of positivism regresses behind Marxist critical theory.

## Critical Theory's Raison d'Être

Ever since Lenin described cognition as the presuppositionless reflection of an objective reality in his 1908 text *Materialism and Empirio-Criticism*, Marxism has been torn internally by epistemological conflicts. Today, these have resurfaced in the split between Herbert Marcuse and many of his critics. Especially notorious are Marcuse's arguments against positivism and for a "new science" based on an epistemology opposed to Marxism-Leninism's reflection theory of knowledge. Essentially, Marcuse and others from the original Frankfurt school (Max Horkheimer, Theodor W. Adorno, Walter Benjamin, Erich Fromm) have tried to broaden the focus of economism in the belief that Marx's critique of domination was definitely not restricted to purely economic factors. So-called critical theory is an attempt to rehabilitate Marx's complex, non-mechanical analysis of relations between economics and culture. Indeed, Marcuse's attack on positivism is a vital dimension of a dialectical social theory that transcends economism and Marxism-Leninism's naturalism systematized by the philosophical Lenin.

Lenin had not yet read Hegel when he helped create positivist correspondence theory in his 1908 text on the empirio-critics. Lenin's *Philosophical Notebooks* were not to appear until later, and the section on Hegel was written in 1914. The *Philosophical Notebooks,* in spite of appearances to the contrary, do not represent a clean break with the naturalism of Lenin's pre-Hegel writings. "Cognition is the eternal, endless approximation of thought to the world" (Lenin 1961, 195). But Lenin also writes, "man by his practice proves the objective correctness of his ideas, concepts, knowledge, science" (1961, 191). In other words, Lenin flirted with a nonpositivist epistemology inspired by Hegel's destruction of the dualism of noumenon and phenomenon. Yet he could not ultimately shed the crude naturalism of his 1908 text. His *Philosophical Notebooks* have been a source of official Soviet Marxism's canonization of the "dialectical method" and logic, almost a religious formula for determining political sin and beatitude. Had Lenin emerged from *Materialism and Empirio-Criticism* to read Hegel's *Phenomenology of Mind* instead of *Science of Logic,* he might have broken through epistemological naturalism and its conversion into a cosmic principle of Soviet Marxism. Critical theory salvages from Hegel not the concept of a "unity of opposites" and its crystallization as the Absolute Idea in *Science of Logic* but Hegel's earlier argument for a negative rationality, a negative philosophy, in *Phenomenology of Mind.*

Unfortunately for Lenin, he chanced on those of Hegel's insights most easily distorted as a tool of Soviet ideologists—a dialectical logic, designed to reconcile all, perhaps irreconcilable, contradictions. It is in the *Phenomenology of Mind* that correspondence theory is given its death blow in Hegel's unremitting critique of Verstand (naive common sense). In Marx's writing, dialectical thought could work for the elimination of exploitation; indeed, Hegelian Marxism is rooted squarely in the *Phe-*

*nomenology of Mind.* Yet dialectical logic found in the Hegel read by Lenin and in Engels's *Dialectics of Nature* was a conservative formula for justifying reality, merely a dialectic of concepts according to which A and not-A are cosmically identical. It was only a short step from Lenin's paean to Hegel in *Philosophical Notebooks* to the official Dialectical Materialism invoked by Stalin (1940) in his crusades against iconoclastic self-criticism such as that of Trotsky and Bukharin. It is especially surprising that Lenin, who in his political practice was highly sensitive to empirical contexts (eschewing pregiven strategies), could have retrieved the speculative and empirically arbitrary "dialectic of matter" from the ontological Hegel. It was impossible for Lenin's hardheaded pragmatism and empiricism in political matters to have had a moderating effect on Stalin when Stalin could turn to the dialectical method canonized in *Philosophical Notebooks* and, on the strength of its authority, legitimize any political strategy.

Below, I want to examine some of Marcuse's views on science and technology in contrast to Habermas's (1971) critique of Marcuse's (1969) concept of a "new science and new technology," a matter I raised in chapter 8. I reject Habermas's position for its failure to appreciate Marcuse's critique of science. Throughout this chapter, I contend that Marcuse is faithful to Marx in reproducing a complex, nonlinear theory of domination combining economic and cultural factors. In analyzing positivist epistemology as a factor in modern domination, Marcuse does not vitiate the basic Marx but only further develops Marx's analysis of the contextualizing effect of ideology, culture, and consciousness on material social relations.

Thus, Marcuse and the critical theorists are not opportunistic social democrats in their critique of science as a hegemonic form of ideology. I maintain that Marcuse is no more utopian or romantic than Marx when he calls for a new science and technology; indeed, Marxism has been crippled by theorists since Lenin who have entertained a crude correspondence theory of knowledge. Critical theory, emanating from the original Institute for Social Research in Frankfurt, arose out of Lukács's (1971) and Korsch's (1970) 1923 attacks on the neo-Kantianism of Eduard Bernstein and on Lenin's naturalism. Lukács, Korsch, and the Frankfurt theorists argued that official Marxism, represented by the Comintern under Zinoviev's and Lenin's direction, was a counterrevolutionary ideology that merely protected bolshevism's political authority. Critical theory opposed a crude naturalist epistemology, according to which concepts reflect given objects, in attempting to rescue Marx's latent theory of a dialectical, postpositivist cognition—what Marcuse calls new science.

My thesis is that Marcuse extends the original Hegelian-Marxian critique of Bernstein's and Kautsky's neo-Kantianism and Bolshevik naturalism; this in no way renders him antimaterialist. I want to show how the argument for a new science is one of the most timely forms of creative Marxian theory—how, indeed, the critique of positivism advanced by Marcuse is one of the most potent forms of the critique of ideology, the model for which is found in Marx's writings on German idealism and religion. I shall argue that to be a Marxist today one must treat cognition and technology as vitally self-expressive forms of human labor that must be freed from the domination of positivism. In other words, positivism is not legitimate epistemologically for theorists who retain Marx's vision of fundamental human liberation.

One of the issues often raised in current discussions of critical theory is the relation of the Frankfurt theorists to Marx, an issue I touched on in chapter 2. As I indicated there, I believe that Marx was not an economic determinist and that his model of relations between "base" and "superstructure" (economics and culture) orients the work of Marcuse, Horkheimer, and Adorno. Marx's model comprehends the reciprocal influences of ideology and economic structures. In this sense, the Frankfurt critique of positivism, exemplified by Horkheimer and Adorno (1972) and Marcuse (1964), is directed at the social function of positivist common sense in diverting attention from the inhumanity and contradictions of domination. Habermas (1971), however, rejects Marx's model of critical theory, arguing that Marx reduced reflection to labor, robbing reflection of its critical function. He believes that Marx did not provide for the function of consciousness in readying revolutionary agents for political practice—indeed, that Marx reduced consciousness to an epiphenomenon automatically springing from economic relations. I believe that Marx provided analytically for the catalyst of self-reflection through his concept of critique. In this vein, as I argued in chapter 2, Marx was the first critical theorist.

Yet Frankfurt critical theory diverges from Marx's historically specific reading of the potentially revolutionary industrial proletariat. Although critical theory accepts Marx's model of the dialectic between theory and practice, it does not necessarily accept as valid today his reading of the revolutionary potential of the blue-collar class. As I argued in chapters 6–9, Marcuse has explicitly tried to go beyond the industrial proletariat in searching for new transitional agents (e.g., 1969, 49–78). He suggests that the "new sensibility," a prefigurative link between rebellion and the creation of a new socialist order, suggests a *new science,* freed from positivist fact fetishism and a dualist theory of knowledge.

The new science is a mode of thought and imagination that engages in speculation for its own sake, a form of nonalienating work activity. This necessarily clashes with Habermas's (1971) notion that cognition is in principle oriented to the mastery of nature (including both society and the environment), and that only "communication" breaks out of what Weber called "purposive rationality." Habermas is significantly less radical than Marcuse in suggesting that the nature of science cannot change—that science is instrumental reason, not a potentially healthy mode of self-expression—but only the uses to which science is put.

Habermas departs from Marx's analysis of the proletarian revolution and from his model of the dialectic of theory and practice. This is complex because Marcuse himself argues that Marx was not bold enough in foreseeing the psychological and social consequences of destroying the division of labor. Yet in Marx's *Grundrisse* (1973) and *Economic and Philosophic Manuscripts* (1961) there are ample hints about a qualitatively different socialist life. Although Marcuse would probably oppose Habermas's reading of Marx as a determinist, preferring to read Marx as a dialectician, he goes further than Marx in sketching how socialism could emerge from the present "damaged life." It does not matter how we return to Marx; what matters is how we preserve Marx's ideal of ending the division of labor and its separation of manual and mental labor while transcending Marx's focus on the industrial proletariat. Neither Marcuse nor Habermas retains Marx's transitional schema in unaltered form; I submit that Marcuse understands better than Habermas the new requirements of subversive practice, namely, that the development of a "new sensibility," able to resist the proscriptions of one-dimensionality and yet always aware of the possibility of happiness, is the most direct way to combat the division of labor.

Adorno's collection of aphorisms (1974) has as its subtitle "Reflections from Damaged Life." All of the Frankfurt theorists believed that capitalism reproduced itself through the creation of distorted needs that prepare the consumer to conform in consumption. Marx did not explicitly foresee the extent to which commodity production could expand unfettered. Adorno's phrase "damaged life" reflects the condition of the subject who has been thus totally manipulated. The nuances of critical theory emerge from differing responses to the phenomenon of heteronomous personality, as I pursue in chapters 12 and 13. In spite of the vulgar reading of Marcuse as irremediably gloomy and therefore non-Marxian, he actually remains the most optimistic of all the Frankfurt-oriented theorists about the autonomy of the subject and its capacity for resisting the damaged life. As I indicate in the next section of this book, some critical theorists relinquish radical hopes and retreat to abstract negation (Adorno) while others reassess Marx's transitional schema and his concept of class (Marcuse and Habermas).

Regrettably, many younger theorists have become preoccupied with textual analysis and the historiographical reconstruction of Hegelian Marxism. This is not wrong, only insufficient; if carried to extremes, it risks becoming a left-wing version of Scholasticism. Partly because the original Frankfurt theorists, especially Adorno, wrote widely on a vast range of subjects, it is wrongly assumed that they have the "last word" on all contemporary issues. The resulting tendency to eschew empirical social research has prompted the charge that critical theory is merely "philosophic" and untrue to its Marxian beginnings, as I discussed and dismissed in chapter 2 and as I address differently in chapter 13. Just as it was necessary during the 1920s and 1930s to lift the dead hands of Marx and Lenin from Marxism, so today must the dead hands of Adorno and Horkheimer be lifted from critical theory. Damaged life must not become critical theory's sole leitmotif, preventing its engagement with contemporary issues of theory and practice and new social movements.

All aspects of society are perceived by the critical theorists as political. The scientific ethos is grounded in the division of labor because the scientist is cast as an expert, hierarchically above citizens. The adoption of the bourgeois concept of science by Marxists has been disastrous because the role of the expert is self-perpetuating. Marcuse in his concept of new science, in contrast to official Marxism-Leninism, treats everyone as capable of profound cognitive activity and thus opposes Lenin's hypothesis that the proletariat could aspire only to trade unionist consciousness and thus needed something "from without," from experts (who quickly become a political elite). Marcuse challenges the role of the expert more directly than does Habermas, who has an emotional affinity for the role of the technocrat, albeit a reformist one. The new sensibility by its very existence challenges the division of labor that remains the primary source of alienation. Marcuse's (1964) Great Refusal essentially denies hierarchies concealed and congealed in the division of labor. Although Marcuse challenges Marx for having been reluctant to speculate about socialism, he shares with Marx the belief that the capitalist (and, I would add, sexist) division of labor is the cause of alienation.

The influence of this debate on critical theory is to demarcate radical reformism, as Habermas calls it, from a thoroughgoing radicalism, a distinction I raised in the preceding chapter. I believe that Marx was such a radical, as *Economic and Philosophic Manuscripts* (1961) suggests; indeed, Marx envisaged a "natural science of history," assuming that nonhuman nature and human nature are tied together and that freedom frees cognition to explore nature's deepest secrets. I side with the radicalism of Marx and Marcuse because it more effectively challenges the social division of labor predicated on a technocratic hierarchy and professionalism. When people who have been excluded from roles of political, economic, and cultural responsibility learn that they can be new scientists, little stands in the way of their destroying the division of labor and transforming alienated labor into an unfettered mode of interaction with the cosmos—an interaction that Marx called praxis.

## The Critique of Science

The contemporary debate within Marxism on the critique of science largely centers around the recent work of Marcuse. In fact, when Louis Althusser (1969; Althusser and Balibar 1970), Lucio Colletti (1973), and Nicos Poulantzas (1973) charge the Frankfurt theorists with Hegelian romanticism, they usually refer to Marcuse. Marcuse has achieved considerable notoriety since *One-Dimensional Man* for his radical critique of science and technology. Habermas (1970b) has criticized Marcuse's conception of science and technology for its alleged identification of domination and technical rationality. Habermas's position is located between Marcuse's radical hopefulness about creating a new science and, for example, the French Marxist-Leninist Althusser's complete mistrust of the "ideological" critique of science. Habermas believes that we can salvage the instrumental rationality of science (and its technical applications in industrial development) without giving up the critical role of social philosophy. Much of his (1971) earlier epistemological work is directed at elaborating such a perspective.

Other friendly critics have attacked Marcuse for his seemingly idealist pre-Marxian critique of science. Offe (1968), in a book on Marcuse edited by Habermas, has criticized Marcuse in much the same way as Habermas does. Schmidt (1968), the recent director of the Institute for Social Research in Frankfurt, has in the same volume examined the putative connection between Heidegger's ontology and Marcuse's version of critical theory. In *Telos,* some have charged Marcuse with an illegitimate borrowing of Heideggerian, Kantian, and Hegelian themes (e.g., see Franklin 1970; Piccone and Delfini 1970). Indeed, Adorno in the 1930s was not completely convinced that Marcuse had yet shed the idealist paraphernalia of Hegelianism, enunciated in Marcuse's *Habilitationsschrift* on Hegel's theory of historicity (see Jay 1973, 28–29).

Marcuse does not have many allies in his critique of science and technological domination. Admittedly, Horkheimer and Adorno's own 1944 (1972) work was based on a critique of enlightenment, which, it appears in retrospect, was itself a thinly disguised critique of the ideological functions of science. Marcuse in his critique of positivism has not attacked all possible forms of cognition as contributing to domination; indeed, he has theorized that we can create a "new" cognition that will no longer satisfy the ideological needs of capitalism. In fact, Marcuse has also conceived a new technology that could liberate nature. In these ways, he is perhaps more hopefully utopian than were Horkheimer and Adorno, as I propose in the next chapter.

Marcuse's concepts of surplus repression and one-dimensionality, discussed earlier in this book, themselves constitute radical innovations in critical theory. Yet the most contentious part of Marcuse's work, for Marxists, is his critique of technical rationality. The most commonly expressed worry is that Marcuse shifts the focus of the traditionally economic analysis of capitalism from a critique of the extraction of surplus value (allegedly Marx's only concern) to a critique of technology and science in general. Thus, it is feared that Marcuse loses the specific weapon of Marxian analysis—the critique of political economy. I shall argue that Marcuse does not reject Marxist political economy (or the critique of domination) but only broadens its focus to include superficially noneconomic factors. This is to defend Marx against his scientistic critics and to supersede a certain tentativeness in his formulations of new science.

It is notable that there are few passages wherein Marcuse explicitly theorizes about science and technology. Over time Marcuse has become progressively more radical in his criticism. *One-Dimensional Man* (1964) contains an attack on the "use" of technology. *An Essay on Liberation* (1969), however, invests technical rationality with an inherent function of domination, leading Marcuse to speculate about a nonexploitative science and technology. Marcuse's (1968b) essay on Weber, which has occasioned so much critical response, echoes the more radical critique of technique. In *One-Dimensional Man,* Marcuse at least gives the impression of being eclectic in assessing the possible uses of technology. Some uses are better than others. Technological domination is another chapter in the development of capitalism. He has never relinquished this view. Yet he has become less eclectic in his attack on science. He views technical rationality as thoroughly pernicious for what it does to the "sensibility" of the person, who apprehends and appropriates the external world under what are believed to be the morally neutral categories of science. For Marcuse it is no longer a question of deciding what the uses of technology should be except in a policy sense. Critical speculation should instead assert that there can be science and technology that respect the rights of nonhuman (and, by implication, human) nature. This is Marcuse's most controversial contention for radicals inasmuch as many social theorists after Weber have been content to view science and technique as unchanging forces in capitalist and socialist development.

Yet Marcuse's concern with technological domination does not divide him from the critique of political economy but adds another dimension to the contemporary critique of domination. In this sense, Marcuse does not recant Marxism; he accepts the materialist dialectic of Marx, the postulate that social being conditions consciousness but that consciousness can alter social being. Yet he is uncommitted to the letter of Marx's class analysis as it has been crudely transported from the mid- and late nineteenth century to the present by certain theorists of the Second International like Bernstein, Kautsky, and Hilferding (who opposed Marx), and by theorists of the Third International like Bukharin, Lenin, and Trotsky (who supported Marx). The critical theory of society has self-consciously connected the critiques of culture and of capital. Marcuse (like Marx) is convinced that capitalism cannot be analyzed simply in terms of its economic dysfunctions. Critique must also attack the cultural and ideological domination that arises in one-dimensional thought, domination that *hides* exploitation. Marcuse views positivism as one of the factors in this ideological hegemony that protects the fundamental structural irrationality of social production for private consumption. He wants to destroy the conservative function of science in analyzing its systemic role as an insidious thought mechanism for hiding domination in mystifications and "natural laws."

In postulating the possibility of a new science Marcuse engages in vitally necessary critical speculation. He sees that domination has penetrated our basic libidinal and psychic constitution. Science and technique as species-specific faculties must become modes of play in the free society. With radical social change, our relation to nature and to our bodies and minds must change. Marx himself envisaged the qualitative transformation of labor, indeed, the elimination of alienated labor. This chapter specifically deals with Marcuse's critique of science. Yet implicit in that critique is an important dimension of critical theory that recognizes that the historical dialectic has not stood still since Marx wrote *Capital*. As Marx recognized even then, economic exploitation is not the only mode of domination. Corporate needs for expanded markets are protected and reproduced by a layer of apparently noneconomic domination, what Horkheimer and Adorno later (1972) called the culture in-dustry. Marcuse sees that the secret of the staying power of capitalism lies in its ability to hide economic exploitation in the cultural myth that the actual is rational. Only by destroying this myth, by showing that sci-ence and technique as forms of human labor can be radically humanized, can we ever begin to attack the structural causes of exploitation. The hegemony of the economy is reaffirmed by a mode of positivist common sense that cannot fundamentally challenge reality's hold on people, as I indicated in chapter 8. We are taught that to be healthy human beings and good citizens we must accept the facts, the everyday. Capitalism sur-vives as long as this myth remains intact. The critique of science is the first step along the road toward the critique and overcoming of domina-tion.

## Marcuse on Science, Technology, and Weber

Until 1969, Marcuse had not written much systematically or specifically about science and technology. *An Essay on Liberation* (1969) contains some of the most explicit and vivid passages. *One-Dimensional Man* (1964) itself prefigures much of his later work on technology. Although Marcuse's remarks are often provocatively allusive, they nonetheless form an important basis for the critique of science. *An Essay on Liberation* contains passages that echo his view that science and technology contrib-ute to the political closure of one-dimensional society. But the oppres-sive functions of science and technology can be broken and these forces pacified and humanized. The root of Marcuse's indefinite, inchoate hopefulness about transforming one-dimensional society is in his opin-ion that science and technology can be fundamentally reconstructed. Al-though he has often been charged with one-dimensional gloom and unwarranted pessimism, it is clear from examining his views on emanci-patory technology that he is far from resigned to the ultimate fate of one-dimensionality. Technology can be qualitatively informed by human de-sign, something that Marx (1973) himself nearly recognized in the *Grundrisse*. It is interesting that Marcuse is one of the very few Marxists to have read and understood the full implications of *Grundrisse* and its passages on technological domination. The orthodox view, given life by Lenin's naturalistic epistemology, is that Marx conceived of science and technology merely as tools for the control of nature and society.

Marcuse links what he calls the new sensibility to the development of a pacified technology and science. His view is that domination infiltrates the psyche, charging the person with the infinite consumption of unneeded goods. The new sensibility is the subject or the organon of new science.

> The liberated consciousness would promote the development of a science and technology free to discover and realize the possibilities of things and men in the protection and gratification of life, playing with the potentialities of form and matter for the attainment of this goal. Technique would then tend to become art, and art would tend to form reality: the opposition between imagination and reason, higher and lower faculties, poetic and scientific thought, would be invalidated. Emergence of a new Reality Principle: under which a new sensibility and a desublimated scientific intelligence would combine in the creation of an *aesthetic ethos*. [1969, 24]

This is one of the most utopian passages in the whole of Marcuse's work. Here he practically identifies a new science and art in terms of the aesthetic ethos. He is influenced by Kant's view in the *Critique of Judgment,* that the ultimate union of moral freedom and necessity is contained in art. Marcuse's idea of desublimated scientific intelligence is no longer congruent only with a science that is responsibly applied. Marcuse does not mean only that nuclear physicists should refuse to engage in war-related research, although he would agree with this as a partial goal. The desublimated scientific intelligence conceives of the natural universe as an object of beauty and mystery, a mirror in which people see their own reflection. By damaging nature, technical rationality damages the human spirit and desire.

The aesthetic posture of Marcuse was influenced by French surrealism and situationism and their recrudescence in the May Movement of 1968. I argue that this concept of new cognition is legitimately compatible with the critique of political economy. Much of Marcuse's writing on science is metaphoric and suggestive. He wants to point out that the reordering of emancipatory priorities will include a new science no longer beholden to the loveless, instrumentalist concept of cognition prevalent since Francis Bacon, who first said that knowledge is power. Although science can be used to dominate nature and society, it can also be used to liberate them, indeed, to be a medium of self-expression once the veil of distorting domination has been lifted. Marcuse does not identify the aesthetic ethos and new science casually. He realizes that he is weakening one of the most deeply ingrained positivist assumptions about how science is a neutral, unprejudiced tool for the architecture and manipulation of society.

The ultimate goal of an aestheticized science would be the attainment of "society as a work of art" (Marcuse 1969, 45). Marcuse is not a casual idealist. "Society as a work of art" is a carefully chosen expression of the possible identity of a heretofore surplus repressive social order and the ideal of beauty. In the 1844 manuscripts Marx (1961) wrote about the same thing. But Marx submerged his own aesthetic vision of a free society in the scientific political economy that was then a more forceful mode of critique. For Marcuse, the concept of an aesthetic politics is the most potent critique by virtue of the way it joins two apparently irreconcilable concepts: society, which demands deference to an oppressive superego, and beauty.

In the same way, by hypothesizing a happy cognition, Marcuse denies that cognition must be a sterile, unmetaphysical business performed without moral or aesthetic consciousness. Marcuse elsewhere calls this a lesson in "political linguistics": we attack one-dimensional ideology by turning its own discourse of facticity against it. By demonstrating that science can be nonrepressively imaginative, we subvert one of the basic assumptions of dominant ideology. Marcuse has, of course, demonstrated nothing, for his is utopian speculation the proof of which will be found only in the future. He is not saying that we can create a new science without effecting simultaneous social change, only that we should treat this as one of the important emancipatory priorities.

But Marcuse is engaged in something more profound than itemizing the goals of the revolution, although that is itself important. He is trying to argue that the dialectic between given conditions and subjective spontaneity can be activated only in the electric moment when people realize that they have nothing to lose but their chains. The chains today include the heavily proscriptive ideology of the division of labor, reinforced and reproduced by the ideology of professionalism and scientism—what Foucault (1977) called discipline. New science is the state of mind of those who recognize their bondage as unnecessary, who choose not to believe that experts and professionals must constitute a political elite.

The then-timely injunction by Marx and Engels against utopian speculation is rejected by Marcuse (1969, 5). Marcuse believes that science and technique contain within themselves the forbidden fruit of freedom. The gloom in some of his earlier work is vitiated by this kind of optimism about reconstructing the very basis of technical rationality according to the needs of the life instincts. It would be useful to return to *One-Dimensional Man,* which is explicit about technological domination as the highest form of exploitation. It is important to note that the whole of the Frankfurt school used "domination" and "exploitation" nearly synonymously. This indicates a subtle revision and extension of Marx's category of the exploitation of labor; no longer is this the only credible mode of dehumanization. Domination involves the self-exploitation of humanity. Technological domination is based on the fetishism of commodities and commodified culture. People buy products and elect politicians because they believe that the products and politicians represent them. The fact that exploitation in the strict economic sense has metamorphosed into the broader category of domination, Marcuse argues, in no way means that it loses its embeddedness in a class structure. Domination is based on profit imperatives, now as before; in advanced capitalism, profit is extracted by promoting false needs and by deluding consumers into infinite consumption as well as political conformity. Domination is the lived ideology that rationalizes and hence reproduces economic exploitation.

In *One-Dimensional Man,* Marcuse presented his critique of technological domination. This is less well developed than his speculation about a new science in *An Essay on Liberation* and *Counterrevolution and Revolt.* Marcuse in 1964 conceived of the Great Refusal as the only credible escape from the mindless quotidian. Writing *One-Dimensional Man,* he is intent on illuminating the weak coalition between reason and unreason that characterizes the dominant ideology of late capitalism. It is fair to say that Marcuse is still agnostic about new or old science. He talks of the "use" of technology. Should we deploy nuclear energy for "peaceful" purposes or harness hydroelectric power? This is surely not a problem any longer in *An Essay on Liberation.* In the earlier book, Marcuse wants to show that technological development can actually bring an end to want and scarcity—but not necessarily a new technology, directed by the cognitive fantasies of non-Cartesian scientists; perhaps the same old technology, yet one which would not spew out useless products and extract the worker's surplus value. At the time *One-Dimensional Man* was written, the critique of technical domination was virtually unheard of on the Left, apart from some of Walter Benjamin's allusive writings (1969) on the technology of culture, which themselves influenced Marcuse. Concern with the foibles of technology was often equated with romantic Luddism.

Yet Marcuse is no Luddite. He wants somehow to preserve the productive function of factories while changing the entire social structure that defines the use of factories. He comes to see, however, that the technology cannot be left intact (e.g., the assembly line would have to be transformed). It would itself have to be reconstructed in terms of the aesthetic ethos, according to the rationality of gratification (1955) discussed in chapter 7. Marcuse has come to see that technology can still be intrinsically oppressive in the matrix of corporate capitalism even if it provides food for all of the world's billions, something it fails to do now. What matters is that the ideological superstructure produces false needs, including positivism, and thus perpetuates capitalism.

Marcuse essentially argues that science and technology have become factors in both the base and superstructure of capitalism. He contends that to disregard the oppressive capacity of technology is wrongly to conceive of the transition to socialism strictly in class terms. According to economistic Marxism, the present-day Soviet Union is a socialist society. While in a certain sense the Bolshevik revolution was politically successful, Marcuse doubts that there has been a qualitative change in the daily life of workers, who are still chained to the oppressive technology established during and after the Stalin period (see Marcuse 1958). This demonstrates Marcuse's distance from orthodox Marxian economics, which fails to conceive of technique and science as factors in the base, the mode of production. Socialized means of production do not by any means guarantee the end of domination, which may live on in the repressed sensibilities of people, but, theoretically, only of the exploitation of labor, defined narrowly in terms of surplus value. Exploitation, however, becomes domination under the command economy of the USSR as well as under state capitalism. Workers do not lose their surplus value in the orthodox sense, but they are nonetheless victims of domination and surplus repression. Their labor is expropriated by the state and turned against them.

Marcuse's aesthetic concerns in *An Essay on Liberation* and *Counterrevolution and Revolt* must be read next to his analysis of technological domination in *One-Dimensional Man*. The present reality is rooted in technical rationalization, which can be exploded only by radical speculation about alternative uses of the productive apparatus and of science. Marcuse's speculation can be summarized in the image of "society as a work of art." This is completely at odds with Habermas's more conventionally Kantian-Weberian position on technique and science.

There is another domain in which Marcuse has advanced his critique of technical rationality. His (1968b) essay on Max Weber concisely raises all of these questions. As we saw in the last chapter, Weber was the sociological metaphysician of rationalization. Although he recognized the dysfunctional tendencies of bureaucratic capitalism, he was a "nostalgic liberal" who could not fundamentally oppose the society to which he was normatively committed. Marcuse has argued that Weber's concept of rationality does not exhaust the universe of possible rationalities. One can conceive of nonexploitive modes of rationality that are not vehicles of domination, such as a rationality of gratification.

Weber, the most prescient prophet of advanced capitalism, eternalizes what is historical. He makes the instrumental rationality of profit maximization based on mathematical accounting procedures and the cultural disenchantment of the world a universal rationality. In the same vein, he conceives science as the most rational mode of social ordering. Value-free science, promulgated by Weber in his writings on the objectivity of science, supports certain political interests. Weber was one of the most perceptively positivist of all sociologists. The concept of a new science, freed from unmetaphysical fetters, might have been developed in opposition to Weber's austere conception of science, a value-free science that sells out its freedom to the highest and most powerful bidder. Not only is science not politically neutral, it may one day embody aesthetic perspectives on a natural world that must not be thoughtlessly plundered. As a willing partisan of bourgeois instrumentality, this would have been lost on Weber.

For Weber, "occidental reason becomes the economic reason of capitalism" (Marcuse 1968d, 205). This "economic reason" is actualized in the "methodical-scientific apparatus" (Marcuse 1968d, 205). Marcuse continues:

> The very concept of technical reason is perhaps ideological. Not only the application of technology but technology itself is domination (of nature and men)—methodical, scientific, calculated, calculating control. Specific purposes and interests of domination are not foisted upon technology "subsequently" and from the outside: they enter the very construction of the technical apparatus. Technology is always a historical-social project: in it is projected what a society and its ruling interests intend to do with men and things. Such a "purpose" of domination is "substantive" and to this extent belongs to the very form of technical reason. [1968d, 223–24]

This summarizes Marcuse's view of science and technology as a transmission belt between human sensibility and the economy. This passage, as we shall see, is the battleground between Habermas and Marcuse. Marcuse asserts that positivist science is a form of domination in that science hides exploitation in ideological mystifications. Science as we currently understand it, with scientists observing a mute, inert universe of exploitable objects, blunts the critical spirit. Indeed, positivist science wants to dominate; it rationalizes domination by offering useful knowledge. New science would shed this quiescent, distorted role; it rejects the reflection theory of knowledge.

There is yet another source of Marcuse's indictment of positivism and technical rationality as vehicles of domination. In his book on Freud, Marcuse (1955) laid the foundation for his critique of technical rationality. While the book treats another theme, it contains the germs of Marcuse's later, more articulate position on science and technology. Marcuse argues that science fetishizes facts and denounces the idea of an "earthly paradise." With the nonsurplus repressive release of the erotic life force, Marcuse believes that science could be transformed into a mode of playfulness, drawing on Schiller's concept of play as a self-expressive form of freedom. Marcuse, in his book on Freud, wants to reverse the cult of instrumental reason by releasing the sensuous capacities of the person. He believes that desire can be released in such a way that our fundamental modes of interacting with nature and concepts would be changed. This is Marcuse's first articulation of the domination of nature. The aesthetic dimension can be one medium for the liberating desublimation of Eros, which would entail the reconstruction of science and technique according to the pleasure principle.

The play impulse is the motive force of human labor, used to build an erotic and liberated society. Nature would become an object of contemplation and fantasy, while cognition would become a productive force of imagination and art. Cognition would refuse to exploit nature for short-run instrumental purposes in pretending that concepts can exhaust an inexhaustible reality. Moreover, the contemplation and adoration of nature would constitute an end, a mode of self-creation. Marcuse does not oppose the domination of nature merely because it causes ecological crises. He is concerned with redirecting the erotic force of labor toward instinctually gratifying tasks. The domination of nature under capitalism is surplus-repressive sublimation, giving rise to what Horkheimer (1974, 92–127) called the "revolt of nature."

## Habermas's Challenge to the Critique of Positivism

Habermas's (1971) critique of Marcuse's "romantic" idealism with respect to science turns on the matter of the relation between work and interaction. Habermas conceives natural science according to a logic that makes it irreducible to communicative rationality. In this, he opposes his conception of science to that of Marcuse, who thinks of science as amenable to retranslation into the communicative situation and the rationality of gratification. As I remarked in the preceding chapter, Habermas accuses Marcuse and the original Frankfurt school of confusing the logic under which nature could be apprehended with the logic under which another person can be understood. Marcuse might not disagree with this. Yet his conception of science would in fact allow for some sort of dialogue between nature and people. Habermas's (1971, 32–33) original idea that the speculative minds from Frankfurt wanted to resurrect nature is incomplete. Marcuse wants to resurrect humanity, including its relation to nature. Only by treating all otherness (be it nature or other people) as potentially intimate with human subjectivity can the person coexist with the rest of the world nondestructively. In the strict sense, the person cannot talk with trees or animals. But in another sense, the person learns to treat other people gently and responsibly by thinking of trees and beasts as possessing some inherent worth, even natural rights (see Leiss 1972). I dispute the claim that Marcuse is concerned with the domination of nature for any reason other than to liberate humanity. Marcuse suggests that science can be made nondominating with respect to its subject matter, that science need not belong to the arsenal stockpiled for the assault on nature. For science itself to engage in a Great Refusal of reflection theory would take us a step closer to the imminent destruction of positivism.

Habermas has ulterior motives for calling Marcuse and the others mystical. He wants to show that Marx himself did not clearly distinguish between the logic of laboring and that of self-reflection. Had Marx done so, according to Habermas, he would not have created a scientism utterly purged of imaginative, creative subjectivity. He would not have licensed a Marxian naturalism. Yet as Habermas himself acknowledges, the "early Marx," too, was party to the mystification of nature. This demands that we decide whether there are two Marxes, a "humanist" and a "scientist." A colleague of Habermas agrees with him about Marx's hidden positivism that emerges in the later economic works (Wellmer 1971). Yet there is also a sizable and authoritative literature that contends that there is only one Marx, including the "mystical" early Marx as well as the later economic one. If this is so, there may not be grounds for charging Marx with hidden positivism or, in Habermas's terms, with the identification of labor and self-reflection. This is not a purely Scholastic quarrel for it is precisely the ground on which Marcuse splits off from critics like

Habermas who wish to preserve positivist epistemology within Marxian critique. Marcuse believes that aesthetic and erotic interests can coexist with instrumental ones in such a way that we can no longer distinguish analytically between the logics of labor and self-reflection.

In an essay entitled "Technology and Science as 'Ideology,' " Habermas (1970b) challenges Marcuse again, but this time with more force. Habermas argues that the Marcuse of *One-Dimensional Man* envisages a "new" technology and science. Habermas is worried that a new science is inconceivable according to certain transcendental criteria. He argues correctly that Marcuse's indictments of science and technology as tools of domination are intimately related (1970b, 87). Habermas in his work has tried to distinguish between two levels of cognition, the one oriented to instrumental control, the other to communicative discourse and enlightenment. But Marcuse wants us to conceive of nature itself as a partner in the human enterprise, albeit a silent partner. This is what Habermas so dislikes about Marcuse's position.

> The idea of a New Science will not stand up to logical scrutiny
> any more than that of a New Technology, if indeed science is
> to retain the meaning of modern science inherently oriented to
> possible technical control. For this function, as for scientific-
> technical progress in general, there is no more "humane" sub-
> stitute. [1970b, 88]

Did Marcuse ever mean to say that the actual nature of tools and machines would change? Yes, he would answer, tools must change. Techniques that are rooted in the domination of nature would have to be abandoned, although technique itself—the very manipulation of nature—would be preserved. He is not saying that we should renounce the mastery of nature but that we must not conceive of nature as something that can be arrogantly exploited. Marcuse proposes an almost theological perspective on nature, yet his is clearly Marxian theology (in the fashion of Ernst Bloch). Why must this theologicospiritual perspective on nature be viewed as either necessarily preindustrial or mystic conservative? After all, as the young Marx said, we too are part of nature. By violating nature thoughtlessly, we violate ourselves as natural subjects.

Habermas reads Marcuse as saying that machines themselves would vanish into thin air. This allows him to dismiss as utopian the idea that we could create a new technology. Marcuse, however, is careful to observe the ban on graven images, the ban against drawing up specific blueprints of the future. Like Marx, he does not want to offer a detailed picture of the future before it is upon us. This Judaic reluctance does not mean that Marcuse is necessarily unrealistic. It may be the only realistic way to confront the complex problems of planning for a new order without violating the self-determining, exuberant nature of radical social change.

Habermas did not have the advantage of having read *Essay on Liberation* when he wrote the essay on science and technology. I have said earlier that *One-Dimensional Man* is vague and rather underdeveloped compared to Marcuse's later, more explicit writings on new science and technique. In *One-Dimensional Man*, he sometimes seems to be saying simply that industrial processes will remain intact but that the stewards of technology must change. Yet in his later work, Marcuse is clearer about the need for new technology and science, technology and science that operate with a new rationality. Marcuse has come to recognize the aesthetic, libidinal potential of politics, science, and industry. He says that the interest in beauty is equally important in a potentially affluent society as the interest in freedom. No longer is he concerned only with reorienting the political uses of technique, as Habermas claims.

Habermas's critique of Marcuse belongs to his overall attempt to reconstruct Marx's critique of political economy in transcendental terms. The attack on Marcuse's concept of new science is a dimension of his general attack on Marx's assessment of relations between base and superstructure. Is Marcuse as radically revisionist as Habermas in reassessing Marx's model of critique? Marcuse retains Marx's categorical framework yet acknowledges the new capacities of the superstructure to veil economic dysfunction in illusions and create false needs. Habermas chooses to elaborate his critique of Marx primarily in terms of the distinction between work and interaction. Marcuse does not share Habermas's view that critical theory needs to revise Marx by truncating Marx's basic category of labor. Marcuse follows Marx in implying that work can be reconstructed to resemble intersubjective discourse, or at least to resemble the aesthetic model of artist and oeuvre. This is the part of Marcuse's and the early Marx's position that Habermas explicitly rejects on transcendental grounds.

What does Habermas reject in Marcuse's position? It is something quite fundamental. Habermas should be read as one of the most perceptive, even dialectical, theorists of technical rationality. It would be superficial to dismiss him as a positivist; he is committed to the critique of domination. Yet Habermas rejects the mystical radicalism of Marx and the original Frankfurt school. Marcuse is only a vehicle for his denunciation of those romantic utopians who believe that they can liberate fundamental human nature, including cognition, as well as labor power.

Habermas has developed a Kantian Marxism. It is Kantian in the way that he transcendentally divides communicative-reflective from material-instrumental rationality. Discourse is not labor, says Habermas. We can fundamentally change the nature of society, making it more enlightened and rational through a therapy that corrects "distorted communication" and overthrows the positivist taboo on metaphysical, political "reflection." Yet we cannot change the relation between humanity and nature by changing the nature of labor *(Arbeit)*. Habermas argues that there will never be a new science or technology, only the same old apparatuses used differently by enlightened technocrats and rational interlocutors. Habermas, as we have seen, criticizes Marx for merging the categories of labor and self-reflection. Marx allegedly contributed to the rise of positivism within dialectical theory by assimilating the self-reflective basis of speech and social philosophy to a crude materialist model of labor. For Habermas, rational self-reflection is designed to reveal the hidden unity of "knowledge" and "interest," illuminating the value commitment and ideological presuppositions of particular cognitive approaches. Marx, by transforming science and self-reflection into a mode of production, dissolved the unity of knowledge and interest, or at least prevented science from reflecting on its own methodological and political auspices.

Habermas rejects Marcuse's position because he wants to reseparate the functions of labor and speech, joined illegitimately by Marx. Yet the Frankfurt approach is to accept Marx's unification of work and science in suggesting that all modes of self-objectifying labor must be liberated under a new order. Marcuse argues that the liberation of science and technology must accompany the liberation of labor; science and technology are not abstract social forces but rather two expressions of the life instinct, two forms of labor and desire.

Science is a surplus repressed form of the cognitive desire, the desire to use the mind freely and creatively. This is where Habermas steps in to remind the Frankfurt theorists that science "as such" must always remain a form of technical rationality, a dispassionate, purposively rational mode of instrumental calculation. No more can science change than the fundamental cosmos can change. Habermas says that we must reserve our energy for the possible tasks, such as transforming political economy and enhancing the rational capacity to engage in undistorted communication. By no means are these trivial or unimportant goals in themselves. Habermas is not a reactionary but a skeptic (at a time when skepticism is virtually a form of radicalism itself, given the momentum behind hype and inflation). Yet his critical perspective is much narrower than that of Marcuse. He does not allow for the liberation of science from positivist fetters for he does not believe that our fundamental relation to the object world can be altered. For Habermas, the primal object will always be a somewhat imposing residue of our inability to know all things; with Kant, we cannot grasp the noumenon, the thing in itself. Therefore, we must restrict our critical commitment to remediable matters of political economy and public policy. Marcuse's "mystical" utopianism with respect to the liberation of cognition and technique (not to mention sexuality—which, interestingly, Habermas rarely mentions) must be rejected.

Habermas reads a Weberian Marx who should have applauded technical rationality and the methodical "disenchantment of the world" while preserving the interest in liberating communication from ideological distortions: Habermas seems to accept the Weberian hierarchy of rationality that places "rational-legal" at the top. His Marx would not change the fundamental nature of human existence; he would only provide a tool for delegitimating positivism and revealing the unity of knowledge and interest, appreciable goals in their own right. Habermas would reject Weber's value freedom but accept Weber's concept of rational-legal authority. Marcuse, in contrast, accepts neither rational-legal authority nor value freedom. For him, there must be a new science as well as a new order of rationality (which, in *Eros and Civilization*, he tellingly calls a "rationality of gratification").

Ultimately, Habermas wants to challenge, not the logic of positivism, but only its hegemony over other forms of cognition (like self-reflection, which positivism disallows). Marcuse, on the other hand, wants to deconstruct positivism by showing that positivism's fact fetishism is a symptom and agent of a one-dimensional social order. Cognition for Marcuse is a form of life-giving self-objectification. Positivism is damaged cognition; accordingly, the cognitive faculty will be liberated only as domination is overcome.

Habermas wants to reserve some of the field for positivism; he argues that dispassionate, objectivist science is one among many legitimate competing epistemological strategies. On the face of it, this seems reasonable. But it is unreasonable if we treat science as another victim and agent of domination. Positivism is a product of the surplus repression of our basic imaginative energies and desire. Marcuse wants to shatter positivism because it is a moment of the general pathology of domination, which, among other things, reduces the mind to mush. Habermas would supersede domination by rational discussions among experts. The fact-fetishizing mentality would then be left intact. Marcuse would challenge this very "human nature" as unnatural by fighting any unnecessarily harsh repression of the basic desires. These desires, when liberated from surplus repression, will issue in rational forms of nonde-structive personality, such as new science. New science will emerge, Marcuse implies, from the abolition of the whole division of labor. Cognition will no longer support the accomplishment of certain technical tasks. Instead, cognition will blossom as an activity enjoyed playfully for its own sake; indeed, science will be transformed from a fragmented form of alienated labor into self-expressive creative praxis.

Habermas is content to preserve structures of expertise and authority as long as technocrats and politicians are democratic in temperament and organization. The concept of a new science is scandalizing because the Left, since Leninism dominated the Communist movement, has promulgated elitist models of theory and practice. The separation of Marxian theory and practice since 1917 and the collapse of the revolutionary proletariat have made it doubly hard to destroy the leftist intellectual's vanguard role. Indeed, by inveighing against new science, Habermas has virtually legitimated the transformation of Marxism into a form of democratic Weberian sociology rooted in the assumption that there must be a division of labor and professionalism, albeit tempered by dialogues between experts and citizens. Critical theory today is divided not merely between different styles of reading Marx but by the issue of the division of labor.

Marxism has contained its own left and right rumps ever since Lukács and Korsch broke from the official Marxism of the Comintern. Initially, the Frankfurt school inherited the mantle of Lukács and Korsch without much difficulty; but in the intervening half-century critical theory has been torn by the emergence of its own right wing, which I have called the Left's Right. While the difference between Habermas and Marcuse may seem to outsiders one of quantity and not quality, there are problems involved that take us back to the original conflict between Marxism and bourgeois social science. Now as before, the central issue is the struggle of reformism against radicalism, this time hinging on Habermas's reaction to Marcuse's critique of the division of labor. Habermas's growing appeal can best be explained by the smoothness with which he reduces revolutionary concepts such as the sameness of manual and mental labor into concepts alien to Marxism. Habermas's (e.g., 1984, 1987a, 1987b) erudition has enabled him to make Marxism acceptable to many pragmatists and bourgeois philosophers of science; yet his translation of orthodoxy, while it has had the salutary effect of diverting attention from "what Marx really said," has expunged orthodoxy's basic radicalism. In other words, Habermas attempts the impossible in aiming at a balance between Marxism's revolutionary appeal and bourgeois social science's acquiescence to the given.

Marxists have found it nearly impossible to relinquish their self-conception as experts, albeit critical ones, in a world wherein they are objectively isolated. By maintaining epistemological barriers between science and philosophy, Marxism necessarily cuts the ground from beneath its own critique of the division of labor, both mental and manual. Habermas goes a long way toward making the Marxist philosophy of history a respectable philosophical alternative to an affirmative positivism; yet in the process he forgets that Marx's ultimate goal was the destruction of social differentiation such as that which exists between the philosopher and the scientist.

> Perhaps the most lasting negative mental effect of oppression is our near inability to discuss seriously the division of labor without either some retreat into utopia or the acceptance of its inevitable anomaly. Domination shrouds the fact of anomaly and mocks utopia as immature fantasy. [Kontos 1975, 220]

The Marcuse-Habermas debate on science and technology, like their debate over work and authority (discussed in the previous chapter), turns on political considerations. Habermas is a radical reformer who does not believe that the mode of production and its operative technical rationality can change, but only the political and intellectual superstructure. My argument has been that Marcuse, like Marx, never separates base and superstructure or technique and communication. Thus, Marcuse hopes to transform the ensemble of capitalist social relations: relations between person and machine, person and nature, person and person, person and concepts. His new science is a form of emancipated intellectual labor, given life through the conquest of reason's reduction to positivist epistemology. Marcuse only broadens Marx's concept of labor in remaining faithful to the early Marx's vision of the emancipation of the five senses and unification of manual and mental labor under socialism.

My discussion of Marcuse and Habermas's views of science and technology in this chapter ends this section of the book on the Frankfurt school. These chapters on Frankfurt critical theory enable me to move beyond exegesis in the concluding section, where I attempt to develop a more positive approach to critical social theory, aided in part by postmodernism. I continue to argue that the depoliticization of the public sphere, celebrated by Bell (1973) and bemoaned by Lasch (1979), can be reversed, especially with the aid of a repoliticized critical theory that fosters oppositional movements wherever it may find them. In this sense, I attempt to develop an applied critical theory that moves beyond texts toward an engagement with the world at large. As I have demonstrated in this section, especially in my discussions of Marcuse, this is the same sort of engagement achieved by the original Frankfurt school in their reappraisal of both capitalism and Marxism after the Great Depression.

PART                    3


BEYOND
THE END
OF IDEOLOGY

# 12

# On Happiness
and
the Damaged Life

C ritical theory is either a museum piece in the hands of its modern
inheritors or a living medium of political self-expression. My argument in this final section is that critical theory can be renewed, as
Marx would have hoped, only by refusing to concentrate on its
philosophical inheritance and instead writing the theory in a direct and
unmediated way. The conviction that to be a Marxist surpasses Marx is
just as true for critical theory: Adorno, Horkheimer, and Marcuse blazed
the trail for a theory of late capitalism, yet now they can be suitably re-
membered only by new formulations of theory responsive to the altered
nature of the sociocultural world. This is the project that I have set for
myself here.

In the four chapters comstituting this section, I work toward *a
lifeworld-grounded critical theory*, drawing from original critical theory,
Habermas's (1984, 1987b) system-lifeworld argument, critical phenomenology (Paci 1972; O'Neill 1972c), postmodernism (see chap. 15) and
feminist theory (Fraser 1989; Agger 1989a, 1989c). This version of critical theory attempts to identify resistances and transformations already
taking place in the quotidian worlds in which all of us live. Although I
appreciate the direness of the political context in which Adorno's type of
critical theory was formulated, that political context has changed dra-

matically. Whereas it is legitimate to talk about the disciplinary society (Foucault 1977; O'Neill 1986; Agger 1989c), there are crucial differences between Adorno's metaphor of society as a concentration camp and Foucault's metaphor of society as a prison that occasion different versions of critical theory as a response. This is not to exaggerate hope; the 1990s may well be a decade of unprecedented regression. Nevertheless, simply to repeat Adorno's (1973b) negative dialectics is a lazy exercise—and quite contrary to his own injunction to think and think and think anew.

The central motif in this task of reinvigoration is that of language or what is fashionably called discourse (see Agger 1990). Critical theory self-consciously employs a vocabulary of political hope and defeat. Marx's great contribution to critical theory was his notion of theory as a stimulant to political action, if not as action's mere reflection. The rhetoric of critical theory emerges from the theorist's sense of the possibility of social change and itself contributes to fostering or deflecting emancipatory activity. In this sense, Adorno's almost unmitigated pessimism contrasts with Marcuse's guarded optimism about cracking open the one-dimensional totality. Although *Eros and Civilization* states that only the "surplus" of ego-constitutive repression can be purposefully eliminated, Marcuse remains hopeful about the prospect of lessening this surplus, as I argued in the preceding section. Similarly, O'Neill's (1974) "wild sociology" defends the commonplaces of everyday life as the inalienable basis of any community, from which all radicalism must inevitably proceed. For Adorno, there was an equivalency between basic and surplus repression and thus few opportunities for social change. In the preceding two chapters I focused on Marcuse's differences with Habermas; here I examine Marcuse's relationship to Adorno inasmuch as it reflects modalities of tone and temperament available to critical theorists today. (It is also important to repeat my observation in chapter 9 that Marcuse [e.g., 1978] had moved closer to Adorno's [1973b] negative dialectics by the end of his career.)

The language of critical theory is its own metalanguage. Objective description already contains a vision of *Aufhebung*, a transcended, reconstructed world. The dialectic is captured in the capacity of objective knowledge for political enlightenment. Critique in Marx meant the imagination and analysis of a world without exploitation, a human world. This must be embodied in the forms of critical expression such as social thought, art, music, and philosophy. A dialectical language both describes the dissonant world and bespeaks the possibility of redemption. As such, theory is political in its own right, as are all public discourses.

The new sensibility and the new consciousness which are to
project and guide such reconstruction demand a new language
to define and communicate the new "values" (language in the
wider sense which includes words, images, gestures, tones). It
has been said that the degree to which a revolution is developing qualitatively different social conditions and relationships
may perhaps be indicated by the development of a different
language: the rupture with the continuum of domination must
also be a rupture with the vocabulary of domination. [Marcuse
1969, 39–40]

Adorno, a quintessential modernist (see Adorno 1974; Huyssen
1986), employed a negative language and favored negative culture. Marcuse was less negative because he glimpsed the point at which evil could
be redeemed. Specifically, Adorno believed that the demise of a politically organized working class sealed the fate of Marxism, whereas Marcuse and O'Neill have responded to the libidinal rebellion of American
youth as a potentially revolutionary phenomenon. However, O'Neill
goes even beyond Marcuse's ingrained preference for high culture in
siding with Norman O. Brown against Marcuse in what he calls "the Left
version of the generation gap" (O'Neill 1972c, 53). Whereas Marcuse
flirted with turned-on 1960s youth, uncertain of their transformational
potential, O'Neill celebrated them. Adorno saw negative theory captured in the mind-boggling staves of twelve-tone music, where Marcuse
and O'Neill hear the crash and flight of rock music as a new promise of
freedom, providing a vision of the aural and carnal grounds of socialism.

For too long, Marxism has been under the sway of a taboo prohib-
iting the depiction of a better society. In Adorno's later work, there is
barely a hint of the promised land. Transplanted from Germany to North
America, critical theory has become a crabbed style of philosophical
analysis, replete with a Scholastic structure of authority. Habermas (e.g.,
1984, 1987b) has further robbed critical theory of its passion, persuasion, and joie de vivre. My thesis here is that this taboo must be lifted and
Adorno's dismal reluctance to sing about socialism opposed, hence repoliticizing critical theory as a deconstructive discourse in its own
right—strange to say (given its academic tone), a mode of cultural resistance and transformation itself. Marxism, under the influence of its
founder, has always assumed that history consisted in radical interruptions; Marx's eschatology revealed a temporal gap between the alienating present and possible future. The taboo on graven images was created
because it was thought that the socialist future was too distant to admit

of sensible description in the here and now. Yet in my opinion, the "moment" of abstract negation, out of which Adorno's theory is built, must be superseded and the temporal model of the long road to a redeemed future scrapped.

Marcuse explicitly rejects the model of critical theory as abstract negation; since his work on Freud he has concerned himself with depicting the body politic of the new society, its politics, sexuality, art, and philosophy. Freud enabled him to translate Marx's rationalism into the body language of a new version of critical theory, replete with the desire to experience and express a new world en route to creating that very world. At the same time, Marcuse also rejected the notion of the long road to socialism and suggested instead that transformational forces could be perceived as emerging prefiguratively in the present society. Adorno's impatience with jazz and rock as culture forms is rejected by Marcuse and O'Neill, who search for oppositional impulses anywhere, even in apparently nonproletarian and nonpolitical forms.

> This potential for transfiguration is not at all obvious amidst
> the vulgarity and garbage of Woodstock or the May revolution.
> But this is the way of wild sociology into the world; it can enter
> only through self-mockery, nihilistic flirtations and the very
> self-violence which it seeks to avoid. Its way is profane because
> its resources are nothing else than the world and its people
> struggling for improvement. It is easy to be cynical about the
> organizational and promotional features of "rock-ins" and
> "maybe's," to dissolve them in a phrase, to empty their logos
> into the waste-bin of fashion. Indeed, the spontaneity, festivity
> and refusals which constitute these events make it inevitable
> that the participants will "blow it," will be unable to sustain
> their enthusiasm and disintegrate as at Altamont, in Paris and
> elsewhere. The critics will observe failure and speak wisely of
> what is to be done within the limits of an untransfigured world
> which lives without fancy and avoids enthusiasm in favor of
> the pigeonholes of politics, history and sociology. [O'Neill
> 1975, 299]

Critical theory in Marcuse and O'Neill has therefore abandoned the traditional model of the politically organized working class. Opposition can come from any quarter; the nature of modern opposition consists in rejecting the division of labor as well as in the actual creation of a new political body. Dialectical thought today rejects the thesis of a long road and indeed all crisis theory rooted in the classical Marxian terms of a proletarian revolution. Instead, critical theory must, as Marx taught time and again, sensitize itself to all ongoing oppositional movements in attempting to channel them in palpably political directions. Critical theory cannot afford to remain in the 1920s and 1930s—when perhaps the original working-class model did apply.

My thesis about Marcuse and O'Neill's sensitivity to nontraditional forms of opposition, in contrast to Adorno's, turns on their approach to certain cultural forms like discourse and music. They have tried to conceive how modes of cultural expression like music and theory themselves constitute a new body politic, auguring the postmodern turn in cultural studies, discussed in chapter 15. Theory is a prefigurative praxis that actualizes and communicates the image of a better world. It contains within itself, as does music, a sense of the future's dialectical emergence from the present. I want to read Marcuse, O'Neill, and Adorno as singing the world in different ways, engaging in different styles of cultural opposition. Marcuse and O'Neill directly attempt to create a socialist body politic through musical and theoretic harmony. Adorno engages in abstract negation through dissonance.

Both body politics and abstract negation must be moments of oppositional practice today. Marx's famous notion of the dialectic between theory and practice bespeaks the practical potential of theory itself as a form of cultural politics. Marcuse and O'Neill's critical theory is the cultural practice of a new sensibility; it is not a form of life separable from political practice. Adorno abjectly resigns before a seemingly intractable world. Marcuse and Adorno cannot be compared according to the lifeless epistemological standard of bourgeois social science but only in terms of their varying styles of cultural opposition. My view is that Adorno is unjustified in resigning from the effort to build a socialist society in the actual lifeworlds of everyday politics, made problematic by Habermas in his *Theory of Communication Action* (1984, 1987b).

One-dimensional society swallows up defiance but leaves the traces of idealism in theory, art, and music through which opposition can find its voice. Derrida and Foucault instruct us that discourse is a legitimate political venue. Inasmuch as the thought of freedom remains conscious, we can create a society grounded in mutuality and dialogue. Once the thought of freedom is buried in the unconscious, hope withers along with the subject of hope. I want to restore the self-consciousness of action and vision to critical theory in turning it toward its own potential for pervasive discourse, thereby combating its ossification as another differentiated form of academic thought.

Marcuse and O'Neill remain hopeful that theory can transcend itself as a new science and technology, as I argued in the preceding chapter, whereas Adorno (1974) wrote of his own irreparably "damaged life." Theory in this vein is but a tragic expression of will, a theme reminiscent of Nietzsche and Schopenhauer. As I develop in chapter 15, Nietzsche's *The Birth of Tragedy* represents one of the discursive options open to critical theory today. Nietzsche writes of the sublation of tragedy by "Socratism," including its destruction of music as a pure expression of the will. Socratic optimism today employs the techniques of opera, romantic classical music, and rock, whereas the tragic version of critical theory takes refuge in the dissonance of twelve-tone music. Adorno is the theorist of atonality, Marcuse the opera buff trying to appreciate the youth culture of rock and resistance. They are split between tragedy and epiphany, the one humbly owning up to its political impotence, the other committing the sin of pride and challenging the world to change. Critical theory has two broad cultural styles, the one tragic or Nietzschean, the other more optimistic or Hegelian-Marxian. For its part, postmodernism returns to Nietzsche, albeit without Adorno's negative dialectic of positive social change. As I discuss in my concluding chapter, there are two readings of Nietzsche that inflect Adorno's type of critical theory, on the one hand, and an affirmative, apolitical postmodernism, on the other.

The negative totality of modern capitalism has reduced criticism to imitation and private language. Marcuse accepts the possibility of a real harmony between subject and object, whereas Adorno rejected all identity theory found in Hegel and Marx. The alternative to the Hegelian optimism of Marcuse is a Nietzschean perspective of tragedy and eternal recurrence for which things either remain the same or get worse. *Dialectic of Enlightenment* by Horkheimer and Adorno (1972) is an echo of *The Birth of Tragedy*. Nietzsche believed that Aeschylus had been eternally wronged by Euripides and Socrates, whereas Horkheimer and Adorno thought that Western civilization began to die with Odysseus' rationalism.

Marcuse was not overly reluctant to hypostatize a 1960s worker–student–Third World coalition as the new collective subject, anticipating Habermas's theory of new social movements. This has been largely a heuristic device in that Marcuse, like Marx and Lenin, never failed to reduce praxis to individuating acts. Hegel's *Phenomenology of Mind* underwrote Marx and Marcuse by offering them an image of the political nature of reflection and cognition. Marcuse's debt to Hegel is revealed in the second preface to *Reason and Revolution* (1960), where he writes that Hegel has restored the "power of negative thinking" at a time when the "second dimension" of transcendent critique has been assimilated to the positive affirmation of the given. But Hegel was not a tragic thinker in the same sense as Nietzsche. Hegel was a dialectical theorist who tried to comprehend how history was animated by its thought of itself, its essentially progressive reflexivity.

Critical theory mediates between the thought of freedom and the actuality of a free world. Its mortal Marxism, as I called it in chapter 9, embodies itself in the struggling but hopeful subject whose mediations can let theory become a practice. The Nietzschean conception of the mortally self-limited subject differs radically from the Hegelian-Marxian idea of the potentially universal subject of world history. For Adorno (1973b), virtually everything we do in the way of politics will end in disappointing failure; rebellion only strengthens the system. For Marcuse and O'Neill, we cannot avoid the attempt to translate emancipatory ideals into the concrete particulars of place, time, desire, and emotion.

> To think sociologically is to dwell upon a question we have answered long ago: How is it that men belong to one another despite all differences? This is the task of a wild sociology,
> namely, to dwell upon the platitudes of convention, prejudice, place, and love; to make of them a history of the world's labor and to root sociology in the care of the circumstance and particulars that shape the divine predicaments of ordinary men.
> The work of sociology, then, is to confront the passionless world of science with the epiphany of family, of habit, and of human folly, outside of which there is no remedy. This is not to deny scientific sociology. It is simply to treat it as a possibility that has yet to convince the world. [O'Neill 1974, 10]

Critical theory either translates the universal telos of freedom into sensible dimensions of experience and language or acts as a fatalistic expression of the heteronomous will. I think it can be argued that Adorno hoped that music itself could express a theory too abstruse for words. Nietzsche heard the sound of tragedy in the choral music of Aeschylus. Tragedy and a certain mortal finitude were expressed through song. Adorno considered Schoenberg to be a prophet of a tragedy essentially beyond the reach of the discursive voice. In the absence of public discourse, the negative dialectic of cultural resistance and transformation bespeaks an evil world.

Marcuse speaks about human tragedy without ascending to Aeschylean heights in forgetting the potential of the positive. He searches for a language with which to express the good contained within the shape of the present. Art and theory prepare us for the time when social relations will not scar the human face, voice, or polity. Yet criticism will also preserve the distance between vital lived experience and the reconstructed experience of language. That is, each society needs critics and artists to idealize a higher order of freedom than that which has actually been attained. Whereas Adorno (1973a) felt that the jargon of authenticity co-opted language, O'Neill and Marcuse want to reserve the most revealing languages for the time when a new social order needs to be invigorated.

> Wild sociology will encourage radicalism. Yet it will be hard on its own radicalism, suspecting further evils from its own activity should it presume upon its relation to the lay community. It may well be that the daily practice of sociology encourages arrogance upon the the part of its members, undermining the very resources of humanism with a numb professionalism or the shrill cry of ideology. If this is not to happen wild sociology must make a place for itself, and to accomplish this it must engage hope and utopia. Hope is the time it takes to make the place in which men think and talk and work together. Thus wild sociology is essentially engaged in the education of the oppressed. [O'Neill 1974, 80]

Praxis, thus, is anything we can do to remain critically alive, responsive to pervasive dissonance and transcendent harmony. As its own political metalanguage, critical theory is a praxis. It talks about the world as it assesses the social potential for freedom. My point is that, for Adorno and Marcuse, theory is not always discursively or strategically articulated but can assume prelinguistic forms. O'Neill rephrases Vico to suggest that critical theory must return to poetry in resurrecting the natural rationality of human expression. Vico implies that humanity can be redeemed because we are the original authors of our own humanity; we can hear the sound of our own humanity in nondiscursive expressions like poetry and music.

> Language fractures in the modern world because our speech is no longer the reflection of anything that is ordered either inside or outside of us. Every historical order ultimately collapses the literary, artistic, and philosophical languages that for a time allowed an age to speak of itself and to gather its particular goods and evils. It is an axiom of Vico's wild sociology that if history is at all saved it is saved by language. For it is in the his-

tory of our language that we recover our humanity. It is in language that we discover the gradual making of the institutions
that have made us human. [O'Neill 1974, 34]

Music, like poetry, is a form of critical theory in that it stimulates
and solicits resignation or rebellion. Adorno felt that twelve-tone music
captured the negative dialectic of an insufferable society, whereas
O'Neill's patience with 1960s rock and drug culture reflects his view that
there is something elementally political in the ecstasy of desire. Marcuse
is located somewhere between Adorno's gloom and O'Neill's song of the
inalienable commonplaces of humanity, less willing than O'Neill to relinquish the Greek ideal of reason in favor of the quotidian rationality of
bodily desire.

Ultimately, critical theory develops an aesthetics of the good life,
which helps it live its own life—the essence of the lifeworld-grounded
critical theory I am trying to develop. Marx resisted writing such an aesthetics, although he gave ample hints in the 1844 manuscripts about the
sense and sentience of socialism. Today, this aesthetic must depict the
form and feel of socialism and feminism, not merely discursively but
through the body and voice of the new person and his or her art, music,
architecture, sexuality. Marcuse was the only Frankfurt theorist to take
the development of this aesthetic seriously, relying heavily on Freud for
the sexual underpinning of a new body politic. O'Neill's concept of the
body politic also formulates this aesthetic in phenomenological terms,
paralleling Marcuse's Freudianization of Marxist critical theory.
O'Neill's vision of a wild sociology is a version of critical theory that sings
of commonplace pain and hope and thus constitutes itself as a form of
civic discourse. The bittersweet harmony of Beethoven or Dylan is
joined with the pretheoretical affirmation of common humanity that
wild sociology provides (see O'Neill 1975, 291–302).

In this sense, critical theory sings, paints, writes, argues, makes
love. In so doing, it evaluates contemporary society against specific criteria of socialist possibility. Marx's ideal of dis-alienation is rendered
phenomenological in the translation of socialism into an actual political
body. The taboo on graven images is explicitly rescinded, for the taboo
robs us of an organizational device with which to redirect resistance into
political channels. Of course, youth music is heavily commodified and
thus co-opted by the culture industry, now as in the 1960s. Yet the libidinal responsiveness of the young to the sights and sounds of their music is
a potential political phenomenon, an essential component of the aesthetic of a new world.

The concept of praxis thus has a more allusive and negative for-mulation in Adorno; Marcuse and O'Neill locate the realm of praxis in the infrastructure of discourse, desire, and the body. I want to focus on the function of art in Adorno's view, a perspective similar to Nietzsche's theory of music expressed in *The Birth of Tragedy*. Adorno says of music:

> Its truth appears guaranteed more by its denial of any meaning in organized society, of which it will have no part—accom-plished by its own organized vacuity—than by any capability of positive meaning within itself. Under the present circumstances it is restricted to definitive negation. [1973c, 20]

"Aesthetic authenticity is a socially necessary illusion: no work of art can thrive in a society founded upon power, without insisting upon its own power" (Adorno 1973c, 216). Art negates only as it promises a different, better world and thereby implodes one-dimensionality by the example of its own abrasive contingency. Yet unlike Marcuse, Adorno does not en-dorse Brecht's concept of the estrangement effect, an art that shocks and thus educates. Atonal music resonated the experience of pain; it was not a pedagogy of the oppressed and philosophy of hope. Marcuse's fond-ness for romanticism contrasts with Adorno's utter lack of sentimental-ity, issuing from his modernist concept of the negative subject. Marcuse's (1955, 1969) subject, rooted in Schiller's play-impulse, suffers greatly at the hands of the world yet can express its suffering in the hope of romantic redemption and political reconciliation, as I argued in chap-ter 9.

As Horkheimer and Adorno wrote in *Dialectic of Enlightenment*, "the triumph of advertising in the culture industry is that consumers feel compelled to buy and use its products even though they see through the advertisements" (1972, 167). Dissonant music serves as revolutionary advertising since it never falls on deaf ears. It insinuates its way into con-sciousness and tries to stimulate the critical spirit of the subject. The clash of cymbals reminds us of the din of the bourgeois city. The twelve-tone scale recalls for us the seriality of our lives. For Adorno, music is a social form because it is an element in a comprehensive social whole, almost a reflex of a noisy society. Music is not simply consumed as use value but gains its allure from its bourgeois purposive purposelessness, as Kant called it. Bourgeois aesthetic theory holds that art has no use value. The oeuvre delights because it represents the affluence of a cul-ture that can afford to employ artists to do nothing in particular.

Theory itself, for Adorno, does not consist in a form of life exuding the positive character and need of its subject. Like dissonant music, it is socially useful noise. Its language cannot fail to be the language of the dominant society, extended to its limit of rationality. Adorno once believed that the social whole contained its own principle of contradiction, to be revealed by a theory that comprehends the untruth of the whole. Theory is the critique of an ideology that does not penetrate its own veneer of half-truths and glosses. Theory opposes the premature harmony of liberal capitalism by denouncing the tragedy of liberalism, its ultimately cheerful seriality. Both Adorno and Nietzsche situated the mythologization of enlightenment in Socrates, who first hoped rationally to eliminate tragedy. *Dialectic of Enlightenment* assumed that Marxism failed by breaking insufficiently with the ethos of the domination of nature and society. *Negative Dialectics* (Adorno 1973b) charts the self-consciousness of enlightened dominion that has produced a thoughtless world. Adorno has rephrased Hegel's cunning of reason as the cunning of unreason: the inexorable progress of enlightenment can be depicted only in an enlightened, disenchanted music. Adorno ultimately abandoned Marx's hope that contradictions within society could be resolved and harmony created.

Like Marx, Adorno was concerned to reveal by reproducing the contradictions of the negative totality through ideology critique. Schoenberg's music became the ultimate critique of ideology in its abrasive reproduction of social dissonance. Art's "penetrating eye of consciousness" bespeaks the world as it has come to be, apparently serving us as the critique of political economy served Marx. Hegelian rationality reveals the essential telos of things by peering behind their commonsense appearances. Adorno believed that a discursive philosophy would fail in this effort, that only art and music could truly disclose the negative inauthenticity of the bourgeois world. "Modern music sees absolute oblivion as its goal. It is the surviving message of despair from the shipwrecked" (Adorno 1973c, 133). Theory is the bottle in which the shipwrecked deposit their plea for help. But no bottle is found until after the shipwrecked have perished. Negative or radical music evokes only negation, hence reproducing it. It provides a mood for the "penetrating eye of consciousness" and enables it to comprehend but not change the depravity of things. If the whole is the untruth, critical theory reproduces by reflecting falsehood, failing to make a political difference.

The subject is so deformed by its presence in a brutalizing, privatizing world that it can never resurrect itself with the aid of theory, art, or politics. Horkheimer and Adorno argue that Socrates tried to comprehend all mysteries, dooming every subsequent generation to the impossible project of seeking apodictic knowledge. The sin of pride scars the subject by forcing it outside itself in the externalizations of technology. Realism overwhelms the subject with things themselves. Adorno contrasts the musics of Schoenberg and Stravinsky:

> Stravinsky does justice to reality. The primacy of specialty over intention, the cult of the clever feat, the joy in agile manipulations such as those of the percussion in *L'Histoire du Soldat*— all these play off the means against the end. The means in the most literal sense—namely, the instrument—is hypostatized: it takes precedence over the music. The composition expresses only one fundamental concern: to find the sounds which will best suit its particular nature and result in the most overwhelming effect. [1973c, 172]

Adorno felt that critical theory could restore the value of intention by asserting the primacy of music over techniques to express sound. Radical music cuts to the heart of instrumentality by following the logic of musical instrumentality to its ultimate conclusion. The "ideal of authenticity" for which Stravinsky's music strives is similar to the authenticity pursued by Heidegger's philosophy. Both discourses are jargons inasmuch as each sublates the objective subject by hypostatizing the abstract importance of technique. Heidegger's *Dasein* is as inhuman as the subject of Stravinsky's composition—if indeed music has any conception of the subject, as Adorno would probably have claimed for it.

Culture is the tip of the iceberg of bourgeois society. But culture "progressively" penetrates downward to affect the base by transforming the sensibilities and expectations of citizens and their received ideology of the work ethic and erotic renunciation. A phenomenology of advanced capitalism reveals the lifeworld ground of the structures we invoke when we speak about a one-dimensional society. Yet theory in Adorno's terms does not enlighten in a hortatory way. Theory merely acts as a bellwether of domination by reflecting the deformations of subjectivity. The more complexly overdetermined is the object of critical theory, namely, late bourgeois society, the more allusive critical theory must be. The more that culture is disenchanted, the more theory will have to be mythological. Just here, dialectical theory in Marx's sense freezes. Allusive theory responds reflexively to the deformations of culture. Adorno understood that theory had become undialectical because the world had been so totalized in its evil that it denied the critical immanence and transcendent quality of thought. Marx's conception of a critical theory that could reveal the telos of deformed social facts has been transformed at a time when the negative totality has lost its principle of dynamic contradiction. Thus the falling rate of profit projected by Marx has not materialized in a final paroxysm as capitalism has checked the disruptive principle of its own self-negation through the interventions of the state and culture industry.

Marcuse (e.g., 1960) always maintained that the "power of negative thinking" contained a rational kernel of hope. In fact, the theory of liberation offered by Marcuse treats the subject as a relatively undamaged agent of transformative praxis. The Hegelian power of reason, its determinate negation of the apparent world, informs Marcuse's hopeful conception of the subject. Even his stark *One-Dimensional Man* holds out the possibility of redemption. "It is only for the sake of those without hope that hope is given to us." In *An Essay on Liberation,* Marcuse (1969) suggests that any future society will have to emerge through a new infrastructure of undistorted human needs and desires. *Counterrevolution and Revolt* (1972) elaborates this through Marcuse's critique of the New Left, which regrettably eschewed the critical function of rationality. He also describes the political aesthetic of a future society and plots a non-antagonistic alliance between humanity and nature. New science can help reconstruct this alliance, as I argued in the preceding chapter. The object world is but a proving ground for liberated subjectivity, which has an ineluctably objective component in the body and desire. Marxian scientism has contributed to the decomposition of Marx's original notion of the possible unity of humanity and nature. The person has been falsely treated as a socioeconomic cipher devoid of intellectual, libidinal, emotional faculties. Mechanical Marxism ultimately has no conception of the objective subject, a conception derived by Marcuse from psychoanalysis.

> Behind these familiar traits of a socialism yet to come is the idea of socialism itself as a qualitatively different totality. The socialist universe is also a moral and aesthetic universe: dialectical materialism contains idealism as an element of theory and practice. The prevalent material needs and satisfactions are shaped—and controlled—by the requirements of exploitation. Socialism must augment the quantity of goods and services in order to abolish all poverty, but at the same time, socialist production must change the quality of existence—change the needs and satisfactions themselves. Moral, psychological, aesthetic, intellectual faculties, which today, if developed at all, are relegated to a realm of culture separate from and above the material existence, would then become factors in the material production itself. [Marcuse 1972, 3]

The historical nature of the subject itself stands at the ideological crossroads between the critical theorists. What is the nature of the subject? Can we even speak about the subject, except by very indirect analogy in our music or our science? Adorno supposed that the subject was an effete residual of bourgeois philosophy that perished in the Nazi death camps. Marcuse and O'Neill, in contrast, argue that the kernel of positive opposition lies in the "libidinal rationality" beginning to emerge from the embodied subject. They have tried to harness the prepolitical reaction of subjectivity against surplus repression in building a new body politic.

Whereas Adorno read Freud as the prescient prophet of the completely eradicated subject, Marcuse employs the gloomy Freud to postulate a buried libidinal substratum capable of healthy creativity as well as socialist and feminist relations. The initial revolt of 1960s youth against an oppressive superego was not dismissed by Marcuse or O'Neill as merely another version of the Oedipal complex but as indicating that desire was beginning to emerge. Marcuse's Freudianism enabled him to harness desire as the new agent of body politics. Marcuse and O'Neill seek to restore the experience and discourse of the embodied subject to Marxism. As I argued in my preceding chapters on Marcuse's Freudianization of critical theory, ideology critique opposes Marxist scientism in arguing that the fate of the subject is important for oppositional activity. Although Hegel spiritualized the subject in terms of a world-historical spirit, Marx reobjectivized the concept of the subject through his labor theory of value. Marx saw that contemplation, as well as discourse, was itself a kind of production, akin to work and possessing the same permanent objectivity. Feminists add that *re*production is production, too, valorizing the realm of unwaged domestic labor. Marx and Engels in *The German Ideology* (1947) relentlessly criticize the spiritualization of the subject in German philosophy and argue that the so-called objective spirit is a product of nineteenth-century idealism as ideology.

For Marcuse and O'Neill, restoring the subject's political desire is tantamount to resuscitating the power of critical rationality. Adorno never believed that Hegel's concept of thought as negation was an adequate form of political activity; but negative thought was better than no thought at all. Marcuse believes that negative reason can actually become a form of praxis, the Great Refusal of domination. Hegel's concept of negation was revised by Marcuse to become a self-sufficient form of critical praxis—negation pregnant with the hidden positive. Marcuse's notion of the political character of sensibility turned the moment of thought in a directly political direction. Surplus repression was the libidinal counterpart of the extraction of surplus value, as I argued in chapters 6 and 7.

Adorno's (1973b) conception of the frozen quality of the social totality denied even the critical power of thought. The subject was so damaged, with no prepolitical potential, that its thought and speech were but reflexes of the dominant ideology and discourse. Total domination could not occasion total opposition unless opposition mirrored the form of domination. Adorno's dialectic was defused and deflected from the social totality. Dialectic no longer reveals the unfulfilled purpose of things but instead simply mirrors a "negative dialectic" of society that successfully reconciles all social contradictions. Dissonant music echoes the prematurely destructured dialectic that becomes sedimented in eternally contradictory social institutions. For example, increasing private leisure time occasions a more thoroughgoing domination of the subject by corporate prerogatives. Indeed, as Horkheimer and Adorno argue in *Dialectic of Enlightenment* (1972), leisure itself is captured by the culture industry as needs are turned into commodities. Critique has no field for its expression but would fall on deaf ears. Everything can be made to seem affirmative, even Marxism.

The aesthetic theories of O'Neill, Marcuse, and Adorno all respond to the premature reconciliation of contradictions in late bourgeois society. O'Neill's turn toward a political aesthetic responds to the deformation of the subject and yet remains sensitive to nascent opposition on the level of body politics. Marcuse's hope of resensitizing the subject lies in an active conception of libidinal rationality and preservation of the transcendent function of art. Adorno argued that the dialectical method was stagnant, archaic; the only possible negation occurs on the mimetic level. Praxis, the self-externalization of the laboring subject, always fails to achieve its purpose, namely, the liberation of other subjects. Thought alone could conceivably remain undamaged by the pernicious totality.

In *Negative Dialectics* (1973b), Adorno argues that the conception of the subject itself is a remnant of bourgeois idealism. The subject cannot be thought without thinking the object that dominates it. To subjectivize social theory was falsely to represent the actual powers of the nearly impotent, voiceless person. Theory was circumscribed by its own inability to include the concept of a separate entity called the human being. In reality, the subject was almost perfectly synonymous with the objects to which it was politically subordinated. Thus, the subject is a trivial and forgotten moment in a dialectical method that charts the progress of the object's preponderance. It is clear that Adorno does not completely banish a concept of the subject from his musicology; music needs an audience. The culture critique of Adorno deals with culture as an objectified domain of spirit that has somehow gone wrong. In *Philosophy of Modern Music* (1973c), Adorno says that the avant-garde's rejection of Schoenberg's music, hiding behind the apology of incomprehension, masks their real hatred of the abrasive atonality of the music. Each sentence in Adorno's work likewise resonates a harshly dissonant quality through which he tries to capture the frozen quality of the dialectic.

Marcuse's theorizing makes thought practical by embedding thinking in the totality of the sensuous person. In O'Neill, "sensibility" is a combination of good sense and good senses, intellectual and libidinal rationality. The ego itself is a dialectic between unfulfilled hopes and concrete possibilities. One thinks of the future and grapples with "the chance of the alternatives" (Marcuse 1964) that springs from the present circumstance. There can be no dialectical movement without the complicity of the self-conscious subject, a subject not so damaged as Adorno supposed. Whereas for Adorno culture was merely a domain for the system's ugly self-reflection, culture for O'Neill and Marcuse is a potential launching pad for oppositional projects.

Negative theory for Marcuse works to create the aesthetic of socialist forms; it contains the positive within the negative. In O'Neill the Great Refusal breaks into song. In Adorno, it peters out in a vague imitation of social insanity by the crazy composer. There is a tendency on the part of Adorno and his followers to reject youth culture as a commodified, co-opted spin-off of the culture industry. Marcuse, in contrast, recognizes the ambivalent nature of the 1960s youth movement. Events like Woodstock are obviously corporate rip-offs, yet they may also represent a real attempt to create a new order of political togetherness, the beginning of a new class consciousness, however inchoate and ephemeral. Woodstock was an ambivalent phenomenon because American youth lacked the political structures (like an organized Left) within which to situate their erotic-aesthetic rejection of inner-worldly asceticism. Marcuse and O'Neill, unlike Adorno, recognize the positive within the negative, the realization of possible transformative experience within an otherwise disorganized, preideological youth movement. This is exactly how a lifeworld-grounded critical theory should proceed.

Rock music and drugs are sources of prepolitical ecstasy that free the person from the space-time of serial bourgeois life. Atonal music merely mocks seriality. Marcuse and O'Neill both attempt to force the moment of prepolitical ecstasy into the mold of a new body politic. The ecstasy of free and easy togetherness experienced at Dionysian 1960s rock concerts can be recollected as an authentic mode of socialist coexistence. Ultimately, the ecstatic forms of youth culture constitute aspects of the everyday life of a socialist body politic. The naive, preideological honesty of gentle folk can thus be preserved as a vital archetype of the postpolitical socialist and feminist personality. Marx's icon of the Paris Commune as the epitome of communism was replaced in the 1960s by the icon of the "be-in"—and perhaps today by the depressing image of youths congregating in shopping malls.

It is insufficient merely to reject these moments of cathartic subjectivity as fodder for the culture industry. Social change is effected between the moments of subjective abandon and objective sobriety; Marx roughly distinguished cultural from economic modes in accepting this motif. Yet nowhere did he rule out the objective potential of initially subjective rebellion. The "counter" culture is not actually against culture; it opposes cultural forms that are divorced from political forms. The archetypal hippie, for all his or her apparent prepolitical innocence, actually rejected the bourgeois segregation of culture from economics and politics, in this way engaging in a quintessentially political form of opposition. The counterculture opposed the categorial boundaries *between* bourgeois culture and society. Indeed, Marcuse's new science and O'Neill's wild sociology are forms of cultural opposition against this very fragmentation of the modern lifeworld. Wild sociology attempts to reunite fractured humanity in rejecting the vulgar Marxist dichotomy between "superstructure" and "base." It is a dialectical sociology because it digs beneath the apparently apolitical surface of phenomena like rock music and turns them toward the political light of day.

In spite of certain dialectical appearances to the contrary, Adorno accepted a quite deterministic model of the relation between economics and culture. Marcuse imputed less determining force to the structure of capital and more to a relatively autonomous cultural sphere. I argue that Marcuse's model is closer Marx's in that Marx also tried to discover prepolitical modes of opposition before they entered the schema of class conflict. Today it is imperative to move further away from Adorno's model of a frozen, totally managed world in reassessing certain nonproletarian cultural forms for their contribution to the creation of a new body politic, precisely the project of cultural studies (see Agger 1991a). It is also imperative that we revise Marx's model of the politically organized working class and the theory of crisis that supports it, especially in light of the feminist challenge. In Marx's spirit, but not slavishly imitating him, we must become sensitive to untraditional modes of political opposition.

For Marxian theory, the location (or rather contraction) of the opposition in certain middle-class strata and in the ghetto population appears as an intolerable deviation—as does the emphasis on biological and aesthetic needs: regression to bourgeois or, even worse, aristocratic, ideologies. But, in the advanced monopoly-capitalist countries, the displacement of the opposition (from the organized industrial working classes to militant minorities) is caused by the internal development of the society; and the theoretical "deviation" only reflects this development. What appears as a surface phenomenon is indicative of basic tendencies which suggest not only different prospects of change but also a depth and extent of change far beyond the expectations of traditional socialist theory. [Marcuse 1969, 58–59]

I have contrasted Adorno, Marcuse, and O'Neill better to comprehend the alternative of critical theory as music and critical theory as the activist sin of pride, even as praxis itself. Adorno thought that everything we do in the way of praxis is wrong, or at best insufficient; theory contemplates freedom that can be expressed only atonally: There is no collective subject anymore. The primacy of the object forces the subject meekly to comply with the interdictions of the object. In late bourgeois society, Schoenberg sings the truth, although in dismal, negative tones. The dialectical blockage of dynamic forces issues in the death of opposition. We can only sing the tragedy of a world that has forgotten tragedy.

Adorno thinks that science has no song but that of mathematics. Nietzschean tragedy has been banished from memory by the instrumental success of scientism. Culture has been made an industry by those who attempt to harmonize the fundamentally tragic universe; culture is a painless ideology, another great myth. Marcuse is less Nietzschean than Hegelian in that he does not accept the inherent tragedy of human existence as an occasion for political resignation. In fact, his conception of the mortal subject is based on Freud's essentially constructive matrix of instincts. His own theorizing presupposes Marx's optimism about eliminating domination. Critical theory can even serve as an expressive medium for the politicization of sensibility, this chapter's thesis. The Great Refusal is a form of praxis, but dissonant music is not. Music is merely negative theory, resigned to its heteronomous quality. Marcuse's theory transcends itself in becoming a form of embodied sensibility, a political structure of needs and feelings. A dialectical theory must herald the negation of contradiction, couched in historically comprehensible terms and forms, which is to say that it must be a discourse of hope.

Adorno's negative theory does not negate dissonance because it cannot rise above the terms of discourse of a dissonant world. O'Neill transcends pain through an optimism rooted in the natural or wild objectivity of the instinctual body. Without this source of desire, critical theory fails to rise above tragedy. Critical theory has become Scholastic because its second generation could not come to terms with psychoanalysis and its theory of objective subjectivity. Marcuse's *Eros and Civilization* (1955) failed to convince enough Marxists that the objectivity of subjectivity was a wellspring of hope, not despair. Therefore, in failing to assimilate Freud, critical theory runs the risk of neglecting vital cultural forms of opposition that utterly repudiate surplus repression. Freud provides what Marx neglected: a transmission belt between economic structure and cultural forms, the objective subject. Ultimately, Marx did not understand why the collapse of capital could emerge in a new order of society; he did not theorize the political sensibility that stands between the moments of structure and consciousness (via discourse). Capitalism survived because workers could not translate the insecurity of wage labor into a sensible language prefiguring a new order of social being.

Today, the one-dimensional totality denies the experiences of imagination and union, experiences that are essential to the nonlinear space-time of rock and drugs. It is in this sense that the language of a critical theory that transcends its own Scholasticism must portray the raw feeling of ecstasy through media that somehow escape the leveling influence of the culture industry. And, as developments in rock culture since the 1960s have shown, the culture industry appears all-powerful: the political ecstasy of the Jefferson Airplane gave way to the grimness of Johnny Rotten, the commodification of Michael Jackson, and the apolitical postmodernization of so-called New Music (the postmodernism of chap. 5, not chap. 15; I use postmodernism as a basis of my lifeworld-grounded critical theory to criticize postmodernism as cultural ideology).

We are not faced with a discrete choice among culture forms like symphony, opera, jazz, or rock. Atonal music recollects the painful dissociation of meaning in an alienating society; rock recollects the libidinal rationality of good times, the promise of living ecstatically beyond instrumental rationality. If critical theory is a discourse, it must talk even when ordinary language has been exhausted. Between Adorno and Marcuse there lies the distance between disappointment and the cautious reawakening of hope, a distance vital for eyes wide open to a history that occasionally delights as well as disappoints.

Critical theory itself is an oeuvre, a product of discourse and desire. In singing the world, this theory chooses either to deny or affirm the possibility of a resurrected humanity arising from this Earth. Atonal music evokes the scream of the tortured, appropriate to its time. Rock sings of sexual rationality and the transcendence of functional differentiation. Between Auschwitz and Haight-Ashbury, critical theory changed its tune, first Adorno, then Marcuse. As I said initially, critical theory must surpass itself in remaining within the dialectic of the real and the possible. New science recovers grounds for positive rebellion in the carnal body and its imagination. "Critical theory" is not a school but the way we choose to oppose inhumanity in different songs of joy. What these songs will be in the 1990s has yet to be determined. The discourse of theory may be theory itself—an interdisciplinary oppositional project grounded in a Habermasian concept of ideal speech (without forgetting the grounding of this project in emancipatory desire).

In this chapter, I have developed the argument that critical theory itself is a mode of political sensibility, a way of life prefiguring a whole new culture, discourse, and polity. I have drawn on Marcuse's politics of subjectivity, explored in the preceding section of this book, in order to make this case. In the next three chapters, I further explore this notion of theory as an intervention in its own right—a moment of radical cultural opposition that repoliticizes the public sphere, hence taking us fruitfully beyond the "end" of ideology. As I shall argue in my concluding chapter, this discussion of the politics of theory is advanced most tellingly by way of a reconstructed, repoliticized postmodernism that in certain respects is already anticipated in Marcuse's own cultural politics of radical sensibility, discussed here.

# 13

# Critical Theory, Scientism, and Empiricism

I shall here sharpen my critique of the Hegelian Marxism of the Frankfurt school, arguing that theorists like Horkheimer and Adorno failed to repoliticize Marxism once they had perceived that the working class would not become a successful revolutionary agent. The redevelopment of Marxism by certain original members of the Frankfurt school exaggerated the extent to which political rebellion could be isolated and contained by dominant interests. I argue that the early Frankfurt school's thesis of the decline of human individuality forced them to deny the possibility of political radicalism largely because it prevented them from recognizing resistance at the level of the lifeworld. This needs to be corrected if critical theory is successfully to challenge the depoliticization of public life today.

I set two tasks for a critical theory that endeavors to repoliticize its orientation to social change, my main project in this book. First, we must develop a concept of human nature that grounds the possibility of political struggle in the capacity of the human being to perceive his or her own exploitation and to envisage and work toward alternative institutions, a project begun by Marcuse. I believe that the assumption of active, constitutive subjectivity must be the foundation stone of contemporary critical theory. In eliminating this assumption and supposing that the human being has become totally dominated, Horkheimer and Adorno deny the possibility of emancipatory struggle. My second task is to reground the theory-practice relation in Marx's concept of the advisory role of critical theory. In this sense, theory follows and guides practice, locating it in an analytic totality and explicating its transformative significance. Horkheimer and Adorno severed the theory-practice relation in arguing that theory could only take the form of ideology critique because human subjectivity was no longer perceived to be capable of revolt.

As I argued in my earlier Marcuse chapters as well as the preceding chapter, Marxism today must not, under the influence of historical pessimism, prematurely abandon the possibility of social change. I reject the thesis of the decline of subjectivity and challenge the overly defeatist attitude of Horkheimer and Adorno to the actuality of constructive change even though I learn a great deal from their dialectical critique of civilization, notably their theory of the culture industry in *Dialectic of Enlightenment* (1972). I apply my insight about critical theory's failure to reengage empirical social research and a praxis orientation to the actual redevelopment of a social science with political implications (of the kind done by the Frankfurt theorists during their most "empirical" phase in the 1940s, e.g., Adorno et al. 1950; Adorno 1945, 1954). I examine certain historical aspects of Marx's theory and suggest ways it could be amended in the light of recent political and economic developments. The result will be a concept of radical empiricism that renews Marx's revolutionary science by enhancing the political significance of contemporary struggle to destroy authority structures and the division of labor (see Marx and Engels 1959, 37–39). Radical empiricism will become a political strategy of dialectical sensibilities who refuse to separate thought and action, even beginning to "live" social change in their own daily activity.

## Origins of Critical Theory: Marxism Redeveloped

As I have explored in chapter 2 and elsewhere in this book, Lukács and Korsch in the 1920s took issue with the Marxism that evolved in the Second International under the influence of theorists like Bernstein and Kautsky. Lukács and Korsch opposed the neo-Kantian reconstruction of Marxism that separated the political from the scientific dimensions of Marx's theory of capitalism. Lukács polemicized against tendencies to conceive of Marxism as a variant of natural science that merely charted "laws" of social motion. In a broader sense, Lukács and Korsch opposed economism, a theory of change that stresses the economic determination of sociocultural and ideological forms. Economism, they believed, degraded the human being's purposeful contribution to the revolutionary process, suggesting instead that capitalism will inevitably collapse, given certain "contradictory" economic circumstances. Lukács and Korsch rejected "automatic Marxism" (see Jacoby 1971, 1975a, 1976, 1981) because it gave too little weight to subjective and ideological factors in social analysis, and thus—they felt—it tended to reinforce a passive, even fatalistic attitude toward social change, eliminating the role of active subjectivity and intersubjectivity.

The philosophical reconstruction of Marxism attempted by Lukács (1971) and Korsch (1970) has been characterized as "Hegelian Marxist" (see Lichtheim 1971). Lukács returned to the theme of Hegel's *Phenomenology of Mind,* which, he believed, was relevant to overcoming the sclerosis of Marxism. Hegel provided an active conception of human consciousness in the *Phenomenology,* opposing the dualism between human consciousness and the sentient world developed by Descartes. Hegel deepened Kant's notion of a constitutive, self-conscious human being who necessarily employs "categories of the understanding" (as Kant called them) with which to perceive and order the objective universe. Hegel went even further than Kant, suggesting that human beings could perceive the essence, or reason, of empirical phenomena, enabling them to go beyond mere commonsense experience. This faculty of reason allowed people to comprehend and indeed to construct their world in accord with its revealed telos.

Lukács argued that this conception of a creative consciousness rested at the core of Marx's dialectical materialism. Moreover, he felt that the concept of subjectivity had been largely eliminated by neo-Kantian Marxists who endorsed deterministic models of social change. Marxism could be revived, Lukács felt, only if the subjective factor were upgraded, giving Marxian theory a new purchase on the psychological dimension of market capitalism that had become increasingly important since Marx's pathbreaking analysis of the reifying effects of commodity fetishism in *Capital.*

"Reification" was a word used by Lukács to describe new conditions in capitalism: alienation, he felt, had become heightened owing to new forces of ideological and psychological manipulation, an analysis later extended by Horkheimer and Adorno in *Dialectic of Enlightenment* and by Marcuse in *One-Dimensional Man.* Indeed, Lukács theorized that the working class failed to rebel between about 1900 and 1920 because it was trapped by a conservative, bourgeois consciousness, a reified consciousness unable to perceive the possibility of a qualitatively different social order and to act on that insight. Lukács called this the "ideological crisis of the proletariat," a concept that directly challenged the economistic assumptions that subjective factors were largely irrelevant to the revolutionary process and that capitalism would collapse without political intervention.

The ideological crisis of the proletariat prolonged the life of capitalism. Western Marxism thus entered a holding pattern, uncertain about its relevance to working-class sensibilities. Lukács felt that the working class could be prepared for its imputed revolutionary potential and even seize power from capitalists only if the grip of reification (or deepened alienation) were challenged. Lukács argued that the crisis of capitalism would be resolved only through "free action" explicitly opposing the deterministic model of social change endorsed by certain Marxists, like Kautsky, that explained the revolutionary delay with reference to purely objective economic factors. Korsch for his part argued that ideology was an important social force and could not be treated only as an epiphenomenon thrown up by the economic substructure. He suggested that Marxism was not deterministic in that Marx took seriously ideological forms like religion and philosophy, refusing to reduce them to mere reflexes of the economic system. Both Lukács and Korsch stressed the importance of conceiving of society as a totality, irreducible to economics. Both believed that Marx was not an economic reductionist and took inspiration from Marx's embryonic theory of ideology in their own attempts to comprehend the developing character of capitalism in the 1920s.

For Lukács and Korsch, the key element in a revised Marxism was the critique of ideology, a critique designed to reveal the depths of proletarian consciousness to which exploitation had penetrated. Exploitation came to have psychological as well as economic significance. Proletarian consciousness could be manipulated by bourgeois ideology; thus exploitation would be occluded and mystified. Neither Lukács nor Korsch relinquished the theories of surplus value put forward by Marx to capture the reality of the exploitation of workers' labor power; they only analyzed new relations between economic infrastructure and ideological superstructure in the context of late or monopoly capitalism that ensued from the ideological crisis of the proletariat.

Lukács in *History and Class Consciousness* (1971) urged that Marxists return to the literal Marx, not as bowdlerized by economic determinists of the Second and Third Internationals. He argued that Marx developed a concept of the social totality stressing the dialectical relationship between economics and ideology. Although he had not seen Marx's 1844 manuscripts when he published the essays constituting *History and Class Consciousness* in 1923, Lukács clearly endorsed Marx's implication that alienation, as Marx called it in 1844, took both economic and psychological forms. Reification, in Lukács's usage, was deepened alienation; Lukács used the term "reification" to describe the naturelike, mechanical quality of social relations under capitalism. He suggested that consciousness itself was being transformed into a dead thing, merely another commodity.

In this sense, it it important to stress the continuity between the first stirrings of Hegelian Marxism in the early 1920s and Marx's critique of alienation. Lukács and Korsch believed that the working class was still a necessary and probable revolutionary agent. The perception of Hegelian Marxism by certain orthodox Marxists (see Althusser 1969; Colletti 1973) as a fundamental departure from Marx's theory of revolution is difficult to sustain in the light of Lukács's and Korsch's 1923 works. Korsch explicitly states that he is faithful to Marx's nondeterministic concept of social change in his revaluation of subjective factors in the historical process (see Korsch 1970, 73, 77). However, Hegelian Marxism, despite the apparent agreement between its cofounders on many issues of substance, is not homogeneous. Its own history is as complex and varied as the history of organized Marxism as a whole. What has come to be called "critical theory," emanating from the Frankfurt Institute for Social Research or "Frankfurt school," founded in 1923, is a variant of Lukács's and Korsch's original work, although there are significant differences that have proved to be very consequential for Marxian theory in the years following World War II.

Lukács and Korsch were fundamentally orthodox in their orientation to Marx's original theory of economic crisis and proletarian revolution. Both were self-consciously engaged in a process of deepening, not fundamentally transforming, Marx's theory. However, the critical theory developed by the Frankfurt circle represented a much more fundamental departure from the original theory than Lukács's and Korsch's work. Critical theory appeared to be more Hegelian than Marxian, more philosophical than political. The Frankfurt theorists were more skeptical in the 1920s about the prospect of proletarian revolution than were Lukács and Korsch. The Frankfurt school initially embraced diverse theoretical perspectives. Orthodox Marxists like Karl-August Wittfogel joined with philosopher-aesthetes like Adorno and with psychoanalytically oriented thinkers like Fromm. However, in the 1930s and early 1940s a distinctive perspective emerged that further demarcated critical theory from Lukács's and Korsch's Hegelian Marxism and from original Marxism.

This perspective shed original Marxism's theoretical allegiance to the working class, an allegiance faithfully maintained by both Lukács and Korsch. Critical theory radicalized Lukács's analysis of the ideological crisis of the proletariat and of false consciousness by suggesting that the working class had utterly lost its potential for revolt. Further, the Frankfurt theorists challenged the Marxian paradigm itself by suggesting that critical theory could no longer achieve a close advisory relation to political practice but would have to play a more circumspect "critical" role. The Frankfurt theorists believed that the prospects for a revolution, which might have appeared greater in the crisis period of the 1920s than in the post-Depression period, had diminished and that the entire relationship between theory and practice had to be revised.

Where Lukács and Korsch attempted to balance the relation between economic and ideological forces (believing that they were faithful to Marx in this), the Frankfurt theorists minimized class struggle. The analysis of false consciousness was extended and radicalized by Horkheimer, Adorno, and Marcuse (Horkheimer 1972, 1974; Adorno 1973b, 1974; Marcuse 1964) so that it was seen by some (e.g., Slater [1977], as I discussed in chap. 2) to usurp the significance of Marx's original economic critique of capitalism. The Frankfurt school theorists did not suddenly abandon the model of proletarian revolution. Initially, in the 1920s and 1930s, Horkheimer and his associates were sympathetic to the revolutionary aspirations of original Marxism. However, it was not long before the Frankfurt circle recognized that capitalism had changed qualitatively, even since the period when Lukács and Korsch had developed their theories of class consciousness. In the institute's journal, *Zeitschrift für Sozialforschung*, articles appeared that suggested that market capitalism had developed into late or monopoly capitalism, requiring new categories of analysis and thus new models of social change (see Marcuse 1968d; Horkheimer 1973).

Where Lukács could still retain the model of a class-conscious collective subject (a class "in and for itself," the working class), the Frankfurt theorists suggested that the entire model of class consciousness needed to be rethought. Indeed, Horkheimer and others went as far as to intimate that human consciousness was far more exploited than Lukács and Korsch had imagined. Lukács believed that the ideological crisis of the proletariat was due to the entrapment of the working class by bourgeois ideology, whereas the Frankfurt thinkers believed that this ideology went far deeper than before, penetrating and distorting the deep subjectivity of the person as well as the intersubjectivity of classes and groups.

Ideology in the original Marxian paradigm was deceptive in that it mystified economic exploitation. Now, under late or monopoly capitalism, ideology has a more insidious function: preventing the development of critical consciousness by occluding the possibility of a qualitatively different social order. The Frankfurt thinkers believed that the human being was nearly incapable of thinking theoretically and critically about his or her own domination. Ideology in this sense penetrated the psychological core of the human being, producing automatons charged with the infinite consumption of commodities and values. Ideology came to have more than the mystifying function it had under market capitalism; it now enhanced profit by guaranteeing that the person would remain a willing adherent and agent of a bourgeois society requiring endless consumption and political conformity. This analysis of the new powers of ideology issued in a different kind of Marxism. The critical theorists no longer assumed that the working class was either the necessary or the probable agent of social change. Ideological pressures to conform and consume deflected political radicalism of the original kind. The Frankfurt theorists felt that consciousness itself was in decline, owing to the harmonizing powers of ideology. Revolt thus was unlikely in both collective and individual terms.

## Scientism as "Para-Ideology": Decline of Subjectivity

The Frankfurt school's thesis of the decline of an autonomous human being went far beyond Lukács's analysis of false consciousness, which could be demystified and reversed through a didactic type of political education, stimulating class consciousness. Hegelian Marxism in its original formulation was mainly concerned to return to Marx's dialectic between economic and ideological forces, opposing economic determinism, which implicitly counseled political passivity. Both Lukács and Korsch suggested that Marxism needed to retrieve its revolutionary focus and praxis orientation.

Critical theory in the Frankfurt formulation, however, was a product of a much more intense pessimism about the possibility of social change. Class consciousness failed to emerge from the post-Depression period, weakening Lukács and Korsch's activist optimism about reinvigorating the working class in Western Europe. Moreover, Marxism-Leninism could no longer convincingly pretend to be a democratizing force in the Soviet Union. Where Lukács could praise Lenin as a great dialectician and revolutionary (1970, 9), the Frankfurt theorists were far less sanguine about Soviet-style Marxism as it was given a Stalinist imprint. Capitalism was further consolidated between the Depression and the end of World War II. The critical theorists stated that the period of sharp contradictions between capital and labor had ended with the widespread unionization of workers and increasing state intervention in the economy. Keynesian economics sanctioned an increased role for the state in stimulating the economy through the creation of jobs and large capital expenditures. This development vitiated Marx's hypothesis that crisis was inevitable in a capitalist system. There *were* mechanisms by which the rate of profit could be sustained and even increased and by which the working class could be gradually enriched, thus ensuring their allegiance, compliance, and consumption.

There is controversy over whether Marx "predicted" the collapse of the system or merely developed several possible scenarios, one of which was heightened class conflict. This is an extremely important issue because the theory of the transition to socialism is tied in with the theory of crises. The concept of the dictatorship of the proletariat, I would argue, was never central to Marx; he was thus far from being a determinist in the sense of having predicted an inevitable collapse. If this reading of Marx is accepted, then the Frankfurt concept of the new powers of ideology and of state intervention in strengthening the economic system can be seen as continuous with the original theory. Also, the critique of Marxist-Leninist state socialism (rooted in the putative necessity of a transitional proletarian dictatorship) is sanctioned if the orthodox transition scheme is rejected or amended. Thus, it is possible to perceive the critical theorists' thesis of the decline of subjectivity (and the major revision of dialectical materialism that it occasioned) as Marxist in spirit. The clash between orthodoxy and revisionism has been productive in that it has cast Marx as having been more ambiguous about the inevitability of social change than many orthodox Marxists have assumed. It can be argued that Marx appeared to stop short of predicting an inevitable collapse, thus supporting the Hegelian Marxist reconstruction of Marx as a dialectical (nonreductionist) theorist of change.

In any case, critical theory (whatever its Marxist credentials) went far beyond Lukács and Korsch's reliance on timeworn models of revolutionary rupture. The philosophical and psychological dimensions of Hegelian Marxism assumed a new significance with the advent of Horkheimer and his associates. The crucial element in the critical theory developed in Frankfurt, and that which distinguishes its brand of Marxism from most earlier versions, was the thesis of declining, damaged subjectivity (see Horkheimer 1974; Adorno 1974). Since ideology was perceived as having developed greater powers of mystification, the concept of the critique of ideology necessarily had to change. Critical theory was not to be didactic in the sense of exhorting workers to revolt; rather, it would prod all human beings to think critically about domination, including self-alienation. The critique of ideology in this sense was transformed from a critique of the ideology of market capitalism and economic exploitation into a critique of bourgeois existence in general.

As I have argued with respect to Marcuse, the Frankfurt theorists believed that the consolidation of capitalism strengthened the system's hold on individual psyches, desires, and discourses. The critical faculty had been weakened by the positivist ideology of advanced capitalism. In 1960, Marcuse suggested that political education—critique—needed to fortify people's powers of "negative thinking." Further developing Weber's theories of instrumental rationality (involving the equation of social rationality with economic rationality such as mathematical accounting procedures), the critical theorists argued that instrumental rationality had become a new ideology to replace liberalism.

Instrumental rationality eliminated the distinction between means and ends. It stressed the importance of economic and bureaucratic efficiency, neglecting the critical examination of the purposes and goals of efficiency. The so-called organization person was a character produced by instrumental rationality. The concern with profit as such has been partly replaced by the values of efficiency and stability in the context of the expansion and consolidation of capitalism. The vast bureaucratization of industrial society has required that people not question the contents of administrative decisions and imperative commands but concern themselves only with accomplishing tasks imposed by custodians of the system. The Frankfurt theorists lamented the development of pervasive instrumental, managerial, and scientific ideologies. They believed that understanding the relationship between means and ends is necessary for assessing the quality of a given social order. They argued that instrumental rationality is fundamentally irrational because it veils embedded values that it secretly values. The apparent concern with only means and technical efficiency conceals the type of ends and social values that bureaucratic capitalism has institutionalized. The critical theorists argued that the so-called rational society is based on particular value constellations such as the belief in private enterprise. Although Weber was not completely sanguine about the existential consequences of thoroughgoing technical rationalization, he was nonetheless a partisan of the superficially value-neutral approach to the problems of social organization represented by instrumental rationality.

Critical theory perceived that "scientism," or the belief that social problems can be solved technically without appeal to normative or political values, has become the new ideology of late capitalism. Liberalism has been superseded by the collapse of market conditions of free competition. Class conflict has been institutionalized and largely (if only temporarily) contained through the rise of big unions and an interventionist state. Liberalism belonged to an earlier period of capitalism, when the ideology of individual initiative was perceived to be more realistic by workers and entrepreneurs. The bureaucratization of capitalism largely rendered liberalism obsolete inasmuch as the concept of individual initiative evidently clashed with the new reality of a bureaucratized economy and polity and a commodifying culture industry.

Mueller (1973) has characterized scientism and instrumental rationality (for my purposes, synonymous terms) as a "para-ideology" (101–12; Habermas 1970b). As a para-ideology, instrumental rationality does not provide the kind of total legitimation of the individual's place in society that religion and liberalism used to provide. Scientism appears to be above the political and ethical considerations that occupied past ideologies. An instrumental rationality that emphasizes technical efficiency depoliticizes decision making and thus seemingly takes social and economic organization outside the realm of ideology and moral choice (a phenomenon that Habermas has called the "scientization of politics"). The function of expertise in resolving social and economic crises becomes paramount because the expert ostensibly is not concerned with higher-order moral issues but only with efficiency. Thus, the para-ideology of instrumental rationality legitimates the essentially powerless position of the individual in face of complex systems that cannot be controlled or even fathomed. This ideology defuses rebellion by convincing the person that dominant interests necessarily act in his or her best interests and that, in any case, there is nothing else to be done.

Critical theorists propose this new analysis of ideology or, indeed, of para-ideology—that is, ideology that does not appear to be such. They argue that social conflicts are contained through the institutionalization of expertise that is fundamentally unchallengeable by powerless citizens, who merely consume decisions and values imposed by economic and sociocultural elites. In this context, the evolution of ideological or critical consciousness is only a remote possibility, given the depoliticization of authority and decision making. The person comes to accept whatever is given in the realm of the quotidian, regardless of its ethical or moral content, believing—trusting—that experts necessarily know best.

Where liberalism used to stress the autonomy of subjective choice and taste, today the illusion of such autonomy has largely disappeared. Conformity replaces individuality as a paramount social value. Political radicalism does not emerge as a salient possibility within the flattened, apparently deideologized universe of technical rationality—Marcuse's argument (see chap. 8 above). The decline of subjectivity emerges from a social context wherein the individual is manipulated by systemic forces that penetrate his or her innermost being, "sensibility." The experience of lack of freedom is justified by an ideology of technocratic control that is seemingly above the dispute about competing ethics and values. The precarious economic position of the average person requires that he or she invest trust in and accord legitimacy to experts who protect him or her against destitution. To do otherwise would be irrational according to the prevalent concept of rationality as involving trust in authorities. Crisis is not eliminated, nor is alienation. However, the causal relationship between capitalism and alienation is now mediated so complexly that the person cannot readily accuse particular people or elites of being oppressive. Domination is flattened into a typical, commonsense reality; it is nearly impossible to imagine a different, better world since the regime of technical rationality is self-perpetuating.

In this context, the concept of damaged life became critical theory's leitmotif in the hands of Adorno (1974). According to Horkheimer and Adorno (1972), there has come to be an equivalency between myth and enlightenment, belief and reason. Progress is debunked as an irrational process of false enlightenment. The aphoristic style of critical theory written between about 1947 and Horkheimer's death in 1973 reveals that the Frankfurt thinkers no longer felt that the causal connection between capitalism and alienation could be systematically severed. Everything is equally reified, including organized Marxism and its causal theory of exploitation.

In his philosophical masterwork, Adorno suggests that Marxism failed to change the world (Adorno 1973b, 3). As I discussed in the preceding chapter, his negative dialectics refuses to emerge in a positive synthesis, a concrete vision of new social life: Philosophy becomes negative in the face of damaged existence. Adorno compared modernity to the concentration camp, unwittingly trivializing the total horror of Nazi genocide. His version of critical theory unintentionally lost the specificity of Marx's critique of exploitation by descending to abstract negation, utilizing the concepts of the totally damaged life and of what may be called spurious subjectivity.

Adorno confused the absence of a philosophical concept of subjectivity with the empirical absence of real human beings (incinerated in the camp ovens). The notion of spurious subjectivity may have had effect as a metaphor for pervasive false consciousness in stressing that organized Marxism had at least temporarily failed. But Adorno intended more than a metaphor in his notion of a negative dialectics. Critical theory abandoned the working class and, with it, Marx's original concept of class revolution. The experience of fascism seemed to reinforce the malaise and cynicism of the critical theorists (except Marcuse, whose deviation from the Frankfurt orthodoxy has been discussed in the preceding section of this book). While Lukács assumed a relatively undamaged, potentially activist human being, Adorno and Horkheimer thought that the human being had gone up in smoke, fully manipulated by imposed authority. In this context, critical theory abandoned its advisory relation to the working class. Theory no longer presaged a qualitatively different social order (as Marx, Lukács, and Korsch definitely intended); it merely reflected the disharmony of late capitalist society, imitating but not overcoming its substantive irrationality.

Adorno's concept of spurious subjectivity made a good deal of sense on empirical grounds. Adorno did not identify a potentially radical working class in the 1940s and 1950s; indeed, he perceived no collective social movements that could be deemed revolutionary. On the basis of what he did see, his idea of critical theory's incipient despair seemed warranted, and the tendentious comparison of liberal democracy to a Nazi concentration camp could be justified, at least as a provocative hypothesis deserving further inquiry. But there was nothing tentative or provisional about the concept of nonexistent subjectivity. Like many postmodernists, the Frankfurt critics were deeply committed to a mode of analysis that abandoned the concept of subjective autonomy, thinking that the individual as a separate monad no longer existed.

The thesis of declining subjectivity was tied in with the analysis of the changing social role of the family and particularly of the father. Since the publication of *Studien über Autorität und Familie* in 1936, the Frankfurt theorists have related the decline of subjectivity to the replacement of the father's function as an effective superego by society as a whole. The Frankfurt thinkers argued that the nineteenth-century bourgeois family provided a haven for the individual, free, to some extent, from social determinations. But, they argued, the individual was no longer insulated by the family, now subject to unmediated domination from without. As entrepreneurial capitalism was transformed into monopoly capitalism, the father lost his earlier economic independence and became merely a fungible quantum of labor, an organization man. Correspondingly, he lost his importance as a feared and respected figure of authority, and the process of socialization gradually became extrafamilial.

Although as I said earlier, this analysis has its place in critical theory, I believe that the decline of the family has not eradicated subjectivity but only produced a different type. The idea that subjectivity has declined as a result of the eclipse of the family assumes that the bourgeois family provided emotional sustenance of a kind that formerly allowed the individual to resist imposed domination. This is a very favorable assessment of the "old" bourgeois family, neglecting especially the damage done to female children and to the mother by the family; here, as in other ways, the nostalgic yearning of the Frankfurt theorists for certain bourgeois institutions like the family distorted their analyses of the present and inured them to the exploitation of women.

Adorno often indicated that contemporary society is completely reified. I submit that this assessment belongs to his nostalgia for the past. He could not ultimately come to grips with the devaluation of intellectuality, which was a by-product of a scientized mass society. Instead of searching for a new kind of intellectuality that overcame the role of the bourgeois scholar—such as Marcuse's new sensibility or my dialectical sensibility, here—Adorno could only fall back on the archetype of the lonely thinker. This aspect of Adorno's self-image was closely related to his attitude toward the alleged demise of subjectivity: in his thesis of spurious subjectivity, Adorno meant to capture his own dissatisfaction with a society that does not listen to intellectuals. If subjectivity, in Adorno's sense, no longer exists, then theory has to abandon its traditional advisory function. No longer can it be conceived as an expressive moment of radical activism, in the way that Marx and Engels suggested in *The Communist Manifesto* (1959, 20). Rather, theory is only to develop the full implications of the completely damaged life, following reification to its ultimate conclusion. Horkheimer and Adorno believed that nothing guarantees a positive synthesis: Subjectivity has been irrevocably lost, and totalitarianism has become eternal.

For Marxist intellectuals who lived through World War II, this kind of pessimism was, perhaps, a prerequisite of spiritual regeneration and hope. Adorno wanted to show that fascism was not an aberration, discontinuous with liberalism, but was immanent in the logic of instrumental rationality that supplanted liberalism. However, the critical theorists did not overcome their deep fatalism after the war but became further entrenched in gloom, rejecting the possibility of revolutionary social change out of hand and thus losing sight of new social movements. The Marxist pedigree of critical theory was correspondingly weakened. In the hands of the original Frankfurt school, Marxism was transformed from a revolutionary science into a critique of total domination. The advisory relationship between theory and practice was subsequently lost; theory became merely a lament for vanished practice.

## Repoliticizing Critical Theory: Beyond the Concept of Spurious Subjectivity

The second generation of the original Frankfurt school included such theorists as Marcuse, Habermas, Schmidt, Wellmer, and Lenk. Although Marcuse was invited to join the Institute in the early 1930s, he belonged more to the second distinct period of critical theory than to the first, led by Horkheimer and Adorno and characterized by the thesis of spurious subjectivity. The depoliticization of Marxism following World War II was a product of new historical circumstances in which radicalism was defused by the rising productivity and affluence generated by a war economy. The productive capacity of American industry was then unrivaled, providing the working and middle classes with goods and services heretofore reserved for elites and thus partially decreasing their resentment of those elites. Adorno and Horkheimer endorsed a negative dialectics to suit this new, seemingly antagonism-free reality. Negative dialectics rejected a systematic concept of political radicalism, attempting to oppose domination philosophically. Critical theory distanced itself from organized Marxism in the belief that philosophy, and not politics, was to become a "radical" battleground. The kind of work produced by members of the original Frankfurt school during the post–World War II years signaled the growing abstraction and political disengagement of critical theory (e.g., Adorno's [1973b] *Negative Dialectics*).

It was left for Herbert Marcuse to reinvigorate critical theory and, if possible, counter its abstract character. I have already interpreted Marcuse's oeuvre as providing a distinct counterforce to the thesis of declining subjectivity put forward by Horkheimer and Adorno (e.g., Horkheimer 1974, 128–61; Jacoby 1975b). Marcuse implicitly opposed the analysis of spurious subjectivity, attempting to reground critical theory in psychoanalysis and a new concept of subjectivity. Marcuse's *Eros and Civilization* was a bold departure from the original Frankfurt reading of Freud as a sophisticated prophet of gloom (see Jay 1973, 103–6) and ultimately served as the point of departure for Marcuse's subsequent work on sexual rebellion and on aesthetics, discussed earlier in this book (Marcuse 1969, 1978). Marcuse did not appear to accept that the human being had been totally captured by bourgeois instrumental rationality. With Freud, Marcuse postulated the existence of a buried libidinal substratum (desire) that defies total manipulation. The sexual constitution of the human being held out against full-blown repression.

Admittedly, Marcuse sometimes repeated Horkheimer and Adorno's thesis about fallen subjectivity, especially in two 1956 essays that are contained in *Five Lectures*. *Eros and Civilization* contains passages about "abolition of the individual" and the "decline in consciousness." *One-Dimensional Man* (1964) suggests that the second dimension of critical consciousness has been lost. Yet I have read Marcuse's more recent works (such as *An Essay on Liberation* [1969] and *Counterrevolution and Revolt* [1972]) as implying that human subjectivity is not yet a victim of total reification. In *Eros and Civilization* he also suggests that an erotic second dimension remains dormant within human beings. This concept of an ineradicable core of desire counters the thesis of heteronomous subjectivity.

The addition of a concept of sexuality to critical theory implicitly challenges the thesis of spurious subjectivity by emphasizing that the human being is an inexhaustible reservoir of desire. As I discussed earlier, Marcuse argued that every human being has the capacity for erotic play and work that can be enhanced in a nonsurplus repressive social order. While accepting the direction of Lukács's analysis of reification, recognizing that capitalism could be sustained by the creation of false or distorted human needs, Marcuse suggested that the subjective capability of constituting, and thus changing, the world is not eliminated by reification but only repressed. In this sense, alienation is a less than total condition that, in spite of being increasingly pervasive, leaves the human being some scope for erotic and, implicitly, political freedoms. Under capitalism, sexuality is often manipulated in such a way that erotic impulses can be inauthentically "liberated" in forms of what Marcuse (1955) calls "repressive desublimation," involving merely superficial types of free sexuality (e.g., mate swapping in a monogamous society).

Marcuse's more recent works, such as *An Essay on Liberation* and *Counterrevolution and Revolt*, develop the insights of *Eros and Civilization*.

In *An Essay on Liberation,* Marcuse outlined the new sensibility to describe a human being who has become a socialist personality in his or her everyday life, refusing to oppress others in the name of distant future liberation. In discussing the significance of the New Left for critical theory, Marcuse stresses the necessity of utopian thinking that refuses to postpone indefinitely the discussion of alternative social institutions. Only by speculating about and attempting to create postcapitalist alternatives can people successfully begin to overcome relations of subservience and authoritarianism in the context of their own lives.

Marcuse further develops his analysis of erotic and aesthetic radicalism in *Counterrevolution and Revolt* (1972). He believes that he salvages and does not subvert the transformative vigor of Marxism by articulating a subjective concept of radicalism—no matter how unorthodox it may appear. Marcuse is more traditionally Marxist than many of his critics suggest in that he explicitly rejects a romantic glorification of irrational, apolitical eroticism (e.g., in his exchange with Norman O. Brown; see Marcuse [1968c]). I have argued throughout this book that Marcuse does not dogmatically renounce orthodox political strategies but only supplements them with a concept of radical subjectivity.

In this sense, the thesis of nonexistent subjectivity is rejected by Marcuse, transcending Horkheimer and Adorno's negativism once and for all. Erotic impulses escape the leveling, homogenizing influence of instrumental rationality, preserving an essential core of unadulterated humanity beneath the appearance of the damaged life. This is extremely significant for critical theory in that it mitigates the pessimism of Adorno and Horkheimer and, most important, because it provides the key to developing more feasible political and theoretical strategies. By going beyond the concept of spurious subjectivity, Marcuse opens the vista of a reengaged Marxism that can again intersect with existing political and social forces.

Russell Jacoby (1975b) in his *Social Amnesia* has criticized the fetishism of subjectivity that has grown out of certain schools of post-Freudian humanistic psychology. Jacoby relies on Adorno and Horkheimer's (1972) thesis of spurious subjectivity in stating that "the subjectivity that surfaces everywhere, be it in the form of human relationships, peak-experiences and so on, is but a response to its demise" (Jacoby 1975b, 17–18). Jacoby extends Adorno's critique of the damaged life in arguing that social change has become nearly impossible. The curious aspect of Jacoby's work is that he also relies on Marcuse, who in the mid-1950s appeared to endorse Adorno's thesis about subjectivity. As I noted above, I believe that Marcuse in his recent work goes beyond this thesis, providing critical theory with a new purchase on emancipatory strategies and a new concept of subjectivity. In an excellent review, Erica Sherover writes:

> Hardly one to be accused of a cheerful positivism, Marcuse is fully aware of the dangers of a falsely happy consciousness. Like Jacoby, he sees the focus on subjectivity among the New Left as a response to objective social conditions, but, unlike Jacoby, he does not view this in a monochromatic fashion. While Jacoby argues too neatly that "the cult of subjectivity is a direct response to its eclipse," Marcuse's discussion is truer to the ambiguous reality. Whereas Jacoby sees the focus on subjectivity simply as the abstract and impotent negation of advanced capitalist society, Marcuse sees the subversive potential of the "new sensibility." [1975, 203]

She adds, "Given that Jacoby's critique of conformist psychology seeks so much support in the writings of Herbert Marcuse, one can only be puzzled by his failure to mention either the *Essay on Liberation* or *Counterrevolution and Revolt*." Sherover shares my view that Marcuse begins to overcome the disengagement of critical theory occasioned by understandable historical pessimism. The concept of a new subjectivity cannot be dismissed but must be viewed as a possibility on the horizon of late capitalism. I argue here that critical theory must further articulate the concept of new sensibility as it struggles to be born, preventing its fetishism and escaping the fate of what Jacoby calls social amnesia.

The usefulness of Marcuse's implicitly creative concept of subjectivity is that it prods critical theory into empirical social research that can identify and foster further new types of political and cultural radicalism. The influence of a Marcusean perspective does not merely vindicate optimism; rather, Marcuse provides a clue that constitutive subjectivity still exists and can be discovered empirically in rebellion as well as in the creation of alternative institutions. By empirical social research I do not refer only to atheoretical fact gathering. Empirical research here refers to a type of historical analysis of contemporary social forces that necessarily brings theoretical and moral perspectives to bear on social investigation. Empiricism has often been equated with atheoretical positivism, giving the impression that there can be no other type of social research. Marcuse analyzes social forces within the parameters of a theory of historical change, assessing the metafactual nature of empirical phenomena (e.g., the transformative potential of unorthodox political forms such as the New Left). Social forces are not simply reflected by Marcuse's empirical methodology but are located in a theoretical totality that goes beyond the factual appearance of the New Left in order to seek its essential historical significance. When I conceive of a renewed empiricism, I distinguish between different types of empirical investigation, some of which eschew atheoretical positivism.

The sclerosis of Marxism resulted from the retention of strictly economic categories of analysis, where Marx did not minimize ideological and psychological forces. If this is accepted as a partial explanation for the irrelevance of orthodox Marxism today—in its deterministic, economistic forms—then efforts to reinvigorate and revise Marxism will deeconomize and feminize the analysis of exploitation (see Agger 1989a). In the hands of the first Hegelian Marxists, this revision proceeded apace. However, in the work of the original Frankfurt school, the revision of Marxism may have gone too far in casting out entirely Marx and Lukács's voluntaristic concept of a revolutionary agent. This development subtly reversed the original relation between theory and practice suggested in *The Communist Manifesto* by Marx and Engels (1959). In their attacks on utopian socialists, Marx and Engels implicitly suggested a concept of radical empiricism that oriented their later work and to which Marcuse returns. In this sense, the critique of scientism and instrumental rationality offered by Horkheimer and Adorno (1972) discarded precisely the kind of radical empiricism that would have repoliticized critical theory and provided the concept of political activism virtually lost by Hegelian Marxism after Lukács and Korsch.

Advocates of either economism or critical theory withdrew them from the imperative of revolutionary practice, the former thinking that the revolution would occur without subjectivity (or, strictly speaking, that the correct subjectivity would arise automatically in response to economic suffering), the latter thinking that subjectivity did not exist. The analysis of captive, damaged subjectivity by the original Frankfurt theorists necessarily discarded the concept of a struggling, rebellious subject capable of throwing off the yoke of domination. Marcuse's work, discussed in chapters 6–11, suggests new concepts of radicalism and, further, of the relation between Marxist social science and political practice.

In *The Communist Manifesto,* Marx and Engels argued that radical theory would stem from and subsequently reflect on given historical circumstances. Marx's famous analysis of the dependence of consciousness on social being (1970, 2) was not a reduction of subjectivity to objectivity but a deep formulation of the dialectical relation between critical theory and political activity. Marx believed that theorizing is a retrospective activity, emergent on the heels of existing struggle and not antecedent to it. Marx criticized the utopian socialists because they tried to draw up blueprints of future communism, viewing theory as a purely projective activity. As a dialectician, Marx suggested that theory could have only a mediating, synthesizing role, following and guiding struggle, rendering it conscious of its motives and objective possibilities. In this sense, Marx did not deny Hegel's formulation in *Philosophy of Right* about the owl of Minerva necessarily taking flight only at dusk (i.e., philosophy emerging only after history had unfolded, as a retrospective activity). I submit that Marx did not deviate from Hegel's essentially retrospective, synthesizing concept of philosophy and theory but only gave this concept of theory a transformative emphasis. For Marx, then, social science was to take flight along with revolutionary activity, theorizing and organizing that activity. Marx's insight, which so influenced subsequent Marxist and bourgeois social science, was his recognition of the revolutionary potential of the urban proletariat. Marx did not impose this on history but extracted it from his analysis of history.

The eleventh thesis on Feuerbach is often taken to be a statement about the revolutionary contribution to be made by a critical social science. However, Marx did not mean that theory alone could change the world. Theory was to follow and to rationalize existing struggle. Indeed, the first thesis states that Feuerbach "sees only the theoretical attitude as the true human attitude." Political practice includes theoretical practice, although Marx implies in places that political and theoretical practice have different revolutionary priorities. Marx's entire critique of German idealism suggests that idealism deflects revolutionary activity; ultimately, Hegel reduced history to the immanent self-reflection of the absolute idea, subordinating practice to theory (and thus countering his own correct insight in *Philosophy of Right* about the subordinate status of thought). Critical theory exaggerated the constitutive function of theory because political radicalism appeared absent during its formative period. Economism discarded the theoretical aspect of radical social change, while the critical theorists discarded the political aspect.

Marcuse implicitly returns to Marx's notion of the advisory, synthetic character of theory, refusing to conceive critical theory as a revolutionary oracle. The perception of Marcuse as a philosopher who relinquishes the political character of Marxism is unjustified in view of this interpretation. In earlier chapters, I have interpreted Marcuse as saying that there is a biological libidinal human nature that provides subjective resources for rebellious political activity. Marcuse goes deeper than the appearance of captive subjectivity in pursuit of a substratum of real autonomy. He endorses a biological concept of this kind of human nature precisely because he does not want to exaggerate the cerebral, theoretical roots of rebellion. He refuses to exhort people to revolt; rather, he develops the consequences of existing, empirically discoverable rebellion, springing from the human being's inability to tolerate exploitation, which is a function of the irrepressibility of desire.

This reading of Marcuse inspires a critique of prior critical theory and helps me better formulate a lifeworld-grounded critical theory open to nontraditional modes of resistance. Horkheimer and Adorno exaggerated the capacity of an overly cerebral concept of reason to be an effective emancipatory stimulus. I read Marx and Marcuse as suggesting that revolt emerges from intolerable suffering caused by crises and contradictions in the social system, not from theory alone. People will not awaken to their revolutionary potential simply by reading *Capital* (or, today, *One-Dimensional Man*) but by reason of their subjectively experienced exploitation and unhappiness, framed for them by theory. Thus, critical theory is to have the function of raising rebellion to the level of full radicalism: this is what it means to mediate existing struggle. As a dialectical theory, Marxism is not unaware of shifts in systemic checks and balances, such as embourgeoisement and enhanced welfare programs and social services. If Marxism is open-minded with respect to such developments, it will not prematurely attempt to take a more active didactic role in exhorting revolt where it is unlikely. The concept of false consciousness is useful when not overstated. People do not rebel or act constructively to transform society merely because they have read works of critical theory but because their current lives are no longer bearable. While critical theory can organize and accelerate the rage behind revolt, it cannot substitute itself *for* revolt because books are not lives.

Horkheimer and Adorno countered the absence of collective subjectivity in Lukács's original sense with cerebral radicalism, fighting fire with fire. But this led nowhere, or at least not toward effective political strategies. The thesis of declining subjectivity involved primarily the decline in consciousness; yet consciousness was given a particularly cerebral meaning by Horkheimer and Adorno. Partisans of cerebral radicalism fought declining subjectivity with negative dialectics, believing that there was nothing else to do but think one's own despair. However, Marcuse avoided the disengagement of cerebral radicalism by developing a concept of subjectivity that was not completely dominated, even engaging in its own self-emancipation. Horkheimer and Adorno theorized total domination, thus retreating into transcendent thought. In contrast, Marcuse's concept of radicalism was developed from the evidence of radicalism, not conjured up through theoretical practice.

Why did Horkheimer and Adorno go as far as to suggest that the alleged demise of subjectivity requires a strictly theoretical radicalism, whether encoded in dense texts or unpopular music? The answer, I believe, lies in their failure to integrate psychological with sociological perspectives in such a way as to comprehend the biological anthropological foundation of human desire. The original Frankfurt thinkers did not develop an adequate concept of human nature—and thus of a new subjectivity—because they rightly accepted Marx's critique of metaphysics and of all theories that tend to hypostatize a static human nature. The Hegelian Marxists were historicist, reluctant to speculate about invariant dimensions of human needs and human nature. The historicist strain in Marxism was inspired by Marx's reluctance to speak about details of life in communist society. Historicism issued in a concept of the reified human being, providing grounds for the thesis of spurious subjectivity. Lacking a definite concept of human nature, Horkheimer and Adorno could not detect the evidence of a subjectivity capable of overcoming reification through its own everyday struggles.

Marcuse, in contrast, was reluctant to endorse the relativistic implications of historicism. His reconstitution of psychoanalysis was meant to introduce into Marxism an empirical concept of human nature, free to some extent from historical determinations. This allowed Marcuse to identify radicalism and resistance at the level of the lifeworld. Moreover, it permitted Marcuse to perceive struggling humanity in the process of its own self-liberation. Marcuse did not attempt to fit a given image of authentic radicalism over existing struggle, necessarily finding it to be insufficient according to the criteria of cerebral radicalism; instead, he allowed ongoing struggle to inform his own theoretical construction of relevant radicalism.

He could therefore overcome the resistance to empirical research of Horkheimer and Adorno in their later years (Institute for Social Research 1973, 123). Akin to the concept of the lifeworld, the "empirical" to Marcuse was the birthplace of potential radicalism, the site of human self-emancipation. Horkheimer and Adorno's thesis of spurious subjectivity necessarily eschewed praxis-oriented research because all social phenomena were perceived to be equally constituted by dominant, dominating interests. The lifeworld appearance of radicalism could thus be discounted as a product of manipulated consciousness, making empiri-

cal research a useless attempt to validate the existence of spurious subjectivity. One even gets the impression that Adorno discounted all
rebellion that did not attain the philosophical erudition of his own work.

A concept of human nature is required by a radical social science
that endeavors to identify and organize ongoing struggle. Otherwise,
struggle will be undetectable in the various formulations and manifestations of its irrepressible desire. A concept of ineradicable subjectivity,
underlying my Marcusean notion of dialectical sensibility, is produced by
insight into the empirical nature of social being. This notion allows critical theory to overcome its resistance to a practice-oriented empiricism
designed to locate and organize incipient radicalism. Foucault offers a
concept of ineradicable subjectivity that repoliticizes critical theory, as I
discuss in my concluding chapter (also see Fraser [1989] and Poster
[1989] on Foucault's possible relevance for critical theory).

## New Epistemological and Political Strategies: The Dialectical Sensibility

Critical theory in Marcuse's hands has begun to transcend pessimism
about effecting social change in late capitalism. The transcendence of
pessimism, as well as the subsequent repoliticization of critical theory,
turns on the concept of desire. If empirical subjectivity still exists, political and cultural radicalism again become meaningful possibilities. I submit that critical theory can overcome its proclivity for abstract
philosophical negation and cerebral radicalism by developing a concept
of subjectivity that allows it to recognize and foster lifeworld instances of
struggle to create new institutions and by returning to an orientation to
the relation between theory and practice that more nearly approximates
Marx's own concept of the advisory role of theory.

Again, I submit that the thoroughgoing critique of scientism by
members of the original Frankfurt school led them to scrap the advisory
role of theory and abandon the prospect of lifeworld radicalism. Adorno
abandoned the advisory role of theory developed by Marx, contending
that human subjectivity was not transformational and thus that theory
could not improve its political possibilities. In overcoming the deep-
seated historicism of the original Frankfurt school, critical theory will be
able to develop a lifeworld concept of radicalism rooted in an image of
active political desire. What I am calling empiricism will take the form of
uncovering the structural potential of incipient radical activity. Radical

social science will identify existing struggle and thus counter its original tendency to view modernity as a self-sufficient, automatic totality capable of integrating all opposition.

A lifeworld-grounded critical theory with an empirical research program will utilize particular examples of quotidian struggle to illuminate a broader theory of change. Epistemological strategies become relevant to political strategies in that critical theory locates empirical instances of rebellion in order to illuminate their radical potential. Theory will allow rebellion to think its own radicalism, to locate its sense of injustice and proposed alternative institutions in a theoretical totality. Out of struggle will spring the resources for creating a better theory to improve and enhance struggle. Radical empiricism becomes a form of political activity as soon as it enters the dialectic of theory and practice. This version of critical social science sheds the disengagement of traditional contemplative theories by taking control of the process of cognition. The division between manual and mental labor is overcome by Gramsci's (1971) "organic intellectuals," intellectuals who refuse to remain aloof from lifeworld struggle.

Radical empiricism is itself a political strategy; it challenges the scientistic concept of disinterested knowledge, taking inspiration from Marx's concept of "practical-critical activity" in theses on Feuerbach. Radical empiricism eschews the abstract tendencies of traditional theory by overturning the dualism between contemplation and action, a dualism that Lukács characterized as an "antinomy of bourgeois thought." Critical theory in this sense can converge with phenomenology and ethnomethodology by endorsing their concepts of cognition as practical, as opposed to transcendental, activity. Although phenomenology and ethnomethodology fail to develop a systematic critique of domination, they both implicitly subvert the contemplative disengagement of the traditional bourgeois intellectual. Radical empiricism is an "everyday" activity, a mode of self-objectification. It relates its theoretical constructs to the lifeworld from which human struggle springs, attempting to develop a structural understanding of the lifeworld location of emancipatory activity. Radical empiricism theorizes subjective radicalism, attempting to articulate a large-scale theory and practice of change, while it is itself a mode of radical subjectivity: this is the ineradicable dialectic between knowledge and action that is at the heart of re-politicized critical theory endorsed in this book.

The radical empiricist is a dialectical sensibility, refusing to separate his or her activity into academic and activist roles. The radical empiricist identifies and attempts to assist human beings in the process of their own quotidian self-emancipation. With dialectical sensibility, the radical empiricist does not separate his or her own liberation from the liberation of others but attempts to provide others with constitutive autonomy so that they may help create a dialogical community. The dialectical sensibility must be empirical because the particular, peculiar circumstances of human beings cannot be ignored by a theory of change. Institutional change is contingent on organizing and developing subjective sources of rebellion, bridging between lifeworld and system in Habermas's (1984, 1987b) terms.

The dialectical sensibility goes beneath the appearances of domination, seeking inchoate prepolitical tendencies toward social change. This version of theoretical sensibility explains how social change—in the abstract—would have actual consequences for particular human experience and discourse. Critical theory will shed formulaic models of change. The models will be suggested by what people already do to improve their own lives. In order to recognize the political potential of lifeworld struggle, theorists must utilize a concept of constitutive subjectivity that provides for the possibility of radicalism, my main thesis in this chapter. The issues here are whether transformative agents do indeed exist and whether their praxis makes a difference (as well as what it means to "make a difference," a left deconstructive concern; see Agger 1989c). Critical theory stands or falls on its estimate of the possibility of social change. A theorist employs insight and imagination in taking a position on the possibility of change and, implicitly, on a concept of subjectivity. Once this step has been taken, certain empirical strategies suggest themselves. These strategies are oriented to developing a theory of change rooted in existing examples of everyday rebellion.

My own position, with Marcuse and others, is that change is currently possible and already taking place in numerous political and prepolitical ways, in a wide variety of venues. Habermas has called these new social movements, although he tends to concentrate on organized movements, hence ignoring more personal struggles, especially on the part of women. My concept of subjectivity, drawn from Marcusean critical theory and a critical version of postmodernism, suggests that people can and do create alternative institutions. I am reluctant to accept the thesis of declining individuality; instead, I am concerned to locate existing rebellion in developing the foundations of a new, more relevant theory of overall social change, using resources from outside traditional Marxism.

However, there is a kind of Marxian empiricism that neither assumes the relevance of constitutive subjectivity nor conceives of theoretical activity as advisory and practice oriented. Within bourgeois social science, Marxism is usually viewed as a variant of value-free social science. I characterize this version as Weberian Marxism because it rests on Weber's concept of value-free scientific objectivity, rejecting Marx's practice-oriented empiricism developed, if briefly, in theses on Feuerbach. Weberian Marxism is a product of the new Kantian Marxism of the Second International, further developing its dichotomy of knowledge and action. The quantitative Marxism of Erik Olin Wright, discussed in chapter 3, is an example of this sort of Marxism (also see Kamolnick 1988).

While Horkheimer and Adorno overstated their critique of scientism, Weberian Marxists have neglected its theoretical significance. Indeed, I have already discussed two problematic manifestations of Weber's influence on Marxism in chapter 3 (on Wright's value freedom) and chapter 10 (on Habermas's theory of organizations). These examples show that Marxist empiricism can take a variety of forms, some of which depart from the dialectical epistemology embraced by Lukács and Korsch. Scientistic Marxism fails to endorse the practice-oriented implications of Marx's critical theory, supposing that Marxian empiricism must take the form of value-neutral social science developed most systematically by Max Weber. I contrapose Weberian Marxism to the dialectical Marxism of critical theory: Weberian Marxism separates Marxian social theory from politics. Sociologists like Bottomore (1975, 47–48, 67) follow Weber in arguing that Marxian empiricism must formulate causal relationships that can provide greater comprehension of social dynamics. Although the radical empiricism that I propose does not abandon the cognitive purpose of science, it is a dialectical empiricism in that it intervenes in the social processes that it studies. Marxist positivism, buttressed by Weber's canon of value-free objectivity, stands in a passive relationship to the social world, failing to adopt the mediating, advisory role with respect to existing struggle that I believe Marx recommended.

Theory and practice are not identical, as certain critical theorists have unwittingly implied, believing that the critique of ideology and of captive subjectivity must replace political activism. But neither are theory and practice unconnected, as Weberian Marxists contend. Dialectical empiricism is unlike non-Marxist social science in that it seeks a particular type of information, namely, how human struggle could change society. Dialectical empiricism seeks to inform rebellion of its political potential. In this sense, Weberian Marxism does not think of itself as a special science struggling to make itself unnecessary by changing society, but only as an instance of value-neutral empiricism. The Weberian Marxist as a scientist does not allow political commitments to affect scientific judgment. However, the radical empiricist does not separate one's life as a scientist from one's life as a political partisan and activist because, as Marx bluntly reminded us, the point is to change the world, not only to interpret it.

Marxist social science either acts as a transformative agent, advising and expediting ongoing rebellion, or reflects social processes, refusing to unify cognitive and political roles (taking us back to issues of Marxist positivism discussed in chap. 3). I submit that the model of a revolutionary working class needs to be replaced by a decentered model of lifeworld self-management and deprofessionalization, blending Habermas's (1984, 1987b) decolonization of the lifeworld with a left-feminist version of the deconstructive program (see Agger 1989a). In this way, the class-specific attack on the capitalist division of labor launched by Marx will be generalized into an attack on all aspects of the division of labor, involving class, gender, and race.

Following Habermas (1975) and Mueller (1973), I contend that economic crises, endemic to an earlier stage in the development of capitalism, have been displaced (but not replaced) by new forms of crisis such as the crisis of legitimacy. This type of crisis has resulted from the near-collapse of liberalism and its ideology of individual initiative, which has eroded the bases of political and cultural legitimacy in late capitalism. Legitimation crisis (Habermas 1975) is peculiar to a form of capitalism that mutes traditional class conflict but expands professional and service sectors as well as a vigorous culture industry. The ideology of liberalism, suitable to an earlier form of market capitalism, no longer elicits mass belief in the rationality of the social system. Affluence has not in its own right guaranteed a stable political system, especially when human dissatisfaction in the spheres of work and leisure has not been mitigated by mere consumption (Leiss 1976). Class conflict is now largely displaced by cynicism about the rationality and humanity of the social system. A postmodern public fails to trust economic, political, and cultural elites and thus rejects imposed authority and retreats from the public sphere.

In this context, resentment of exploitative economic elites is displaced by resentment of imposed authority in general. People feel that they cannot contribute to complex decision-making processes or control their workplaces, communities, social services, culture, and bodies. The world appears beyond subjective control, an illusion sustained by the ideology of scientism and technocracy that has largely superseded liberalism. Marxist critical theory thus can be most effective by enhancing the struggle to take control over private and public existences, including discourse and desire—my argument in the preceding chapter. The rebellion against authority imposed from above can be mediated and organized by lifeworld-grounded critical theory. Instead of searching for the traditional revolutionary working class, Marxists and feminists will seek to identify new social movements that take control of social and political processes at the level of the lifeworld. This provides a theoretical framework within which ongoing efforts to decentralize and deprofessionalize modern life can be perceived as radical and hence further radicalized. Theorists will refuse to minimize the transformative importance of these lifeworld rebellions and resistances, abandoning the vanguard discourse of economistic radicalism perhaps more appropriate to an earlier stage of capitalism. Paradoxically, the original Frankfurt theorists remained more traditional in their concept of radical scholarship than appearances perhaps indicated. The pessimism that I have attributed to critical theory was a product of disappointment about a quiescent working class. Although the thesis of declining subjectivity seems to apply to all social groups, members of the middle class, proletarians, and houseworkers alike, it was really meant to apply only to the integrated working class.

Unless critical theory sheds its thesis of declining individuality and regains its advisory relationship to struggle, it will remain politically irrelevant. Marxists can either await a delayed revolution to be carried out by the traditional male blue-collar working class, or they can return to Marx's idea that radicalism provides theory with empirical and political resources and not vice versa. Critical theory seeks the promise of emancipation in unorthodox forms of struggle, Habermas's new social movements, putting intellectual radicalism to the test of social and political practice. In this sense, the Marxist intellectual can develop a dialectical sensibility, engaging in his or her own particular type of revolt against imposed authority, including bureaucratized academia. The dialectical sensibility does not separate theory and practice, envisaging instead a radical intellectuality that itself contributes to social change. It remains for this type of theoretical practice to be more fully articulated, as I attempt to do in the next two chapters, first via the Frankfurt school and then via postmodernism.

I have argued here that it is not enough to identify new social movements. We must learn from their very existence that Marxist critical theorists need to theorize the lifeworld in order to politicize its prepolitical rebellions and resistances. This is not to propose a radical ethnography or ethnomethodology (e.g., see Mehan and Wood [1975]; but for a feminist-postmodern version of ethnography that converges with my argument here, see Richardson [1988, 1990a, 1990b, 1990c, 1991]); that would only introduce another set of insuperable problems. Where structuralist Marxism ignores the lifeworld, ethnography and phenomenology tend to ignore the influence of large-scale social structures on people's quotidian experiences and discourses. Only a lifeworld-grounded critical theory remains dialectical enough to bridge what Alexander (see chap. 4 above) calls the micro and macro (albeit from his neo-functionalist point of view). As I have argued in this and the preceding chapter, the elaboration of that grounded critical theory requires us to reinvent the very activity of intellectuality—perhaps our biggest challenge in repoliticizing critical theory.

# 14

# Toward
# a New
# Intellectuality

In chapter 13, I suggested a new version of a lifeworld-grounded critical theory's empirical research program appropriate to late capitalism. I returned to Marx and Marcuse's concept of the advisory and prefigurative roles of critical theory in its relation to lifeworld efforts to overcome alienation. In this chapter, I develop further the concept of "dialectical sensibility" as it may inform the activity of radical intellectuals—preparing the way for a discussion of postmodern intellectuality in my final chapter. Instead of submerging theory in the tactics of revolutionary transformation, I argue for a theory that does not pretend either value neutrality or disengagement in its orientation to the possibility of change. The dialectical sensibility, as I conceive of it, democratizes critical intellectuality as a way of creating social change from within, countering what Weber so perceptively called bureaucratic "imperative coordination." In this regard, I do not wish to imply that the deconstruction of bourgeois concepts of scholarship is a sufficient form of practice today: we must still produce a theory that explains and accelerates utopian possibilities contained in the empirical present.

## Cognitive Self-Management

The dialectical sensibility begins to live social change in the midst of the everyday lifeworld, which includes the activity of theorizing. In this sense, intellectuals do not "merely" talk or write but exemplify in their own activities the order of a new society, refusing to be bound by imposed standards of truth and value. What I call cognitive self-management involves the deconstruction of imposed intellectual authority; it is an activity of what Foucault (1977) might have called *dedisciplining*, one of my central concerns (see Agger 1989b, 1989c, 1990). But cognitive self-management is more than mere thought; it also changes the very activity of cognition. The radical intellectual portrays dialectical sensibility, demonstrating to the powerless that they need not live forever under the tyranny of self-imposed ignorance and passivity. The radical intellectual in this sense begins to live the revolution by becoming less isolated, refusing to stay within the narrow confines of the academic role. It is this multidimensionality of role-playing that I contend is transformative, challenging the very essence of technocratic society that counsels people only to consume (commodities and commands). It would be hypocritical to preserve the role of the traditional Marxist intellectual while counseling others to destroy the division of labor. The dialectical sensibility must transform itself while trying to transform society, an argument I advance in the next chapter, where I consider the postmodernist contribution to the reformulation of critical intellectuality. Unless radical intellectuals develop this type of sensibility, the notion of cognitive self-management would rest on precarious foundations: everyone but intellectuals would be exhorted to engage in the merging of theory and practice.

Cognitive self-management will take the form of what Marcuse calls "new science" (chap. 11) or what I have called "radical empiricism" (chap. 13). The idea of a new science is a metaphor that stimulates political imagination, furnishing a workable image of a dedifferentiated, demystified society. In this context, new science is an essential mode of free human activity, practiced for its own sake, without reference to externally imposed purposes. I have developed the idea that cognition can become a form of mental play, reiterating Marcuse's vision that alienated work can be eliminated and thus fundamentally transformed under a different social order. New science is crucial here because it stimulates human beings to take control of cognition and discourse—no longer activities reserved for experts.

I do not believe that modern capitalism is moving toward inexorable collapse. History is open to both tragedy and epiphany, stasis and transformation; frequently, history is ordinary, requiring us to seek the possibilities of tragedy and epiphany in the routines in which people live their lives (see O'Neill's [1974] wild sociology). This does not mean, however, that change is impossible or even improbable, for the psychic costs of domination are mounting rapidly, especially as capitalism is increasingly capable of satisfying basic material needs while people still go hungry and work at unsatisfying jobs (Marcuse's assumption in *Eros and Civilization*). Marcuse has explicitly suggested that subversive forces are already being produced by capitalist society, albeit in forms that differ from orthodox Marxian models of change. I accept that this trend exists; the question facing critical theory today is how we recognize and enhance these "ambiguous" forces, as Marcuse (1964) has called them.

At this juncture, a dialectical sensibility engaging in what I call cognitive self-management is a reasonable place to carry on the theoretical and political struggle. Since the struggle is already happening in multifarious forms as human beings attempt to overcome alienation in their own lives, this is a place for radical intellectuals to join the process of self-transformation. While this process may be painful and troubled, I can think of no better way of contributing to social change than to transform the traditional disengagement of the lonely scholar, in the process creating an archetype of dialectical sensibility engaged in revolutionary self-management, a theme I pursue further in the next chapter. As radical intellectuals carry out their own critical activity, they will necessarily engage in political education that explicates the possibility of what I am calling cognitive self-management. Instead of merely revealing the fact of domination, political education will demonstrate potentials for changing society in feasible and comprehensible ways. In demonstrating these potentials, dialectical sensibilities will draw on existing examples of rebellion and struggle, not invent unrealistic, improbable scenarios in acts of sheer projection. Political education will engage with existing lifeworld resistance in attempting to raise its radicalism to a higher, more theoretically coherent level.

The radical intellectual thus will help organize ongoing efforts to resist the division of labor between expert and nonexpert, encouraging radical democracy as the most direct means of creating a new order and avoiding vanguardism. Although the radical intellectual is an "expert" of sorts, he or she is only too willing to abandon expertise in the interest of liberating others perhaps less theoretically and politically articulate from the tyranny and hegemony of hierarchical expertise. The radical intellectual is not opposed to specialized knowledge but only to the type of specialized knowledge that, through mystification, becomes politically dominating. Significant social change will occur, I submit, only when human beings become able to articulate reasons for alienation and the possibility of a new social order. The radical intellectual helps to provide the language and theoretical system through which that type of transformative comprehension can take place.

At this time, political resistance is fragmented and scattered. It may be organized by providing a model of change through which each otherwise isolated and therefore impotent pocket can be orchestrated. This type of orchestration can avoid the perils of vanguardism by encouraging resistance to develop its own self-confidence and political freedom of choice: this is the emancipatory content of the notion of cognitive self-management. Freire's (1970) pedagogy of the oppressed was designed to raise political consciousness by teaching peasants the rudiments of literacy, giving them self-esteem and thus political efficacy (Freire 1970; O'Neill 1976; Agger 1991a). This can serve as an archetype of the political education that dialectical sensibilities will conduct. Instead of learning to read and write, people in advanced industrial societies will be shown the possibility of becoming "new scientists," free from being coerced into coordination by experts. Indeed, Freire's literacy techniques are a good example of cognitive self-management, giving citizens a practical opportunity to control their own intellectual and political destinies. This type of political education differs from earlier forms in that it relates lifeworld struggle to the evident prospect of a qualitatively different society. Instead of merely projecting a new order in speculative fashion, political education will articulate the dialectic between empirically discoverable struggle—no matter how reformist it may appear—and the prospect of a new order. Following Marcuse's model of engagement with heterodox forms of resistance, the dialectical sensibility recognizes the subjective roots of objective social change: emancipation will not fall from the sky.

A lifeworld-grounded critical theory becomes the practice of thinking and living the discourse of radicalism; a new order cannot be separated from the movement to achieve it. I have implied that the dialectical sensibility would become a living theorist, free from guilt about appearing politically inactive in the usual sense. This type of guilt plagued the original critical theorists, pushing them further away from engagement with new social movements. Adorno (1973b) wrote, "My thought is driven to [negative dialectics] by its own inevitable insufficiency, by my guilt of what I am thinking." The concept of dialectical sensibility entails a "sufficient" intellectuality, a dialectics that breaks out of the confines of isolated thought without losing its reflective moment.

We can thus overcome critical theory's dichotomous approach to thought and action, reminiscent of philosophical dualism—the same dualism that Hegelian Marxism originally opposed.

Dialectical sensibility will perceive the positive within the negative, domination producing its transcendence: this is the foundation of the radical intellectuality that I am proposing. Horkheimer and Adorno were overwhelmed by the appearance of the negative totality. As I discussed in chapter 12, Adorno, paraphrasing Hegel, identified the totality with falsehood, declaring everything equally reified and thus intractable. To be sure, even critical thought tends to be degraded into a commodity by market pressures and the cultural star system. Adorno failed to recognize, however, that human beings do not always acquiesce to their bondage. They have not surrendered. And it is the task of lifeworld-grounded critical theory to locate that resistance within a conceptual totality and discourse that give it political voice, moving beyond its initial isolation and fragmentary quality.

Marx's analytic treatment of the Paris Commune is an example of this kind of intellectuality: he seized on the commune as the harbinger of future world communism, not minimizing its importance merely because it began as an isolated movement. That the commune failed to realize communism does not vitiate Marx's attitude toward it. Opposition forces were stronger than the original communists. Theory must be analytically scrupulous in assessing the political potential of resistance: as often as not, it will arrive at a pessimistic conclusion, discovering that resistance and struggle are purely reformist, auguring no fundamental alternative to the present. Adorno could not see the positive penumbra surrounding the shadow of domination. The radical intellectual, in contrast, refuses to see only gray on gray, and goes beyond the appearance of heteronomy in search of alternatives produced from within the seemingly total darkness of the present.

## Contraorthodoxy

By stressing the initial importance of cognitive liberation, we do not ignore more material modes of change involving political and economic institutions. In the previous chapter, I reformulated cognition as involving the sensibility (Marcuse 1969, 59) of the person, combining mental and manual activity. Thus, cognitive liberation goes beyond the traditional concept of disengaged intellectuality, auguring more than a purely privatized freedom. This blossoming of mental into material liberation is what Marcuse (1969) intends when he argues that "social change becomes an individual need."

It may be objected that critical theory will fail to change the world because it remains isolated in the university. Allegedly, we fail to consider the strategic question of how to produce a world of dialectical sensibilities: we are "idealists." This type of criticism is a product of the mechanistic tendencies in Marxism that critical theory opposes. Theory works by thinking about how the division of labor can be overcome by thinkers and actors. Questions of strategy can be answered only in the particular contexts of contemporary experience, not from above. The point is that social change will always fail in its ultimate aims if it is imposed; dialectical sensibility *prefigures* the revolution in counterhegemonic institutions and thus heads off the self-perpetuating, self-institutionalizing tendencies of authoritarian socialism and feminism. Cognitive self-management guarantees that theoretical vanguardism will not crystallize in a dictatorship over the proletariat, as Korsch called it.

Questions of strategy are not immaterial; neither can they be resolved in orthodox terms. It is not a matter of drawing up new blueprints of society, to be submitted to the "executive committee" of critical theory and then automatically carried out (see Agger 1979). Socialism must begin with the lifeworld, even if it produces deep and unsettling contradictions between old bourgeois and new socialist and feminist existence. Counterhegemonic institutions are not the end-all and be-all of critical theory; counterinstitutions must ultimately be institutionalized in their own right. But in the interim, between domination and freedom, counterinstitutions can harbor fragile human beings and also augur a possible future (see Jacoby 1981).

Orthodox Marxists require the destruction of private productive property. Since I do not equate exploitation only with private productive property, I have a different vision of the new society, one that necessarily includes the destruction of capitalism as its precondition. For example, feminists argue that we must also abolish reproductive relations that promote both sexism and capitalism. I contend that it is possible to live social change prefiguratively, in terms of a socialist and feminist ethics rooted in mutual respect for humanity and nature. Orthodox Marxism has ignored a prefigurative ethics and notion of the quotidian because it was more concerned with changing economic structures than with changing human beings, as if this is a disjunctive alternative. Marxists assumed that humanity would automatically be transformed (for the better) after private property was abolished.

A socialist and feminist ethics has a number of features. It involves respect and care for the being of others; it involves a "rationality of gratification," as Marcuse (1955) calls it, treating others as sensuous beings; it also involves a new relation between human and nonhuman nature—an ethics governing our attitudes toward the environment. These features of ethical praxis are truer to Marx's vision of communism than the economistic identification of communism with the collective ownership of the instruments of production. (I believe that the notion of public ownership is implied in the type of ethics emanating from dialectical sensibility and does not have to be introduced from the outside.)

Orthodox Marxists ridicule such discussions of prefiguration because in their own lives they give value to the legitimacy of their own specialized authority, which they derive from their own vanguard theories of the role of the expert. They believe that their time is better spent on scholarship than in unifying their fragmented activities. They fail to recognize that the dialectical sensibility does not abandon theorizing but rather integrates theory into the totality of human existence. The orthodox Marxist scholar rationalizes disengagement by saying that conditions are not ripe for personal liberation; but, as Marcuse has so powerfully shown, today social change in a total sense begins with personal liberation. Only by guaranteeing quotidian change can the authoritarian tendencies of traditional socialism be effectively challenged "from below." Orthodox Marxists pursue the roles of traditional scholarship, separating their thought and action, because orthodoxy sanctions the dictatorship of the proletariat and thus the concept of revolutionary professionalism. Allegedly, Marx sanctioned the traditional role of the vanguard intellectual, theorizing that the revolution would occur automatically and would then go through two distinct stages, with communism to be reached only in the distant future (when intellectuality could become generalized). Orthodoxy in this sense repeats orthodox social relations, reproducing the fateful dualisms of contemporary experience that function ideologically to keep people in their place.

Agreeing with Habermas (1984, 1987b) and feminists (e.g., Fraser 1989; Marshall 1988), I contend that the only way to create a new order is to begin with the lifeworld, creating new sensibilities capable of engaging in cognitive and political self-management of both production and reproduction. This is precisely the unified agenda of a lifeworld-grounded feminist critical theory. Hegel thought that the dialectic reveals the general in the particular. Today this means that domination must be read in the "fates" of people, thus deconstructing the notion of fate as a deceptively dehistoricizing construct. Further, liberation must be conceived as involving struggling human beings, not taking place behind their backs or on a cosmic, transpersonal level. We need not retain Hegel's fatalistic concept of the cunning of reason but can instead rely on his notion of the dialectic. Hegel suggested that the whole is the truth, indicating that personal liberation requires human liberation. Similarly, as Marcuse shows, the dialectic between personal and societal change cannot be abrogated. When Marxism and feminism become a living theory, *a form of personality,* the entire nature of intellectuality will change, calling into question deep-seated emotional preferences and habits. The dialectic requires that one regard thought as an activity, oriented to generating a truly democratic intellectuality as a route to significant social change.

## The Dualisms of Oppression

Radical social scientists will unite activities heretofore conceived as separate. These separations between work and play, science and common sense, reflection and action protect dominant interests by legitimating expertise and imposed authority. Knowledge is produced by experts and consumed by nonexperts in capitalism: this is the sense of Lukács's (1971) concept of reification as involving the transformation of social relations, mental processes, and ideas into things, even commodities (in this echoing Marx's notion of commodity fetishism). In challenging certain dualisms, the radical intellectual does not go overboard and reduce everything to subjectivity. The nonidentity between subject and object will be preserved: activity produces objectivity, creating a continuum between humanity and the world. The radical intellectual attacks only those dualisms, such as oppressor and oppressed, that are historical and can be eliminated. The dialectic between subject and object is not a dualism and cannot be effaced. Theories that reduce everything to subjectivity (see Jacoby 1975b) gloss over contradictions and tensions in objective reality, pretending that the world can be changed heroically, an issue noted at the end of chapter 13, where I traced the outline of lifeworld-grounded critical theory and its empirical research program. Rather, the subject must interact with the world in transforming its historical character.

While radical intellectuals will engage in unifying activity—making nonexperts experts, capable of comprehending and overcoming their own domination—they will preserve the essential difference between subject and object that makes social change possible. It is not enough that nonexperts think that they are experts; they must act expertly, wresting control of productive and reproductive processes from the guardians of discipline. In overcoming the duality of oppressor and oppressed (the expert and the nonexpert), we eliminate all hierarchizing difference, a central Derridean concern (see Agger 1989a). Subjectivity will sustain itself by recognizing its dialectical dependence on the objective world, free, for the first time in human history, to interact with the world in its own chosen ways.

Difference is eternal, impervious to theoretical unification through totalizing word play. Domination, however, is tractable. Critical theory analyzes the difference between the eternal and the ephemeral in developing a concept of the possible, refusing utopia because it attempts to change everything—thus changing nothing. I have developed a lifeworld-grounded critical theory because I want to emphasize that a new order must be depicted in prefiguratively comprehensible metaphors that relate to the lives people lead and want to change. I do not oppose dualism in total but only particular dualisms, such as oppressor-oppressed and expert-citizen. The shape of the new society can be captured in images that borrow from present concepts and experience: dialectical sensibility allows concepts to point beyond themselves, bringing out their hidden content in new, even unforeseen directions.

Critical theory in the hands of Horkheimer and Adorno (1972) has tended to portray the new order as entirely unimaginable by contrast to the present damaged life—hence Adorno's (1973c) descent into dissonant music, the veritable apotheosis of the reason he so cherished. I oppose this because I believe it is imperative to think through the possibility of a new world in lifeworld terms, thereby alerting people to the possibility of their own liberation from within the forms of life (Wittgenstein 1953) of their everyday experience and discourse. This is how we can attain a new world, not heroically or apocalyptically, but through changes in the ways people do things. There will not be a quantum leap between the present and the future, as Engels suggested in his notion of the transformation of necessity into freedom. Instead, people in a new order will still confront complex problems of social organization and administration that they must face with seriousness as well as a sense of irony. A lifeworld-grounded critical theory works through these problems. Damaged life will not automatically repair itself into utopia; it will only produce alternative social forms, none of them ideal. Automatic Marxism has tended to endorse an image of automatic social change. Both are irresponsible, neglecting the necessity of decision and desire.

## Deconstructive Radicalism

I envisage a deconstructive radicalism, learning from the experience of creating a new order by continually interrogating what it means to create a new order. Deconstructive interrogation is a vital factor in this process of theoretical self-education. Social existence is so complex as to prevent theorists from planning or predicting every detail of the new life; most of these details will have to be clarified by experiments with alternative social forms, not foisted on people from the beginning. A salient example of self-interrogating experimentation in this sense involves the future of the family. It is difficult to state with certainty which forms of child raising and adult cohabitation would be appropriate to a self-managed social order. We have had insufficient experience with forms like the kibbutz in Israel or the Serbian extended family (the *zadruga*) to project a communist/feminist family, if there is to be any family at all. Similarly, a psychoanalytically informed Marxism will recognize that the "pain" of growing up cannot be avoided under a new order; children and adolescents must undergo at least a modicum of what Freud called repression and sublimation. As Marcuse (1968c) stated in his debate with Norman O. Brown, the point is not to eliminate the reality principle but only particular realities such as domination and oppression. A deconstructive radicalism can determine what the psychological and socioeconomic limits of change will be.

A lifeworld-grounded critical theory must not have a purely anticipatory element, awaiting a different future. People are already beginning to create a "different" society in their own lives. It is imperative that this different society include institutionalized mechanisms to enable people to interrogate the meaning of difference as an important social value in its own right. The notion of a long road to social change is abandoned (even if it is truthful, given the numerous political obstacles today) because the concept has traditionally legitimated severely hierarchical forms of political discipline. But neither is dialectical sensibility merely a parliamentary socialist sensibility for it refuses to postpone fundamental personal changes until that magic moment of parliamentary success. Bolshevik and parliamentary strategies end up changing very little for the better.

Finally, a lifeworld-grounded critical theory is unwilling to delay revolutionary gratification, awaiting "future" liberation to be paid for by present discipline. The concept of the dictatorship of the proletariat is unnecessary; it trades future benefits against present sacrifices. This sacrificial model of social change is renounced by the dialectical sensibility, and in its place a more self-serving model of transition is conceived. Marcuse (1969) makes us wonder, *why* must we await the millennium? How different will the future be? Economism and Adorno's critical theory both deny that a qualitatively different society may not be entirely different from the present. Avoiding the questions "how much difference?" and "What difference?" will only lead to quagmires in which human beings do nothing to change their own lives in the expectation that real change will only come from above—either from the vanguard party or from the cosmic clash of self-contradictory economic structures.

The radical intellectual leans hesitatingly toward the future, recognizing that the preservation of humanity (albeit "damaged" to some extent) requires that we not renounce suddenly everything we have been and known. How will our lives as individual producers, reproducers, and consumers change under a new order? How can we preserve aspects of present happiness? The Adornoian believes that little can be saved; the orthodox Marxist believes that change will be largely economic. A lifeworld-grounded critical theory, blending Marcuse, the Habermas of new social movements theory, postmodernism, and feminism, recognizes the truth of each of these positions, orchestrating them in order to produce a life worth living as well as a society worth fighting for. This version of critical theory ultimately begins by reformulating what it means *to begin*. In this way, the dialectical sensibility may produce a dialectical social order, a new order beyond the reification that today weighs so heavily upon all of us.

In my concluding chapter, I further develop my notion of a deconstructive intellectuality through the emerging program of a politicized postmodernism. Where in this and the preceding chapters I have worked strictly within the Frankfurt framework, which informs much of my thinking about an enduring critical theory, in the next chapter I attempt to blend critical theory and postmodernism. As we shall see, critical theory and postmodernism have a good deal in common, even though postmodernism is sometimes formulated in distinct contrast to Marxism, as I discussed in chapter 5. I argue that Marxism and postmodernism can be read as particular versions of critical theory, which remains the most global philosophy of emancipation to which these particular versions are mutually edifying contributions. In making this claim, I risk Lyotard's (1984) condemnation as an author of grand narratives. I am willing to accept this risk because I believe that without a social theory of the totality, we make little headway, either intellectually or politically.

# 15

# Postmodernism: Ideology or Critical Theory?

n this chapter, I attempt to theorize critically about the public world, keeping in mind the status of critical theory in that world. I pursue themes raised in the preceding three chapters about the transformation of intellectual life. Postmodernism is reappraised for its theoretical and political contribution to what I call lifeworld-grounded critical theory—a critical theory that begins with everyday experience and discourse, including its own. For the most part, this chapter is written in straightforward descriptive and analytic prose, turning away from the density of some of my earlier, more traditional theoretical formulations; I do not presuppose a deep grounding in recondite European social theory, whether the critical theory of the Frankfurt school or postmodernism and poststructuralism. In fact, as I argue in this concluding chapter, high theory is often so incomprehensible that the very theory capturing the decline of discourse ironically ends up facilitating it. Much of my own past work as well as the work I have discussed in this book has risked this, although one can defend dialectical complexity's appropriateness to a dialectically complex world (as Adorno has done).

In this chapter, I conclude my argument for a new theoretical discourse of lifeworld-grounded critical theory. In no way am I suggesting that world problems would be solved if theory were clearer by the standards of British analytic philosophy (Gellner 1959). I am trying to theorize the decline of discourse without allowing such theorizing to contribute to it. This is a tall order, given the difficulty of Barthes, Adorno, Derrida, Kristeva. It is tempting to spend one's time simply explicating these important sources. But that would neglect empirical analysis and diagnosis, as well as political recommendation, the tasks of this book. I want to understand how what writers write is conditioned by large, often invisible forces and then to help them—us—better protect ourselves against our own commodification and stupefaction. In the process, I will examine one of the central legitimating ideologies of cultural production and reception today, postmodernism.

As I indicated in chapter 5, there is no single or simple postmodernism but only versions. Indeed, I want to reclaim postmodernism for the project of radical social theory by carefully examining postmodernity (Habermas 1981a), a civilizational stage in which we are supposed to believe that all fundamental social problems have been solved. This will involve me in a theoretical discussion of the meaning of words like "postmodernism" and "postmodernity." This concluding chapter extends my argument for a repoliticized critical theory, adding certain postmodern insights to Marcuse's version of critical theory. Interestingly, postmodernism comes in two versions—one that endorses the end of ideology, discussed in chapter 5, the other (from which I draw and which I attempt to extend) arguing that ideology simply recurs in new forms scarcely imagined by Marx, requiring new theoretical articulations.

Theory declines in exact proportion to its academization. When theory becomes a body of knowledge to be carved up, dissected, and then mummified by disciplinary museum keepers, it loses its ability to sharpen insight. Unfortunately, this is the fate of much theory today, including oppositional theory. Indeed, the Left perpetuates its own obscurantism by canonizing great books that once provoked radical opposition. Today books like *Capital* and *The Second Sex* inspire term papers or yawns, not political activism. Cells have become study groups. This is not to say that we should forgo reading dense works of world-historical significance. One cannot understand the present without having grappled with Kant, Hegel, Marx, Freud, Wittgenstein, Husserl, Beauvoir, Sartre, Adorno, Marcuse—the list is virtually endless, as is the hermeneutic work required to master these difficult sources. But academization is the subtraction of Dionysian passion from thought; scholarship reduces thought to method, killing it.

I do not dispense with references to other writers; some of these aid archaeological investigation and extrapolation by curious readers. Referenceless writing pretends sheer originality and thus claims unchallengeable authority. But too often these citations burden one's argument so much that one ends up arguing nothing in particular; writing merely repeats the tried and true—the tired—albeit in a trivial revisionism deriving its license from the rearrangement of other people's footnotes and references. Ironically, the analysis of the decline of discourse presented here must pass through the very theories that hasten discourse's decline, often in spite of themselves. One of my main topics (as well as opportunities) in this chapter is postmodernism—not the critical theory of modernity and postmodernity so abundant with insights into what is going wrong with the world, especially in the realm of culture, but the fashionable theory authorizing the fashionable literary life-style of cosmopolitanism. I want to use postmodernism against itself, rescuing it from its own sloganizing. People talk of postmodern this and postmodern that—art, architecture, advertising. But that only reduces the critical analysis of modernity to trendy cultural taxonomy.

One of the central valences of postmodernism is its fungibility, as I argued in chapter 5. Everyone claims it, but few have read in its sources. It is much harder to claim Marxism and feminism while ignoring their roots in radical opposition, although many academics try (see Jacoby 1987). Postmodernism is postured by all sorts of Establishment interests, who only deepen what Gramsci (1971) called hegemony. I want to unpack postmodernism by way of empirical categories like literary political economy (see Agger 1990), thus liberating its critical insights from the culture industry (Horkheimer and Adorno 1972, 120–67). My central claim is that postmodernism in its best sense is a radical theory of society, not a mindless vehicle of cultural production and consumption (see Wolin 1984). Better, postmodernism must be written and rewritten as critical theory and not allowed to slip frictionlessly into the maw of cultural, political, and economic co-optation.

We are in serious trouble when Jay McInerney and Tama Janowitz are lauded as postmodern writers, or Lyotard and Baudrillard elevated above Marx and Marcuse; or when a powerful editor sponsoring the so-called New Fiction takes on the moniker "Captain Fiction" and thus shapes literary taste and practice; or when advertising agencies and architects churn out "postmodern" copy, text, image, design, better to grease the wheels of capitalist culture, consumption, and urban life. But my aim is not only to salvage the concept of postmodernity in terms of modernism's own revolutionary ethos; that is precisely what is wrong with the academic project: footnotes fail to do our creative intellectual work for us. Intellectual pedigree is no substitute for intellectuality. Rather, having debunked an Establishment version of postmodernism in chapter 5, I want to deploy postmodernism here as a mode of empirical description, analysis, and diagnosis, allowing its dialectical comprehension of the inner tendencies of modernity—capitalism—to issue in rigorous social science that can guide reconstructive activities of all sorts, especially cultural ones.

Of course, few American social scientists would regard this book as an example of either rigor or social science. It will be dismissed impatiently as densely essayistic and carping, anathema to the number crunchers and survey researchers ever in pursuit of better techniques, measures, hypotheses. So be it. Social science lost its mind long ago, at least in positivist America. It must be reinvented by writers unafraid to bridge the social sciences and humanities in order to search the social world for its deepest meanings and structures. I have already developed arguments for a literary social science, borrowing from the Frankfurt school's critical theory, feminist theory, poststructuralism, and postmodernism (Agger 1989a, 1989b, 1989c, 1991b). Those were largely programmatic arguments for an analytic discourse that neither embraces positivism nor renounces empirical social understanding, what Marcuse (1969), following Nietzsche, called new science, discussed in chapter 11.

In this chapter, I try to write discourse, not merely theorize it, showing the possibility of a lifeworld-grounded critical theory composed for a broad critical readership—not only other academics; I analyze the decline of discourse using insights from discourse theory. This is ironic only because so much contemporary theory is incredibly obscure, doing little to rebuild the public sphere by its own example. Having said this, I feel it is worth noting that the plain-language theorists who lambaste Adorno and Derrida for their impenetrability fail to attend to the parallel obscurity of mainstream quantitative empiricism (which takes its own license from the British analytic philosophy laying waste to Teutonic thought and writing). Nevertheless, there is something regrettable about discourse theory that fails to be discourse itself—an ironic insensitivity to its own audience.

In this final chapter I survey the contributions of postmodernism to critical theory's understanding of the decline of public discourse, which I regard as a serious social problem today. One way to think about the logic of my argument is to view this chapter as a defense of postmodern critical theory that responds to my critique of postmodernism in chapter 5, where I discussed the cosmopolitan life-styles pursued by those who live in order to dress. I want to distinguish carefully between postmodernity and postmodernism. The former is a civilizational stage; the latter is a theory of culture and society, adaptable to my version of critical theory. Obviously, the two are connected inasmuch as theory enters into the cultural discourses of the moment. But I want to situate postmodernism outside the cultural mainstream in order to utilize its critical distance from the so-called postmodern world it diagnoses. Postmodernism, properly understood, helps reverse the direction of postmodernity, notably what I call the decline of discourse. Postmodernism can go beyond the thesis of the end of ideology by deconstructing it as being, itself, ideological.

## Does Postmodernity Exist?

Let me offer some initial clarification of the ways in which I use the main theoretical categories employed here. Unfortunately, imposters threaten to usurp the legitimate meanings of these words, homogenizing them into safe, system-serving ciphers. By postmodernity I am referring not to a concrete stage of civilization somehow set apart from modernity, notably capitalism. Postmodernity ideologically postures as a postmodern stage of world history in order to suggest the end of class, race, gender, and geographic inequalities; in this, it serves exactly the same purpose as Bell's earlier (1960) notion of the end of ideology. But just as ideology is still with us, now notably in the very concept of the postmodern or postmodernity, so history has not recently transcended itself into a frictionless, fractiousless, classless, raceless, genderless epoch. Postmodernity is myth. In its name people (e.g., Lyotard 1984) justify their opposition to Marxism. Lyotard rejects "metanarratives" that would privilege one form of radicalism or another; but this privileging, in the name of putative postmodernity, is every bit as much a metanarrative as the ideological systems it opposes.

Partisans of postmodernity like Lyotard (1984) define the postmodern in terms very reminiscent of Bell's earlier argument. Postmodernity is supposedly characterized by postindustrialism (Bell 1973), the resulting end of class conflict, a consumers' cornucopia of limitless goods and services, high technology as a panacea for all social problems, the end of ideology, and universal global modernization. In this, Lyotard adds nothing to Bell. But postmodernity also suggests a kind of centerlessness to world history that serves as an axial moral and political principle of a new individualism. Where Bell (1976) decried the "adversary cultures" of narcissistic New Leftists, Lyotard and his ilk embrace an apparent eclecticism of personal, cultural, and political styles. This New Individualism formulates itself partly in neoconservative economic and political theory (e.g., Nozick 1974; Gilder 1981). Postmodernism is its cultural expression, although, as I argue, this is not really postmodernism at all but only warmed-over end-of-ideology theory appropriate to post-1950s capitalism.

New Individualism is continuous with the "old" version: Mill, Locke, Coolidge, Frederick Taylor. It is different in that it is situated in a more affluent stage of capitalism—affluent at least for tenured intellectuals and Yuppies. Postmodernity enshrines individualism on the ground that what Lyotard calls the grand "metanarratives" are no longer relevant to middle-class individuals. C. Wright Mills's *White Collar* (1951) remains a cogent response to this overly optimistic perspective on universal embourgeoisement, just as it contains a pithy discussion of modern intellectuals in the section on "Brains, Inc." Mainstream sociology has always foretold the postindustrial future in which people would not lack for basic necessities but could spend their lives cultivating their own spiritual (and real) gardens; in this view, Marxism is not so much wrong as out of date. The notion of postmodernity approaches this sociological formulation of a post-Marxist future in largely cultural terms, making way for "postmodernist" strictures about urbane life-styles discussed earlier.

Postmodernity is a term used apologetically to describe and defend late capitalism (Mandel 1975). There is absolutely nothing "post" about the current modernity, which is fundamentally continuous with the capitalism of the mid-nineteenth century in the sense that capitalism is characterized by private property, sexism, racism, and the domination of nature. Saying that does not mean we should not theorize and retheorize late capitalism; there are some significant differences between capitalism then and capitalism now. But this rethinking should be done within Marxism and feminism, not outside of them. Postmodernity theory (see Kellner 1988) is fundamentally opposed to the utopian prospect of a new world beyond class, gender, and race oppression. It formulates the future in terms of New Individualism, as such leaving the capitalist, sexist, and racist edifice intact. Freedom is characterized in terms of individual expression, taste, consumption, travel, leisure, clothing, life-style. Postmodernity theory is the latest alternative to radical social thought and action, not a successful undermining of them. Postmodernity theory is a more cosmopolitan version of the earlier, more puritanical postindustrialism (e.g., Bell 1973); it is centered in New York City, the cultural lodestone. Of course, its pretended cosmopolitanism is really parochial, as indicated by global Americanization.

## Postmodernism as Ideology

Having essentially rejected the concept of postmodernity, I shall extend my discussion in chapter 5 of the work postmodernism does in the Establishment end-of-ideology theory prevailing in the culture industry as well as in non-Marxist literary theory and cultural studies. To talk about a mainstream postmodernism seems ludicrous; Baudrillard, Barthes, Foucault are impossible to commodify and co-opt. Or are they? The local television critic in *The Buffalo News* occasionally writes of Foucault and Barthes, if only to show the local university community that he knows what is going on as well as to elevate his chatter about network television into high cultural criticism. And postmodernism abounds on Madison Avenue as the latest signifier of cultural trendiness (e.g., Newman 1985). It moves products, not minds.

This discussion of "bad" postmodernism, the kind that informs cultural production in capitalist countries today, suggests the possible development of a "good" postmodernism, what I call postmodernism as critical theory. I organize this comparison around six axial themes characterizing their different positions on issues of intellectual and social substance: values, history, politics, subjectivity, modernity, and reason. I am going to simplify in order to make my point that postmodernism contains a powerful liberating element largely suppressed by the culture industry's version of postmodernism, which is really only veiled capitalist modernism. My interest in this comparison is not Scholastic for I maintain that postmodernism as critical theory issues in a politically relevant empirical sociology of culture for which the central concept is literary political economy, a concept I discuss in the last section of this chapter. I want these critical concepts to do empirical and political work; before they can, I must disentangle subversive from affirmative postmodernism.

### The Rejection of Absolute Values

An ideological postmodernism, the kind dispensed in cosmopolitan magazines and taught in mainstream literary theory classes, maintains that there are no absolute values, in this drawing on a version of Nietzsche. Nietzsche encompasses both postmodernism and poststructuralism on the one hand and critical theory on the other. For Derrideans and Foucaultians, Nietzsche is the author of anti-Enlightenment, an emblem of the futility of (Western) reason. For Adorno and his Frankfurt colleagues, Nietzsche is a profoundly dialectical critic of the Enlightenment, a harbinger of "playful science"—both new cognition and new society, discussed in chapter 11. Of course, this second Nietzsche is the more difficult to exhume from his books. But no matter whatever/ whomever the "real" Nietzsche, I believe that Adorno's attempt to ground a materialist concept of reason in Nietzsche's (1956) Dionysian attack on the Apollonian frigidity and rigidity of Western rationality makes eminent sense. And it helps define a critical postmodernism with which to navigate the roiling waters of the contemporary culture industry.

Returning to my theme, an ideological postmodernism uses Nietzsche among others as buttress for the notion that, because absolute values have disappeared, anything goes. Or, at least, the establishment of values in a postmodern period is not to draw on what Lyotard (1984) calls the grand "metanarratives" of Marxist and feminist reason. The rejection of absolute values (notably, for Nietzsche, Platonism) results in nihilism—the rejection of all values (e.g., Rosen 1969). This is the conventional reading of Nietzsche and one, it must be noted, amply plausible on the textual evidence. In any case, mainstream postmodernism (like poststructuralism, if one distinguishes between the two) rests heavily on the premise that one cannot locate an Archimedean point outside history from which to glimpse or postulate world-historical meanings, ethics, values, truth. Nietzsche's nihilism is converted into relativism by these postmodernists, thus casting doubt on the standard left-wing attempts to specify definitive values, whether a classless society or mother right.

## The Eternal Present

Postmodernism also contains a conception of history that notably breaks with the eschatologies of classical Western thought or, better, serves as their completion. Postmodernists reduce the future orientation so typical of Western eschatology to a kind of eternal present, a philosophical posture reminiscent of the sociological announcement of a postindustrial society (Bell 1973). The future is now; technology has set us free;

culture is so rich that we no longer have to search outside of time—in the future, a time that has not happened—for the riddle of history. Indeed, this Establishment postmodernism obliterates history in a grandiose gesture of self-satisfaction. Of course, this bespeaks a thoroughgoing optimism about the distance we have come. And it generalizes (I would say overgeneralizes) the good fortunes of Western cultural, economic, and political elites—call them Yuppies—to all of humanity. Support for this comes from what Baudrillard (1981) calls the political economy of the sign, notably the proliferation of Western products and advertising in poor countries, "texts" that Western postmods "read" to indicate global modernization—the veritable end of history prophesied by all eschatology.

This notion of an eternal present not only overestimates the glories of the present, it also forecloses the possibility of radical interventions. The end of history is also the end of hope, of utopian imagination. Postmodernism in its Establishment version is at once blissfully cheerful about how good things are and world-weary, disdainful of the radical metanarratives that still seek a heaven on earth in the fashion of every utopia. The beats called this attitude "cool" or "hip," precisely the stance of postmods in the late 1980s and early 1990s. Indeed, fashionable men's magazines sell sneakers once popular in the 1950s under the sign of James Dean, the enfant terrible of 1950s avant-gardism. Hip endures as the quintessential postmodern sensibility, expressing a combination of self-satisfaction and aversion to the passions and polemics of the political.

### Antipolitics

The third dimension along which one can evaluate affirmative and critical postmodernism is politics. Whether postmoderns express their disdain for the political in terms of James Dean's nonchalance or the rock musician Stephen Stills's 1960s opinion that "politics is bullshit," it is clear that affirmative postmodernism rejects politics as a venue of meaning. Of course, if history has ended, the telos of political activism—social change—is chimerical, archaic. One risks little generational oversimplification if one observes that members of the baby boom generation, all now thirtysomething, were the exception, not the rule, in twentieth-century America in terms of their political engagement around issues like the war in Vietnam, civil rights, and the women's movement. The

Ozzie-and-Harriet generation—their parents—share with the post-1960s generation a quiescence about politics, indeed an antipolitics grounded in an aversion to eschatology. Young people curry cool, not the transformation of the world. This does not ignore a kind of social liberalism whereby people care about the environment, the rebellious students in China, animal rights, etc. As I noted in chapter 5, the thirtysomething generation helped mainstream a certain social liberalism fundamentally unthreatening to the dominant capitalist order, notably including the right of women to regulate their own reproductive systems as well as to work outside the home.

But this social liberalism, like all liberalism, is essentially privatized; it says little about how social structures should be changed. Postmodernism shuns politics as the site of venality, corruption, cynicism: images all the way from Watergate to Iranscam drum this lesson into our heads; politics is equivalent to a sick messianism. "Healthy" people seek careers, mortgages, perfect children, cultural status, spiritual plenitude. Thus, postmodernism contains powerful assumptions about the nature of politics that are fundamentally hostile to the left-wing metanarratives, like Greek thought, seeking redemption in politics (e.g., Arendt 1958). Politics today is widely viewed as an open sewer, not as the basis for a decent public life. Traditional conservatives join with radicals in lamenting the decline of the public sphere—here, the decline of discourse, one of its central aspects. Politics is shunned mainly by neoconservatives who are disappointed liberals. The welfare state is viewed widely as the source of significant social problems, not their remediation, as originally it was for Keynes and FDR. This is a postmodern attitude par excellence: the best politics is antipolitics, an impugning of politics, politicians, and all social movements seeking the truth in one or another concept of social justice.

### New Individualism

Established postmodernism enshrines a revamped individualism, a post-liberalism, according to which the traditional democratic social contract (e.g., Rousseau 1973) is reformulated so that individuals can "take" from the collectivity but need not "give" something in return, especially popular legitimation. Habermas (1975) already identified this "legitimation crisis" as one of the potential undoings of welfare capitalism. Possessive individualism (Macpherson 1962) is nothing new; indeed,

Macpherson shows that it is present in Locke from the beginning. But the New Individualism is even more possessive than ever, largely responding to the perceived failures of the welfare state to keep poor urban blacks and other minorities in check. New York liberals become neoconservative when Farrakhan embraces Hitler and when it is no longer safe to jog in Central Park at night. Bernhard Goetz, the subway desperado, epitomizes this postmodern New Individualism: when accosted by youthful black muggers, he drew his gun and blew them away. Interestingly, Goetz was heroized not only by working-class NRA rednecks; he was supported by all sorts of "sophisticated" liberals (i.e., neoconservatives) who were sick and tired of affirmative action, welfare safety nets, overall social permissiveness.

The sociology of race and racism is an interesting barometer of this New Individualism, as Feagin (1989) demonstrates. Gone are systematic appraisals of the structural roots of racism; in their place, we find various condemnations of the black family, black character structure, black language, black music. The New Individualism in this regard can be traced back to Banfield's (1970) *The Unheavenly City* as well as to work by Moynihan (1969). What distinguishes it today, though, is its pervasiveness in the race relations literature. White racism is replaced by black sloth as an explanation of persistent and increasing economic inequalities between blacks and whites. Worse, there is a growing perception among commentators and social scientists that blacks are actually demonic, even wild animals (viz., the recent attacks of "wilding" where roving gangs of black youth terrorize random passersby).

The New Individualism cowers before this savagery, ignoring its own responsibility for bringing it about. This is not to reduce character structure to social structure (Gerth and Mills 1946) but to acknowledge the complex mediations between the two (e.g., Wexler 1982). The brutalizing gang members are as much (or as little) products of their society as Bernhard Goetz. What is new about postmodern individualism is its defensive posture; earlier possessive individualism (Macpherson 1962) attempted to better itself by striking out in wagon trains for the West Coast, construing the future as a time ahead. The New Individualism protects its fiefs against the dispossessed, in the process theorizing its just deserts with various neoconservative defenses of property, family, state. Where original individualism was self-interested but optimistic, the New Individualism is both self-interested and cynical. It is precisely this cynicism that characterizes the mien of the mainstream postmodern; self becomes the central social agenda for late twentieth-century rationalists (Lasch 1984).

## Occidentalism/Modernization

I have already discussed aspects of the postmodernity thesis that closely resemble Bell's (1973) earlier notion of a postindustrial society. Postmodernism theorizes postmodernity, notably in terms of the six axial dimensions I am discussing here. In particular, mainstream postmodernism is a version of occidental modernization theory, in spite of its pretension to be pluralist or "decentered" (Luke 1991). In fact, the occidentalism of postmodernism is concealed in the superficial valorization of "difference." Difference is but a slogan; deconstruction reveals it to be a myth, an ideologizing defense of the provinces, regions, languages, cultures, and peoples colonized by America International. Where old-fashioned liberals construed American freedom as the freedom to dine out in ethnic restaurants, contemporary postmodernism pretends a global diversity just as it purports to borrow eclectically from different historical epochs, styles, value systems. What used to be called pluralism by old-guard liberals is now characterized by postmodernists as "difference." But there is no difference.

Postmodernism's conception of modernity is not eclectic but Eurocentric, indeed American. Economic imperialism is now matched by cultural imperialism, including an imperialism of the zeitgeist. The Americanization of the planet proceeds apace, even in the Soviet Union and China. Few countries continue to hold out against Coca-Cola, blue jeans, and superficial democratization. Of course, state socialist countries democratize in order to modernize economically (Marcuse 1958). Central planning does not work, as the Soviets and Chinese are now discovering. Hence they rush to loosen the constraints on personal expression in order to foster a character type suited to participation and productivity in the "new" socialist economies dominated by market production and frenzied consumption. The upheavals in the Soviet Union and China were virtually inevitable: people inculcated to be self-sacrificing "new men and women" are suddenly unleashed on a statist system that bends only gradually to the press of popular "participation," even if the participation is as fraudulent as it is in the capitalist West.

Where 1950s modernization theory (e.g., Parsons 1951) recognized the colonizability of the Third World, postmodernism recognizes that colonization is complete or nearly so. The Iron and Bamboo Curtains have largely come down; even the Berlin Wall, symbolically and physically separating capitalist and communist worlds, has come down. This is not to say that East-West relations are entirely without vicissitudes; occasionally, global crises spark when the Soviets shoot down an unarmed airliner or Americans become too aggressive in pursuit of oil. In the postmodern world, the more relevant structuring hierarchy is vertical rather than horizontal, north-and-south, rich-and-poor. Monopoly capitalism and monopoly socialism are instances of an overarching state capitalism, although many postmodernists and even some critical theorists characterize this emerging global monolith in deideologized terms (e.g., Sarup 1989). Recall that postmodernity is a positive valuation among many mainstream postmodern theorists like Lyotard.

## Postrationalism

Finally, postmodern theory suggests a concept of reason fundamentally different from that of Hegelian Marxism (Marcuse 1960). Here the role of Nietzsche is central, especially the question of which Nietzsche is being used as authority, the irrationalist relativist of *Beyond Good and Evil* (1955) or the more dialectical critic of *The Genealogy of Morals* (1956). I do not want to labor over Nietzscheology but simply to note the centrality of Nietzsche's irrationalism and cynicism for postmodernism, notably for Foucault, Derrida, and Lyotard. In attacking the Enlightenment as mythologizing, Nietzsche suggests an antirationalism or postrationalism fundamentally at odds with the left projects of Marxists, feminists, and opponents of racism. Indeed, the "other" left Nietzsche has already been rendered by Horkheimer and Adorno (1972) in their *Dialectic of Enlightenment*, where they explicate a dialectic of myth and enlightenment grounding their critical theory. In particular, the Frankfurt school has used Nietzsche as a linchpin of its critique of positivism, indicating the extent to which positivism is the most recent and effective form of ideology in late capitalism as well as state socialism.

Now postmodernism in its affirmative formulation is antipositivist, too. Derrida's critique of the metaphysics of presence is an unrelenting attack on positivism; indeed, in many ways it is an ingenious one, as is his deconstruction of Western dualism. One can effectively radicalize deconstruction by using its interpretive methodology to show that apparent dualities are really hierarchies, thus buttressing the critique of ideology. But the efforts to radicalize deconstruction (e.g., Ryan 1982; Eagleton 1983) recognize that Derridean poststructuralism is not particularly radical at the outset, even though one can point out, as Ryan has done, his filiation to Adorno's project in critical theory. Radicalizing deconstruction threatens to deconstruct deconstruction, leaving little but the ashes of yet another failed critique of positivism.

The postrationalism of postmodernism is not explicitly irrationalist or antirationalist in the fashion of earlier romantic critiques of enlightenment, science, reason. I use the term postrationalism because it seems that when Lyotard (1984) argues against grand "metanarratives" of history he is not so much denying their rationality per se but simply their grandiose sweep, their Archimedeanism and Prometheanism. Or perhaps he is denying their attempt to impose reason's order on the recalcitrant, bitter world. Whatever the truth (and, after all, there are many contending postmodernisms available in the cultural marketplace), postmodernism does not choose against reason so much as it locates a sufficient reason in the here and now—late capitalism. Instrumental rationality in Weberian terms is not recanted (instrumental reason does give us high technology, a staple of postmodern cosmopolitanism's obsession with electronic media connections and entertainments); it is supplemented with expressive embellishments, whether spirituality or religion, that somehow extend reason into the region of the irrational, notably the extrasensory. Postmodernism equals modernity plus New Individualism (see, e.g., Kroker and Cook 1986).

Derrida's (1976) critique of metaphysical dualism does not pose another lasting way to view dualities and thus to create a nondualist, nonhierarchical social order. Deconstruction in Nietzschean fashion becomes methodology, technique, obsession. The potentially ideology-critical program of deconstruction makes itself absolute, neglecting its own undecidability in Derrida's terms (see Fraser 1984; Jameson 1984a). Postmodernism and critical theory differ most markedly over Derrida's claim that "the text has no outside." As materialists, critical theorists recognize that the text is a world, an ensemble of substantive social relationships (here addressed in terms of literary political economy, particularly relations among writers, publishers, and readers). But they also recognize that all the world is not text, especially where people break their backs and minds in waged and unwaged labor. Postmodernism is cultural reductionist, ignoring the productive and reproductive infrastructure of capitalism and patriarchy, respectively. Of course, this "discourse" is rejected out of hand as emblematic of old-age Marxism, one of those *grands récits* so despised by the postmodernists.

But reason in Plato, Hegel and Marx's sense is a *grand récit*, a metanarrative. It aims to produce a world in its image, notably in terms of various criteria of truth, beauty, and justice. Abjuring reason as a metanarrative implicitly endorses unreason, the stance of all mythology. Derrideans reject absolutism absolutely, thus reproducing only the fatefully cyclical nature of Enlightenment's reversion to myth (Lenhardt

1976). This is not to say that anyone can simply posit a rational order and then attempt to bring it about, heedless of the consequences. As Habermas (1979) suggests, we must argue about reason until we achieve real consensus about it. Critics of Hegelian Marxism have never accurately understood that Marx's version of Hegel's reason was not simply speculative but firmly anchored in Marx's empirical reading of history's unfolding (Lichtheim 1971). This is not to assume that Marx is right about the vector of that unfolding, although I think he largely is. But the postmodernist aversion to world-historical narratives misses, and misunderstands, the historical-materialist effort to place such narratives on the firm footing of empirical social analysis. Marx anointed the proletariat as the world-historical agent of reason because he thought this was "necessary" historically, given the evolving internal contradictions of capitalism. Although his empirical version of history may have been mistaken in some respects, postmodernists cannot simply reject out of hand his attempt to reason history. To avoid grand narratives endorses the very ones playing out behind our backs, what Hegel called the "cunning of reason."

## Postmodernism as Critical Theory

Having examined postmodernism's affirmative, apologetic version, I want to argue for a radical concept and practice of postmodernism that preserves the continuity between a rebellious modernism (e.g., Marx, Adorno, Kafka, Beckett) and a postmodernism that eschews the cultural conformity and self-inflation of the American culture industry (Horkheimer and Adorno 1972, 120–67). Huyssen (1986) leads the way in his dextrous treatment of postmodernism as radical cultural theory; others follow his lead (e.g., Kellner 1988, 1989a, 1989b, 1989c; Ryan 1989). Huyssen suggests that one can use postmodernism both as a critique of the present and as a sketch programming utopia; in particular, postmodernism locates the liberating potential of modernity—industrial capitalism—as well as of its modes of consciousness (e.g., democratic theory) while attacking the insufficiencies of modernity in a dialectical way. After all, Marx was a modernist; he valued capitalism as a prolegomenon to communism, nothing less. In this way, postmodernism functions as critical theory, thawing the social facts frozen by positivism into the dialectical pieces of history they really are.

In particular, this radicalized postmodernism opposes the conservative tendencies of modernism and modernity in much the way Marx did. The notion of the modern, like that of postmodernity, is fraught with difficulty. "Modern" in popular culture connotes positive social value—modern appliances, modern culture, modern consciousness. In this vein, modernity gives rise to modernization theory, the dominant mode of positivist social science since Comte. Modernization theorists suggest that history is moving forward unilinearly toward a postindustrial outcome; this postindustrial order is depicted in the local terms of American sexist and racist capitalism (e.g., Parsons 1951; Bell 1973), confusing the particular and the general. As I said, postmodernity is just another term for postindustrialism; it adds a certain cosmopolitanism to the homelier, homier images of 1950s modernization theory: "Leave It to Beaver," the epitome of suburban modernity in the 1950s and early 1960s, is replaced with the violence and fashion of "Miami Vice," the quintessential American postmodern television show (see Best and Kellner 1988a, 1988b; Luke 1989).

Now this shift from the modern to the postmodern seems truly wrenching from the perspective of narrow cultural focus. Some loathe it, especially neoconservatives wary of the New Individualism; others applaud it as progressively avant-gardist. Huyssen points out that postmodernism, in its authentic sense, draws heavily on the left avant-gardism of forces like surrealism, Dadaism, and situationism, giving the lie to the claim that cultural forms like "Miami Vice" or the Trump Tower are before their time—avant-garde. American senators' wives crusade to rid the airwaves of the more demonic expressions of the avant-garde, fearing the corruption of children. As I said in chapter 5, more cosmopolitan postmoderns would probably view this as a silly excrescence of the Old Individualism; they celebrate the decentered orgy of postmodern significations as the latest in cultural enlightenment, gleaning this from *Vanity Fair*, *Rolling Stone*, even *The New Yorker*—all the places where the culture industry theorizes and elevates itself.

Having contrasted postmodernity, a myth invented by the ideologues of New Individualism to vanquish radical thought yet again, with a genuinely political postmodernism, let me briefly sketch the diverse resources of this postmodernism. Defining postmodernism is as difficult as dodging raindrops; nevertheless, it is an important task, especially given the co-opting way in which anyone and everyone claims postmodernism for one cultural fad or gadget after another. One can read in Hassan (1987), Jameson (1981), Eagleton (1985), Spivak (1988), or Huyssen (1986) for different perspectives on postmodernism; indeed, postmodernism has become a veritable cottage industry, spawning primers purporting to simplify an incredibly ingrown subject (Klinkowitz 1988; Sarup 1989). In trying to "define" postmodernism, I am not simply summing others' usage of the term for there is too little commonality of usage to make that effort worthwhile. My definition of postmodernism helps it do useful critical and political work. Let others add to a trendy cultural glossary (e.g., Gitlin 1988) indispensable for Sunday *New York Times Book Review* readers and others who aim to be in the know about the latest twists and turns of the zeitgeist.

## The Absolute within Relation

In comparing postmodernism as critical theory to its affirmative mainstream version, I shall move along the six axial dimensions on which I located the first version of the postmodern. To some extent, this is an artificial exercise in that the different varieties of postmodernism are complexly entwined with each other. Where some call Foucault a neoconservative (Sarup 1989), others regard him as a first cousin of the Frankfurt school (Smart 1983; Dews 1984, 1987; Agger 1989c). There is continuity as well as rupture between the two senses of postmodernism I identify here, just as there was continuity as well as contradiction between capitalism and socialism for Marx. Even a fanatical exercise in "scholarship" would not resolve the issue for, above all, commentators on postmodernism have not yet discovered a key with which to code one author, writing, or theory as genuinely postmodern whereas others are merely pretenders.

First, a critical postmodernism differs from its affirmative companion version on the issue of the absolutism of values. Where Lyotard rejects the axiological absolutism and Archimedeanism involved in the *grands récits* of world history, a critical postmodernism would not simply reject the notion of stable values with which to orient both theory and practice. This is very much the Nietzsche question raised earlier: can one read or write a Nietzsche who not only railed against the pretensions of the Enlightenment but who also implied a new order of value free of mythic residues? Of course, no amount of interpretive casuistry will make Nietzsche into a Marxist and feminist, even if one takes seriously Adorno's sympathy for him. Yet it seems to me that a postmodern critical theory can suggest a concept of the normative that neither succumbs to unreflected absolutism (e.g., Platonism) nor embraces relativism willy-nilly as a counterposition, especially inasmuch as relativism is absolute in its own right.

Many on the Left (e.g., Kamenka 1962; Heller 1976) have speculated about appropriate standards of value with which to guide the construction of socialism. Feminists have been debating this issue vigorously
(Gilligan 1982). A left and feminist version of postmodernism could well
propose a notion of values that appear absolute (i.e., nonnegotiable,
fundamental to the creation of a new order) but are in fact situational
(Weedon 1987). One might well disqualify the death penalty as barbaric
but recognize that the very discourse of "death penalty" is an artifact of
a society legitimizing certain kinds of death (e.g., from starvation or war).
This is very much how I read the Foucault (1977) of *Discipline and Punish*, where he argues convincingly that criminality is an historical product
of criminologists and of the state.

In fact, Foucault's writings about the relation among knowledge,
discipline, and power strike me as eminently a contribution to an empirical and political critical theory. One could read Foucault as a Marxist
who borrows from what sociologists would call labeling theory. In any
case, a relational view of absolute values could serve critical theory well,
suggesting the discursive and epistemic grounds of values and thus helping us deconstruct them. Postmodernism offers Marxism and feminism
an internal method of self-interrogation with which to examine fossilized
assumptions about the nature of oppression and freedom. Call this
deconstruction; call it immanent critique; or call it self-criticism. Names
do not matter. The point is that critical theory must be equipped to posit
a rational society without losing sight of its own investment in particular
modes of rationality that are not treated simply as incommensurable language games (Wittgenstein 1953) but can be argued for, defended reasonably. As I understand it, this is the sense of Habermas's recent (1984,
1987b) contributions to the reconstruction of historical materialism as
communication theory, from which I draw in the formulation of my own
lifeworld-grounded critical theory.

## An Unfulfilled Present

Where mainstream postmodernism views the present as eternal, the end
of ideology and of industrialization having been reached, a more critical
postmodernism regards the present as somehow connected dialectically
both to past and present. This is the sense in which I understand Marx to
have written a theory of modernity; he favored modernity—the technological and civil infrastructure of industrial capitalism—but he wanted
to push one stage beyond modernity toward socialism. This is a crucial

source of confusion for postmodernists: on the one hand, the depiction of postmodernity is not always sanguine, especially where postmodernity connotes cynicism, pessimism, the New Individualism, red-baiting. On the other hand, the diagnosis of postmodernity often tends to become postmodernism, negation fatefully turning into its opposite, even unconsciously. Indeed, mainstream postmodernism endorses the postmodern scene (Kroker and Cook 1986), reveling in the erosion of meaning, hope, utopia. But even left postmodernisms risk conflating themselves with the sorry social condition they explore and reject. Thus, Marxist postmodernists forget that Marx would have reserved the term "postmodernity" only for the end of prehistory—socialism. Late capitalism is precisely not postmodern but modern, as Habermas (1987a) and Kellner (1988, 1989a, 1989b, 1989c) have pointed out.

## Redefining the Political

Where poststructuralists and postmodernists like Derrida and Lyotard seem to endorse an antipolitics, rejecting both dominant institutions and oppositional social movements (or at least those that theorize themselves in terms of metanarratives like Marxism and feminism), left postmodernists (e.g., Aronowitz 1981; Agger 1989a, 1989c, 1990) attempt to redefine the political. My (1989a) argument about a "fast capitalism" in which image and thing blur, thus reducing the critical distance of thought and writing, suggests that we can find politics today everywhere but in the traditionally defined political arena. Left postmodernism does not abandon political praxis. Chic postmodernism endorses postmodernity, where left postmodernism regards postmodernism as yet another ideology cloaking the real in sheer appearance (although I [1989a] argue that it is harder than ever to disentangle reality and appearance, the special nature of fast capitalism).

Postmodernists like Foucault (1977, 1980) who rethink the nature of power in a disciplinary society (O'Neill 1986) also seem to shun large-scale social movements that seek to shift power. Again, this reflects the political ambivalence of the postmodernity/postmodernism problematic: that power takes new forms not imagined by prior radical critics like Marx does not mean it is impregnable. Here, postmodernism (Foucault, Lyotard) borrows heavily from poststructuralism (Derrida, Barthes, French feminism, Lacan). Derrida and Barthes posit the death of the subject, suggesting an antisubjectivism that permeates all poststructural and postmodern thought. However valid this may be on the evidence (after all, the Frankfurt school theorists also suggested the "decline of the individual" [Horkheimer 1974] as a tendency in late capitalism, discussed and rejected in chap. 13), poststructuralists and postmodernists ontologize the death of the subject, thus fatefully depoliticizing their own critique of dominant culture and society. Habermas's own (1984, 1987b) reconstruction of critical theory as communication theory indefatigably defends the notion of personal and interpersonal agency (notably through his "universal pragmatics" of communicative competence) as an indispensable condition of any critical theory and hence critical social practice. It is one thing to note that people are less and less in control of their discourses, lifeworlds, and productive/reproductive activities; it is altogether another thing to chill this disempowering into a veritable social metaphysic in the fashion of both poststructuralism and postmodernism.

Laclau and Mouffe (1985), among others, seek alternative "subject positions" from which alienated but constitutive individuals can launch oppositional projects. Although they abandon Marxism, they also resist the fatalizing assumptions of poststructuralists and postmodernists who reject any talk of constitutive subjectivity as metaphysical treason. They try to redefine the political, although not in a way that is ultimately successful given that they jettison so much of the materialist apparatus. But that is precisely what left postmodernism must do—reconceive of politics in a way that we can formulate and enact new modes of opposition and reconstruction. The death of the subject is only temporary. Once we historicize subjectivity, we can rethink the modalities of personal and public life in an energizing way.

### Objective Subjectivity

This rethinking of the political gives rise to, and is reflected in, a left postmodernist conception of subjectivity. For the most part, I find this concept of an objective subjectivity already available in the Freudian Marxism of the Frankfurt school (e.g., Jacoby 1975b), although a left feminism has important things to say about the matter, too (Jaggar 1983; Fraser 1989). The New Individualism of neoconservative postmodernism is contrasted with an objective concept of subjectivity grounded in one or another depth psychology connecting psychological and social-structural dynamics, whether Freudian, Freudian-Marxist, or feminist-Marxist. The American women's movement says it best: the personal is political. The psyche and family are legitimate political agenda items. The Frankfurt theorists (Marcuse 1955), with their heterodox version of psychoanalysis, suggested some private-public links quite unconventional by orthodox Marxist standards. Marcuse (1969) recognized that revolutionary product must be borne of revolutionary process lest the "revolution" turn out to be what Korsch called a dictatorship over the proletariat as horrifying as the capitalism it replaces.

Western Marxism (Agger 1979) (including phenomenological Marxism [Piccone 1971; Paci 1972]) joins left feminism in making the personal-political link thematic, both for theory and practice. Together they help fertilize a critical postmodernism that refuses to dispense with a concept of the subject; instead, together, these theoretical currents suggest a notion of objective subjectivity, of historical subjectivity, and a notion of intersubjectivity (Piccone 1971) that provide a semblance of radical energy in an overstructured, overdetermined world. As I argued in chapter 13, the Left has been unable to relinquish an active concept of subjectivity without descending into either fatalism or authoritarianism. State socialism is all state and no socialism, just as democratic centralism, Lenin's euphemism, was very short on democracy. A critical postmodernism rebuts left determinism yet again, whether it is structuralism (Althusser 1969) or garden-variety economism (Mandel 1968). One may imagine that poststructuralism in its very nature would reject the structuralism of Lévi-Strauss (1963, 1966). But it also turns its back on subjectivity and thus political activism. Derrida's claim that he is a Marxist and the promise of a book by him called *The Political Derrida* are not convincing. Either political transformation is present in theoretical concepts from the beginning or it is not; it cannot be imported.

### The Nonmodern

Luddism is antimodern; modernism ambivalently values capitalist progress but, in its avant-garde formulation, rages against it (e.g., Dadaism, situationism [Debord 1983], surrealism); an establishment postmodernism endorses the present as a plenitude of postmodernity—the eclipse of the old isms (like Bell in his "end of ideology" thesis). What, then, of a critical postmodernism? How does it conceive of a post-postmodern future? Theoretically, we can say this: a left postmodernism rejects the whole continuum of modernity, modernization, and postmodernity as a fatefully teleological discourse. Left postmodernism poses the possibility of a future stage of social history characterized neither by antimodernism nor promodernism (given the ambivalent status of modernism—both capitalism and Adorno) but by nonmodernism.

I reject the notion that we are now in a stage of postmodernity fundamentally discontinuous with earlier capitalist modernity. Jameson (1984b) and Kellner (1988) are among the left theorists who support this contention. Aronowitz (1981, 1990), too, suggests that postmodernism and poststructuralism are often faddish and betray the historical materialist project, although he takes the lead in showing how we can learn from them in deepening our own version of the totality. Indeed, his 1988 book on science agrees largely with the sense of my argument here for a renewed form of public reason within a materialist framework. Ryan (1982) and Eagleton (1983) join this discussion about how to salvage the critical and dialectical insights of French social theory, notably deconstruction. In many ways, Huyssen (1986) has gone the furthest toward embracing postmodernism as critical theory, although he may well have passed the point of no return beyond which postmodernism's neoconservatism swallows its avant-gardist radicalism. This largely depends on how we define postmodernism and then what we take from it in the way of ideology-critical resources. Kellner (1988) is correct to note that there is no systematic postmodern social theory but only various people who claim postmodernism in the frenzy of intellectual trendiness, particularly in France.

For my part (Agger 1989a, 1989c), I have tried to formulate a postmodern Marxism in terms of what I call disciplinary reading. What I call a critical theory of significance broadens disciplinary reading from sociology per se to what Foucault (1977) called the disciplinary society in general. Fast capitalism is my term for our present social formation; in it I attempt to preserve the sense of continuity between modernity and postmodernity as well as to suggest its distinctive features: "fast" capitalism speeds up the rate at which concepts and images blur with the reality to which they bear a representational relationship, a twist of Adorno (1973b), Baudrillard (1983), and others who have theorized the relationship between ideas/ideology and reality. In Jacoby's (1976) terms, fast capitalism causes the "rate of intelligence" to decline, thus checking the tendency of the rate of profit to fall.

But words cannot do our thinking for us, let alone our political work. Jameson (1981) struggles to elaborate a total theory of political unconsciousness; Aronowitz (1990) attempts to restore radical democracy to a Marxism nearly overtaken by the secret vanguardism of French social theory, particularly postmodernism. All of us struggle to retain a notion of totality, resisting the decenterings of our grand narratives by those (e.g., Lyotard 1984) who may well have neoconservative motives (as Habermas [1981b] has cogently argued in his original piece on modernity and postmodernity). Adorno (1973b, 1974) suggested the inversion of positive totality into the negations of postfascist capitalism: "The whole is the untruth." Although at a certain level it is difficult to deny the absolute nature of world horrors, especially in the nuclear age, Adorno himself (e.g., 1973b) attempted to render negation and negativism dialectical. I think of my own effort to redevelop left-feminist postmodern critical theory as an example of "negative dialectics," combining a Hegelian-Marxist foundationalism with methodical circumspection about the pitfalls of totality. Sartre (1963, 1976) also offers a theory of totalization largely ignored by the postmodern Left, ironic—considering how his version of political existentialism energized a variety of currents of political dissent in France (e.g., the 1968 May Movement) that both directly and indirectly issued in more recent theoretical developments around postmodernism and poststructuralism.

## Dionysian Reason

The antirationalism of Establishment postmodernism can be countered by a new formulation of reason that in significant respects makes good the search for a non-Archimedean, non-authoritarian concept of totality. Reason in Hegelian-Marxist terms is a way both of conceiving and of working toward a good society; it has both subjective and objective components. Habermas's continuing effort to think through the communicative as well as institutional requirements of the "rational society" (e.g., Habermas 1970c, 1971, 1984, 1987b) reflects the double character of reason in the Frankfurt tradition, as does Marcuse's (1960) book on Hegel. There appear to be three choices of a concept and practice of rationality available to postmodern theory: we could decide to embrace the dualism of technical/instrumental and self-reflective/communicative rationalities, in the fashion of Habermas's essentially Kantian Marxism (see chap. 10); or we could dispense with the concept of reason and its metanarrativeness altogether, as Nietzschean postmodernists like Lyotard do. Or, finally, as I propose, following the Freudian Marxism of the Frankfurt school (see chap. 7) as well as the Frankfurt reading of Nietzsche, left existential phenomenology (Merleau-Ponty 1964), and left feminism (Jaggar 1983; Donovan 1985), we can heal the reason/desire split in a new concept of rationality that is both libidinal and cognitive/communicative. Although Habermas (1971, 32–33) rejects this tendency in the original Frankfurt School as "mysticism," I embrace Marcuse, Adorno, and Horkheimer's attempts to formulate a nondualist rationality that preserves the concept of a redeemed totality and helps provide bridging principles between the levels of personality and social structure.

Whether or not one invests doctrinally in a left psychoanalysis (e.g., Jacoby's [1975b] discussion of "negative psychoanalysis") or for that matter in left existential phenomenology and socialist feminism, I believe it is possible and necessary for critical theory to develop a notion of rationality that staunchly defends itself against the postrationalism of Lyotard's postmodernism. In Nietzsche's terms, this rationality combines Dionysian passion and Apollonian intellection, precisely the nondualist rationality of Marx (1961) in the 1844 manuscripts. Without the conceptualization of reason in these terms, critical theory is defenseless against the rising tide of antisubjectivism, antirationalism, neoconservatism, and New Individualism—all virtually endorsing postmodernity as the world-historical solution to capitalism, sexism, racism, and the domination of nature.

For these reasons, it is imperative to address directly how large institutional forces press down on writers who write to make a difference, to initiate social change as well as answer to their own creative muses. This is the task of cultural studies, as I understand it. Writers who refuse to submit to the commodifying forces of popular culture and academia need some actual notion of how to think and live in order to survive the corporate and profit impulses of the culture industry. They need a Dionysian rationality alert to the irrepressible requirements of the writer's desire to think, write, and live free of the commodifying, hegemonizing forces of postmodern textual politics. There must be hope, as well as a concept of the hoped for, in addition to the hard materialist analysis of how to make a living, start bookstores and journals, create community. As much as anything, critical writers need a source and focus of dialectical imagination (Jay 1973) to encourage their lonely dissent. The decline of discourse can be countered by articulate, activist writers who engage in the creation of what Sartre (1965) called committed literature. But the first problem is how to generate commitment; from that follows a practical conception of what is to be done in the way of dehegemonizing the literary, hence public, world.

## Literary Political Economy: Toward a
## Dialectical Sociology of Culture

I derive categories of an empirical sociology of culture from my general postmodernist framework, albeit the postmodernism of critical theory and not Lyotard's affirmative postmodernism denying the *grands récits* of Marxism and feminism. I characterize this sociology of culture as literary political economy, building on the Frankfurt analysis of the culture industry (Horkheimer and Adorno 1972, 120–67) as well as Jameson's (1984b) discussion of postmodernism as the "cultural logic of late capitalism." This is in aid of a real discussion and diagnosis of the falling fortunes of literary and hence public intelligence, framed in terms of the phenomenological experiences of writers struggling both to survive and to make a difference. As for all Marxism, the central analytical category of literary political economy is commodification, capturing the idea that writing increasingly trades only through its "exchange value," as Marx called it (e.g., see Best 1989). This is obviously true of writing in the realm of popular culture, including advertising, television, journalism, film, and trade fiction. It is also true of academic writing where we understand that journal and monograph space is a scarce resource and thus becomes a necessary value for those who would rather publish and prosper than perish (Brodkey 1987).

Commodified discourse is displaced from the realm of authentic writing proper, whatever that may mean, into the regions of popular culture and academia (Ross 1988). The displacement of discourse definitely lowers the level of public intelligence in that writers write, not for expressive and political reasons, but to please editors and publishers concerned both to maximize profit and to enforce social control. Discourse's displacement is a structural tendency in a commodified literary world; this tendency must be examined in terms of its real influence on writers' lives. The commodification of discourse exacts grievous costs from writers who come to their craft to ventilate a certain aesthetic and political desire.

My version of literary political economy derives from what I have characterized as a left and feminist version of postmodernism or simply critical theory. One of the tensions in my argument is the alternation between the trendy, glitzy postmodernism of the culture industry and an academic world that endorses the commodification and displacement of literary craft and an alternative, fugitive postmodernism that criticizes literary postmodernism as both faddish and ideologizing. Although this issue turns on how one defines postmodernism, I am convinced that a discussion of literary political economy cannot address only the political economy of trade publishing, television, advertising, movies, journalism, and academia without also examining the legitimating ideologies, increasingly self-styled "postmodern," attending on the economic ramifications of the commodification and corporate control of discourse. In other words, we need to "deconstruct" the stories publishers, producers, editors, and even authors tell themselves and others about the nature of postmodern literary life-styles as a way of piercing the haze surrounding what is really happening in literary political economy on a structural level. As Horkheimer (1972) and his Frankfurt colleagues (Horkheimer and Adorno 1972, 120–67) knew from the beginning, an adequate analysis of the culture industry cannot neatly separate infrastructural from superstructural phenomena, even less in "postmodern" or "fast" (Agger 1989a) capitalism.

Postmodernism as a legitimating ideology in contemporary literary political economy justifies all manner of authorial self-sacrifice and conformism. Its peculiar nature is that it does this behind the facade of literary desublimation that, as ever, proves to be repressive (Marcuse 1955). The postmodern auteur is portrayed as cosmopolitan, networked and networking, brazen, supremely self-confident. In fact, this conceals a hollowness and insecurity only exacerbated by life in the literary fast lane. This holds true for academia as well as for popular culture—perhaps more for academia where "points" are tallied entirely in reputation and citations if not also sales and dollars. Everybody is running scared, although by the look of things people seem to be enjoying these halcyon days of limitless literary opportunities and upward mobility. Postmodernity is the best and worst of times: writers wear a brave front but inside they feel empty. Bravado is both a survival strategy, part of the repertoire of coping and people-handling skills of the late twentieth-century rationalist, and ideology, an index of one's belief in the world's fundamental goodness. Unfortunately, few see this for what it is: as the Frankfurt school knew, the culture industry proceeds through people's obliviousness to it, the nature of contemporary ideology.

In this sense, my empirical and political aim is to formulate a mode of counterhegemony, of literary resistance, to the culture industry and its postmodern patina. This is one way to understand the research agenda of a lifeworld-grounded critical theory that functions as a radicalizing cultural studies and cultural critique. What can writers do to avoid being crushed by the logos of the postmodern? What can writers write in order to change the world? Of course, these are portentous questions, and I have few definitive answers. I am not unduly hopeful.

But neither am I hopeless a priori. Articulating the problem of the decline of discourse this way helps slow it, if infinitesimally. At least, we writers, by framing our own complicity in literary political economy in terms of our susceptibility to its postmodernist ideologization, can avoid the worst aspects of false consciousness, what Nietzsche called the love of fate. Whether capitalism is destined to survive attempts to rebel against it is an empirical question; but we know with certainty that fate is redoubled by fatalism, the stance of the postmodern who rejects subjectivity, reason, totality—optimism.

Saying this suggests self-help—for writers. There is nothing wrong with self-help except its institutional housing beside the other deceptive mechanisms of third-force and New Age affirmation and acquiescence. We have to help ourselves and others. Community begins at home, in neighborhoods and classrooms, between couples, and among small handfuls of souls struggling to overcome their mortal and political isolation. And social change movements in their full-blown nature are nothing more than communities arrayed together strategically. If this is self-help for radical writers, it wants to extend that help into a larger framework of literary and political community in which people can cluster together for shelter and perhaps even the first halting steps of social change. There is nothing wrong with a radical concept of subjectivity as long as we realize that subjectivity is already objective (Adorno 1978) and intersubjective (Husserl 1965). In fact, we cannot do without a notion of struggling, imaginative subjects—writers and readers. Lacking such a notion, we on the Left fail to take existential responsibility for changing our own worlds. The powers will not do it for us.

Writers must write through it all, neither heroizing themselves nor reveling in their isolation. Literary work can be political especially where politics is found everywhere but in the traditionally defined political arena. And where politics is increasingly textual politics, we simply cannot afford to ignore literary political economy and its accompanying postmodernist ideology out of economistic prejudices. By now, the analysis of the culture industry has become an integral part of Western Marxism and left feminism, whether as critical theory, Birmingham cultural studies, left deconstruction, feminist literary criticism, Marxist aesthetic theory, or the radical sociology of culture. My version of critical theory contributes to that tradition, reformulating some of the categories of culture-critical analysis in the direction of recent postmodern critical theorists like Jameson (1984a, 1984b), Huyssen (1986), and Kellner (1988), among others. The decline of discourse is a factor, a moment, in overall domination. It can be slowed, perhaps even reversed, as long as literary workers, both popular and academic, recognize and reorder their own roles in the textual politics enmeshing us in the overall political fabric.

The culture industry is a vehicle of mass unconsciousness today. But it is not a deus ex machina. The logic of cultural capital does not transpire above the heads of men and women, readers and writers. As such, it can be transformed, if not heroically through singular expressions of outrage or optimism. At issue here are writing and reading, publishers and producers, the literary labor market, the role of the intellectual, the nature and future of ideology—public culture. Critical theory can make use of postmodernism in developing a concept of public life that celebrates critique and revivifies consciousness. The end of ideology is not just yet. The world is not seamless; dissonance and dissent abound. Culture reproduces the quotidian, hence reproducing power. It can be deconstructed, hence democratized. A postmodern critical theory contributes to this deconstruction, reading politics into culture in order to create a new culture, hence a whole new world.

In this book I have outlined a postmodern critical theory that functions empirically and politically. Although I have derived this theory largely from the work of members of the Frankfurt school, this chapter makes it clear that the original Frankfurt theory needs to be revitalized from sources outside it. Although I have taken issue with Habermas at various points in the book, Habermas is clearly at the forefront of this effort to reformulate the categories and emancipatory objectives of critical theory. I believe that the reconstruction of historical materialism—of emancipatory theory, broadly understood—is crucial at this stage in world history, where the political is found everywhere but in the official political arena, which is increasingly dominated by the rituals of pseudodemocracy. The Frankfurt school theorists, especially Marcuse, always insisted that politics is found in culture as well as in desire. As I have argued, this does not deeconomize Marxism, which still pivots around Marx's analysis of commodity fetishism in *Capital,* but extends the analysis of the logic of capital to realms unforeseen by Marx.

*Pace* Bell (1973), ideology has not ended. It is all around us (and within us). It suffuses us with the various discourses of the quotidian, notably positivism, which counsels an acquiescent fact fetishism. Yet as Marcuse (1964) convincingly argued in *One-Dimensional Man,* one-dimensionality does not exist outside of history. Hence, it can be cracked as people seize "the chance of the alternatives." That remains a very real possibility today as people's struggle takes the form of new social movements (Habermas 1981b), including feminism, antiracism, environmentalism, and antinuclearism. Marcuse would have been among the first to recognize these formulations of resistance as politically relevant. Like Habermas, he would have theorized them. That is the sort of work theorists should be doing in the years ahead. Again—ideology, which functions to conceal and legitimate domination (Marx and Engels 1947), only ends with domination. Once translated into the discourses and practices recognizable as politically inflected, ideology can be debunked, now as before.

# Bibliography

The years given in the Bibliography and text are those of the editions used by the author and not necessarily the dates of the original publications.

Ackerman, B.
1980    *Social Justice in the Liberal State*. New Haven: Yale University Press.

Adorno, T.
1945    "A Social Critique of Radio Music." *Kenyon Review* 8 (2): 208–17.
1954    "How to Look at Television." *Quarterly of Film, Radio and Television* 3: 213–35.
1967    "Sociology and Psychology I." *New Left Review* 46: 67–80.
1968    "Sociology and Psychology II." *New Left Review* 47:79–97.
1969    "Scientific Experiences of a European Scholar in America." In *The Intellectual Migration*, edited by D. Fleming and B. Bailyn. Cambridge: Harvard University Press.
1973a   *The Jargon of Authenticity*. Evanston, Ill.: Northwestern University Press.
1973b   *Negative Dialectics*. New York: Seabury.
1973c   *Philosophy of Modern Music*. New York: Seabury.
1974    *Minima Moralia*. London: New Left Books.
1978    "Subject and Object." In *The Essential Frankfurt School Reader*, edited by A. Arato and E. Gebhardt. New York: Urizen.
1984    *Aesthetic Theory*. London: Routledge & Kegan Paul.

Adorno, T. W.; H. Albert; R. Dahrendorf; J. Habermas; H. Pilot; and K. Popper
1976    *The Positivist Dispute in German Sociology*. London: Heinemann.

Adorno, T. W.; E. Frenkel-Brunswik; D. Levinson; and R. N. Sanford
1950    *The Authoritarian Personality*. New York: Harper & Row.

Agger, B.
1975    "On Science as Domination." In *Domination*, edited by A. Kontos. Toronto: University of Toronto Press.

1979            *Western Marxism: An Introduction.* Santa Monica, Calif.: Good-
               year.
1981            "A Critical Theory of Dialogue." *Humanities in Society* 4: 7–30.
1985            "The Dialectic of Deindustrialization: An Essay on Advanced
               Capitalism." In *Critical Theory and Public Life*, edited by J. For-
               ester. Cambridge: MIT Press.
1989a           *Fast Capitalism: A Critical Theory of Significance.* Urbana: Univer-
               sity of Illinois Press.
1989b           *Reading Science: A Literary, Political and Sociological Analysis.* Dix
               Hills, N.Y.: General Hall.
1989c           *Socio(onto)logy: A Disciplinary Reading.* Urbana: University of Illi-
               nois Press.
1990            *The Decline of Discourse: Reading, Writing and Resistance in
               Postmodern Capitalism.* London and Philadelphia: Falmer.
1991a           *Cultural Studies as Critical Theory.* London and Philadelphia:
               Falmer.
1991b           "Critical Theory, Poststructuralism and Postmodernism: Their
               Sociological Relevance." *Annual Review of Sociology* 17: 105–31.

Agger, B., and S. McDaniel
1982            *Social Problems through Conflict and Order.* Toronto: Addison-Wes-
               ley.

Alexander, J. C.
1982            *Theoretical Logic in Sociology,* 4 vols. Berkeley: University of Cali-
               fornia Press.

Alexander, J. C., ed.
1985            *Neofunctionalism.* Beverly Hills: Sage.

Alexander, J.C.; B. Giesen; R. Munch; and N. J. Smelser, eds.
1987            *The Micro-Macro Link.* Berkeley: University of California Press.

Althusser, L.
1969            *For Marx.* London: Allen Lane.

Althusser, L., and E. Balibar
1970            *Reading "Capital."* New York: Pantheon.

Anderson, P.
1976            *Considerations on Western Marxism.* London: New Left Books.

Antonio, R.
1983            "The Origin, Development and Contemporary Status of Critical
               Theory." *Sociological Quarterly* 24: 325–51.

Arendt, H.
1958            *The Human Condition.* Chicago: University of Chicago Press.
1964            *Eichmann in Jerusalem.* New York: Viking.

Aronowitz, S.
1981        *The Crisis in Historical Materialism.* New York: Praeger.
1988        *Science as Power: Discourse and Ideology in Modern Society.* Minneapolis: University of Minnesota Press.
1990        *The Crisis in Historical Materialism,* 2d ed. Minneapolis: University of Minnesota Press.

Banfield, E.
1970        *The Unheavenly City: The Nature and Future of Our Urban Crisis.* Boston: Little, Brown.

Baudrillard, J.
1981        *For a Critique of the Political Economy of the Sign.* St. Louis: Telos.
1983        *Simulations.* New York: Semiotext(e).

Becker, H.
1986        *Writing for Social Scientists.* Chicago: University of Chicago Press.

Bell, D.
1960        *The End of Ideology.* Glencoe, Ill.: Free Press.
1973        *The Coming of Post-Industrial Society.* New York: Basic.
1976        *The Cultural Contradictions of Capitalism.* New York: Basic.

Benhabib, S.
1987        *Critique, Norm and Utopia.* New York: Columbia University Press.

Benjamin, W.
1969        *Illuminations.* New York: Schocken.

Berger, P.; B. Berger; and H. Kellner
1973        *The Homeless Mind.* New York: Random House.

Bernstein, B.
1971        *Class, Codes and Control.* London: Routledge & Kegan Paul.

Bernstein, E.
1961        *Evolutionary Socialism.* New York: Schocken.

Best, S.
1989        "The Commodification of Reality and the Reality of Commodification: Jean Baudrillard and Post-Modernism." *Current Perspectives in Social Theory* 9: 23–51.

Best, S., and D. Kellner
1988a       "(Re)Watching Television: Notes toward a Political Criticism." *Diacritics* 17: 97–113.
1988b       "Watching Television: The Limits of Postmodernism." *Science as Culture* 4: 44–70.
1991        *Postmodern Theorizing.* London: Macmillan.

Bottomore, T.
1975            *Marxist Sociology*. London: Macmillan.

Bourdieu, P.
1988            *Homo Academicus*. Cambridge, England: Polity.

Breines, P., ed.
1970            *Critical Interruptions*. New York: Herder & Herder.
1985            "Redeeming Redemption." *Telos* 65: 152–58.

Brodkey, L.
1987            *Academic Writing as Social Practice*. Philadelphia: Temple University Press.

Buck-Morss, S.
1977            *The Origins of Negative Dialectics*. New York: Free Press.

Burawoy, M.
1982            "Introduction: The Resurgence of Marxism in American Sociology." *American Journal of Sociology* 88: S1–S30.
1985            *The Politics of Production*. London: New Left Books.
1987            "The Limits of Wright's Analytical Marxism and an Alternative." *Berkeley Journal of Sociology* 23: 51–72.

Cleaver, H.
1979            *Reading "Capital" Politically*. Austin: University of Texas Press.

Colletti, L.
1973            *Marxism and Hegel*. London: New Left Books.

Collins, R.
1975            *Conflict Sociology*. New York: Academic.

Connerton, P.
1980            *The Tragedy of Enlightenment*. Cambridge: Cambridge University Press.

Culler, J.
1982            *On Deconstruction: Theory and Criticism after Structuralism*. Ithaca, N.Y.: Cornell University Press.

Dahrendorf, R.
1959            *Class and Class Conflict in Industrial Society*. Palo Alto: Stanford University Press.

Davis, K., and W. E. Moore
1945            "Some Principles of Stratification." *American Sociological Review* 10: 242–49.

Debord, G.
1983            *Society of the Spectacle*. Detroit: Black & Red Press.

Derrida, J.
1976          *Of Grammatology*. Baltimore: Johns Hopkins University Press.

Dews, P.
1984          "Power and Subjectivity in Foucault." *New Left Review* 144:
              72–95.
1987          *Logics of Disintegration: Post-Structuralist Thought and the Claims of
              Critical Theory*. London: Verso.

Diamond, S.
1974          *In Search of the Primitive*. New Brunswick, N.J.: Transaction.
1987          "The Beautiful and the Ugly Are One Thing, the Sublime An-
              other: A Reflection on Culture." *Cultural Anthropology* 2:
              268–72.

DiTomaso, N.
1982          " 'Sociological Reductionism' from Parsons to Althusser: Link-
              ing Action and Structure in Social Theory." *American Sociological
              Review* 47: 14–28.

Djilas, M.
1964          *The New Class*. New York: Praeger.

Donovan, J.
1985          *Feminist Theory*. New York: Ungar.

Durkheim, E.
1950          *The Rules of Sociological Method*. Glencoe, Ill.: Free Press.

Eagleton, T.
1976          *Marxism and Literary Criticism*. London: Methuen.
1983          *Literary Theory: An Introduction*. Minneapolis: University of Min-
              nesota Press.
1985          "Marxism, Structuralism and Poststructuralism." *Diacritics* 15:
              2–56.

Feagin, J.        "The Future of Blacks in America: Race and Class in American
1989          Cities." Albert A. Levin Lecture Series, Cleveland State Univer-
              sity, May 18.

Fischer, E.
1969          *Art against Ideology*. New York: Braziller.

Foucault, M.
1970          *The Order of Things*. New York: Pantheon.
1976          *The Archaeology of Knowledge*. New York: Harper & Row.
1977          *Discipline and Punish: The Birth of the Prison*. London: Allen Lane.
1978          *The History of Sexuality*, vol. 1. New York: Pantheon.
1980          *Power/Knowledge*. New York: Pantheon.

Franklin, M.
1970            "The Irony of the Beautiful Soul of Herbert Marcuse." *Telos* 6:
               3–35.

Fraser, N.
1984            "The French Derrideans: Politicizing Deconstruction or Decon-
               structing the Political?" *New German Critique* 33: 127–54.
1989            *Unruly Practices: Power, Discourse and Gender in Contemporary So-
               cial Theory.* Minneapolis: University of Minnesota Press.

Freire, P.
1970            *Pedagogy of the Oppressed.* New York: Seabury.

Fromm, E., ed.
1965            *Socialist Humanism.* Garden City, N.Y.: Doubleday.

Gellner, E.
1959            *Words and Things.* London: Gollancz.

Gerth, H., and C. W. Mills
1946            *Character and Social Structure.* New York: Harcourt, Brace.

Giddens, A.
1973            *The Class-Structure of the Advanced Societies.* London: Hutchinson.

Gilder, G.
1981            *Wealth and Poverty.* New York: Basic.

Gilligan, C.
1982            *In a Different Voice.* Cambridge: Harvard University Press.

Gitlin, T.
1987            *The Sixties: Years of Hope, Days of Rage.* New York: Bantam.
1988            "Hip-Deep in Postmodernism." *The New York Times Book Review*
               (6 November) 1, 35–36.

Gottdiener, M.
1991            "Space, Social Theory and the Urban Metaphor." *Current Per-
               spectives in Social Theory* 11: 295–311.

Gouldner, A.
1970            *The Coming Crisis of Western Sociology.* New York: Basic.
1976            *Dialectic of Ideology and Technology.* New York: Seabury.
1980            *The Two Marxisms: Contradictions and Anomalies in the Development
               of Theory.* New York: Seabury.

Gramsci, A.
1971            *Selections from the Prison Notebooks.* London: Lawrence & Wishart.

Habermas, J.
1970a           "On Systematically Distorted Communication." *Inquiry* 13:
               205–18.

1970b          "Technology and Science as 'Ideology.' " In *Toward a Rational Society*. Boston: Beacon.
1970c          *Toward a Rational Society*. Boston: Beacon.
1970d          "Towards a Theory of Communicative Competence." *Inquiry* 13: 360–75.
1971           *Knowledge and Human Interests*. Boston: Beacon.
1973           *Theory and Practice*. Boston: Beacon.
1975           *Legitimation Crisis*. Boston: Beacon.
1976           "Some Distinctions in Universal Pragmatics." *Theory and Society* 3: 155–67.
1979           *Communication and the Evolution of Society*. Boston: Beacon.
1981a          "Modernity versus Postmodernity." *New German Critique* 22: 3–14.
1981b          "New Social Movements." *Telos* 49: 33–37.
1984           *The Theory of Communicative Action*, vol. 1. Boston: Beacon.
1987a          *The Philosophical Discourse of Modernity*. Cambridge: MIT Press.
1987b          *The Theory of Communicative Action*, vol. 2. Boston: Beacon.

Harvey, D.
1989           *The Condition of Postmodernity*. Oxford: Basil Blackwell.

Hassan, I.
1987           *The Postmodern Turn: Essays in Postmodern Theory and Culture*. Columbus: Ohio State University Press.

Hayek, F.
1944           *The Road to Serfdom*. Chicago: University of Chicago Press.
1964           *The Counter-revolution of Science*. New York: Free Press.

Hegel, G. W. F.
1920           *The Philosophy of Fine Art*. London: Bell.
1966           "Preface to *Phenomenology of Mind*." In *Hegel: Texts and Commentary*, edited by W. Kaufman. Garden City, N.Y.: Anchor.

Held, D.
1980           *An Introduction to Critical Theory*. Berkeley: University of California Press.

Heller, A.
1976           *The Theory of Need in Marx*. New York: St. Martin's.

Horkheimer, M.
1972           "Traditional and Critical Theory." In *Critical Theory*. New York: Herder & Herder.
1973           "The Authoritarian State." *Telos* 15: 3–20.
1974           *Eclipse of Reason*. New York: Seabury.

Horkheimer, M., and T. W. Adorno
1972           *Dialectic of Enlightenment*. New York: Herder & Herder.

Horowitz, G.
1977            *Repression: Basic and Surplus Repression in Psychoanalytic Theory.*
                Toronto: University of Toronto Press.

Hughes, H. S.
1975            *The Sea Change: The Migration of Social Thought, 1930–1965.* New
                York: Harper & Row.

Husserl, E.
1965            *Phenomenology and the Crisis of Philosophy.* New York: Harper &
                Row.

Huyssen, A.
1984            "Mapping the Postmodern." *New German Critique* 33: 5–52.
1986            *After the Great Divide: Modernism, Mass Culture, Postmodernism.*
                Bloomington: Indiana University Press.

Hyppolite, J.
1970            *Studies on Marx and Hegel.* New York: Basic.

Institute for Social Research
1973            *Aspects of Sociology.* Boston: Beacon.

Jacoby, R.
1971            "Towards a Critique of Automatic Marxism." *Telos* 10: 119–46.
1975a           "Politics of the Crisis Theory." *Telos* 23: 3–52.
1975b           *Social Amnesia.* Boston: Beacon.
1976            "A Falling Rate of Intelligence?" *Telos* 27: 141–46.
1981            *Dialectic of Defeat.* New York: Cambridge University Press.
1987            *The Last Intellectuals: American Culture in the Age of Academe.* New
                York: Basic.

Jaggar, A.
1983            *Feminist Politics and Human Nature.* Totowa, N.J.: Roman & Al-
                lenheld.

Jameson, F.
1981            *The Political Unconscious: Narrative as a Socially Symbolic Act.* Ith-
                aca, N.Y.: Cornell University Press.
1984a           "The Politics of Theory: Ideological Positions in the
                Postmodernism Debate." *New German Critique* 33: 53–65.
1984b           "Postmodernism, or the Cultural Logic of Late Capitalism." *New
                Left Review* 146: 53–93.

Jay, M.
1973            *The Dialectical Imagination.* Boston: Little, Brown.
1975            "Marxism and Critical Theory: Martin Jay and Russell Jacoby."
                *Theory and Society* 2: 257–63.
1984            *Marxism and Totality.* Berkeley: University of California Press.

Kamenka, E.
1962      *The Ethical Foundations of Marxism.* New York: Praeger.

Kamolnick, P.
1988      *Classes: A Marxist Critique.* Dix Hills, N.Y.: General Hall.

Keane, J.
1984      *Public Life and Late Capitalism.* Cambridge: Cambridge University Press.

Kellner, D.
1975      "The Frankfurt School Revisited: A Critique of Martin Jay's *The Dialectical Imagination.*" *New German Critique* 4: 131–52.
1988      "Postmodernism as Social Theory: Some Challenges and Problems." *Theory, Culture and Society* 5 (2/3): 239–69.
1989a      "Boundaries and Borderlines: Reflections on Jean Baudrillard and Critical Theory." *Current Perspectives in Social Theory* 9: 5–22.
1989b      *Critical Theory, Marxism and Modernity.* Cambridge: Polity.
1989c      *Jean Baudrillard: From Marxism to Postmodernism and Beyond.* Cambridge: Polity.

Kidder, T.
1985      *House.* Boston: Houghton Mifflin.

Klinkowitz, J.
1988      *Rosenberg/Barthes/Hassan: The Postmodern Habit of Thought.* Athens: University of Georgia Press.

Kontos, A.
1974      "Between Memory and Dream." In *Thinking about Change,* edited by D. Shugarman. Toronto: University of Toronto Press.
1975      "Domination: Metaphor and Political Reality." In *Domination,* edited by A. Kontos. Toronto: University of Toronto Press.

Korsch, K.
1970      *Marxism and Philosophy.* New York: Monthly Review Press.

Kroker, A., and D. Cook
1986      *The Postmodern Scene.* New York: St. Martin's.

Laclau, E., and C. Mouffe
1985      *Hegemony and Socialist Strategy.* London: Verso.

Lasch, C.
1977      *Haven in a Heartless World: The Family Besieged.* New York: Basic.
1979      *The Culture of Narcissism.* New York: Norton.
1984      *The Minimal Self.* New York: Norton.

Leiss, W.
1972      *The Domination of Nature.* New York: Braziller.

1976        *The Limits to Satisfaction: An Essay on the Problem of Needs and Com-
            modities.* Toronto: University of Toronto Press.

Lenhardt, C.
1975        "Anamnestic Solidarity: The Proletariat and Its *Manes*." *Telos* 25:
            133–54.
1976        "The Wanderings of Enlightenment." In *On Critical Theory*, ed-
            ited by J. O'Neill. New York: Seabury.

Lenin, V.
1952        *Materialism and Empirio-Criticism.* Moscow: Foreign Languages
            Publishing House.
1961        *Philosophical Notebooks.* Moscow: Foreign Languages Publishing
            House.

Lenski, G.
1966        *Power and Privilege: A Theory of Social Stratification.* New York: Mc-
            Graw-Hill.

Lévi-Strauss, C.
1963        *Totemism.* Boston: Beacon.
1966        *The Savage Mind.* Chicago: University of Chicago Press.

Lewis, L.
1975        *Scaling the Ivory Tower: Merit and Its Limits in Academic Careers.*
            Baltimore: Johns Hopkins University Press.
1988        *Cold War on Campus.* New Brunswick, N.J.: Transaction.

Lichtheim, G.
1961        *Marxism.* London: Routledge & Kegan Paul.
1971        *From Marx to Hegel.* New York: Herder & Herder.

Lukács, G.
1970        *Lenin: A Study on the Unity of His Thought.* London: New Left
            Books.
1971        *History and Class Consciousness.* London: Merlin.

Luke, T.
1989        *Screens of Power: Ideology, Domination and Resistance in Informa-
            tional Society.* Urbana: University of Illinois Press.
1991        "The Discourse of 'Development': A Genealogy of 'Developing
            Nations' and the Discipline of Modernity." *Current Perspectives in
            Social Theory* 11: 271–93.

Lyotard, J.-F.
1984        *The Postmodern Condition: A Report on Knowledge.* Minneapolis:
            University of Minnesota Press.

McCarthy, T.
1978        *The Critical Theory of Jurgen Habermas.* Cambridge: MIT Press.

Macpherson, C. B.
1962            *The Political Theory of Possessive Individualism.* Oxford: Claren-
                don.

Mandel, E.
1968            *Marxist Economic Theory.* New York: Monthly Review Press.
1975            *Late Capitalism.* London: New Left Books.

Marcuse, H.
1955            *Eros and Civilization.* New York: Vintage.
1958            *Soviet Marxism.* New York: Vintage.
1960            "Preface: A Note on Dialectic." In *Reason and Revolution: Hegel
                and the Rise of Social Theory.* Boston: Beacon.
1964            *One-Dimensional Man.* Boston: Beacon.
1968a           "The Affirmative Character of Culture." In *Negations.* Boston:
                Beacon Press.
1968b           "Industrialization and Capitalism in the Work of Max Weber." In
                *Negations.* Boston: Beacon.
1968c           "Love Mystified: A Critique of Norman O. Brown." In *Negations.*
                Boston: Beacon.
1968d           *Negations.* Boston: Beacon.
1969            *An Essay on Liberation.* Boston: Beacon.
1972            *Counterrevolution and Revolt.* Boston: Beacon.
1973            "The Foundations of Historical Materialism." In *Studies in Criti-
                cal Philosophy.* Boston: Beacon.
1978            *The Aesthetic Dimension.* Boston: Beacon.
1978–79         "Theory and Practice: A Discussion." *Telos* 38: 123–52.

Marcuse, H.; R. P. Wolff; and B. Moore, Jr.
1965            *A Critique of Pure Tolerance.* Boston: Beacon.

Markovic, M.
1974            *From Affluence to Praxis.* Ann Arbor: University of Michigan Press.

Marshall, B.
1988            "Feminist Theory and Critical Theory." *Canadian Review of Soci-
                ology and Anthropology* 25 (2): 208–30.

Marx, K.
N.D.            *Capital,* vol. 1. Moscow: Progress.
1961            *Economic and Philosophic Manuscripts of 1844.* Moscow: Foreign
                Languages Publishing House.
1970            *A Contribution to the Critique of Political Economy.* New York: Inter-
                national.
1973            *Grundrisse.* New York: Vintage.

Marx, K., and F. Engels
1947            *The German Ideology.* New York: International.
1959            *The Communist Manifesto.* In *Marx and Engels: Basic Writings on*

*Politics and Philosophy*, edited by L. Feuer. Garden City, N.Y.: Doubleday.

Mattick, P.
1972        *Critique of Marcuse.* New York: Herder & Herder.

Mehan, H., and H. Wood
1975        *The Reality of Ethnomethodology.* New York: Wiley.

Merleau-Ponty, M.
1964        *Sense and Non-Sense.* Evanston, Ill.: Northwestern University Press.

Mills, C. W.
1951        *White Collar.* New York: Oxford University Press.
1959        *The Sociological Imagination.* New York: Oxford University Press.

Misgeld, D.
1985        "Education and Cultural Invasion: Critical Social Theory, Education as Instruction and the 'Pedagogy of the Oppressed.' " In *Critical Theory and Public Life*, edited by J. Forester. Cambridge: MIT Press.

Mitchell, J.
1974        *Psychoanalysis and Feminism.* New York: Pantheon.

Mitzman, A.
1971        *The Iron Cage.* New York: Grosset & Dunlap.

Moynihan, D. P.
1969        *Maximum Feasible Misunderstanding.* New York: Free Press.

Mueller, C.
1973        *The Politics of Communication.* New York: Oxford University Press.

Neumann, F.
1957        *The Democratic and the Authoritarian State.* Glencoe, Ill.: Free Press.

Newman, C.
1985        *The Postmodern Aura: The Act of Fiction in an Age of Inflation.* Evanston, Ill.: Northwestern University Press.

Nietzsche, F.
1955        *Beyond Good and Evil.* Chicago: Regnery.
1956        *The Birth of Tragedy and the Genealogy of Morals.* Garden City, N.Y.: Doubleday.

Norton, T. M., and B. Ollman, eds.
1978        *Studies in Socialist Pedagogy.* New York: Norton.

Nozick, R.
1974            *Anarchy, State and Utopia.* New York: Basic.

Offe, C.
1968            "Technik und Eindimensionalitat. Eine Version der Technokra-
                tiethese?" In *Antworten auf Herbert Marcuse,* edited by A. Schmidt.
                Frankfurt: Suhrkamp.
1984            *Contradictions of the Welfare State.* Cambridge: MIT Press.
1985            *Disorganized Capitalism.* Cambridge: MIT Press.

O'Neill, J.
1972a           "The Hobbesian Problem in Parsons and Marx." In *Sociology as a
                Skin Trade.* New York: Harper & Row.
1972b           "Public and Private Space." In *Sociology as a Skin Trade.* New
                York: Harper & Row.
1972c           *Sociology as a Skin Trade.* New York: Harper & Row.
1972d           "On Theory and Criticism in Marx." In *Sociology as a Skin Trade.*
                New York: Harper & Row.
1974            *Making Sense Together: An Introduction to Wild Sociology.* New
                York: Harper & Row.
1975            "Gay Technology and the Body Politic." In *The Body as a Medium
                of Expression,* edited by J. Benthall and T. Polhemus. London: Al-
                len Lane.
1976            "On Critique and Remembrance." In *On Critical Theory.* New
                York: Seabury.
1981            "Marxism and the Two Sciences." *Philosophy of the Social Sciences*
                11: 281–302.
1984            *For Marx against Althusser.* Washington, D.C.: University Press of
                America.
1986            "The Disciplinary Society: From Weber to Foucault." *British
                Journal of Sociology* 37 (1): 42–60.
1991            "Is There a Class in This Text?" In *Interpretation and Discipline.*
                Norman: Oklahoma University Press.

O'Neill, J., ed.
1973            *Modes of Individualism and Collectivism.* London: Routledge &
                Kegan Paul.

Paci, E.
1972            *The Function of the Sciences and the Meaning of Man.* Evanston, Ill.:
                Northwestern University Press.

Parsons, T.
1937            *The Structure of Social Action.* New York: McGraw-Hill.
1951            *The Social System.* Glencoe, Ill.: Free Press.
1990            "Prolegomena to a Theory of Social Institutions." *American Soci-
                ological Review* 55: 319–33.

Parsons, T., and R. Bales
1955        *Family, Socialization and Interaction Process*. Glencoe, Ill: Free
            Press.

Piccone, P.
1971        "Phenomenological Marxism." *Telos* 9: 3–31.
1976        "Beyond Identity Theory." In *On Critical Theory*, edited by J.
            O'Neill. New York: Seabury.
1978        "The Crisis of One-Dimensionality." *Telos* 35: 43–54.

Piccone, P., and A. Delfini
1970        "Marcuse's Heideggerian Marxism." *Telos* 6: 36–46.

Popper, K.
1961        *The Poverty of Historicism*. London: Routledge & Kegan Paul.
1963        *The Open Society and Its Enemies*, 2 vols. New York: Harper & Row.

Poster, M.
1989        *Critical Theory and Poststructuralism*. Ithaca, N.Y.: Cornell Univer-
            sity Press.

Poulantzas, N.
1973        *Political Power and Social Classes*. New York: Routledge & Kegan
            Paul.

Richardson, L.
1988        "The Collective Story: Postmodernism and the Writing of Sociol-
            ogy." *Sociological Focus* 21: 199–208.
1990a       "Narrative and Sociology." *Journal of Contemporary Ethnography*
            19: 116–35.
1990b       "Speakers Whose Voices Matter: Toward a Feminist Postmodern-
            ist Sociological Praxis." *Studies in Symbolic Interactionism*, in press.
1990c       *Writing Strategies: Reaching Diverse Audiences*. Newbury Park, Ca-
            lif.: Sage.
1991        "Value Constituting Practice, Rhetoric and Metaphor in Sociol-
            ogy: A Reflexive Analysis." *Current Perspectives in Social Theory*
            11: 1–15.

Roemer, J.
1981        *Analytic Foundations of Marxian Economic Theory*. New York: Cam-
            bridge University Press.
1982        *A General Theory of Exploitation and Class*. Cambridge: Harvard
            University Press.

Roemer, J., ed.
1986        *Analytical Marxism*. Cambridge: Cambridge University Press.

Rosen, S.
1969        *Nihilism: A Philosophical Essay*. New Haven: Yale University Press.

Ross, A.
1988  "The New Sentence and the Commodity Form: Recent American Writing." In *Marxism and the Interpretation of Culture*, edited by C. Nelson and L. Grossberg. Urbana: University of Illinois Press.

Rousseau, J.-J.
1973  *The Social Contract and Discourses*. London: Dent.

Ryan, M.
1982  *Marxism and Deconstruction*. Baltimore: Johns Hopkins University Press.
1989  *Politics and Culture*. Baltimore: Johns Hopkins University Press.

Sarup, M.
1989  *An Introductory Guide to Post-Structuralism and Postmodernism*. Athens: University of Georgia Press.

Sartre, J.-P.
1963  *Search for a Method*. New York: Vintage.
1965  *What Is Literature?* New York: Harper & Row.
1976  *Critique of Dialectical Reason*. London: New Left Books.

Schaff, A.
1970  *Marxism and the Human Individual*. New York: McGraw-Hill.

Schmidt, A.
1968  "Existential-Ontologie und historischer Materialismus." In *Antworten auf Herbert Marcuse*, edited by A. Schmidt. Frankfurt: Suhrkamp.

Schrecker, E.
1986  *No Ivory Tower: McCarthyism and the Universities*. New York: Oxford University Press.

Schroyer, T.
1973  *The Critique of Domination: The Origins and Development of Critical Theory*. New York: Braziller.
1978  "Review of O'Neill's *On Critical Theory*." *American Journal of Sociology* 83: 1033–35.

Sher, G.
1978  *Praxis*. Bloomington: Indiana University Press.

Sherover, E.
1975  "Review of Jacoby's *Social Amnesia*." *Telos* 25: 203.

Sica, A.
1983  "Parsons Jr." *American Journal of Sociology* 89: 200–219.

Slater, P.
1977            *Origin and Significance of the Frankfurt School*. London: Routledge
                & Kegan Paul.

Smart, B.
1983            *Foucault, Marxism and Critique*. London: Routledge & Kegan
                Paul.

Sober, E.; E. Levine; and E. O. Wright
1987            "Marxism and Methodological Individualism." *New Left Review*
                162: 67–84.

Spivak, G. C.
1988            "Can the Subaltern Speak?" In *Marxism and the Interpretation of
                Culture*, edited by C. Nelson and L. Grossberg. Urbana: Univer-
                sity of Illinois Press.

Stalin, J. V.
1940            *Dialectical and Historical Materialism*. New York: International.

Turner, B. S., ed.
1985            *Theories of Modernity and Postmodernity*. Newbury Park, Calif.:
                Sage.

Turner, S.
1985            "Reviews of Alexander's *Theoretical Logic in Sociology*." *Philosophy
                of the Social Sciences* 15: 77–82; 311–16; 365–68; 513–22.

Weber, M.
1947            *The Theory of Social and Economic Organization*. Glencoe, Ill.: Free
                Press.
1968            *The Methodology of the Social Sciences*. New York: Free Press.

Weedon, C.
1987            *Feminist Practice and Poststructuralist Theory*. Oxford: Basil Black-
                well.

Wellmer, A.
1971            *Critical Theory of Society*. New York: Seabury.
1976            "Communications and Emancipation: Reflections on the Lin-
                guistic Turn in Critical Theory." In *On Critical Theory*, edited by J.
                O'Neill. New York: Seabury.

Wexler, P.
1982            *Critical Social Psychology*. London: Routledge & Kegan Paul.
1987            *Social Analysis of Education: After the New Sociology*. London: Rout-
                ledge & Kegan Paul.

Wittgenstein, L.
1953            *Philosophical Investigations*. Oxford: Basil Blackwell.
1981            *Tractatus Logico-Philosophicus*. London: Routledge & Kegan Paul.

Wolin, R.
1984            "Modernism versus Postmodernism." *Telos* 62: 9–30.

Wright, E. O.
1976            "Class Boundaries in Advanced Capitalist Societies." *New Left Review* 98: 3–41.
1978            *Class, Crisis and the State.* London: New Left Books.
1985            *Classes.* London: Verso.
1987            "Reflections on *Classes.*" *Berkeley Journal of Sociology* 23: 19–49.

Wright, E. O., and L. Perrone
1977            "Marxist Class Categories and Income Inequality." *American Sociological Review* 42: 32–55.

Wright, E. O.; C. Costello; D. Hachen; and J. Sprague
1982            "The American Class Structure." *American Sociological Review* 47 (6): 709–27.

# Index

Absolute Refusal. *See* Great Refusal
Absolutism, 291, 294–95
Academia, 268, 301–3
Academic McCarthyism, 64–65
Academic (University) Marxism, 44,
46–47, 51, 53–55, 65, 72, 272–73.
*See also* Intellectuality: radical
Action: instrumental, 64
Adorno, Theodor W., 6, 9–10, 29, 71,
151, 166, 270; aesthetic theory,
228–30, 233; cerebral radicalism,
258–60; critical theory, 12, 20–21,
157, 219; culture industry theory, 80,
91; on "damaged life," 195, 249–50,
275; on decline of the individual, 12,
110; interpretation of Freud, 25, 102;
on Marcuse's Hegelianism, 197;
Marxism, 5, 37, 194, 239; on music,
24, 221–25, 227–30, 233–34;
negative dialectics, 219–22, 225, 252,
271, 300; Nietzsche's influence, 285,
290; on reification, 251–52; response
to absence of answers, 50–51; Slater
on, 24–25, 27; theories compared
with Marcuse's and O'Neill's, 220–28,
232–38; theory for, 195–96, 228–31,
236. *See also* works by name
Adulthood, mature, 111, 114–16
Advanced (Late; Monopoly) capitalism,
99, 135, 146–47, 219, 250, 260, 283,
290
—celebration of enlightenment, 138
—collapse of not inevitable, 268–69
—counterhegemony in terms of, 100
—culture and political economy in,
132–34

—displacement of opposition to militant
minorities, 236
—domination based on profit
imperatives in, 203
—early (1930s to early 1960s), 135,
145, 147, 242
—for Establishment postmodernism,
291
—fast capitalism as stage, 8–9, 73, 80,
269, 299
—Frankfurt school's response to, 16–17,
29, 37, 131, 184, 244–45, 247
—instrumental rationality in, 247–49
—legitimation crisis, 264
—for Marcuse, 98, 112–13, 121,
136–37, 154; alienation of the
individual in, 95–96; false needs in,
134, 144–45
—negative totality of, 224
—New Individualism in, 283
—phenomenology of, 230
—postmodernity theory on, 283
—revolutionary struggle as nonexistent,
46
—Weber as prophet of, 205
—*See also* Capitalism; Mobilization, total
Advertising, 284, 286, 302–3
*Aesthetic Dimension, The* (Marcuse), 13,
25, 150–51, 153–58, 163–70
Aesthetics, 227–28, 233; of Adorno,
228–30, 233; of the Frankfurt school,
6, 22, 37; of Marcuse, 88, 108–9,
118, 141, 150–51, 153–71, 201–2,
204, 253. *See also* Art
*Aesthetic Theory* (Adorno), 24, 166
Affirmative postmodernism. *See*
Establishment postmodernism